The Personnel of George Rogers Clark's Fort Jefferson

and the

Civilian Community of Clarksville, Kentucky

1780–1781

Based on the Lost Vouchers of George Rogers Clark

Kenneth Charles Carstens

HERITAGE BOOKS
2011

HERITAGE BOOKS
AN IMPRINT OF HERITAGE BOOKS, INC.

Books, CDs, and more—Worldwide

For our listing of thousands of titles see our website
at
www.HeritageBooks.com

Published 2011 by
HERITAGE BOOKS, INC.
Publishing Division
100 Railroad Ave. #104
Westminster, Maryland 21157

Copyright © 1999 Kenneth Charles Carstens

Other books by the Author:

*George Rogers Clark's Fort Jefferson, 1780–1781:
Kentucky's Outpost on the Western Frontier*

*The Calendar and Quartermaster Books of General George
Rogers Clark's Fort Jefferson, Kentucky, 1780–1781*

All rights reserved. No part of this book may be reproduced or transmitted in any form or by any means, electronic or mechanical, including photocopying, recording or by any information storage and retrieval system without written permission from the author, except for the inclusion of brief quotations in a review.

International Standard Book Numbers
Paperbound: 978-0-7884-1183-0
Clothbound: 978-0-7884-8969-3

About the Author

Kenneth C. Carstens received a B.S. in Liberal Arts from Central Michigan University (1971). He did graduate course work in anthropology at Western Michigan University, then took his M.A. (1974) and Ph.D. (1980) degrees in anthropology from Washington University-St. Louis, concentrating on eastern U.S. prehistory. He has been the director of the Murray State University anthropology program since 1978 and the MSU Archaeology Service Center since 1987. The Fort Jefferson research project, of which this book is a part, began during the early 1980s. The program involves the search for archaeological evidence of the fort as well as archival and historical studies directed toward reconstructing every facet of life associated with this late eighteenth century Kentucky military and civilian frontier settlement. Dr. Carstens has authored more than 30 journal articles about Fort Jefferson and has written three book-length manuscripts about the fort's history. He is the co-author of an edited volume (with Patty Jo Watson), Of Caves and Shell Mounds (1996; University of Alabama Press).

Table of Contents

	Page
Acknowledgements	i
Introduction	iii
Introduction, Part II: List of Companies	viii
Introduction, Part III: List of Families	xiv
Introduction, Part IV: List of Deaths	xv
Introduction, Part V: Fort Jefferson Chronology	xvi
Fort Jefferson Personnel	1
Index	184

Acknowledgements

Many individuals assisted with the archival portion of the Fort Jefferson project and have affected to varying degrees my perception, compilation, interpretation, and presentation of information within this book.

Individuals at other institutions and archives who assisted me include Jane H. Pairo, Conley L. Edwards, III, and Paul I. Chestnut, Virginia State Library, Archives Division, Richmond; James J. Holmberg, The Filson Club, Louisville, Kentucky; Robert B. Kinnaird and Thomas Applegate and their staff at the Kentucky Historical Society, Frankfort; Ms. Kandie Adkinson, Land Office, Secretary of State's Office, Frankfort, Kentucky; Mr. Richard K. Boyd and Ms. Sandra S. Jones, Public Relations Managers, Westvaco, Wickliffe, Kentucky; Dr. William S. Coker, University of West Florida; Dr. Light T. Cummins, Austin College, Texas; Ms. Linda R. Baumgarten, Colonial Williamsburg Foundation; Ms. Josephine L. Harper, State Historical Society of Wisconsin, Madison; Dennis J. Latta and Pamela A. Nolan, George Rogers Clark National Historical Park, Vincennes, Indiana and Robert J. Holden, Historian and former employee at GRC National Historical Park; Ms. Wilma L. Dulin, Program Archivist, Indiana Historical Society, Indianapolis; Janice C. Fox, Archivist, Missouri Historical Society, St. Louis; Mr. William E. Lind, Military Reference Branch, National Archives, Washington, D.C.; and David Hamilton, Greg Holm, and William Potter, former Board of Director Members, Northwest Territory Alliance, Decatur, Illinois, Cleveland, Ohio, and Palos Hills, Illinois, respectively.

Financial support for many different aspects of the Fort Jefferson research project came from various administative offices at Murray State University, but especially the Office of the Provost (formerly Dr. James L. Booth); Office of the Dean, College of Humanistic Studies (initially Dr. Kenneth E. Harrell; subsequently Dr. Joseph Cartwright), and from the Department of Sociology, Anthropology and Social Work (first, the late Dr. Dennis Poplin, then Dr. Frank W. Elwell, chairmen). The MSU Committee on Institutional Studies and Research (C.I.S.R.), chaired by Dr. Peter W. Whaley, consistently provided support since 1986 for the Fort Jefferson project. J. William Young and George P. Crounse,

Paducah, Kentucky, provided private funds to support the Fort Jefferson research program at the request of Mr. Bill Black, Jr., also of Paducah.

Artwork for the figures was accomplished by Richard J. Mjos, Murray. Richard Day, Vincennes, Indiana, drew the artist's reconstruction of Fort Jefferson used for the cover jacket. This volume is better than it would be because of the inclusion of the artwork accomplished by these two individuals.

Throughout this project, tens of Murray State University students logged thousands of hours helping me transcribe, translate, and triplicate the Fort Jefferson records. To those students I am truly appreciative. A special thank you is extended to Cathy Biby who typed the original version of the Fort Jefferson manuscripts before it became fashionable to use personal computers.

A special thank you is extended to Dr. Robert R. Rea, Hollifield Professor of Southern History at Auburn University, for commenting on an earlier draft of this manuscript and for his earlier research assistance with the Fort Jefferson project.

Last, but not least, I wish to acknowledge my two sons, Jason Lee and Jameson Tranter, and my wonderful wife, Nancy June, all a source of inspiration and love. This Fort Jefferson book is dedicated to my parents, Calvin Z. and Dorothy M. Carstens, Pinconning, Michigan, who encouraged and supported me to pursue my interests in archaeology and history, and to the heroic men, women and children who made the history at George Rogers Clark's Fort Jefferson.

The Personnel of George Rogers Clark's
Fort Jefferson, 1780-1781

Kenneth C. Carstens, Ph.D.

Murray State University

Introduction

George Rogers Clark built Fort Jefferson at the mouth of the Ohio River in April, 1780, by orders of Governor Thomas Jefferson. The fort and civilian community of Clarksville were the first Virginian settlements sanctioned by the Virginian government to be located in, what today is, western Kentucky.

In 1984 I traveled to the State Archives in Virginia to examine several thousand documents that had been lost at the end of the American Revolution. Those documents were George Rogers Clark's lost vouchers, his economic records from the Kentucky and Illinois country areas. Of the twenty thousand estimated documents in the collection, approximately 4000 papers pertained to Clark's Fort Jefferson. They are, for the first time, reproduced here in an edited and synthesized format. And as a result, a new and exciting history about Fort Jefferson can be gleaned from the records that correct and amplify the fort's previously written history, part of which previously claimed no more than 35 persons ever occupied the fort! The attached records demonstrate that more than 500 persons garrisoned, lived, farmed, and died in that remote and westerly-located region of Kentucky. Genealogists particularly will be pleased with the following pages, as will historical re-enactors who wish to re-create exactly, 18th century life on the Kentucky/Illinois frontier and know exactly the type of clothing worn, the fabric used, and type of issues given to the soldier, Indian, everyday frontier person.

The *Personnel* volume provides an alphabetical listing of every individual known to have either set foot in Fort Jefferson or to have had direct ties with the fort (such as sending items to the post or receiving correspondence from its inhabitants). Every activity recorded for each person at the fort, or for the civilian community of Clarksville, is noted. The vast majority of those entries are based on data contained in manuscripts in the unpublished George Rogers Clark Papers at the Virginia State Library (herein referenced as VSA, followed by a volume number, e.g., VSA-12). That record has been supplemented by other Fort Jefferson documents found in archives at Kentucky's Filson Club, the Kentucky Historical Society, the William Clark Papers in the Missouri Historical Society (St. Louis), and several previously published sources, especially Margery Harding's 1981 <u>George Rogers Clark and His Men Military Records, 1778-1784</u>, James Alton James's 1912 (reprinted 1972 AMS Press) <u>George Rogers Clark Papers 1781-1784</u>, and Katherine Seineke's 1981 <u>The George Rogers Clark Adventure in the Illinois and Selected Documents of the American Revolution at the Frontier Posts</u>.

The following pages demonstrate that more than 500 persons participated in the Fort Jefferson experience between 1780 and 1781. Of that number, 548 persons are named. Sixty-five persons belonging to the friendly Kaskaskia Indians remain unnamed to history, but they were instrumental in the rescue of the post with Captain Richard McCarty, who helped defend the post from the British-supported Chickasaw, and who were given permission and assistance to launch attacks on the Chickasaw by Captain Robert George, the post commander, and Leonard Helm, Superintendent of Indian Affairs. Other Native Americans, whose individual names have been lost to history, include members of the Sauk, Ottawa, Kickapoo, Delaware, and Peoria who were also defending <u>and</u> fighting against Fort Jefferson, but unlike the Kaskaskia, no specific number is associated with their presence; therefore other native groups are obviously under-represented at the post as are the actual numbers of Chickasaw who attacked the post under the combined leadership of Lt. William Whitehead (British Southern Indian Dep't) and James Colbert (a local Chicakasaw "Big Man" from Mussel Shoals).

Similarly under-represented are children and, most likely, adult women. Although more than 40 families were present at the post, the number of children in each family is known only for a few families. Even fewer of the children's names are known. It would not be out of the question to assume the presence of an additional 40 children at this outpost, figuring one child per family. Indeed, if the Andrew McMeans family of seven children was typical of the population, the total number of persons at Fort Jefferson would be considerably larger than that which is now recorded.

Adult women, although present in considerable numbers, are certainly underrepresented in the written records. If a woman participated in the post's barter system, or if her daily activities brought her some notoriety (i.e., testifying during a court of inquiry), or if she received goods from the public store, her name was recorded. Otherwise, it was not. In several cases, only the initial of the first name is known; in some cases, her presence is indicated only by association with her husband. How many men had wives at Fort Jefferson is not known, but vastly more information is provided about the women of Fort Jefferson in this volume than in any other published work about western Kentucky frontier.

Slaves represent another category of persons present at the post. Too few slaves at Fort Jefferson were recorded by name; several are known only by their owner's name or by a racist-reference to their presence (e.g., wench); the majority of slaves left no written documentation whatsoever, a reflection of 18th century life as well as social position within a highly stratified society. One black man, named Cesar, was a considerably-skilled artisan, who served as an artificer and who helped build the fort. Because of his skills, it is not surprising a record of his presence at the fort remains. Yet, the number of slaves at Fort Jefferson is unknown. It should be pointed out that numerous slaves certainly existed at nearby (120 miles north) Kaskaskia in 1778. Clarence Alvord (1907:xv-xvi) stated that Kaskaskia's population of 1,000 persons was nearly evenly divided between whites and slaves. Could the same be true of Fort Jefferson two years later? Although there is no indication that the slave population at Fort Jefferson was comparably as large, the Kaskaskia example accurately reflects the great number of persons lost to history and the role of the slave trade in Clark's 18th century frontier life (note also at the end the reference to slaves owned by Clark).

Finally, a clarification should be made regarding information provided about officers and others holding positions of authority at the post. Their entries, unlike those of enlisted personnel or civilians, include, in addition to issues for themselves, issues they ordered for their companies as a whole and issues to unnamed individuals in their companies. Issues and orders affecting named persons appear with the person named.

The significance and utility of the <u>Personnel</u> volume lies in its alphabetical presentation of individuals known to have been actively involved with George Rogers Clark's Fort Jefferson and the recording of 548 "named" persons of Fort Jefferson. By recovering the names of the Fort Jefferson personnel from original vouchers, payrolls, and other documents, the identity of these men and women has been saved for history. At least a part of their story now has been recorded for posterity. The size of the Fort Jefferson-Clarksville population was significantly larger and more diverse than earlier historians suggested. Clark, and the government of Virginia, obviously had great plans for this military post and civilian community. Therefore, Fort Jefferson's role in the American Revolution should be rethought in light of the overwhelming evidence which now indicates the site was of greater strategic importance to the western theatre than was previously believed. Fort Jefferson was not a small, undermanned garrison of no consequence, in spite of its eventual failing. Ample evidence now indicates that Fort Jefferson was the very hub of George Rogers Clark's Illinois Battalion between 1780 and 1781. This book, which is meant to compliment other volumes I have written about Ft. Jefferson, will be of particular use to those individuals interested in genealogy. Herein they may find a previously lost ancestor or add greater detail to that ancestor's life. For the historian, anthropologist, and sociologist, important data for research about day-to-day lives of individuals and populations on the 18th century American frontier should prove to be highly significant. For the historical re-enactor, the accoutrements of 18th century life are vividly described and can now be recreated.

A list of works cited in the <u>Personnel</u> volume appears at the end of this section. Abbreviations for several of the references used in the body of the volume are as follows: MHS, represents the William Clark Collection at the Missouri Historical Society (followed by B for Box and F for Folder number); GRC I or GRC II refers to James Alton James' edited version of the George Rogers

Clark Papers (1972 AMS reprint); and VSA indicates the unpublished George Rogers Clark papers in the Archives Division of the Virginia State Library.

References Cited

Alvord, Clarence W.
1907 Collections of the Illinois State Historical Library, Volume II: Cahokia Records, 1778-1790. Illinois State Historical Library, Springfield, Illinois.

Draper, Lyman C.
n.d. The Draper Manuscripts. Wisconsin Historical Society, Madison.

Harding, Margery Heberling
1981 George Rogers Clark and His Men Military Records, 1778-1784. The Kentucky Historical Society, Frankfort.

James, James Alton, editor
1972 George Rogers Clark Papers, 1771-1784, Vols. I and II. Originally published in 1912. Reprinted by AMS Press, New York.

Jamison, Ann McMeans
n.d. The Personal Narrative of Ann McMeans Jamison. Unpublished manuscript, The Filson Club, Louisville.

Missouri Historical Society
n.d. The William Clark Papers. The Missouri Historical Society, Forest Park, St. Louis.

Seineke, Kathrine Wagner
1981 The George Rogers Clark Adventure in the Illinois and Selected Documents of the American Revolution at the Frontier Posts. Polyanthos Press, New Orleans.

Sioussat, St. George L.
1915 The Journal of General Daniel Smith, one of the Commissioners to Extend the Boundary Line between the Commonwealths of Virginia and North Carolina, August, 1779, to July, 1780. The Tennessee Historical Magazine, 1(1): 40-65, Nashville.

Virginia State Library
n.d. The Unpublished Papers of George Rogers Clark. Virginia State Library, Archives Division, Boxes 1-50 (now available on microfilm but not indexed), Richmond.

Fort Jefferson Personnel

Introduction, Part II: Companies

The following rosters of men are based on information contained primarily within the unpublished George Rogers Clark papers from the archives division of the Virginia State Library (VSA). In most instances, the rosters were created from lists that were used by military unit captains to denote which of the men in their unit had received their clothing issue/allotment. Where noted, a reference to the box of the Virignia papers is provided (e.g., VSA 50). Other references used include Harding's 1981 <u>George Rogers Clark and His Men</u>, and the Missouri Historical Society's William Clark collection (Box #, Folder #). No attempt has been made to correct spelling as spellings from different contexts varied, and although a preferred spelling may be suggested, the actual spelling of the person's name may never be known. References given below should be checked against the Bibliography in Part I.

<u>Captain Robert George's Company of Artillery</u> (VSA 50)
Capt. Lt. Richard Harrison
Andrews, Joseph
Armstrong, G.
Ash, John
Babu, Daniel
Bakley, John
Balsinklee, Vallintine
Bolton, Daniel
Brian, John
Burk, Charles
Bush, Drury
Bush, John
Carney, Martin
Cesar
Clark, Andrew
Damewood (also Dance), Bostin
Daughterty, John
DeLany (also Lany), Thomas
DeMore, Mary (washerwoman)
Ditterin, Jacob
Fabers (also Fever), William
Fair, Edmund
Gilbert, John
Grimshaw, J.
Hacketon, Michel
Hacker, John
Hazard, John
Hern, Jeremiah
Hopkins, Richard
Hup, Phil
Jones, Matthew
Kening, Lazarous
Kennada, David
Kenon, Lawrance
Layarous, Ryon
Litle, Francis
Long, Philip
McCalley, Patrick
McDaniel, James
McMullen, J.
Marr, Patrick
Mathews, E.
Megarr, John
Miller, Abraham
More, William
Morgan, C.
Murray, Matthew

Pittman, Buckner (boatmaster)
Posey, William
Postin (also Pastin), William
Pruit, Isaac
Quibes, Paul
Ramsey, James
Rogers, Patrick
Smith, George
Smothers, John
Taylor, Travis (?)
Tinklee, Michel
Turpin, Richard
Win, Thomas
Wagner, Peter
Wheat, Jacob
White, William
Win, Thomas

<u>Captain Richard Brashear's Company</u> (VSA-11)
Ensign Jerit Williams
Allen, Isaac
Allen, Samuel (sgt.)
Bartholomew, William
Blair, John
Boils, John
Brown, James
Cowen, John
Curry, James
Curry, Patrick
Dawson, James
Elms, James
Elms, John
Elms, William (sgt.)
Flarry, James
Howell, Peter
Joins, John (sgt.)
LePaint, Lois
Mackever, John
Mayfield, Cagy
McMichael, John
Moneral, Joseph
Morgan, Charles
Morris, James
Ouneler, Charles
Ross, Joseph
Rubedo, Francis
Rubedo, Jache
Snellock (also Snarlock), Thomas
Tyger, Daniel
Wallis, David

<u>Captain John Rogers, Virginia Light Dragoons</u> (VSA-12)
Lt. James Merriwether
Coronet John Thruston
Barnit, Robert
Blankinship, Henry
Bootin, Travis
Bootin, William
Bredin, Francis
Cailer, Casper
Cambell, William
Curtis, Rice
Dohaty, Frederick

Frogget, William
Glass, Mikiel
Goodwin, William
Bruin, William
Hammit, James
Irwin, Joseph
Jones, John
Key, George
Key, Thomas
Kindall, Williams
Leer, William
Martin, Charles
McDonald, David
Mershom, Nathaniel
Meriwether, William
Murphey, John
O'Harrah, Mikel
Pagan, David
Snow, George
Spillman, Francis
Spillman, James
Welch, Dominick
Wigins, Barney

Captain Edward Worthington's Company of Regulars
(William Clark Collection, MHS, Box 1, Folder 20)
Lieutenant Richard Clark
Allen, David
Anderson, John
Bowdery, John (fifer)
Brading, William
Bryant, James
Cox, Thomas
Crump, William
Dewit (also Dewitt), Henery
Estis, James
Evans, Charles
Gilmore, George
Hargis, John
Harris, Francis
Hatton (also Hutten), Christopher
Jewell, John
Johnson (also Johnston), Andrew (drummer)
Johnson, Edward (corporal)
Kemp (also Camp), Reubin
Kerkely, James
Leviston, George
Lockart, Archibald
Lundsford, Moses
McKensey, Mordiack
Moore, John (sgt)
Nelson, Enoch
Nelson, John
Nelson, Moses
Robison, John
Sertain (also Certain), Page
Sutherland, Lawrance
Swordkin, Jonathan
Thorninton (also Thornington), Josias (Joseph)
Tulfor (also Tulford), John
White, John
Williams, Daniel
Williams, Zachariah

Willis, Jacob
Wilson, John
Yeates, Isaac
Yeates, John (drummer)

Captain Richard McCarty's Company (VSA-13; Harding 1981:21-22)
Lieutanant John Girault
Lieutanant Michael(?) Perrault
Andre, Jean (sgt.)
Bennoit, Francis
Blanchard, (?)
Gagnus (also Gagnier), Jacque
Gagnus (also Gagnier), Louis
Grolet, Francis (father)
Grolet, Francis (son)
Harrison, James
Laform, (?)
L'Enfant, Francois
La Marine, John
LaRichardy, John
Lovin (also Loving), Richard
McLaughlin, Charles
Metivce, John
Metivce, Ps.
Mulboy (also Mulby), William
Pepin, John(?), Peter(?)
Piner, Jesse
Pipin, John
Pursley, (?)
Villier, Francis (sgt.)

Captain Abraham Keller's Company (VSA-12)
Brown, James (sgt.)
Chappel, John
Cooper, Barney
Cooper, Joseph
Crawley, John
Davis, James
Decart, Jacob
Dasker, Jacob
Duly, Haymore
Duly, Philip
Eagle, Harmon
Hays, Thomas
Hoit, George
Humber, David
Kearns, James or John
Kellar, John
Laycore, Francis
Montroy, Anthony
Panther, Joseph
Pritchet, James
Raper (also Rahr?), Baptist
Russill, David
Shank, John
Smith, George
Thompson, James

Captain John Bailey's Company (VSA-12)
Lieutenant William Clark
Ensign Laurence (also Lawrence) Slaughter
Ballenger, Larken
Bell, William

Fort Jefferson Personnel

Bravly, William
Buchanan, William
Burk, Nicholas
Bush, William
Carr, William
Clark, John
Conner, John
Horden, Frances
Hays, James
Jarril, James
Johnston, John
Lunsford, Anthony
Lunsford, George
Morris, Graves
Murray, Edward
Parker, Edward
Philaps, Henery
Shaver, David
Shepard, Peter
Theel, Levi
Thomson, William
Trent, Beverly (sgt.)
Tuttle, Nicholas
Vaugh, John
Waitt, Robert
White, Randel
Whitehead, Robert
Whitehead, William
Young, Hugh

Captain Jesse Evans Company (men discharged at Ft. Jefferson; VSA-12)
Brown, Lou
Chapman, Richard
Clark, Andrew
Hollis, Joshua
Huffman, Jacob
Lastly, John
McGuire, John
Potter, James
Shoemaker, Leonard
Smith, Joseph

Captain George Owens (also Oins) Company of Militia (VSA-12)
Aldar, John
Archer, Joshua
Barnet, James
Burk, John
Ciblet, Francis
Cooper, Samuel
Craten, Robert
Ford, John
Ford, Joseph
Ford, Robert
Graffen, Daniel
Groats, Jacob
Harlan, Silas
Hellebrandt, Peter
Hunter, Joseph
Hutsil, John
Hutsil, William
Johnston, John
Ker (also Ilor), Conrad
Ker (also Ilor), Henry

Ker (also Ilor), Jonas
Ker (also Ilor), Mark
King, Charles
King, James
McCan, Moses
McCormack, John
McMeans, Andrew
McMeans, James
Merridith, Daniel
Nedinger, Nicholas
Phelps, Anthony
Phelps, George
Phelps, Josiah
Phister, John
Reid, William
Shilling, Jacob
Smith, Edmund
Springer, Enoch
Steward, Henry
Wiley, James
Wilson, Edward
Wilson, John
Wolf, Michael
Young, James
Young, John

Captain Isaac Taylor's Company Discharged at Fort Jefferson
(VSA-12; Harding 1981:13)
Anderson, John
Bell, William
Brawly, William
Freeman, Peter
Hart, Miles
Hayes, James
Meadows, Josiah
Murray, Thomas
Oater, Samuel
Senet (also Sinnat), Richard
Taylor, Edward
Tennell, Richard
Thomson, William
Tiburn, Christopher
Tuttle, Nicholas
Tygar, Daniel
Wicks, Mordicai
Willson, John (sgt.)

Other Soldiers (several enlisted men below traveled to FJ for discharge)
Colonel John Montgomery
Major Thomas Quirk (also Kirk)
Major John Williams
Ballenger, James
Cox, John
Duncan, Joseph
Hall, William
Johnston, Samuel
Ozala, John (Captain ?)
Pines, Lewis
Roberts, John
Suverns, Ebenezer
Tolley, Daniel
Watkins, Samuel

Quartermaster/Commissary Corps (VSA-50)
John Dodge (to be paid at rate of Captain)
Blackford, Zephaniah
Carney, Martin
Dalton, Valentine Thomas (also in Indian Department)
Dodge, Israel
Donn, John
Finn (also Finz), James
Kennedy, Patrick (assistant deputy conductor)
Lindsay, Joseph
Roberts, Benjamin (Captain in George Slaughter's Quartermaster Corps)
Shannon, William (Captain, Conductor)

Artificers
Butcher, Gasper
Caesar (also Sezor) (also listed in Captain Robert George's Company)
Clark, Andrew (also listed in Captain Robert George's Company)
Thornton, Joseph (also listed in Captain Edward Worthington's Company)

Indian Department/Affairs
Leonard Helm, Superintendent
Dalton, Valentine Thomas (also Deputy Conductor in Quartermaster Corps)
Dalton, Hannah (wife of Valentine; interpreter)
Sherlock, James (interpreter for French and Indians)

Armorer and Smithy
Harris, John
White, John (listed in Captain Worthington's Company)

Tailor
Bryan, John
Bryan (also O'Brian and OBryan), Mrs. (no first name give)

Prisoners at Fort Jefferson
DeJean, Mr. (no first name given)
Wilson, Thomas (Lieutenant)

Friendly Indians
Batisst (Chief of Kaskaskia Indians)
"Joseph," a friendly Indian
65 unnamed Kaskaskia Indians

Slaves
George Rogers Clark's slaves (unspecified)
Captain (no first name given) Smith's slaves

Doctors at Fort Jefferson
Ray (also Rey), Andrew
Smyth, Samuel (surgeon)

Introduction, Part III: A List of Families at Fort Jefferson, 1780-1781
(Based on information taken from the Unpublished George Rogers Clark Papers in the Virginia State Library.)

Last Name	Wife's Name	Husband's Name	Reference to Family
Asher	Widow	William	Unknown
Brashears	Unknown	Richard	Unknown
Breeding	Hanah	Francis	Unknown
Bryan	Unknown	John	Yes, numbers unknown
Burks	Elizabeth	John	Unknown

Fort Jefferson Personnel   xv

Dalton	Hannah	Valentine T.	Unknown
Damewood	Mary	Boston	Yes, two children
Daughterty	Unknown	John	Unknown
Donne	Martha	John	Unknown
Elms	Ann	See Note #1	Yes, one daughter
Hellebrant	Mary	Peter	Unknown
Hughes	Martha	Unknown	Yes, numbers unknown
Hunter	Marah	Joseph	Yes, Nancy & Mary
Hutsel	Widow	John	Yes, numbers unknown
Johnston	Ann	Ezekiel	Unknown
Jones	Elizabeth	Matthew	Yes
Kennedy	Rachel	Patrick	Unknown
Lockard	Unknown	Archibald	Yes, numbers unknown
Lunsford	Mary	Anthony	Yes, numbers unknown
McAuley	Mary	Patrick-?	Unknown
McCormack	Unknown	John	Unknown
McMeans	Ann	Andrew	Yes, Mary, John, James, Isaac, Jane, Robert, & Anne
Mains	Unknown	Patrick	Yes, one child
Mayfield	Unknown	Micajah	Yes, unknown
Meredith	Mrs. (Widow)	Daniel-?	Unknown
Meredith	Luvana	See Note #2	Unknown
Miles	Unk./Deceased	Michael	Yes, one son
Murray	Unknown	Matthew	Unknown
Oiler	Unknown	Unknown	Yes, seven children
Owens	Charaty	George	Yes, unknown
Phelps	Elizabeth	Thomas-?	Yes, six children
Piggott	Eleanor	James	Yes, Levi & William
Quirk	Unknown	Thomas	Yes, two children
Rion/Ryan	Unknown	Lazurus-?	Unknown
Shilling	Mary	Jacob	Yes, unknown
Smith	Mary	Henry-?	Yes, one daughter, Sarah or Sidy (?)
Trent	Sarah	Mr. Beverly	Unknown
Watkins	Elizabeth	Samuel-?	Unknown
Witzel	"The Widow"	Unknown	Unknown
Young	Margery	James	Unknown

Note #1: Her husband may be William, John, or James Elms.
Note #2: Her husband may be Laurence or James Meredith.

Introduction, Part IV:
A Chronological Order of Recorded Deaths at Fort Jefferson, 1780-1781

Date	Individual	How Death Recorded	Military Company
6/2/80	Estes, James	Killed	Worthington
6/2/80	Gilmore, George	Killed	Worthington
6/3/80	March (Marak?), John	Deceased	George
6/7/80	Certain, Page	Killed	Worthington
6/7/80	Ker, Conrad (also Ilor)	Killed	Owen's Militia
6/7/80	Ker, Henry (also Ilor)	Killed	Owen's Militia
6/7/80	Ker, Mark (also Ilor)	Killed	Owen's Militia
6/8/80	Haul, Henry	Killed	George
7/15/80	Dean, James	Killed	Worthington
7/17/80	Aldar, John	Killed	Owen's Militia
8/12/80	Blair, John	Deceased	Brashear
8/27/80	Female Slave	Killed	Belonged to Captain Smith
8/27/80	Snowden (Swordin?), Jon.	Deceased	Worthington
8/27/80	Hutsill, John	Killed	Owen's Militia
8/27/80	Hatton, Christopher	Killed	Worthington
8/28/80	Laney, Thomas	Killed	George
9/4/80	Fair, Edmund	Deceased	George
9/5/80	Whitacre, Dan	Killed	George

Fort Jefferson Personnel

Date	Name	Status	Company
9/23/80	Rubido, Frank	Deceased	Brashear
9/24/80	Unnamed soldier	Dies	Rogers
9/28/80	Robeson (Robson?), Wm.	Deceased	Worthington
9/30/80	Unnamed soldier	Dies	Kellar
10/4/80	Brown, James	Killed	Worthington
10/4/80	Thorington, Joseph	Killed	Worthington
10/4/80	Ditterin, Jacob	Deceased	George
10/5/80	Wilson, Edward	Killed	Owen's Militia
10/7/80	Decker (Deckar), Jacob	Deceased	Kellar
10/10/80	Crawley, John	Died	Kellar
10/10/80	Villier, Francis	Killed	McCarty
10/10/80	Papin, John	Killed	McCarty
10/14/80	Hardin, Francis	Deceased	Bailey
10/17/80	Davies, James	Deceased	Kellar
10/20/80	Thompson, James	Deceased	Kellar
10/25/80	Waggoner, Peter	Deceased	George
11/2/80	Harrison, Richard	Deceased	Brashear
11/9/80	Williams, Daniel	Dead	Worthington
11/12/80	Morris, James	Deceased	Brashear
11/19/80	Turpin, Richard	Deceased	George
12/26/80	Horn, Jeremiah	Deceased	George
1/2/81	Smith, George	Died	George
1/15/81	Fever, William	Died	George
1/24/81	Carr (Kerr), William	Deceased	Bailey
3/28/81	Piner, Jesse	Killed	McCarty
4/12/81	Cooper, Joseph	Died	Kellar
5/28/81	Slaughter, Laurence	Killed	Bailey
6/2/81	McCarty, Richard	Killed	McCarty
6/5/81	Murray, Edward	Deceased	Bailey
3/28-6/7/81	Mrs. Michael Miles	Deceased	Civilian

Introduction, Part V: A Calendar of Fort Jefferson Activities

The following chronology provides a list of activities that led to the establishment, use, and abandonment of Fort Jefferson. The reader may find the timeline useful as an outline of events for the Fort Jefferson activities described in greater detail within the body of this book.

Summer, 1777   Clark sends spies into the Illinois posts

Fall, 1777   Spies return stating that Illinois country can be taken; Clark takes information to Governor Patrick Henry

January, 1778   Clark receives government okay with plans to fortify mouth of Ohio River

July, 1778   Clark takes Kaskaskia and other French towns along Mississippi and Vincennes along the Wabash

August-November, 1778   Henry Hamilton takes Vincennes

February, 1779   Clark takes Vincennes from Hamilton then plans to build garrison at mouth of Ohio after writing Daniel Broadhead, Silas Harlan

November, 1779   Clark holds meeting with his junior officers in a "Council of War" at Louisville to determine necessary number and strength of new garrisons, including garrison at mouth of Ohio

Fort Jefferson Personnel

January, 1780	Jefferson writes Joseph Martin to have Martin seek permission from Indians claiming land around the mouth of the Ohio; Jefferson also writes to Thomas Walker, surveyor, asking for plat of intended garrison at mouth of Ohio
March, 1780	Inducements to populate mouth of Ohio area by offering free land to civilians and military recruits, and reduce the number of posts and garrisons in the Illinois country and center population at mouth of Ohio
April, 1780	Clark procures goods for new fort at mouth of Ohio with plans and provisions for 1000 men for six months
April 19, 1780	Jefferson proposes Shawnee expedition to Clark; Clark and about 150 soldiers arrive at the mouth of the Ohio to establish Fort Jefferson and the civilian community of Clarksville; Clark writes John Dodge in Kaskaskia for supplies
April 20, 1780	Thirty-men from Vincennes (O'Post) leave to join garrison at mouth of Ohio; more civilians from Illinois country, Louisville (Falls of the Ohio), Central Bluegrass (Harrodsburg-Boonesborough), and others from Holston Valley begin arriving at mouth of Ohio
May 20, 1780	Clark and majority of soldiers leave Fort Jefferson to go to Cahokia to assist against British-Indian attack on St. Louis (Pancore) and vicinity
June 1, 1780	Consolidation of forces from Illinois country continues at Fort Jefferson
June 4, 1780	Captain Robert George, commander of Fort Jefferson, writes to Clark about completion of stockade around the post, clearing of farmland and planting by civilians, and assistance of inhabitants; Robert George notes early on that provisions are low
June 7, 1780	Chickasaw Indians, allied to the British, begin "marauding" around Fort Jefferson killing the Ker brothers
June 10, 1780	Clark at Fort Jefferson preparing for Shawnee expedition; Clark leaves ahead of troops and will be taking Richard Harrison's Company, one-half of Captain George Company of artillery, Captain Bailey's Company, and Captain Shannon's Company
June 10-14, 1780	Clothing issued to soldiers at garrison; expresses (messengers) sent ahead to the Falls of the Ohio
June 13, 1780	Civilians Piggott, Johnson, Smith, Hunter, Iles write petition to Virginia government to recognize civilian community of "Clarksville" as new county of Virginia
June 14, 1780	Expedition to Falls of Ohio begins from Fort Jefferson
June 15, 1780	Payments from Quartermaster stores at Fort Jefferson begin to seamstresses at Fort Jefferson for sewing of soldiers clothes
June 20, 1780	Fort Jefferson issued food to help inhabitants of Kaskaskia

Fort Jefferson Personnel

July, 1780	More issues of clothing at Fort Jefferson to soldiery; more payments to seamstresses; Ensign Jarret Williams Company at Kaskaskia preparing to go to Fort Jefferson
July 13-16, 1780	Sgt. Matthews and Major Harlan are bringing corn and a swivel from Falls of the Ohio to Fort Jefferson
July 14, 1780	Captain John Rogers' Light Dragoons at Fort Jefferson are about to leave for Cahokia; Col. John Montgomery prepares to leave Fort Jefferson for Fort Clark (Kaskaskia)
July 17, 1780	Chickasaw Indians attack Clarksville community at daybreak killing two of the militia and wounding several others
July 20, 1780	Expresses (Lawrence Keenan and Joshua Archer) are sent to Col. Montgomery at Fort Clark for assistance
July 31, 1780	Kaskaskia Indians-allies of the Americans--arrive from Fort Clark to assist Fort Jefferson. Captains Bailey and William Clark arrive from Fort Clark with 1400 lbs of flour, 50 bushes corn and 28 men from Bailey's Company
August, 1780	Kaskaskia Indians stay at Fort Jefferson and hunt for garrison; Lt. Timothy Montbreuen and Captain Richard McCarty and Company arrive at Fort Jefferson from Fort Clark
August 12, 1780	Thomas Bentley (a double agent) writes Haldimand in Detroit that all American troops are at Fort Jefferson and that the Illinois Country is free for Haldimand's taking; Fort Jefferson returns to "normalcy;" distribution of ammunition and rifles
August 27, 1780	A larger force of Chickasaw Indians attack civilian town of Clarksville killing a Negro "wench," and Private John Hutsil; attack widens and encapsulates Fort Jefferson and civilian settlement; attack continues three days; this attack led by Lt. James Whitehead from Southern British Indian department; attack continues four days; Captain Bailey's hunting party is intercepted; four killed, one, taken prisoner
September 1, 1780	Chickasaw withdraw from post and community after burning corn crop and killing majority of livestock; Jack Ash, messenger for Captain Robert George sent to Fort Clark for assistance; Lt. Helm and William Clark assess damage done to 45 acres of corn crops; Col. Montgomery arrives Fort Jefferson with ten soldiers and 65 Kaskaskia Indians sometime before September 6th for assistance
September 6, 1780	Boat from New Orleans arrives with 12 kegs of gunpowder amounting to 1200 lbs and other supplies
September 7, 1780	Sickness among soldiers and civilians prevails, mostly malaria and flu; large quantities of sugar and tafia issued for the sicknesses
September 10, 1780	Montgomery preparing to return to Kaskaskia; Kaskaskia Indian revenge party leaves Fort Jefferson to find Chickasaw after being armed with 10# gunpowder and 20# lead and taking barge with swivel gun; many blankets are issued to sick persons
September 12, 1780	Twenty civilian families (of the 40 known) move from Fort Jefferson; all had been members of George Owens Clarksville

Fort Jefferson Personnel

militia; move occurred because of "few provisions" and "poor prospect of getting more" now that corn crop was destroyed

September 13, 1780 Four more families move

September 16, 1780 Sickness increases around the fort and community

October 4-5, 1780 Four more people at Fort Jefferson are killed by marauding Indians; more ammunition is issued to soldiers and civilians; sickness continues; soap is issued; desertion is frequent among the soldiers

October 22-23, 1780 Col. Montgomery and Captain John Williams arrive from Kaskaskia; Montgomery wants Williams to take command from Captain George; Captain George refuses to relinquish command unless so ordered by George Rogers Clark

October 29, 1780 Montgomery leaves Fort Jefferson for New Orleans. Montgomery notes that Fort Jefferson is being reduced by famine, desertion, and dying

November, 1780 Major Harlan and members of the garrison are out hunting; sickness continues; dry goods and brass kettles arrive from New Orleans

December, 1780 John Donne's letter to George Rogers Clark paints a bleak picture of Fort Jefferson, describes successful hunting (more than 8000 lbs of meat), but still not enough for remaining civilians and soldiers

December 7, 1780 Tafia issue for 152 persons in the outposts and garrison

December 12, 1780 Cargo from New Orleans arrives; mostly munitions

December 15, 1780 Cargo from the Falls of the Ohio arrives; mostly dry goods; men were issued shoes

December 25, 1780 (Christmas) Canon salute in garrison and in town of Clarksville

January 1, 1781 Cargo of goods arrive from New Orleans; Robert George signs note for items as $237,320 hard specie even though cargo valued at only $25,000; most of cargo dry goods and tafia; Kaskaskia revenge party supplied with gunpowder, lead and flint; hogsheads of tafia sent to Falls of Ohio and Illinois Country for supplies; shipment of swords received at Fort Jefferson and issued to soldiery; officers receive annual allotment of clothing; John Dodge becomes universally-disliked by all at Fort Jefferson

January 23, 1781 Boat with supplies arrives at Fort Jefferson

January 30, 1781 Tafia ration given to 110 men at Fort Jefferson

February, 1781 Kickapoo and Perorian Indians at Fort Jefferson. Tafia and whiskey rations allotted to 110 men; Supplies (most ammunition) sent to O'Post in Vincennes with Major Linctot

February 15, 1781 Bailey's Company goes to O'Post

February 26, 1781 A Court of Inquiry is looking into Captain Worthington's conduct; John Williams writes, "How dry I am;"

Fort Jefferson Personnel

February 28, 1781	A Court of Inquiry examines Captain McCarty's conduct
March 7, 1781	A Court of Inquiry continues to examine Captain McCarty's conduct; McCarty is found guilty for threatening to leave the service and Virginia; a general Court Martial is recommended; McCarty also found guilty of threatening a fellow officer; other charges against McCarty are dropped
March 9, 1780	Court of Inquiry examines Captain Rogers conduct during command at Kaskaskia; court found no evidence of misconduct; acquitted; 100 lbs of gunpowder sent to Kaskaskia for its defence; only 50 men receive tafia rations
March 17, 1781	Much drinking to St. Patrick's health; 90 men now in garrison receiving tafia ration (Captain Bailey's Company has returned); received from hunters 1652 lbs buffalo meat and 188 lbs bear meat
March 18, 1781	Drinking to the health of St. Patrick's wife (Shealy)
March 19, 1781	Lt. Girault writes George Rogers Clark for permission to go on an expedition and leave Fort Jefferson; Captain John Rogers' Company goes to the Falls of the Ohio
March 20, 1781	Court martial proceedings against David Allen and James Taylor for beating servants, robbing Major Williams kitchen, and speaking disrespectfully to an officer; Taylor acquitted; Allen found guilty of speaking disrespectfully and given 50 lashes on his bare back; William Clark, John Dodge and others leaving Fort Jefferson for Louisville and Virginia to procure supplies and settle accounts respectively
March 29, 1781	Kaskaskia revenge party has returned
April, 1781	Drinking continues, tobacco issued, seining for fish begins
April 15, 1781	George Rogers Clark's letters forwarded by Captain James Sullivan to Fort Jefferson from Beargrass Station near the Falls
April 20, 1781	George Washington writes to the Board of War stating that George Rogers Clark intends an expedition against Detroit
April 22, 1781	Martin Carney writes George Rogers Clark and asks to be relieved of his position at Fort Jefferson
April 25, 1781	High water at Fort Jefferson necessitates stores moved out of garrison; 43 men receive tobacco ration
May, 1781	Ninety-five persons (76 men, 9 women, 10 children) of the Illinois Regiment at Fort Jefferson receive a sugar ration; additional issues of rum and tobacco given
May 10, 1781	Col. John Montgomery arrives
May 23, 1781	Sixty-nine men, eight women, and 10 children present
May 25, 1781	Sixty-four men present; break-in at public store; situation at Fort Jefferson getting desperate
June, 1781	Garrison strength at 58

June 5, 1781	Issues of ammunition are given to hunting parties for Kellar's Company on its way back to the Falls of the Ohio; much tobacco and sugar being issued to garrison and civilians
June 7, 1781	Fifty-seven troops in garrison
June 8, 1781	Fort Jefferson evacuated (troops leaving include members of Worthington's, Kellar's, George's, and Brashear's companies)
July 12, 1781	Troops arrive at the Falls of the Ohio

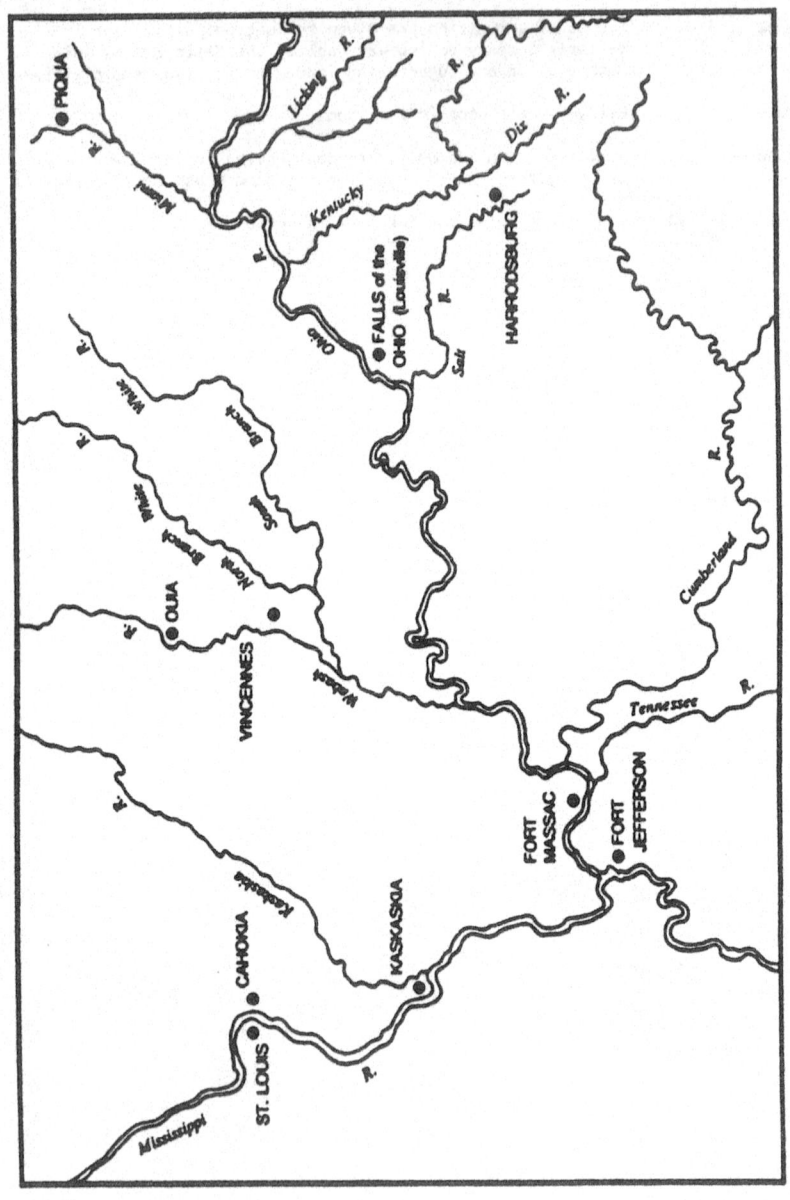

Figure 1: Sites associated with George Rogers Clark's Fort Jefferson.
Artwork by Richard Mjos of Murray, Kentucky.

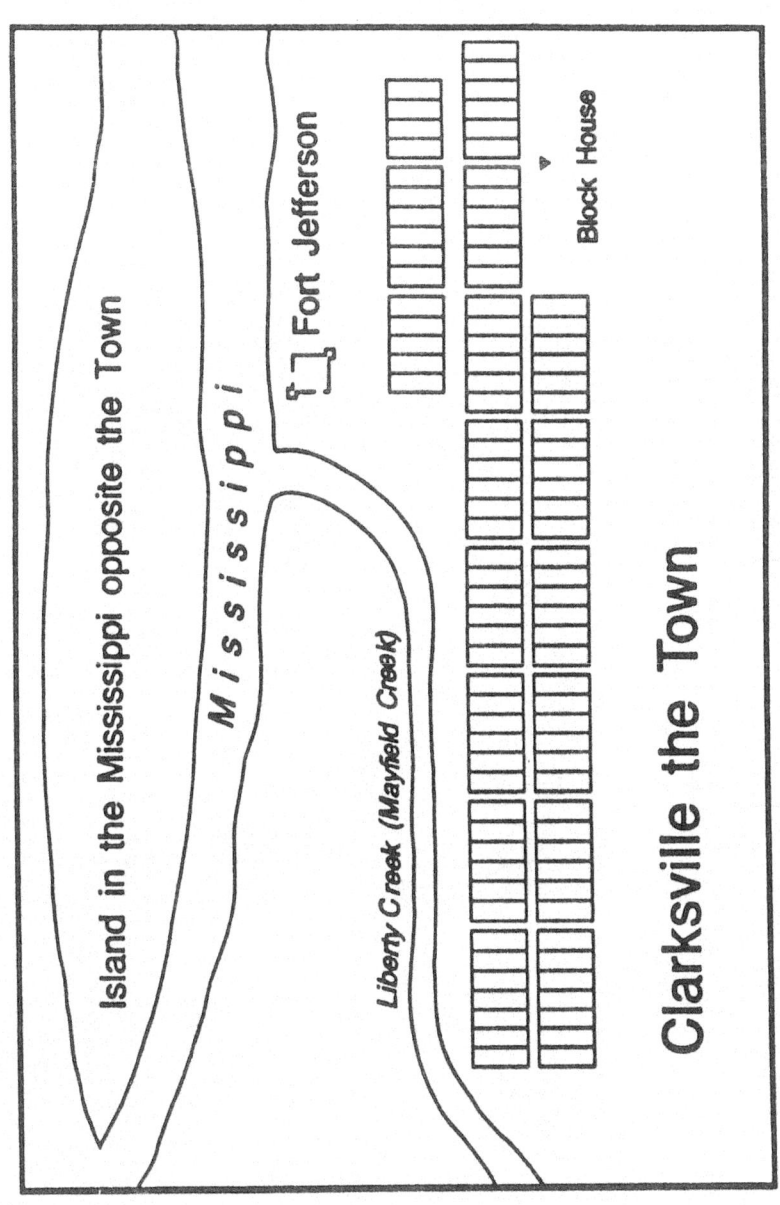

Figure 2: A redrawn version of the William Clark map of Fort Jefferson. Source: Draper Manuscripts, 1M11. Artwork by Richard Mjos of Murray, Kentucky.

Fort Jefferson Personnel

Aldar, John
05/01/80 Enlisted on this date as Private in Capt. George Owens' Co. of Militia of the District of Clarksville in the State of Virginia (GRC Papers, I 464; Harding 1981: 48-9).
07/17/80 Killed (Harding 1981: 49) (DMS 26J28).

Allen, David
06/10/80 A. Gamelin signs he received of Sgt. Moore of Capt. Worthington's Co., two soldiers of the same company: Louis Brown and David Allen. They are to be delivered to the commanding officer. [This probably occurred at FJ although not stated] (MHS: B1, F20).
07/15/80 In Capt. Worthington's Company (MHS B1, F20) (VSA-12).
08/12/80 Issued for Capt. Worthington's Company, two plain shirts for David Allen per Lt. Clark's receipt and Capt. George's order (VSA-48).
09/09/80 Account of sugar delivered by Martin Carney by order of Col. Montgomery at Fort Jefferson, to David Allen, a soldier in Worthington's Company, one lb (VSA-50).
03/20/81 Underwent Court Martial Proceedings at FJ for having robbed Major Williams' kitchen, beaten his servants, and for verbally abusing Maj. Williams after being arrested; he was acquitted of all charges except for speaking disrespectfully of Major Williams and was sentenced to receive "50 lashes on his bare back well laid on" (DMS 56J40).

Allen, Isaac
06/12/80 Issued two shirts, entitled by law, at FJ as member of Ensign Williams' Company (VSA-12).
09/18/80 Listed as one of five sick men of Capt. Brashears' Company to receive a share of five lbs of sugar issued by order of Capt. George to Quartermaster M. Carney (VSA-13).
09/25/80 Paid Isaac Allen for 12 days work per order Lt. Col. Montgomery, one blanket (VSA-48).

Allen, John
08/10/80 Enlisted in Capt. Kellar's Co. (Harding 1981: 24).
10/25/80 Deserted (Harding 1981: 24).
11/22/80 Status changed to killed [Body found?] (VSA-14).

Allen, Nathan
09/09/80 Received two lbs sugar and one pint tafia from the Quartermaster by order of Col. John Montgomery valued at 13 shillings. Referred to as an "inhabitant of this place" [F.J.] (VSA-13).
09/09/80 Account of sugar delivered by Martin Carney by order of Col. Montgomery at Fort Jefferson, to Nathan Allen of militia, two lbs (VSA-50).

Allen, Samuel
05/30/80 Enlisted on this date as a sergeant in Capt. Brashears' Company (Harding, 1981: 51).
06/12/80 Issued two shirts, entitled by law, at FJ as member of Ensign Williams' Company (VSA-12).
09/14/80 Issued a share of two lbs sugar along with James Brown for being sick (VSA-13).
09/25/80 Two yds linen paid Sam Allen for five days work per order of Col. Montgomery (VSA-48).
10/10/80 J. Donne signs that he received 496 lbs beef from Samuel Allen, to be paid at current rate (VSA-13a).
10/14/80 Robert George requests Capt. Dodge to issued Samuel Allen 1/2 yard stroud in part of payment for beef delivered; Samuel Allen acknowledged to have received 12 yds flannel (VSA-13a).
10/14/80 Samuel Allen signs he received the within order from Israel Dodge (VSA-13b).

Fort Jefferson Personnel

10/14/80 Account of ammunition delivered by Martin Carney by order of Capt. George to Sgt. Allen of Capt. Brashears' Co., 1 1/2 lbs powder, three pounds lead (VSA 50).

Allin, Jon
05/30/80 Enlisted on this date as a private in Capt. Brashears' Company (Harding 1981: 51).
09/11/80 Issued as a Soldier in Capt. Brashears' Co., two shirts, one pair breeches, one jacket, and one coat (VSA-13a).
11/12/80 Deserted (Harding 1981: 51).

Alison, John
09/30/80 Thirty yds osnaburgs paid John Alison for 25 bushels of corn (VSA-48).
09/30/80 Two check handkerchiefs paid Alison for carting 25 bushels of corn (VSA-48).

Anderson, John
Enlisted as Matross [Corporal] in Capt. Robert George's Company of Artillery in the Service of the Commonwealth of Virginia and Illinois Department (Harding 1981: 29-30).
11/29/79 On a return signed by R. George and dated 12/10/80, John Anderson enlisted on this date, for three years or during the wary by Lt. V.T. Dalton into Capt. Robert George's Company of Artillery (MHS: F1, B23).
12/09/80 Robert George requests of Israel Dodge to pay John Anderson out of the public store for making one suit of clothes for a soldier of George's Co. (VSA- 14a).
12/09/80 John Anderson signed that he received of Israel Dodge three yds flannel and a skein of thread in full of Anderson's demands for making a suit of clothes (VSA-14b).

Anderson, John
07/15/80 In Capt. Worthington's Company (MHS B1, F20) (VSA-12).

Anderson, Joseph [also Andrews and Andrewson]
06/04/79 Enlisted as Sergeant in Capt. Robert George's Company of Artillery in Service of the Commonwealth of Virginia and Illinois Department (Harding 1981: 29-30).
06/19/80 At FJ and issued two shirts per Capt. George's orders for being enlisted during the war (VSA-11).
06/22/80 One brass ink stand per order and receipt of Joseph Anderson (VSA-48).
06/23/80 Capt. Robt. George requests of John Dodge by Col. Clark's orders to issue one brass inkstand to Sgt. Anderson (VSA-11).
06/23/80 Joseph Anderson signs that he received the above (VSA-11b).
06/23/80 Account of ammunition delivered by Martin Carney by Capt. Robert George's order at Camp Jefferson, to Sgt. Anderson, 1/2 lb lead and one flint (VSA-50).
06/30/80 Account of ammunition delivered by Martin Carney by Capt. Robert George's order at Camp Jefferson, to Sgt. Anderson for the use of the garrison, 4 1/2 lbs powder, nine lbs lead, and eight flints (VSA-50).
06/30/80 Account of ammunition delivered by Martin Carney by Capt. Robert George's order at Camp Jefferson, to Sgt. Anderson, 1/2 lb lead and one flint (VSA-50).
07/03/80 Capt. Robt. George requests of John Dodge to issue one pair of leggings of half-thicks each to Sgt. Anderson and Michael Hacketon of George's Co., going on command, by Col. Clark's orders (VSA-12a).
07/03/80 2 1/2 yds half-thicks per order and receipt of Joseph Anderson (VSA-48).
07/15/80 Account of arms delivered by Martin Carney to Capt. George's Company of Artillery of the Illinois Virginia Regiment, delivered to Sgt. Anderson, five muskets and five carabines (VSA-50).
07/17/80 Acc't of ammunition delivered by Carney by Capt. George's order at Camp Jefferson, to Sgt. Anderson for the defense of this place (VSA-50).

Fort Jefferson Personnel

07/26/80 Issued along with John Ash, Matthew Jones, James McDaniels, William Posten, and Richard Hopkins, three carots of tobacco (VSA-12a).
07/28/80 Acc't of tobacco delivered by M. Carney by order of Capt. George at this place, to Sgt. Anderson in George's Company, three carots weighing nine lbs (VSA-50).
08/03/80 Account of ammunition delivered by Martin Carney by Capt. George's order to Sgt. Anderson for the use of some of the soldiers, one lb powder and two lbs lead (VSA-50).
08/03/80 Account of tobacco delivered by Martin Carney by order of Capt. Robert George at this place, to Sgt. Anderson, 1 1/2 carots weighing 4 1/2 lbs (VSA-50).
08/17/80 Account of arms delivered by Martin Carney to Capt. George's Company of Artillery of the Illinois Virginia Regiment, delivered to Sgt. Anderson for Capt. Worthington, one rifle gun (VSA-50).
08/26/80 Issued 1/2 carot of tobacco (VSA-12a).
08/26/80 Account of tobacco delivered by Martin Carney by order of Capt. Robert George at this place, to Sgt. Joseph Anderson for his own use, 1/2 carot and 1 1/2 lbs (VSA-50).
09/03/80 Account of tobacco delivered by Martin Carney by order of Capt. George at Fort Jefferson, to Sgt. Anderson for Capt. George's Company, 5 1/2 carots weighing 16 lbs (VSA-50).
09/13/80 Account of sugar delivered by Martin Carney by order of Capt. George at Fort Jefferson, to Sgt. Anderson of Capt. George's Company, two lbs (VSA-50).
09/26/80 Robert George requests the Quartermaster to issued one lb powder and two lbs lead to Sgt. Anderson (VSA-13a).
10/23/80 By order of Col. Clark, Robert George requests J. Dodge to issue cloth and trimmings for nine men, one is Joseph Anderson, issued for enlisting (VSA-13a).
10/23/80 R. George signs he received the above cloth and trimmings for the nine men (VSA-13b).
10/28/80 Account of ammunition delivered by Martin Carney by order of Capt. George, to Anderson for going express to the Falls of Ohio, 1 1/4 lbs powder, three lbs lead (VSA-50).
10/22/81 Deserted (Harding 1981: 29-30).

Andre, Jean [also Andres, John] [SGT]
09/10/80 Member of Capt. Richard McCarty's Co. Issued full clothing for enlisting (VSA-13).

Angley, Peter
02/04/80 Enlisted on this date as a Private in Capt. John Bailey's Company of the Illinois Regiment in the Virginia State Service (Harding 1981: 45-46).
04/19/80 Deserted on this date from Capt. John Bailey's Company (Harding 1981: 46).

Archer, Jane
06/24/80 One blue cotton handkerchief, one linen handkerchief, three yds ribbon, one paper pins, and one pair scissors paid Jane Archer for making six ruffled shirts (VSA-48).

Archer, Joshua
05/01/80 Enlisted on this date in Capt. George Owens' Company of Militia of the District of Clarksville in the State of Virginia (Harding 1981: 48-49).
05/01/80 Enlisted on this date as Private in Capt. George Ownes' Company (GRC, I: 465).
07/21/80 2 1/2 yds half-thicks, one yd blue stroud, and one linen handkerchief per order and receipt of Joshua Archer (VSA-48).
09/01/80 [?] Farmed with Joseph Hunter, had 1 3/4 acres [45 bushels] destroyed by Indians (DMS 1M8).
09/02/80 5 1/2 yds linen per order paid to J. Archer per receipt for going express to Kaskaskia in time of an attack (VSA-48).

Fort Jefferson Personnel

09/09/80 Account of sugar delivered by Martin Carney by order of Col. Montgomery at Fort Jefferson, to Joshua Archer, three lbs (VSA-50).
09/10/80 Issued three lbs sugar for behaving himself when an express (VSA-13a).
11/25/80 Account of sugar delivered by Martin Carney by orders of Capt. George, to Joshua Archer of Militia, one lb (VSA-50).
11/26/80 Account of ammunition delivered by Martin Carney by order of Capt. Robert George at Fort Jefferson, to Mr. Archer, a militia man, one lb powder (VSA-50).
12/25/80 Joshua Archer should be paid ten shillings and four pence for buffalo and bear meat furnished Capt. George's troops (GRC, PapersII: 334).
03/23/81 Ammunition delivered by order of Capt. George, to Mr. Archer, 1/2 lb powder (VSA-50).
05/03/81 To Mr. Archer, militia of Clarksville, per orders, three lbs sugar and one carot of tobacco (VSA-49).
05/03/81 Tobacco issued to sundry persons per order of Capt. George, Commandant, to Joshua Archer, three lbs (VSA-50).
06/05/81 To Mr. Archer, militia of Clarksville, per orders, 12 lbs sugar (VSA-48).
06/05/81 Account of ammunition delivered by Martin Carney by order of Capt. Robert George and Col. Montgomery, to Mr. Archer, one lb powder, one lb lead (VSA-50).

Armstrong, George
06/04/79 Enlisted as matross [corporal] on this date in Capt. Robert George's Company of Artillery in the Service of the Commonwealth of Virginia and Illinois Department (Harding 1981: 29-30).
09/11/80 Issued one blanket with ten others of Capt. George's Co., for being enlisted for three years or during the war. Issued two shirts for enlisting for three years or duration into Capt. George's Co. (VSA-1a).
09/13/80 V. T. Dalton requests John Dodge to issue two shirts to George Armstrong for enlisting (VSA-13a).
09/13/80 V. T. Dalton signs that shirts were received for George Armstrong (VSA-13b).

Ash, John [also Ashe] [possibly Jack]
06/04/79 Enlisted as matross [corporal] on this date in Capt. Robert George's Company of Artillery in the Service of the Commonwealth of Virginia and Illinois Department (Harding 1981: 29-30).
06/19/80 Issued two shirts by order of Capt. George for being enlisted during the war (VSA-11).
07/26/80 One of six men issued three carots of tobacco (VSA-12).
08/18/80 Issued one coarse comb, one fine comb, and one butcher knife (VSA-12a).
08/19/80 One ivory comb, one horn comb and one scalping knife per order and receipt of John Ash (VSA-48).
08/27/80 1 1/4 yds blue stroud and three pair moccasins to John Ash per order (VSA-48).
09/01/80 [?] Possibly "Jack" Ash left Ft. Jeff for Kaskaskia for help (DMS 26J24).
09/10/80 Issued one blanket and one shirt for going express to Kaskaskia (VSA-13a).
09/11/80 One, 2 1/2 point blanket and one shirt per order of Lt. Col. Montgomery paid John Ash for going express (VSA-48).
09/12/80 Four yds flannel paid John Ash for going express (VSA-48).
09/25/80 One blanket and one shirt issued to Ash per order Lt. Col. Montgomery (VSA-48).
10/11/80 Account of ammunition delivered by Martin Carney by order of Capt. George, to John Ash, a soldier in Capt. George's Company, 1 1/2 lbs powder, three lbs lead (VSA-50).
10/12/80 Robert George requests M. Carney to issue one lb soap to John Ash (VSA-13).

Fort Jefferson Personnel

10/22/80 Account of soap delivered by Martin Carney by order of Col. Montgomery and Capt. George at Fort Jefferson, to John Ash a soldier in Capt. George's Company, one lb (VSA-50).
12/07/80 John Montgomery at Fort Jefferson "orders" the quartermaster to issue to John Ash on gill of tafia for every man belonging to the garrison [Reverse states 78 quarts and six gills] (VSA-14a,b).
10/08/81 Discharged (Harding 1981: 29-30).

Asher, Mrs. William [wife of Ensign Wm Asher] [Widow]
07/23/80 Husband [in Capt. Benjamin Roberts' Co.] killed (Harding 1981: 37).
01/01/81 Issued provisions for four days [Jan 1 - Jan 4] per Prockter Ballard [Sgt.] and George Slaughter's order to the Quartermaster (VSA-15).

Baber, Daniel [also Babu]
02/03/80 Enlisted as Matross [Corporal] in Capt. Robert George's Company of Artillery in the Service of the Commonwealth of Virginia and Illinois Department (Harding 1981: 29-30).
06/12/80 Going to Falls of Ohio with Capt. Harrison; George requests clothing issue for list of men who will be going on expedition (VSA-11).
08/04/80 Deserted (Harding 1981: 29-30).

Bailey, John [also Bakley, Bayley]
05/24/79 Edward Murray enlisted on this date in Capt. Bailey's Company as a private (Harding, 1981: 46).
09/20/79 Mathias Prock enlisted on this date as a Private in Capt. John Bailey's Company of the Illinois Regiment in the Virginia State Service (Harding 1981: 45-46).
11/17/79 Beverly Trent enlisted on this date as a Sergeant in Capt. John Bailey's Company of the Illinois Regiment in the Virginia State Service (Harding, 1981: 45-46).
02/04/80 Peter Angley enlisted on this date as a private in Capt. John Bailey's Company (Harding 1981: 45-46).
03/24/80 Larken Ballenger enlisted on this date as a private in Capt. John Bailey's Company (Harding 1981: 45- 46).
03/26/80 Peter Blain enlisted on this date as a Private; William Carr enlisted as a private; and James Hays enlisted as a private in Capt. John Bailey's Company of Illinois Regiment in the Virginia State Service (Harding 1981 45-46).
03/29/80-11/30/81 Listed as Captain. Payroll (Harding 1981: 45-46).
04/12/80 Account of arms delivered to Capt. John Bailey's Company: delivered to Sgt. Trent by Col. Clark's verbal orders, two rifles (VSA-50: 4).
04/19/80 Private Peter Angley, Private Ephraim Dragoon, and Private Mathias Prock deserted on this date from Capt. John Bailey's Company (Harding, 1981: 46).
04/26/80 Account of arms delivered to Capt. John Bailey's Company: delivered to Ensign Slaughter, one rifle (VSA-50: 4).
04/26/80 Account of arms delivered to Capt. John Bailey's Company: delivered to Capt. Bailey, one rifle (VSA-50: 4).
04/26/80 John Bailey signed that he received of Martin Carney one rifle gun for the use of Bailey's Company (VSA-10).
05/01/80 Private Peter Blain deserted on this date from Capt. Bailey's Company (Harding, 1981: 46).
05/08/80 Account of arms delivered to Capt. John Bailey's Company: delivered to Ensign Slaughter, one rifle (VSA-50: 4).
05/08/80 John Bailey signs request to the Quartermaster to issue one gun to one man of Bailey's Company (VSA-11a; filed as May 9, 1780).
05/09/80 John Bailey signs that he received the within contents from Martin Carney (VSA-11b).
05/12/80 John Bailey signs that he received of Martin Carney, three fusees for Capt. Worthington's Company (VSA-11a).

Fort Jefferson Personnel

05/19/80 Account of ammunition delivered by Martin Carney by order of Col. Clark: to Capt. John Bailey of regulars at Kaskaskia, 9 1/2 lbs powder and 19 lbs lead (VSA-50: 8).

05/26/80 Account of ammunition delivered by Martin Carney by order of Col. Clark: to Capt. John Bailey at Cahokia, 4 1/2 lbs powder and nine lbs lead; to Capt. John Bailey at Cahokia, 9 1/2 lbs powder and 19 lbs lead (VSA-50).

05/31/80 Account of arms delivered to Capt. John Bailey's Company: delivered to Capt. Bailey, one carabine (VSA-50: 4).

06/12/80 Going on expedition with Harrison to Falls of Ohio; George requests clothing to be issued for the list of men going with Harrison (VSA-11).

07/10/80 Capt. Robt. George requests by Col. Clark's orders, that John Dodge issue Capt. John Bailey and Ensign Slaughter their full quota of clothing which they are entitled to by law (VSA-12a).

07/12/80 Issued 1 1/2 yds brown broadcloth 7/4 wide, 1 1/2 yds scarlet broadcloth 7/4 wide, one stick silk twist, eight skeins silk, 2 1/4 yds thickset for one vest or breeches, two yds toile gris for one vest or breeches, 2 1/2 yds shalloon, two yds toile gris for one vest or breeches, 4 1/2 yds check linen for two vests or breeches, 3 1/8 yds calender for three vests or breeches, 5/8 yd sycee, two yds chintz for two vests or breeches, 19 1/2 yds white linen for six shirts, two yds muslin for six stocks, 3/4 yd fine holland for ruffling, nine skeins white thread, one silk handkerchief, one Indian handkerchief, four linen handkerchiefs, two pairs thread hose, one hat fine -- returned, 3 1/2 yds coarse linen for lining, three yds broadcloth 7/4 wide, 2 3/4 yds calamanco for one vest or breeches, 3/4 yard spotted flannel for one vest or breeches (VSA-48).

07/12/80 Ensign Slaughter, Illinois Battalion signed in behalf of Capt. John Bailey that the above goods were received from Capt. John Dodge, Agent in part of the clothing allowed Bailey by law. Attested by J. Donne (VSA-48).

07/12/80 Four yds osnaburg and 5/8 yd stroud for leggings, issued to and overdrawn by Capt. Bailey. Neither article appeared on the July 12 list of sundry goods issued to Bailey (VSA-48).

07/12/80 Capt. Robert George requests of John Dodge, by order of Col. Clark, that Ensign Slaughter be given 44 shirts for 22 men of Capt. Bailey's Company which are enlisted during the present war. List of the 22 men:

John Vaughan	Larken Ballenger	Wm. Brauly	David Shaver
Graves Morris	Randel White	James Jarrell	Henry Philips
George Shepard	Wm Care	Robert Waitt	Nic'las Tuttle
Frances Harden	Edward Thurry	James Hays	Wm Thomson
Levi Theel	Hugh Young	John Comier	Wm Brush
Peter Shepard	(VSA-12).		

07/13/80 Issued to Capt. Bailey for his company 43 plain shirts and one ruffled shirt per Ensign Slaughter (VSA-48).

07/13/80 Issued to Ensign Slaughter for Capt. Bailey's company by order of Col. Montgomery, two shirts (VSA-48).

08/01/80 Arrived with Lt. Clark [probably Richard] and brought 1400w of flour and 50 bushel of corn and 28 men (Seineke 1981: 449).

08/01/80 Account of ammunition delivered by Martin Carney by Capt. George's order to Sgt. Vaughan of Capt. Bailey's Company, seven lbs powder and 14 lbs lead (VSA-50).

08/05/80 Account of tobacco delivered by Martin Carney by order of Capt. Robert George at this place, to Sgt. Vaughan of Capt. Bailey's Company, 3 1/3 carots weighing ten lbs (VSA-50).

08/13/80 One ruffled and one plain shirt for a soldier per Capt. Bailey (VSA-48).

08/24/80 Account of ammunition delivered by Martin Carney by Capt. George's order, to a man of Capt. Bailey's Company, 1/4 lb powder and 1/2 lb lead (VSA-50).

08/27/80 Bailey's hunting party encounters hostile Indians; four men killed, one captured (Seineke 1981: 458).

08/29/80 Bailey returns to Ft. Jefferson with hunting party, reports encounter to Capt. Robert George (Seineke 1981: 458).

Fort Jefferson Personnel

09/02/80 Letter from George to Montgomery states that four unnamed soldiers in Capt. Bailey's Co. were killed on 08/27/80 (MHS B1, F21).

09/03/80 Account of tobacco delivered by Martin Carney by order of Capt. Robert George at Ft. Jefferson, to Sgt. Vaughan for Capt. Bailey's Company, five carots weighing 16 lbs (VSA-50).

09/08/80 Account of sugar delivered by Martin Carney by order of Col. Montgomery at Fort Jefferson, to three men of Capt. Bailey's Co., 3 lbs (VSA-50).

09/09/80 Account of sugar delivered by Martin Carney by order of Col. Montgomery at Fort Jefferson, to Groves Morris, a man in Capt. Bailey's Company, two lbs; to two men of Capt. Bailey's Company, two lbs; to two men of Capt. Bailey's Company, one lb; to George Lunsford of Capt. Bailey's Company, 1/2 lb; to five men of Capt. John Bailey's Company, 2 1/2 lbs (VSA-50).

09/10/80 Issued two blankets: one for himself and one for Ensign Slaughter (VSA-13).

09/10/80 One blanket per receipt of E. Slaughter and order of Lt. Col. Montgomery, five yds white flannel, 40 continental dollars to enlist a recruit issued to and overdrawn by Capt. John Bailey. These articles did not appear with the July 12th list of sundry goods issued to Capt. Bailey (VSA-48).

09/12/80 Account of sugar delivered by Martin Carney by order of Col. Montgomery at Fort Jefferson, to a man of Capt. Bailey's Company, 1/2 lb (VSA-50).

09/13/80 Listed as one officer of the mess who received a share of 60 lbs of sugar (VSA-13b).

09/13/80 Account of soap delivered by Martin Carney by order of Col. Montgomery and Capt. George at Fort Jefferson, to Capt. Bailey's Company, 12 lbs (VSA-50).

09/15/80 John Bailey writes a return [George signs] to the Quartermaster for five lbs powder and thirty-two lbs lead for the use of ten men of his company (VSA-13a).

09/15/80 Reverse: John Bailey requests [George signs] the Quartermaster to issue five lbs powder and eleven lbs lead for use of his company (VSA-13b).

09/15/80 Account of ammunition delivered by Martin Carney by Capt. George's order to Capt. Bailey's company, 5 1/2 lbs powder and 11 lbs lead (VSA-50).

09/15/80 Account of sugar delivered by Martin Carney by order of Capt. George at Fort Jefferson, to Edward Murray, a soldier in Capt. Bailey's Company, two lbs (VSA-50).

09/16/80 John Bailey requests [Robert George signs] the Quartermaster to issue to four sick men of his company, two lbs sugar (VSA-13a).

09/16/80 Account of sugar delivered by Martin Carney by order of Capt. George at Fort Jefferson, to four men of Capt. John Bailey's Company, two lbs (VSA-50).

09/26/80 John Bailey requests [R. George signs] one lb powder and two lbs lead issue to two men of Bailey's company "from the Illinois" (VSA-13a).

09/26/80 Account of ammunition delivered by Martin Carney by Capt. George's order to two men of Capt. Bailey's Company, one lb powder and two lbs lead (VSA-50).

09/27/80 John Bailey requests [George signs] Quartermaster to issue one lb sugar to two sick men of Bailey's company (VSA-13a).

09/27/80 Account of sugar delivered by Martin Carney by order of Capt. George at Fort Jefferson, to two men of Capt. John Bailey's Company, one lb (VSA-50).

10/01/80 Account of sugar delivered by Martin Carney by order of Capt. George at Fort Jefferson, to Edward Murray, a soldier in Capt. Bailey's Company, 1/2 lb (VSA-50).

10/06/80 John Bailey requests [George signs] the Quartermaster to issue 1/2 lb sugar to Edward Murray (VSA-13a).

10/06/80 John Bailey requests [George signs] the Quartermaster to issue 1/2 lb sugar to a man of Bailey's company "long sick" (VSA-13a).

10/06/80 Account of sugar delivered by Martin Carney by order of Capt. George at Fort Jefferson, to William Carr of Capt. Bailey's Company, 1/2 lb (VSA-50).

Fort Jefferson Personnel

10/09/80 John Bailey requests [George signs] the Quartermaster to issue John Bailey eight lbs soap from the public store (VSA-13a).
10/09/80 Account of soap delivered by Martin Carney by order of Col. Montgomery and Capt. George at Fort Jefferson, to Capt. Bailey for his own use, eight lbs (VSA-50).
10/12/80 John Bailey writes that Mrs. Johnes [?] made five shirts for the men of Bailey's company and she is to be paid in goods from the public store [George signs] (VSA-13a).
10/15/80 By order of Col. Clark, George signs that John Bailey requests for J. Dodge to issue to Levi Theel and John Clark, cloth and trimmings to produce a suit, each required by law for their enlistment (VSA-13a).
10/18/80 Account of ammunition delivered by Martin Carney by order of Capt. George, to two men of Capt. Bailey's Company, 1 1/2 lbs powder, one lb lead (VSA-50).
10/19/80 Sometime after this date, one lb soap and one pair mockisons are issued for one man of Bailey's Company per order of Col. Montgomery. One pint tafia, one weight sugar and 1/2 weight coffee issued for a sick man of Capt. Bailey's Company per Col. Montgomery's order (VSA-48: 111).
10/19/80 Sometime after this date, 400 continental dollars are advanced Capt. Bailey for the recruiting service (VSA-48: 118).
10/20/80 Account of ammunition delivered by Martin Carney by order of Capt. George, to four men of Capt. Bailey's Company, one lb powder, two lbs lead (VSA- 50).
10/28/80 Account of ammunition delivered by Martin Carney by order of Capt. George, to Sgt. Vaughan of Capt. Bailey's Company, 1/4 lb powder, 1/2 lb lead (VSA-50).
11/09/80 Account of ammunition delivered by Martin Carney by order of Capt. George, to two men of Capt. Bailey's Company, one lb powder, two lbs lead (VSA-50).
11/15/80 Account of sugar delivered by Martin Carney by orders of Capt. George, to five sick men of Capt. Bailey's Company, five lbs; to a sick woman of Capt. Bailey's Company, one lb (VSA-50).
11/15/80 Account of brass kettles delivered by Martin Carney by order of Capt. George at Fort Jefferson, to Ensign Lawrence Slaughter for Capt. Bailey's Company, two lbs (VSA-50).
11/17/80 Account of sugar delivered by Martin Carney by orders of Capt. George, to a soldier of Capt. Bailey's Company, one lb (VSA-50).
11/19/80 Account of soap delivered by Martin Carney by order of Capt. George at Fort Jefferson, to Capt. Bailey's Company, 12 lbs (VSA-50).
11/28/80 Account of sugar delivered by Martin Carney by orders of Capt. George, to Capt. Bailey and Mr. Slaughter, 12 lbs (VSA-50).
11/29/80 Account of ammunition delivered by Martin Carney by order of Capt. Robert George at Fort Jefferson, to two men of Capt. Bailey's Company, 1/2 lb powder, one lb lead (VSA-50).
12/03/80 John Bailey and Robert George sign request of Israel Dodge to issue Levi Theel of Bailey's Company, two yds damaged blue cloth for enlisting for three years or during the war (VSA-14).
12/07/80 Account of ammunition delivered by Martin Carney by order of Capt. Robert George at Fort Jefferson: to one man of Capt. John Bailey's Company, 1/4 lb powder and 1/2 lb lead; to two men of Capt. Bailey's Company, 1/2 lb powder and two lbs lead (VSA-50: 29).
12/15/80 Statement concerning Fort Jefferson in which Capt. George had an inventory of a quantity of tafia delivered to Martin Carney and another for a quantity of broad cloth with a receipt signed by Israel Dodge and dated Fort Jefferson 12/15/80. It was witnessed by Capt. Bailey and Leonard Helm (GRC, Papers II: 315).
12/18/80 Account of ammunition delivered by Martin Carney by order of Capt. Robert George at Fort Jefferson: to Capt. Bailey, 1/2 lb powder and one lb lead (VSA- 50: 29).
12/24/80 John Bailey and Robert George sign request of Israel Dodge to issue enough linen to make two shirts each for 25 men of Bailey's Company for the ensuing year (VSA-14a).

Fort Jefferson Personnel

12/24/80 John Bailey signed that he received of Israel Dodge 162 1/2 yds linen agreeable to the within order (VSA-14b).

12/25/80 Account of ammunition delivered by Martin Carney by order of Capt. Robert George at Fort Jefferson: to Capt. Bailey's Company, six lbs powder and 12 lbs lead (VSA-50: 29).

12/29/80 John Bailey and Robert George sign request for an issueance of two yds flannel for Bailey's own use (VSA-14a).

12/29/80 Bailey signed that he received of Dodge the two yds of flannel (VSA-14b).

12/29/80 Stores issued by order of Capt. Robert George: to two men of Capt. Bailey's Company, two muskets (VSA-50: 37).

12/29/80 Account of ammunition delivered by Martin Carney by order of Capt. Robert George at Fort Jefferson: to Capt. Bailey's Company, 36 flints (VSA-50: 31).

12/30/80 Stores issued by order of Capt. Robert George: to Capt. Bailey's Company, one kettle (VSA-50: 37) (VSA-14; misfiled).

12/31/80 John Bailey signed that he received of Israel Dodge one pair of shoes upon a certificate given Bailey by John Dodge (VSA-14c).

01/08/81 Account of ammunition delivered by Martin Carney by order of Capt. Robert George at Fort Jefferson, to three men of Capt. Bailey's Company, one lb powder, two lbs lead; to Capt. Bailey and Owens, going express to the falls, 1 1/2 lbs powder, four lbs lead (VSA-50).

01/11/81 Stores issued by order of Capt. Robert George, to a soldier of Capt. Bailey's Company, one musket and one bayonet with belt (VSA-50).

01/11/81 Account of ammunition expanded by the artillery at sundry times by order of Capt. Robert George, Commandant at Fort Jefferson, issued Capt. Bailey for the use of the artillery at O'post, three yds flannel (VSA-50).

01/12/81 Account of ammunition delivered by Martin Carney by order of Capt. Robert George at Fort Jefferson, to Capt. Bailey's Company, six flints (VSA-50).

01/12/81 Stores issued by order of Capt. Robert George, to Capt. Bailey's Company, 23 swords (VSA-50).

02/04/81 Stores issued by order of Capt. Robert George, to a soldier of Capt. Bailey's, one musket and one bayonet with belt (VSA-50).

02/08/81 Account of ammunition delivered by Martin Carney by order of Capt. Robert George at Fort Jefferson, to Capt. Bailey's hunting party, 12 lbs powder, 24 lbs lead (VSA-50).

02/13/81 Stores issued by order of Capt. Robert George, to Capt. Bailey, one axe (VSA-50).

02/16/81 Ammunition delivered by order of Capt. George, to Capt. Bailey for the defense of Opost (Vincennes), 150 lbs powder, 100 lbs lead, and 100 flints (VSA-50).

02/22/81 Ammunition delivered by order of Capt. George, to three men of Capt. Bailey's Company, 1 1/2 lbs powder, three lbs lead (VSA-50).

03/06/81 Ammunition delivered by order of Capt. George, to three men of Capt. Bailey's Company, six flints (VSA-50).

Balfau, Petter
06/02/80 Capt. Kellar lists 17 men who had served in his unit at one time or another during the war. Balfau is among that list [NOTE: no other record of him in relation to Ft. Jeff] (MHS: B1, F19).

Ballanger, James [also Ballenger, Ballinger]
01/19/79 Enlisted on this date as a member of Capt. Robert Todd's Company of foot. Believe Ballanger was discharged at Fort Jefferson (Harding 1981: 11-12).

12/01/79 Enlisted on this date as a member of Capt. Mark Thomas' Company of Infantry commanded by Col. George Slaughter [the spelling of Ballanger's name is different for this entry and above entry. Not positive it is same person] (Harding 1981: 37).

06/23/80 Issued shirt at FJ to go to Illinois for provisions (VSA-11).

Fort Jefferson Personnel

07/14/80 Among list of men being issued one shirt per Col. Montgomery's orders at FJ (VSA-12).
07/14/80 James Ballenger received either one shirt or linen to make shirt from Capt. John Dodge per Capt. George's orders at FJ for having gone to Kaskaskia for provisions for FJ [Accompanied by Richard Sennet, Peter Freeman, and Jacob Hoffman] (VSA-12).

Ballenger, Larken [Lankin, Larkin]
03/24/80 Enlisted on this date as Private in Capt. John Bailey's Company of the Illinois Regiment in the Virginia State Service (Harding 1981: 45-46).
07/12/80 Among list of men receiving two shirts each as they are enlisted during the war in Capt. Bailey's Co. (VSA-12).
05/28/81 Taken prisoner (Harding 1981: 46).

Balsinger, Valentine [also Balsinklee, Vallintine]
06/04/79 Enlisted on this date as Sergeant in Capt. Robert George's Company of Artillery in the Service of the Commonwealth of Virginia and Illinois Department (Harding 1981: 29-30).
06/12/80 Going on expedition with Capt. Harrison to Falls of Ohio; request for clothing for soldiers who will be going with Harrison (VSA-11).
03/20/81 Gave testimony at FJ during Court Martial Proceedings of David Allen and James Taylor that while he was Centry of the guard house he heard one of the prisoners speak disrespectfully of Maj. Williams (DMS 56J41).
11/15/81 Deserted (Harding 1981: 29-30).

Barbeau, Jean Baptist
08/23/80 Paid Jean Baptist Barbeau for four sides of tanned leather for use of the light dragoon by order of Col. Montgomery (VSA-48).
10/09/80 One snaffle bridle paid Barbeau per order Col. Montgomery on behalf of Col. Todd (VSA-48).

Barbour, Philip [also Barber]
09/19/80-04/07/81 Sometime between these dates, tobacco is issued to sundry persons per order of Capt. George, Commandant to Philip Barbour, four lbs (VSA-50: 13).
12/07/80 In a letter from Capt. Richard Harrison at the Falls to Col. Clark in Richmond or "elsewhere," Capt. Barbour is expected to bring a very large cargo from New Orleans to Fort Jefferson for the state (GRC, I: 468).
12/12/80 Account of ammunition received by Martin Carney at Clarksville (Ft. Jefferson), received of Capt. Philip Barbour, 472 lbs powder and 300 lbs powder damaged (VSA-50: 5).
12/12/80 Account of arms received by Martin Carney in this department, the property of the Commonwealth of Virginia: received of Capt. Barbour, 120 muskets (VSA-50: 16).
12/12/80 List of articles brought to Fort Jefferson by Capt. Barbour as public store property: 12 cases of arms or chests, 120 stand, three cases of cartridge boxes, belts, one trunk of cartridge boxes and belts, 261 cartridge boxes, 422 bayonetter belts, 300 lbs damaged gunpowder and 14 oil cloths or Spanish [illeg.], and an eight lb bar of steel (VSA-14).
12/15/80 Delivery made (GRC Papers, II: 315).
12/24/80 Letter from Capt. Robert George at Fort Jefferson to George Rogers Clark. George tells that the greatest part of the cargo sent to Clark for use of the state was lost in a hurricane. The remainder of Capt. Barbour's goods were purchased as a result (MHS: B1, F23) (Seineke, 1981: 468-469).
01/01/81 Capt. Robert George at Ft. Jefferson writes to Oliver Pollock at New Orleans. Letter sent with two sets of exchange for $237,320 in favor of Capt. Philip Barbour who furnished a large cargo of liquors and dry goods which George says has saved the post. George states that he called a council and consulted them about the sum. The council and George felt it was a reasonable amount considering the difficulties Barbour encountered in getting the cargo to Fort Jefferson. George begs

Fort Jefferson Personnel

Pollock to pay for the cargo in gold or silver coin so that Barbour can supply Fort Jefferson in the future (GRC, I: 496-497).

01/01/81 Robert George requests of Oliver Pollock [Agent at New Orleans] to pay Capt. Philip Barbour 5000 Spanish milled dollars for liquor and clothing furnished George for use of the troops of the Illinois Department (VSA-15; misfiled).

01/01/81-01/19/81 Sometime between these dates, a letter was written from John Donne at Fort Jefferson to George Rogers Clark in Richmond. John Donne had been gone to Kaskaskia. While Donne was away, Capt. Barbour arrived from New Orleans with a quantity of goods, part of which Capt. George intends to use for the purchase of provisions (MHS: B1, F23; filed as Misc. FJ Doc.).

Barnett, James
05/01/80 Enlisted on this date as Private in Capt. George Owens' Company of Militia of the District of Clarksville in the State of Virginia (Harding 1981: 48-49).
09/12/80 Moved (Harding 1981: 48).

Barnit, Robert
07/10/80 Member of Capt. John Rogers' Co. Among list of men being issued two shirts and two stocks at FJ per Capt. George's orders to John Dodge (VSA-12).

Bartholomew, William [also Betholomew]
04/21/80 William Bartholomew, John Breeding, George King, Bob Logan, William Bohman, John Deck, John Cowan and Daniel Tyger are mentioned as being at Ft. Clark, some later are at Fort Jefferson (VSA-10: Non-FJ Document).
05/30/80 Enlisted on this date as a private in Capt. Richard Brashears' Company of the Illiois Regiment (Harding, 1981: 51-52).
07/12/80 Among list of men receiving two shirts each which they are entitled to by law as members of Williams' Company; had previously received clothing (VSA-12).
07/12/80 Received flannel, blue cloth and thread and buttons (VSA-12).
07/12/80 Jarrett Williams certifies that James Curry, William Elms, James Morris, William Barthalomew, James Dawson, James Elms, and John Elms are enlisted during the war (VSA-12).
09/18/80 Listed as one of five sick men of Capt. Brashears' Company to receive a share of an issue of five lbs sugar by order of Capt. George to M. Carney (VSA-13).
10/02/80 Deserted from Capt. Brashears' Co. (Harding, 1981: 51-52).

Beauvais, Marguerite
07/19/76 Sometime after this date, Marguerite married Thomas Bentley (Seineke, 1981: 69).

Bell, William
03/10/80-11/30/81 Listed as Private in Capt. John Bailey's Co. of the Illinois Regiment in the Virginia State Service. Payroll (Harding 1981: 45-46).

Benoit, Francis
05/30/79-06/02/81 Listed as a Private in Capt. Richard McCarty's Co. of the Illinois Regiment. Pay Abstract (Harding 1981: 27).
07/12/80 Capt. Robert George requests that four enlisted men be issued to serve all during the war, full clothing by Lt. Girault. The four men being: Francis Villier, Charles M. Laughlan, John LaRichardy, and Francis Benoit. Lt. Girault certifies that the above mentioned are all enlisted to serve during the war (VSA-12).
11/20/80 Deserted (Harding 1981: 27).

Fort Jefferson Personnel

Bentley, Thomas
Paid Thomas Bentley on account, 530 livres cash (VSA-48).
07/19/76 Sometime after this date, Thomas Bentley married Marguerite Beauvais (Seineke 1981: 69).
Spring 77 Thomas Bentley is spoken of as being a merchant along with Daniel Murray who had lived in the French villages for several years and provided information to Col. Clark (Seineke 1981: xxi).
04/19/80 George Rogers Clark at Mouth of Ohio writes to John Dodge stating he arrived at Mouth of Ohio yesterday [4-19-80] and that Dodge should sent Clark furniture, seeds for garden, and "beans the French plant to make shades." Clark states that Capt. Bentley will give Dodge the news (GRC Papers, I: 417-418).
04/20/80 Listed as Captain. Carried letter from Ft. Jefferson for George Rogers Clark to John Dodge at Kaskaskia (GRC, Papers I: 418).
09/09/80 Issued in the Indian Department, paid Bentley for his account, 93 (VSA-48).
10/10/80 Montgomery requests the Quartermaster to issue 73 lbs powder to Thomas Bentley (VSA-13a).
10/26/80 J. Dodge signs above quantity of powder delivered to I. Dodge on Thomas Bentley's account (VSA-13b, Filed as 10 October 80).
10/26/80 Account of ammunition delivered by Martin Carney by Col. Montgomery's orders to Israel Dodge upon Mr. Bentley's account, 73 lbs powder (VSA-50).
01/01/81 Received of Capt. John Dodge, Agent, for the State of Virginia three quarts of tafia for use of the Commissary Department, also two quarts spirits for use of a fatigue party on command going for provisions which he has purchased from Mr. Thomas Bentley at J. Donne's desire. In the form of a letter and signed by J. Donne Deputy Conductor WD. (VSA-48).

Blackford, Zephaniah
04/20/80 John Ozala signed that he received of Zephaniah Blackford 230 lbs of Indian meal for a command of 30 men going from Fort Patrick Henry to the Mouth of Ohio (VSA-10).
06/20/80 Issued to Mr. Blackford Deputy Commissary of Issues, 3 3/4 yds sycee for three vests, issued for three pair trousers 5 1/4 yds cottonade and 2 1/2 yds toile gris, 9 3/4 yds white linen for three shirts, 1 1/2 yds muslin for three stocks and ruffling, two linen handkerchiefs, nine skeins white thread, one ink pot - brass, 3 3/4 yds linen for lining for jackets (VSA-48).
06/20/80 List of goods issued by Capt. Robert George's order as per Mr. Z. Blackford's receipt on said orders (VSA-48).
06/20/80 One pair damask 5 1/8 yds, one pair flowered lawn 13 yds, five ells ribbon, one dozen check linen handkerchiefs, one piece chintz no. 12, one piece chintz no. 6, one piece chintz no. 10 issued to Zeph. Blackford by order Capt. George to purchase provisions, and disposed of agreeable to the return made me for 187 hard dollars (VSA-48).
06/20/80 Capt. Robt. George writes to John Dodge by Col. Clark's orders to ask him to deliver to Mr. Blackford 187 hard dollars worth of bread and such goods for the use of Kaskaskia and its neighborhood (VSA-11a).
06/20/80 Zephaniah Blackford signed that he received the above (VSA-11b).
06/20/80 Capt. Robt. George requests of John Dodge to issue Mr. Blackford [Commissary], linen for three shirts, stuff for three summer jackets and trousers, two pocket handkerchiefs with thread to make them, one ink pot, and stuff for three stocks by order of Col. Clark (VSA-11a).
06/20/80 Zephaniah Blackford signed that he received the above (VSA-11b).
06/20/80 Capt. Robert George asks of John Dodge to issue Zephaniah Blackford with trimmings for three jackets by order of Col. Clark (VSA-11a).
06/20/80 Z. Blackford signed that he received 3 3/4 linen (VSA-11b).
07/02/80 Zephaniah Blackford requests at Fort Clark [V.T. Dalton signs] an issuance of rations for 10 men for six days [July 2 - July 7] going from Fort Jefferson to get provisions for the Fort (VSA-13a misfiled).

Fort Jefferson Personnel

07/05/80 Zephaniah Blackford requests [John Montgomery] an issuance of two days allowance of beef for ten men on command from Ft. Jefferson (VSA-12a).
08/19/80 Issued twenty-nine ells blue cloth and 85 ells white flannel per Z. Blackford's receipt, paid to Madam Valle for 52 bushels of corn, 1417 weight flour, and six empty barrels paid by order Lt. Col. Montgomery (VSA-48).
08/20/80 Forty ells white linen delivered in lieu of 100 dollars worth of goods to Z. Blackford per receipt and voucher to purchase provisions for Fort Jefferson (VSA-48).
09/11/80 Received one lb sugar and one lb soap (VSA-13a).
09/11/80 Account of soap delivered by Martin Carney by order of Col. Montgomery and Capt. George at Fort Jefferson, to Zephaniah Blackford, one lb (VSA-50).
10/24/80 J. Montgomery writes to Oliver Pollack to pay V.T. Dalton for provisions received of Zephaniah Blackford (VSA-16b, Misfiled).
11/18/80 Account of soap delivered by Martin Carney by order of Col. Montgomery and Capt. George at Fort Jefferson, to Mr. Blackford, Commissary, three lbs (VSA-50).
12/05/80 Letter from John Donne at Fort Jefferson to George Rogers Clark. Donne tells that Mr. Blackford arrived after Clark's departure and will be attending to the issues in Donne's absence (MHS, B1: F23).
12/07/80 Robert George requests of Israel Dodge to issue two ounces of thread fit to make a pair of leather breeches to Zephaniah Blackford and charge it to his account (VSA-14a).
12/07/80 Zephaniah Blackford signed he received of Israel Dodge six skeins of thread (VSA-14b).
02/12/81 Account of ammunition delivered by Martin Carney by order of Capt. Robert George at Fort Jefferson, to Z. Blackford, 1/4 lb powder, 1/2 lb lead (VSA-50).

Blain, Peter
03/26/80 Enlisted on this date as Private in Capt. John Bailey's Company of the Illinois Regiment in the Virginia State Service (Harding 1981: 45-46).
05/01/80 Deserted on this date from Capt. Bailey's Company (Harding 1981: 46).

Blair, John
05/30/80 Enlisted on this date in as a private in Capt. Brashears' Company (Harding 1981: 51-52).
07/12/80 Among list of men receiving two shirts each which they are entitled to by law as members of Williams'] Company (VSA-12).
08/12/80 Deceased (Harding 1981: 51-52).

Blanchard, [no first name given]
09/10/80 Member of Capt. Richard McCarty's Company (VSA-13).
09/10/80 Issued full set of clothing for enlisting (VSA-13a).

Blankinship, Henry
07/10/80 Member of Capt. John Rogers' Co. Among list of men being issued two shirts and two stocks at FJ per Capt. George's orders to John Dodge (VSA-12).

Bohman, William
04/21/80 William Bartholomew, John Breeding, George King, Bob Logan, William Bohman, John Deck, John Cowan, and Daniel Tyger are mentioned as being at Ft. Clark, some later travel to Ft. Jefferson (VSA-10; Non-FJ Document).

Boils, John [also Bills]
07/12/80 Among a list of men receiving two shirts each which they are entitled to by law as members of Williams' Company (VSA-12).
12/27/80 Richard Brashears and Robert George sign request of Israel Dodge to issue 12 needles to John Boils for making clothes (VSA-14a).

Fort Jefferson Personnel

12/27/80 John Boils signed his "mark" that he received of Israel Dodge the within contents (VSA-14b).

Bolton, Daniel [also Boblar] [note discrepancies in desertion dates]
05/30/80 Enlisted in Capt. Richard Brashears' Co. (Harding 1981: 29-30).
06/04/79-12/03/81 Listed as Corporal in Capt. Robert George's Co. of Artillery in the Service of the Commonwealth of Virginia and Illinois Department (Harding 1981: 29-31).
06/04/79-12/03/81 Listed as Gunner in Capt. Robert George's Co. of Artillery in the Service of the Commonwealth of Virginia and the Illinois Department. Muster Roll (Harding 1981: 31-33).
06/16/80 Delivered munition supplies to Lawrence Keinan in Capt. George's Co. (VSA-11).
06/16/80 Issued 2 1/2 yds white flannel, 2 1/2 yds osnaburg, one pair scissors, eight skeins twine, two needles per order Capt. George, Commandant, and receipt of Daniel Bolton, to make cartridges for the cannon (VSA-48).
06/19/80 Issued two shirts by order of Capt. George for being enlisted during the war (VSA-11).
06/29/80 Account of ammunition delivered by Martin Carney by Capt. Robert George's order at Camp Jefferson, to Daniel Bolton, Gunner, 15 lbs powder (VSA-50).
07/20/80 Three yds white linen paid by order of Col. Montgomery to D. Bolton in lieu of 15 days public work per his receipt (VSA-48).
08/14/80 Issued 2 1/2 yds toile gris per order and receipt of D. Bolton (VSA-48).
08/15/80 Issued as much toile gris or other sort linen as will make a pair of trousers by order of Capt. George (VSA-12a).
08/19/80 Issued one suit of clothing (VSA-12a).
10/02/80 Deserted [Capt. Brashears' Co.] (Harding 1981: 51).
10/15/80 Deserted (Harding 1981: 29-30).

Bolton, M. [also Bolting]
06/16/80 Issued three yds calico to Margaret Bolton for making six plain shirts (VSA-48).
06/19/80 Issued two yds white linen for washing stains out of damaged linen (VSA-48).

Bolton, Thomas [?]
01/01/80 On a return signed by Robert George and dated 12/10/80, Thomas Bolton has enlisted for three years or during the war by Lt. V. T. Dalton into Capt. Robert George's Company of Artillery (MHS: B1, F23).

Bond, Shadrack [Shadrach]
04/28/80 Richard Brashears and George Rogers Clark sign request to let Shadrack Bond, one of the artificers have one suit of clothing and flannel for one shirt (MHS: B1, F16).
07/13/80 Col. J. Montgomery, sigining as commandant, requests of Capt. John Dodge to issue two shirts and as much coarse lining as will make a pair of trousers in part of an account Bond has against the state, for which he is to be paid from the country store (VSA-12a).
07/13/80 Bond signed that he received the within contents (VSA-12b).
07/13/80 Issued 6 1/2 yds linen, 2 3/4 yds osnaburg, and four skeins thread per order of Col. Montgomery and receipt of Shadrack Bond, per account for public services (VSA-48: 78).

Boofry, Petter
06/02/80 Capt. Kellar listed 17 men who had served in his unit at one time or another during the war. [NOTE: Boofry is not mentioned in relation to Ft. Jefferson] (MHS: B1, F19).

Fort Jefferson Personnel

Bootin, Travis
07/10/80 Member of Capt. John Rogers' Co. among list of men being issued two shirts and two stocks at Fort Jefferson per Capt. George's orders to John Dodge (VSA-12).

Bootin, William
07/10/80 Member of Capt. John Rogers' Co. among list of men being issued two shirts and two stocks at Fort Jefferson per Capt. George's orders to Capt. John Dodge (VSA-12).

Bosson, [Bosron, Bosseron, F. ?] Paid Major Bosson for sundries for use of the savages and troops per his account and receipt, 1018 livres peltry (VSA-48). By John Dodge's certificate on the state in favor of Major Bosson, 272 livres of peltry (VSA-48).
09/04/80 Issued in the Indian Department, four ells cotton of 16 Sachaque given Major Bosson for assisting Helm in the Indian Department at Opost (Vincennes)(VSA-48).

Bouden, John
04/20/80 On a return signed by Robert George and dated 12/10/80, John Bouden has enlisted for three years or during the war by Lt. V.T. Dalton into Capt. Robert George's Company of Artillery. Not included on payroll because Dalton neglected to give account of what has become of him or where or how his time expired [possibly a different person?] (MHS: B1, F23).

Bowdery, John
07/15/80 Listed in Capt. Worthington's Company (MHS B1, F20; VSA-12).

Brading, William
07/15/80 Listed in Capt. Worthington's Company (MHS B1, F20; VSA-12).

Brady, T.
05/26/80 Account of ammunition delivered by Martin Carney by order of Col. Clark: to Mr. Brady for Indians at Cahokia, three lbs powder and four lbs lead (VSA- 50: 8).
08/23/80 Paid T. Brady for carting per receipt (VSA-48).

Brashears, Richard [also Brashers] [discrepancies of rank after deserting] Three yds white linen paid Richard Brashears for making six shirts (VSA-48). Two lbs sugar and 1/2 lb coffee delivered to two sick of Capt. Brashears' Company per order of Col. Montgomery, two weight soap to one man of Capt. Brashears' Company, four weight soap sugar to four sick of Capt. Brashears' Company per order Col. Montgomery, five dressed deer skins for Capt. Brashears' Company per Col. Montgomery's order, three weight sugar and 1/2 weight coffee for three sick of Capt. Brashears' Company per Col. Montgomery's order, three weight sugar and 3/4 weight coffee for three sick of Capt. Brashears' Company per Col. Montgomery (VSA-48). One pair moccasins and one weight soap for Brashears' Company per order of Col. Montgomery, 1 1/2 weight coffee, one weight sugar to Brashears for his Company per his order, one bottle tafia and one lb sugar for Brashears' Company per order of Col. Montgomery (VSA-48).
04/25/80 Col. John Montgomery at Ft. Clark [Kaskaskia] writes George Rogers Clark at Mouth of Ohio. Montgomery is pleased Clark has arrived. Lt. Brashears delivers letter and awaits at Fort Jefferson for Clark's response. Montgomery states condition at Fort Clark not good but he will do all he can in bringing Clark goods (MHS: B1, F16).
04/28/80 Richard Brashears and George Rogers Clark sign request to let Shadrack Bond, one of the artificers, have one suit of clothes and flannel for one shirt (MHS: B1, F16).
04/28/80 George Rogers Clark requests that Mr. Brashears be issued 20 suits of soldiers clothes and take his receipt for the same. Also issue flannel for ten shirts (MHS: B1, F16).

Fort Jefferson Personnel

04/28/80 Lt. Brashears signs that he received the within contents from William Clark (MHS: B1, F16).

05/11/80 Listed as Lieutenant (GRC Papers, I: 418-419).

05/18/80 Richard Brashears signs request to the Quartermaster to issue one case bottle of tafia for Brashears' own use (VSA-11).

05/26/80 Account of ammunition delivered by Martin Carney by order of Col. Clark: to Capt. Richard Brashears at Cahokia, 4 3/4 lbs powder and 9 1/2 lbs lead; to Capt. Richard Brashears at Cahokia, five lbs powder and 11 lbs lead (VSA-50: 8).

05/30/80 Jon Allin, Jon Blair, Mark Foley, Richard Harrison, James Morris, Francis Rubedo and Samuel Allen enlisted on this date in Capt. Brashears' Company (Harding, 1981: 51-52).

05/30/80 William Bartholomew enlisted on this date as a private in Capt. Richard Brashears' Company (Harding 1981: 51-52).

06/03/80 Letter from John Montgomery saying Capt. Brashears enlisted 24 men to the Illinois Regiment, and is entitled to receive his commission if the commander-in-chief of the Regiment approves it. Written at Cahokia. G.R. Clark was notified of this letter (MHS: B1, F19).

06/10/80 Six gallons tafia issued to GR Clark were taken to Fort Jefferson by Capt. Brashears (VSA-48).

07/04/80 Richard Underwood's receipt for one land warrant, dated 4 July 1780 at Cahokia for enlisting for three years [Company not specified], attested by Capt. Richard Brashears (MHS: B1, F20).

07/11/80 Capt. Robt. George requests of John Dodge that Capt. Richard Brashears be issued his full quota of clothing which he is entitled to by law agreeable to Col. Clark's orders at FJ (VSA-12).

07/12/80 Issued to Capt. Brashears, 1 1/2 yds scarlet cloth 7/4 wide, 1 1/2 yds broadcloth 7/4 wide, 2 1/2 yds shalloon, two yds calender for two small garments, four yds toile gris for two small garments, eight yds toile gris for four small garments, three yds gray cloth 7/8 wide for two small garments, 19 1/2 yds white linen for six shirts, 3/4 yd fine holland for ruffling, two yds muslin for six stocks, ten skeins thread, 2 1/2 check for one small garment, 2 1/2 yds coarse linen for lining, one pair thread hose, one silk handkerchief one Indian handkerchief, four linen handkerchiefs, four skeins silk, one hat, 2 3/4 calamanco for one small garment, three yds blue cloth 7/4 wide (VSA-48).

07/12/80 Ensign Jarret Williams, Illinois Regiment, apparently signed in behalf of Brashears that he received from Capt. John Dodge, Agent a list of goods in part of the clothing allowed Brashears by law, attested by J. Donne (VSA-48).

07/12/80 John Williams signs that one man of Capt. Brashears' Company is issued provisions at FJ (VSA- 12).

07/12/80 Robt. George requests of John Dodge by order of Col. Clark, that full clothing be issued for James Curry, William Elms, James Morris, William Barthalomew, James Dawson, James Elms, and John Elms of Capt. Brashears' Company (VSA-12).

07/13/80 Issued to Ensign Jarrett Williams for 25 men of Capt. Brashears' Company, one ruffled shirt, 49 plain shirts, 21 yds flannel, 24 1/4 yds blue cloth, thread and buttons and one ink pot to Sgt. Brown by Col. Montgomery's order (VSA-12; VSA 48).

07/14/80 Jarrett Williams and John Montgomery sign request for one man of Capt. Brashears' Company to be issued five days' provisions from July 14 - July 18 at Fort Jefferson (VSA-12).

08/03/80 Account of tobacco delivered by Martin Carney by order of Capt. Robert George at this place, to Sgt. Elms for Capt. Brashears' Company, one carot and three lbs (VSA-50).

09/09/80 One English blanket per receipt and order of Lt. Col. Montgomery, issued to and overdrawn by Capt. Brashears. Blanket not listed on Brashears' July 12th list of goods issued to him (VSA-48).

09/09/80 Account of sugar delivered by Martin Carney by order of Col. Montgomery at Fort Jefferson, to a sick woman and children of Capt. Brashears' Company, two lbs; to Capt. Brashears and Doctor Ray, three lbs (VSA-50).

Fort Jefferson Personnel

09/10/80 Account of ammunition delivered by Martin Carney by Col. Montgomery's orders, to Capt. Brashears' Company, five lbs powder, ten lbs lead; to Capt. Brashears for the troops at Cahokia, 100 lbs powder, 200 lbs lead (VSA-50).

09/11/80 Capt. Brashears issued one lb powder and two lbs lead for his own use (VSA-13a).

09/11/80 Account of ammunition delivered by Martin Carney by Col. Montgomery's orders, to Capt. Brashears for his own use, one lb powder, two lbs lead; to two men of Capt. Brashears' Company, one lb powder, two lbs lead (VSA-50).

09/12/80 Issued three lbs sugar and one lb soap to the Doctor and Capt. Brashears (VSA-13).

09/13/80 Four blankets per receipt and order of Lt. Col. Montgomery, issued to Ensign Williams for 25 men of Capt. Brashears' Company (VSA-48).

09/13/80 Account of soap delivered by Martin Carney by order of Col. Montgomery and Capt. George at Fort Jefferson, to Capt. Brashears' Company, 8 1/2 lbs; to Capt. Brashears and Doctor Ray, one lb (VSA-50).

09/13/80 Listed as one officer of the mess who received a share of 60 lbs of sugar (VSA-13b).

09/14/80 Account of sugar delivered by Martin Carney by order of Capt. George at Fort Jefferson, to two sick soldiers of Capt. Brashears' Company, two lbs (VSA-50).

09/18/80 Account of sugar delivered by Martin Carney by order of Capt. George at Fort Jefferson, to five men of Capt. Brashears' Company, five lbs (VSA-50).

09/25/80 Issued 100 nails for repairing a public boat per order Capt. Brashears (VSA-48).

09/27/80 Account of ammunition delivered by Martin Carney by Capt. George's order to two men of Capt. Brashears' Company, one lb powder and two lbs lead (VSA-50).

09/28/80 Issued one ivory comb, one horn comb, 3 1/2 gallons rum, eight weight sugar, four weight coffee, six weight soap to and overdrawn by Capt. Brashears. Articles are not listed on Brashears' July 12th list of goods issued to him (VSA-48).

09/30/80 Two yds linen per order favor of Capt. Brashears issued to and overdrawn by Lt. Col. John Montgomery beyond his quota of clothing (VSA-48).

09/30/80 Ten lbs soap per order Capt,. Brashears and receipt of John Gils issued to Ensign Jarret Williams for 25 men of Capt. Brashears' company (VSA-48).

10/06/80 Two blankets per order favor of Capt. Brashears issued to and overdrawn by Col. Montgomery. Blankets did not appear on the July 12 list of goods issued to Montgomery (VSA-48).

10/09/80 Issued 1/2 weight sugar to one sick man of Capt. Brashears' Company (VSA-48).

10/14/80 Account of ammunition delivered by Martin Carney by order of Capt. George, to Sgt. Allen of Capt. Brashears' Company, 1 1/2 lbs powder, three lbs lead (VSA-50).

10/16/80 Account of ammunition delivered by Martin Carney by order of Capt. George, to Sgt. Elm of Capt. Brashears' Company, 1/2 lb powder, one lb lead (VSA-50).

10/24/80 According to Richard Winston Letter (to Todd?), Capt. Brashears left Kaskaskia to go to Fort Jefferson on 19 September with Col. Montgomery, Brooks and Family; Montgomery left with large quantities of provisions (boats deeply loaded) and five black slaves... Also, Capt..Brashears has left the service, and married Brook's daughter (Seineke 1981: 463-465).

10/27/80 Richard Brashears requests [George signs] two skeins of thread to be issued to Mayfield to repair his clothes (VSA-13).

11/02/80 Account of ammunition delivered by Martin Carney by order of Capt. George, to three men of Capt. Brashears' Company, 1 1/2 lbs powder, three lbs lead (VSA-50).

Fort Jefferson Personnel

11/03/80 Account of ammunition delivered by Martin Carney by order of Capt. George, to one man of Capt. Brashears' Company, 1/2 lb powder, one lb lead (VSA-50).

11/09/80 Account of ammunition delivered by Martin Carney by order of Capt. George, to two men of Capt. Brashears' Company, one lb powder, two lbs lead (VSA-50).

11/15/80 Account of brass kettles delivered by Martin Carney by order of Capt. George at Fort Jefferson, to Capt. Richard Brashears, one kettle (VSA-50).

11/17/80 Account of sugar delivered by Martin Carney by orders of Capt. George, to two men of Capt. Brashears' Company, two lbs; to a sick woman and child of Brashears' Company, two lbs (VSA-50).

11/19/80 Account of soap delivered by Martin Carney by order of Capt. George at Fort Jefferson, to Capt. Brashears' Company, 4 1/2 lbs (VSA-50).

11/29/80 Account of sugar delivered by Martin Carney by order of Capt. George, to Capt. Brashears for his use, six lbs (VSA-50).

11/29/80 Account of soap delivered by Martin Carney by order of Capt. George at Fort Jefferson, to Capt. Brashears for his own use, six lbs (VSA-50).

12/01/80 Stores issued by order of Capt. Robert George: to Capt. Brashears' Company, two tomahawks (VSA-50: 40).

12/09/80 Stores issued by order of Capt. Robert George: to Capt. Brashears' Company, two tomahawks (VSA-50: 37).

12/21/80 Capt. Richard Brashears and Robert George sign request of Israel Dodge to issue eight pair of shoes to eight men in Brashears' Company (VSA-14a).

12/21/80 Richard Brashears signed that he received of Israel Dodge the within contents (VSA-14b).

12/21/80 Richard Brashears and Robert George sign request of Israel Dodge to issue two shirts each to 13 men of Brashears' Company (VSA-14a).

12/21/80 Richard Brashears signs that he received of Israel Dodge 84 1/2 yds linen agreeable to the within order (VSA-14b).

12/26/80 Account of ammunition delivered by Martin Carney by order of Capt. Robert George at Fort Jefferson, to Capt. Brashears' Company, two lbs powder, four lbs lead (VSA-50).

12/27/80 Richard Brashears and Robert George sign request of Israel Dodge to issue 12 needles to John Boils for making clothes (VSA-14).

12/29/80 Account of ammunition delivered by Martin Carney by order of Capt. Robert George at Fort Jefferson: to Capt. Brashears' Company, 20 flints (VSA-50: 31).

12/30/80 Account of ammunition delivered by Martin Carney by order of Capt. Robert George at Fort Jefferson: to two men of Capt. Brashears' Company, one lb powder and two lbs lead; to Capt. Brashears, one lb powder and four lbs lead (VSA-50: 30).

12/31/80 Stores issued by order of Capt. Robert George: to Capt. Brashears, one tent or cloths (VSA-50: 37).

12/31/80 Capt. Richard Brashears signed that he received of Israel Dodge one pair of shoes upon a certificate given Brashears by John Dodge (VSA-14c).

01/01/81 Richard Brashears and Robert George sign request of the Quartermaster to issue two pairs overalls for two men of Brashears' Company who enlisted for three years or during the war going down river on a purigee [pirogue] (VSA-15a).

01/25/81 Stores issued by order of Capt. Robert George, to Capt. Brashears' Company, ten swords (VSA-50).

02/13/81 Stores issued by order of Capt. Robert George, to a soldier of Capt. Brashears, one musket and one bayonet with belt (VSA-50).

03/02/81 Stores issued by order of Capt. Robert George, to Capt. Brashears' Company, three muskets or smoothed guns (VSA-50).

05/03/81 Per order brought from day book, four gallons, one quart, and one pint rum and five lbs sugar (VSA-49).

05/15/81 Ammunition delivered by order of Capt. Robert George at Fort Jefferson, to Capt. Brashears, 1/2 lb powder, 1/2 lb lead (VSA-50).

05/19/81 Per order to a man of Capt. Brashears' Company, two lbs sugar (VSA-49).

Fort Jefferson Personnel

05/26/81 Per order brought from day book, ten lbs sugar (VSA-49).
06/05/81 Per order brought from day book, 20 lbs sugar (VSA-49).
06/07/81 Per order brought from day book, one carot of tobacco (VSA-49).
06/07/81 Per order for hospital or sick accounts, to one woman of Capt. Brashears, four lbs sugar (VSA-49).

Brauley, William
03/29/80-11/30/81 Listed as Private in Capt. John Bailey's Co. of Illinois Regiment in the Virginia State Service (Harding 1981: 45-46).
07/12/80 Among list of men receiving two shirts each for being enlisted during the war in Capt. Bailey's Co. (VSA-12a).
09/09/80 Issued [along with John Johnston 1 pint of tafia and 1lb sugar due to being "very sick." Member of "Capt. John Bailey's Company" (VSA-13).
11/15/81 Deserted (Harding 1981: 46).

Bredin, Francis [also Breeding, Breedin] Probably wife of Richard
Issued 2 1/2 yds linen and four yds flannel paid F. Bredin for making six shirts (VSA-48: 88).
06/16/80 Issued 1 1/2 yds chintz, one linen handkerchief one horn comb, and one pair scissors paid F. Bredin, for making seven plain shirts (VSA-48: 80).
07/06/80 Issued five linen handkerchiefs and one yd ribbon paid F. Bredin for making ten plain shirts and one pair leggings (VSA-48: 82).
08/18/80 Issued one linen handkerchief paid F. Bredin for making two hunting shirts (VSA-48: 83).
09/15/80 Capt. John Bailey certifies that Mrs. Bredin made four shirts, one coat and one waistcoat for Bailey's Company, who are enlisted for three yrs. or during the war (VSA-13).
09/15/80 Robert George requests that John Dodge pay for the above mentioned work, out of the public store (VSA- 13a).
09/26/80 Francis Bredin signs her mark that she received 19 1/2 yds of linen and six skeins thread to make shirts for troops (VSA-13a).
09/26/80 Reverse acknowledges that six shirts were made and should receive [?] 1/2 yds linen and four yds flannel for making six shirts (VSA-13b).
09/30/80 Francis Bredin signs her mark [on reverse of 09/15/80] that she received four yds of flannel in payment for the coat and waistcoat (VSA-13b).
10/04/80 Francis Bredin signs her mark [on reverse of 09/15/80] that she received four yds of flannel as full payment (VSA-13b).
10/26/80 Paid 25 shillings for making two suits of clothes for Capt. McCarty's Company (VSA-13).
12/07/80 Capt. Abraham Kellar and Robert George sign request of Israel Dodge to pay Mrs. Francis Bredin out of the public store for making four soldier coats for Kellar's Company (VSA-14a).
12/07/80 Francis Bredin signs her "mark" that she received of Israel Dodge eight yds white flannel in full of her demands for making the coats (VSA-14b).

Bredin, Richard [also Bradin]
06/23/80 Capt. Robt. George requests of John Dodge, by Col. Clark's orders to issue 16 shirts to Reuben Camp, Daniel Williams, Richard Bredin, Charles Evans, Andrew Johnston, Isaac Yeates, and William Nelson who are members of Capt. Worthington's Co. (VSA- 11) (VSA-48).
09/19/80 "A Breden & family" were sick and were issued two lbs sugar out of the public store at Fort Jefferson (VSA-13).
09/19/80 Account of sugar delivered by Martin Carney by order of Capt. George at Fort Jefferson, to Bredin of Worthington's Company, two lbs (VSA-50).
11/18/80 Enlisting (Harding 1981: 47).

Breeding, Mrs. Hanah [also Bredin] Made soldier shirts at Ft. Jefferson (GRC, II: 326). Probably married to John Breeding.

Fort Jefferson Personnel

Breeding, John
01/10/79 Enlsited as a sergeant in Capt. Quirk's Co. of the Illinois Regiment (Harding, 1981: 16).
04/21/80 William Bartholomew, John Breeding, George King, Bob Logan, William Bohman, John Deck, John Cowan and Daniel Tyger are mentioned as being at Ft. Clark, some are later at Fort Jefferson (VSA-10; Non-FJ Document).

Brien, Mary
06/16/80 Paid M. Brien 3 1/4 yds calico for making six plain shirts, three yds calico for making six plain shirts, 3 1/4 yds calico for making seven plain shirts (VSA-48).
07/05/80 Two Indian handkerchiefs and two coarse check handkerchiefs paid M. Brien for making eight plain shirts (VSA-48).

Brown, James
04/15/80 Enlisted on this date as a private in Capt. Worthington's Company (Harding 1981: 47).
07/14/80 Lt. Col. John Montgomery issues at FJ 1/8 lb powder and 1/4 lb lead to each of the 14 men going from FJ to Kaskaskia. James Brown signs for materials received (VSA-12).
10/04/80 Killed (Harding 1981: 47).

Brown, James [Sergeant]
05/09/79-02/09/81 Enlisted, member of Capt. Kellar's Company (Harding 1981: 22-23).
07/14/80 Signs for 1/8 lb powder and 1/4 lb lead each for 14 men going to Kaskaskia (VSA-12).
07/14/80 Account of ammunition delivered by Martin Carney by Col. Montgomery's orders, to Sgt. Majr. James Brown, Illinois Regiment, 3 1/2 lbs powder, seven lbs lead (VSA-50).

Brown, James [Sergeant]
07/12/80 Capt. R. George requests of J. Dodge by order of Col. Clark, that Joseph Momeral, Louis Lepaint, James Brown, and Jacke Rubedo, four soldiers of Capt. Williams' Company be issued cloth and trimmings for a complete suit of clothes each and two shirts each, they being entitled to the same by law, having more than one year to serve (VSA-12).
07/13/80 Lt. Col. John Montgomery, signing as commandant, requests of Capt. Dodge by Col. Clark's order, to issue James Brown, a Sgt. in Brahsears' Company, one ink pot. James Brown signs that he received the within contents (VSA-12).
07/13/80 One ink pot to Sgt. Brown by Col. Montgomery's order issued to Ensign Jarrett Williams for men of Capt. Brashears' Company (VSA-48).
09/13/80 Issued a share of two lbs sugar along with Sam Allen for being sick (VSA-13).

Brown, Lewis
07/10/80 In Capt. Worthington's Company (VSA-12).
07/10/80 A. Gamelin signs that he received of Sgt. John Moore of Capt. Worthington's Co., two soldiers of the same company: Louis Brown and David Allen. They are to be delivered to the commanding officer (MHS: B1, F20).

Brown, Loue
Listed as Private in Capt. Jesse Evans' Co. (Harding 1981: 14).
07/13/80 Discharged (Harding 1981: 14).
07/14/80 Among list of men being issued one shirt at FJ per Col. Montgomery's order (VSA-12).

Fort Jefferson Personnel

Bryan, John [civilian]
06/19/80 John Bryan is issued two shirts per Capt. George's request of John Dodge for being enlisted during the war (VSA-11b).
06/20/80 Capt. Robert George requests of John Dodge to pay John Bryan 15 pounds four shillings, and six pence in goods for making clothing for Capt. George's Co. (VSA-11a).
06/20/80 John Bryan signs his mark that he received the following goods in full of his demand: one piece chince, 6 3/4 yds linen, one paperfold of pins, two silk handkerchiefs, 1 1/2 yds ribbon (VSA-11b).
06/20/80 John Nash is mentioned as being a soldier in Capt. Shelby's Co. Received suit of clothing made by J. Bryan, Tailor at FJ (VSA-11).
06/21/80 One pair chintz no. 23, 6 3/4 yds white linen, one paper pins, two silk handkerchiefs, 1 1/2 yds ribbon per order of Capt. George and receipt of John Bryan for making up clothing (VSA-48).
08/18/80 Issued 3/4 yd black persian, 1/2 yd thickset, six yds binding, and two linen handkerchiefs for making a suit of clothes for the interpreter (VSA-48).
09/08/80 Received one quart tafia for use of his sick family (VSA-13).
09/09/80 Account of sugar delivered by Martin Carney by order of Col. Montgomery at Fort Jefferson, to John Bryan of Capt. George's Company, three lbs (VSA-50).
10/20/80 Account of ammunition delivered by Martin Carney by order of Capt. George, to Bryan, a soldier in Capt. Worthington's Company, 1/4 lb powder, 1/2 lb lead (VSA-50).
11/16/80 Is the tailor at Fort Jefferson (VSA-14).

Bryan [Mrs. and family] [John ?]
09/08/80 Received one quart tafia for sick family (VSA-13).

Bryant, James
07/15/80 Listed in Capt. Worthington's Company (MHS B1, F20) (VSA-12).
10/04/80 Listed as one of three men in Capt. Worthington's Company to receive one lb powder and [one lb beef?] per request of Robert George (VSA-13).

Buchannon, William
07/12/80 Capt. Robt. George requests of John Dodge by order of Col. Clark, that full clothing be issued for three men enlisted during the war, who have never received any part thereof. Also for one man enlisted for one year. The men were recruited by Col. Montgomery: William Buchanan, Robert Whitehead, William Whitehead, John Robert. John Roberts enlisted for one year; the others during the war (VSA-12a).
11/30/80 Enlistment. Listed as Private in Capt. John Bailey's Co. of the Illinois Regiment in the Virginia State Service. Payroll (Harding 1981: 45-46).
11/15/81 Deserted (Harding 1981: 46).

Burk, Charles
06/04/79-12/03/81 Listed as Matross [Corporal] in Capt. Robert George's Co. of Artillery in the Service of the Commonwealth of Virginia and Illinois Department. Pay Abstract (Harding 1981: 29-30).
06/19/80 Issued two shirts by order of Capt. George (VSA-11).
11/15/81 Deserted (Harding 1981: 29-30).

Burk, John [also Burks]
Deposition in court case regarding his being present at Fort Jefferson through evacuation; return trip to Louisville took 32 days [Brooks vs Edwards Bullitt, Circuit Court; Jefferson County Court House]. [discrepancies of four days re: ETS]
04/19/80-06/08/81 Furnished Ft. Jefferson with 365 lbs beef and 35 lbs venison (GRC Papers, II: 363).

Fort Jefferson Personnel

05/01/80-12/25/80 Listed as Private in Capt. George Owens' Co. of Militia of the District of Clarksville in the State of Virginia [Jefferson Co.]. Pay Abstract (GRC Papers, I: 465; Harding 1981: 48-49).
09/01/80[?] Farmed one acre [potential of 20 bushels] which was burned by Indians (DMS 1M8).
11/19/80 Account of sugar delivered by Martin Carney by orders of Capt. George, to John Burks, sick militia man, one lb (VSA-50).
03/09/81 Ammunition delivered by order of Capt. George, to John Burks, Militia man, 1/4 lb powder (VSA-50).
06/05/81 To John Burks, Militia of Clarksville, six lbs sugar (VSA-49).
06/06/81 Issued six lbs sugar for use of his family "of militia" (VSA-20).

Burks, Mrs. Elizabeth [probably married to John]
06/16/80 Five yds calico paid E. Burk for making six ruffled and six plain shirts per receipt (VSA-48).
01/17/81 Mrs. E. Burks received 15 skeins of thread for payment for making two shirts for Capt. Brashears' Company as attended by James Williams and Capt. George (VSA-15).
05/23/81 Mrs. E. Burks received five lbs sugar for making eight shirts for Capt. George's Company at Fort Jefferson (VSA-19).
05/23/81 Per order to Mrs. Burks for making shirts for Capt. George's Company, five lbs sugar (VSA-49).

Burk, Nicholas
08/13/80-11/30/81 Listed as Private in Capt. John Bailey's Co. of the Illinois Regiment in the Virginia State Service. Payroll (Harding, 1981: 45-46).
08/13/80 Enlistment (VSA-12).

Burk, Sarah
06/16/80 Two yds calico and two linen handkerchiefs paid Sarah Burk for making six ruffled and one plain shirt (VSA-48).
06/21/80 Two silk handkerchiefs, one India handkerchief paid S. Burk for making 11 shirts plain (VSA-48).

Burney, Simon
11/05/80 Account of ammunition delivered by Martin Carney by order of Capt. George, to Simon Burney in lieu of 380 lbs of beef, six lbs powder (VSA-50).

Bush, Charles
06/19/80 Charles Bush is issued two shirts per Capt. George's request of John Dodge for being enlisted during the war (VSA-11b).

Bush, Drury
06/04/79-12/03/81 Listed as Matross [Corporal] in Capt. Robert George's Co. of Artillery in the Service of the Commonwealth of Virginia and Illinois Department. Pay Abstract (Harding, 1981: 29-30).
06/12/80 Going on expedition with Capt. Harrison to the Falls of Ohio; George requests clothing to be issued for the list of men who will be going (VSA- 11).

Bush, John
06/04/79-12/03/81 Listed as Matross [Corporal] in Capt. Robert George's Company of Artillery in the Service of the Commonwealth of Virginia and Illinois Department. Pay Abstract (Harding, 1981: 29-30).
06/12/80 Going on expedition with Capt. Harrison to the Falls of Ohio; George requests clothing issue for those going with Harrison (VSA-11).

Bush, William
05/10/79-11/30/81 Listed as Private in Capt. John Bailey's Company of the Illinois Regiment in the Virginia State Service. Payroll (Harding, 1981: 45-46).

Fort Jefferson Personnel

07/12/80 Among list of men receiving two shirts each for being enlisted during the war in Capt. John Bailey's Company (VSA-12).

Butcher, Gasper [Bucher]
05/0?/80 Discharged from Capt. Thomas Quirk's Company at Fort Clark. Came to Fort Jefferson with Col. Montgomery (VSA-13a).
05/11/80 Col. John Montgomery signs request to John Dodge to except [accept] and pay the within contents [not mentioned]. Gasper Butcher signs that he received the goods from Dodge (VSA-11a).
05/11/80 Richard Clark and John Montgomery sign that Butcher was employed as artificer repairing Fort Clark at Kaskaskia for three days in March at 3/day payable in goods as they were sold in 1772 (VSA-11b).
09/10/80 Issued on shirt as serving 20 months in the service (VSA-13a).
09/10/80 Three plain shirts per order for Thomas Kirk, Gasper Butcher, and Stephen Stephensen issued to Col. Montgomery for part of clothing for four men of Capt. Quirk's Company (VSA-48).
09/11/80 Received $6 of goods for artificer work done in Kaskaskia (VSA-13a).
09/25/80 Issued 3 1/2 yds white flannel and five yds white linen to Gasper Butcher per order of Col. Montgomery (VSA-48).

Cailev, Casper
07/10/80 Member of Capt. John Rogers' Company. Among list of men received two shirts and two stocks each at Fort Jefferson per Capt. George's orders to Capt. John Dodge for having more than one year to serve (VSA-12).

Callaghan, Patrick
06/07/81 Account of ammunition delivered by Martin Carney by order of Capt. Robert George and Col. Montgomery, to Patrick Callaghan, one lb powder, two lbs lead (VSA-50).

Calvit, Lt. Joseph
01/0?/81-02/0?/81 Apparently accompanied Capt. Edward Worthington by boat from Falls of Ohio to Fort Jefferson (DMS 56J28).
01/27/81 Stores issued by order of Capt. Robert George, to Lt. Calvit one kettle (VSA-50).
02/03/81 Stores issued by order of Capt. Robert George, to Lt. Calvit, three swords and two axes (VSA-50).
02/03/81 Account of ammunition delivered by Martin Carney by order of Capt. Robert George at Fort Jefferson, to Lt. Calvit for his use, 1/2 lb powder and one lb lead (VSA-50).
02/16/81 Ammunition delivered by order of Capt. George, to Lt. Calvit, 1/2 lb powder (VSA-50).
02/26/81 Served on Court of Inquiry board at Fort Jefferson (56J27).
02/27/81-03/03/81 Served on Court of Inquiry Board at Fort Jefferson regarding Capt. John Dodge's charges against Capt. Richard McCarty (DMS 56J29).
03/03/81 During Court of Inquiry against Capt. McCarty, Lt. Calvit was ordered by Capt. Robert George to leave Board of Inquiry and go to Illinois for provisions for Fort Jefferson (DMS 56J34).
03/09/81 Ammunition delivered by order of Capt. George, to Lt. Calvit command to the Illinois, 3 3/4 lbs powder, 7 1/2 lbs lead (VSA-50).
03/10/81 Stores issued by order of Capt. Robert George, to Lt. Calvit's Command, four tents or oil cloths (VSA-50).
03/28/81 Ammunition delivered by order of Capt. Robert George at Fort Jefferson, to Lt. Calvit and bowman, one lb powder (VSA-50).
05/03/81 Per orders brought from day book, two gallons and one quart rum and eight lbs sugar (VSA-49).
05/14/81 Ammunition delivered by order of Capt. Robert George at Fort Jefferson, to Lt. Calvit, 1/2 lb powder and one lb lead (VSA-50).
05/23/81 Per orders brought from day book, eight lbs sugar (VSA-49).
06/05/81 Per orders brought from day book, 20 lbs sugar (VSA-49).
06/07/81 Per orders brought from day book, two carots of tobacco (VSA-49).

Fort Jefferson Personnel

Camp, Ichabod
Paid Doctor Ichabod Camp for medicines for the light horse men per account per order of Capt. John Rogers, Commandant, 332 livres in peltry; two check handkerchiefs paid Camp for a pickle cask; 11 yds linen and three yds chintz paid Camp for making an Indian coat; 30 bags and 20 shirts (VSA-48).
09/04/80 Issued in the Indian Department, paid I. Camp for medicine for the interpreter, 16 livres peltry; paid I. Camp for a keg for the savages, 12 livres peltry (VSA-48).

Campbell, William
07/10/80 Member of Capt. John Rogers' Company. Among list of men receiving two shirts and two stocks at Fort Jefferson per Capt. George's orders to Capt. John Dodge for having more than one year to serve (VSA-12).

Canada, Nicholas [also Canadaw]
08/29/80 Issued in the Indian Department, paid Nicholas Canada for his account of Smith work per receipt, 40 (VSA-48).
09/04/80 Issued in the Indian Department, paid Canada for repairing Indian Arms and 200 flour per receipt 120 livres peltry (VSA-48).

Canore, Andrew [?]
03/20/80 Enlisted for three years or during the war by Lt. V. T. Dalton into Capt. Robert George's Company of Artillery (MHS: B1, F23).

Carmack, William
07/14/80 Among list of men being issued one shirt each at Fort Jefferson per Col. Montgomery's orders (VSA- 12).
07/14/80 Discharged (VSA-12).

Carney, Martin
Listed as quartermaster at Fort Jefferson 1780-81 (GRC Papers, II: 315; 325).
03/01/80 Account of arms received from Mr. Donne, Commissary at Falls of Ohio, two rifles and three muskets (VSA-50: 16).
04/05/80 Articles purchased by Martin Carney for the State of Virginia: one ugn and gears, and four gallons tar, value at 1148 pounds; purchased five flat bottomed boats for sake of the plank to build a garrison and barracks at or near the mouth of the Ohio River (VSA-50:2).
04/06/80 Articles purchased for the State of Virginia: one bateau for 275 pund to be paid to Eliasha Freeman (VSA-50: 2).
04/07/80 Articles purchased for the State of Virginia: from William Papo, two muskets and a rifle for 330 pounds (VSA-50: 2).
04/08/80 Articles purchased for the State of Virginia: one rifle gun, the property of Nathanal Randal, valued at 180 pounds (VSA-50: 2).
04/08/80 Account of arms received in this department, the property of the Commonwealth of Virginia: three rifles and 27 muskets (VSA-50:16).
04/10/80 Articles purchased for the State of Virginia: one large bateau, paid to John A. Johns per receipt, 1000 pounds (VSA-50: 2).
04/12/80 Account of arms delivered to Captain George's Company of Artillery: delivered to Sergeant Walker, two rifle guns (VSA-50: 3).
04/22/80 Articles purchased for the State of Virginia: taken into service, two horses the property of Captain Worthington, valued at 1800 pounds (VSA 50: 2).
Daily issues from 04/26/80 to 05/14/80 (VSA-3, 11 16, 50).
05/14/80 Received at Fort Jefferson: from the French boats ten kegs gunpowder said to contain 100 weight each, three kegs, none of them full. Received from Captain Dodge, 21 piggs lead said to be 1600 lbs lead (VSA-50: 5).
Daily issues from 05/17/80 to 05/19/80.
05/19/80 Account of ammunition delivered by Carney by order of Col. Clark to Captain Richard Harrison at Kaskaskia, 23 1/2 lbs gunpowder; to Major

Fort Jefferson Personnel

Harlan of militia, three lbs gunpowder and six lbs lead; to Captain John Bailey of regulars at Kaskaskia, 9 1/2 lbs gunpowder and 19 lbs lead; to Lt. Perrault of regulars at Kaskaskia, 1/2 lb gunpowder; to the Doctor and Lt. Girault at Kaskaskia, one lb gunpowder and two lbs lead (VSA-50: 8).

05/26/80 Account of ammunition delivered by Carney by order of Col. Clark: to Captain Richard Brashears at Cahokia, 4 3/4 lbs gunpowder and 9 1/2 lb lead; to Captain Richard Brashears at Cahokia, five lbs gunpowder and 11 lbs lead; to Captain John Rogers at Cahokia, six lbs gunpowder; to Captain Richard Harrison at Cahokia, 136 lbs gunpowder; to Captain John Bailey at Cahokia 4 1/2 lbs gunpowder and nine lbs lead; to Mr. Brady for Indians at Cahokia, three lbs gunpowder and four lbs lead; to John Duff, spy at Cahokia, 1/4 lb gunpowder and 1/2 lb lead; to Captain John Bailey at Cahokia, 9 1/2 lbs gunpowder and 19 lbs lead; to Captain McCarty at Cahokia 4 3/4 lbs gunpowder and 9 1/2 lbs lead; to Ensign Jarrett Williams at Cahokia, 3 1/2 lbs gunpowder and seven lbs lead; to Captain Richard Harrison at Cahokia, 21 lbs lead (VSA-50: 8). Daily issues from 05/29/80 to 06/06/80 (VSA-50, 50: 5;8).

06/07/80 Martin Carney balances records of "ammunition received" and "ammunition issued" finding a mistake in the "issued" records. Carney is charged with 3235 weight gunpowder and 4145 weight lead. The issues exceed that amount by 46 1/2 weight in gunpowder and 149 1/2 weight in lead (VSA-11). Daily issues from 06/07/80 to 06/09/80 (VSA-11; 48; 50).

06/09/80 Col. George Rogers Clark at Fort Jefferson requests Captain George to allow Quartermaster Carney the same clothing privileges as an officer of the regiment (VSA-11). Daily issues from 06/09/80 to 06/13/80 (VSA-11; 48; 50).

06/13/80 Account of ammunition delivered by Captain Robert George's order at Camp Jefferson, to Josiah Phelps and John Montgomery, one lb gunpowder and two lbs lead; to Captain Harrison 1/2 lb lead; to Captain Harrison to take to the Falls of Ohio, 500 lbs gunpowder and 1000 lbs lead; t o Captain George for the use of the troops, 3/4 lbs gunpowder and 1 1/2 lbs lead (VSA-50).

06/13/80 Account of tobacco delivered by Carney by order of Captain Robert George at this place, to Captain Lt. Harrison going up the Ohio, six carots weighing 18 lbs (VSA-50).

06/13/80 Captain Robert George requests Martin Carney to purchase tobacco from Mr. Lindsay for the use of the troops in this department (VSA-11).

06/13/80 Joseph Lindsay received of Martin Carney a receipt for 161 lbs of tobacco equal to 240.50 livres in peltry (VSA-11; 50).

06/13/80 Captain Richard Harrison writes he received from Martin Carney one large barge, one small canoe, 28 oars, 13 fathom cable, and one grapling [hook] (VSA-11).

06/14/80 Issued to Martin Carney, Deputy Quartermaster, three yards brown broadcloth 7/4 wide and three yards shalloon, issued for six vests and six pair breeches; five yards spotted cotton velvet, six yards casimir, 2 1/2 yards thickset, 4 1/2 yards cottonade and five yards sycee, 2 1/4 yards linen for lining for vests and breeches, 19 1/2 yards linen for six shirts, two yards muslin for six stocks, 3/4 yard fine holland for ruffling six shirts, one silk handkerchief, one India handkerchief, one red cotton handkerchief, one blue cotton handkerchief, two check linen handkerchiefs, two sticks silk twist, two skeins silk, 12 skeins thread, one pair knee garters, five dozen metal buttons, one fine hat (VSA-48). Daily issues from 06/14/80 to 06/19/80 (VSA; 11; 48; 50).

06/19/80 Received one brass ink pot, one large clasp knife, one ivory comb, one horn comb, and six yards ferret (VSA-48). Daily issues from 06/20/80 to 07/13/80.

07/13/80 Carney is a participant in a Court of Inquiry at Fort Jefferson (Draper Manuscripts 56J22-24). Daily issues from 07/13/80 to 07/17/80.

Fort Jefferson Personnel

07/13/80 Account of ammunition delivered by Carney by Col. Montgomery's orders to James Finn, Quartermaster Illinois Regiment, 20 lbs gunpowder and 40 lbs lead (VSA-50).

07/13/80 Account of arms received by Martin Carney in this department, the property of the Commonwealth of Virginia, received of Lt. Wilson at ﬩ Jefferson, five muskets (VSA-50).

07/14/80 Account of ammunition delivered by Martin Carney by Captain Robert George's order at Camp Jefferson, to Captain John Rogers going to Cahokia, one lb gunpowder and one lb lead (VSA-50).

07/14/80 Account of ammunition delivered by Carney by Col. Montgomery's orders to Ensign Slaughter, going to Oka [?], 1/4 lb gunpowder and 1/2 lb lead; to James Brown, Sergeant Majr. in Illinois Regiment, 3 1/2 lbs gunpowder and seven lbs lead; to Lt. Girault, Illinois Regiment, 1/4 lb gunpowder and 1/2 lb lead; to Sgt. Wilson, Illinois Regiment, 5 1/2 lbs gunpowder and 11 lbs lead (VSA-50).

07/15/80 Account of arms delivered by Carney to Captain George's Company of Artillery of the Illinois Virginia Regiment, delivered to Sergeant Anderson, five muskets and five carabines (VSA-50).

07/17/80 Account of ammunition delivered by Martin Carney by Captain Robert George's order at Camp Jefferson, to Sergeant Anderson for the defense of this place, 22 lbs gunpowder and 104 lbs lead (VSA-50). Daily issues from 07/21/80 to 08/09/80.

08/09/80 Account of ammunition delivered to Captain George Owens' Company of Militia, 11 1/2 lbs gunpowder and 46 lbs lead (VSA-50).

08/14/80 Account of ammunition delivered to Sergeant Anderson, for a hunter at this place, 1/2 lb gunpowder and one lb lead; for Lawrence Keinan (Keenan), gunner at this place, 13 1/2 lbs gunpowder and 2 1/2 yard flannel (VSA-50). Daily issues from 08/16/80 to 08/26/80.

08/26/80 Ammunition delivered to Thomas Laney, gunner at the blockhouse, one b gunpowder and two lbs lead (VSA- 50).

08/27/80 Two yards flannel and thread per order delivered for use of the artillery per receipt of Martin Carney (VSA- 48).

08/27/80 Ammunition delivered by Martin Carney by Captain George's order to the soldiers and inhabitants at this place, 22 lbs gunpowder and 44 lbs lead; to the artillery men at this place, 25 lbs gunpowder and 50 lbs lead (VSA-50). Daily issues from 08/28/80 to 09/09/80 (VSA-13; 48; 50).

09/09/80 Account of sugar delivered by Martin Carney by order of Col. Montgomery at Fort Jefferson, to Nelly Lewis a soldier's widow, two lbs; to David Allen a soldier in Worthington's, one lb; to Thomas Kirk, one lb; to Archibold Lockard in Worthington's, two lbs; to Col. Montgomery's order, three lbs; to Groves Morris a man in Captain Bailey's, three lbs; to a man and his sick children, one lb; to Thomas Kirk, two lbs; to eight sick people of the inhabitants, four lbs; to a sick woman and children of Captain Brashears', two lbs; to Lt. James Merriwether of Cavalry, four lbs to two men of Captain Bailey's, two lbs; to Matthew Jones a soldier in Captain George's Company, two lbs; to Mr. Donne, Commissary, four lbs; to Mayfield and children, two lbs; to two men of Captain Bailey's, one lb; to Col. Montgomery's order, one lb; to John Bryan of Captain George's Company, three lbs; to Anthony Lunsford and family, two lbs; to Joshua Archer, three lbs; to George Lunsford of Captain Bailey's, 1/2 lb; to Mary Demore, a soldier's wife, two lbs; to Henry Steward, a militia man, one lb; to five men of Captain John Bailey's, 2 1/2 lbs; to Mrs. Witzel a widow of militia, three lbs; to Nathan Allen of Militia, two lbs; to Captain Kellar for his own use, four lbs; to Mr. Oiler's sick family, four lbs; to Jacob Ditterin, one lb; to Charles Evans a soldier in Captain Worthington's, one lb; to the widow Meredith, two lbs; to two wounded militia men, two lbs; to Captain George Owens of militia, two lbs; to Jacob Shilling a militia man, two lbs; to Ezekiel Johnston, a militia man, four lbs; to Joseph Hunter, a militia man, three lbs; to Francis Gamlin, a militia man, 2 1/2 lbs; to

Fort Jefferson Personnel

the widow Hughes of militia, three lbs; to Captain Brashears and Doctor Ray, three lbs (VSA-50).
Daily issues from 09/09/80 to 09/13/80.

09/13/80 Sugar delivered by order of Col. Montgomery at Fort Jefferson, to Captain Helm for his use, four lbs; to Captain Dodge, Agent, for his use, four lbs; to Lt. Dalton, for his own use, 20 lbs; to Col. Montgomery for his own use, three lbs; to Reuben Kemp, of Worthington's, 1 1/2 lbs; to Col. Montgomery's order, two lbs; to Robert Ford, a militia man for 57 lbs beef for public use, seven lbs; to James Young a militia man, three lbs; to ten officers in Col. Montgomery's mess, 60 lbs; to Captain Dodge's order by Frank Little, 5 1/2 lbs; to Carney's own use, four lbs; to Mr. Graffen for a handmill for public use, six lbs; to the widow Witzel for a flat bottomed boat for public use, seven lbs; to James King and company for a flat bottomed boat, seven lbs (VSA-50).

09/13/80 Soap delivered by order of Col. Montgomery and Captain George at Fort Jefferson, to Captain Bailey's Company, 12 lbs; to Captain Robert George's Company, 16 lbs; to Captain Edward Worthington's Company, 9 1/2 lbs; to Captain Brashears' Company, 8 1/2 lbs; to Mr. Donne, Commissary, three lbs; to Captain McCarty's Company, 15 lbs; to Lt. Williams for his use, one lb; to Captain Brashears and Doctor Ray, one lb (VSA-50).

09/14/80 Account of sugar delivered by Martin Carney by order of Captain George at Fort Jefferson, to James Thomson, a soldier in Captain Kellar's Company, one lb; to two sick soldiers in Captain Kellar's Company, two lbs; to two sick soldiers of Captain Brashears'Company, two lbs; to Joseph Hunter of Militia, three lbs (VSA-50).

09/15/80 Account of ammunition delivered by Martin Carney by Captain George's order, to Capt John Bailey's Company, 5 1/2 lbs gunpowder and 11 lbs lead; to John Hazard of Artillery, 1/4 lb gunpowder and 1/2 lb lead; to two men of Captain McCarty's Company, one lb gunpowder and two lbs lead; to the artillery at this place, 16 lbs gunpowder, 32 lbs lead and six yards flannel (VSA-50).

09/15/80 Account of sugar delivered by Martin Carney by order of Captain George at Fort Jefferson, to John Hazard of Captain George's Company, one lb; to William Creton of militia, one lb; to Paul Quibea of Captain George's Company, one lb; to William McCauley of militia, one lb; to John Johnston of militia, one lb; to Jacob Ditterin of Artillery, one lb; to John Reed of militia, one lb; to Zachariah Williams, soldier in Worthington's, one lb; to John Grimshaw and Mr. Mullens of Capt. George's Company, two lbs; to Edward Murray, a soldier in Captain Bailey's, two lbs (VSA- 50).

09/16/80 Sugar delivered by order of Captain George at Fort Jefferson, to Andrew Clark, Artificer at public work, two lbs; to Joseph Panther a soldier in Captain Kellar's Company, one lb; to Peter Helebrand, a militia man, two lbs; to four men of Captain John Bailey's Company, two lbs (VSA-50).
Daily issues from 09/16/80 to 09/19/80 (VSA 13; 50).

09/19/80 Sugar delivered by Martin Carney by order of Captain George at Fort Jefferson, to Mr. Donne, Commissary for his family, four lbs; to James Thomson a soldier in Captain Kellar's, one lb; to Matthew Jones of Captain George's, one lb; to John Daughterty of Captain George's, two lbs; to Bredin of Worthington's, one lb; to William Crump a soldier in Worthington's, two lbs (VSA-50).
Daily issues from 09/19/80 to 10/28/80.

10/28/80 Articles purchased by Martin Carney for the state of Virginia by order of Col. Clark. Purchased of the Widow Hughes, hard money price to one iron pick for keeping the hand mills in order, value 1/2 pound. Purchased this same date of Archibold Lockard at the same price, value 1/2 pound (VSA-50).
Daily issues from 10/28/80 to 11/02/80.

11/02/80 Ammunition delivered by order of Captain George, to Mr. Sherlock for the use of the Kaskaskia Indians, 80 lbs gunpowder and 89 lbs lead; to Captain Helm for his own use, two lbs gunpowder and two lbs lead; to

Fort Jefferson Personnel

	three men of Captain Brashears' Company, 1 1/2 lbs gunpowder and three lbs lead (VSA- 50).
11/03/80	Account of ammunition delivered by Martin Carney by order of Captain George, to one man of Captain Brashears' Company, 1/2 lb gunpowder and one lb lead (VSA-50).
11/05/80	Account of ammunition delivered by Martin Carney by order of Captain George to Simon Burney in lieu of 380 lbs of beef, six lbs gunpowder; to Major Harlan for hunting, one lb gunpowder and two lbs lead (VSA-50).
	Daily issues from 11/05/80 to 11/15/80.
11/15/80	Sugar delivered by Martin Carney by orders of Captain George to Nelly Lewis, a soldier's widow, one lb; to five sick men of Captain Bailey's, five lbs; to eleven sick men of Captain George's, 11 lbs; to a sick woman of Captain Bailey's, one lb (VSA-50).
11/15/80	Brass kettles delivered by order of Captain George at Fort Jefferson, to Captain Robert George and Company, three kettles; to Captain Leonard Helm for his use, one kettle; to Captain Abraham Kellar and Company, two kettles; to Major John Williams for his use, one kettle; to Lt. Richard Clark for Captain Worthington's Company, two kettles; to Ensign Lawrence Slaughter for Captain Bailey's Company, two kettles; to Captain Richard Brashears, one kettle; to John Harry, armourer at this place, one kettle; for Carney's own use, one kettle (VSA-50).
	Daily issues from 11/16/80 to 12/04/80 (VSA 50: 29; 52).
12/04/80	Robert George requests of Martin Carney to issue four lbs gunpowder and eight lbs lead to Major Harlan and his hunting party as they are going to hunt meat for Fort Jefferson (VSA-14).
	Daily issues from 12/04/80 to 12/12/80.
12/12/80	Ammunition received from Captain Philip Barbour 472 lbs gunpowder; received of Philip Barbour 300 lbs gunpowder damaged (VSA-50: 5).
12/12/80	Arms received from Captain Barbour, 120 muskets with bayonets and belts (VSA-50: 16).
12/12/80	Martin Carney attests a memorandum of weights of stores brought to Fort Jefferson from New Orleans: one Spanish musket and bayonet; one cartridge box and bayonet belt; one arms chest; one belt chest and one large trunk. Also listed are articles brought by Captain Barbour as public store property: 12 cases of arms or chests; 120 stand, three cases of cartridges boxes and belts; one trunk of cartridge boxes and belts, 261 cartridge boxes and 422 bayonet belts; 300 lbs damaged gunpowder; 14 oil cloths or Spanish tents; and an eight lb bar of steel (VSA-14).
	Daily issues from 12/15/80 to 12/23/80.
12/23/80	Issued Silas Harlan one barrel rum, three lbs coffee, and six lbs sugar from Martin Carney (VSA-14).
	Daily issues from 12/23/80 to 1/1/81.
01/01/81	Buckner Pittman signed he received from Martin Carney three barges and piroques, 120 oars, one iron grapple, one pittaugree, one canoe and 12 fathon new cable rope (VSA- 15).
	Daily issues from 01/04/81 to 2/07/80 (VSA-50).
02/07/81	Ammunition delivered by order of Captain Robert George at Fort Jefferson, to three men of Captain George's Company, 3/4 lb gunpowder and 1 1/2 lb lead; to the Kickapoo Indians, seven lbs gunpowder and four lbs lead; to two militia men going to the Falls, two lbs gunpowder and one lb lead (VSA-50).
	Daily issues from 02/08/81 to 3/09/81.
03/09/81	A "Lt." Carney served on the Board of the Court of Inquiry at Fort Jefferson regarding Captain John Rogers' conduct while in command at Kaskaskia (Draper Manuscripts 56J45).
03/20/81	A "Lt." Carney is listed as participating in the Court Martial proceedings of David Allen and James Taylor (Draper Manuscripts 56J40).
	Daily issues from 3/20/81 to 6/7/81.
06/07/81	Ammunition delivered to six men going to the Falls by land, three lbs gunpowder and six lbs lead; to Patrick Calaghan, one lb gunpowder and

Fort Jefferson Personnel

two lbs lead; to Dapiae Whitegar, one lb gunpowder and two lbs lead (VSA-50).

Carr, William
03/26/80 Enlisted as a private in Captain John Bailey's Company (Harding 1981: 45-46).
07/12/80 Received two shirts for enlisting (VSA-12).
10/06/80 Sugar delivered at Fort Jefferson to William Carr of Captain Bailey's Company, 1/2 lb (VSA-50).
01/24/81 Deceased (Harding 1981: 46).

Certain, Page [Sertain]
03/10/80 Enlisted as a private in Captain Worthington's Company (Harding 1981: 47).
06/07/80 Killed (Harding 1981: 47).
07/15/80 Listed in Captain Worthington's Company of regulars [obviously a discrepancy] (MHS B1, F20; VSA-12).

Chapeau
09/04/80 Issued from the Indian Department, three check handkerchiefs for carrying a speech to the Savages (VSA-48).

Chapman, Richard
07/13/80 Member of Captain Jesse Evans Company. Discharged at Fort Jefferson (Harding 1981: 14).
07/14/80 Issued one shirt (VSA-12).

Chappel, John
06/02/80 Was present at Fort Jefferson and a member fo Captain Kellar's Company (MHS: B1, F19).
07/12/80 Received clothing issue at Fort Jefferson (VSA-12).

Cimblet, Francis
05/01/80-12/21/80 Listed as a private in Captain George Owens' Company of Militia (Harding 1981: 48-49).
09/12/80 Moved (Harding 1981: 49).

Clark, Andrew (artificer)
Note: Discrepancies in dates of enlistment.
01/04/78-07/13/80 Listed as Sergeant in Captain Jesse Evans' Company (Harding 1981: 14).
06/04/79-12/03/81 Listed as matross [corporal] in Captain Robert George's Company of Artillery (Harding 1981: 29-30).
06/19/80 Issued two shirts for enlisting (VSA-11).
06/22/80 Charged at public store, two pair trousers, one check handkerchief, one small tooth comb, one large tooth comb (VSA-11).
06/22/80 Charged at public store, five yards toile gris, one check linen handkerchief, one ivory comb, one horn comb, and two skeins thread (VSA-48).
07/28/80 Issued 1/2 carot of tobacco (VSA-12).
07/28/80 Tobacco delivered to Andrew Clark, artificer, 1/2 carot weighing 1 1⁄2 lbs (VSA-50).
09/16/80 Sugar delivered to Andrew Clark, artificer at public work, two lbs (VSA-13; 50).

Clark, Andrew, (Sergeant)
07/13/80 Member of Captain Jesse Evan's Company; discharged at Fort Jefferson (Harding 1981: 14).
07/14/80 Received one shirt (VSA-12).

Fort Jefferson Personnel

Clark, George Rogers
Received one large chest for public papers at Fort Jefferson from New Orleans, valued at 401 continental dollars (VSA-48).

Spring 1777 Clark is preparing plans to seize the British posts of Kaskaskia, Cahokia, and Vincennes. He obtained information from Thomas Bentley and Daniel Murray who are merchants and had lived in the French villages for several years (Seineke 1981: xx-xxi).

09/24/79 Letter from George Rogers Clark at the Falls of Ohio to Col. Daniel Broadhead. Clark mentions he will station a small floating battery at the Mouth of Ohio whenever it can be built (Seineke 1981: 401-402).

09/30/79 Letter from George Rogers Clark to Silas Harlan. Clark states a fort will be built near the Mouth of Ohio "immediately." Clark orders Harlan to raise settlers to live at the post. The settlers will be paid as militia for as long as necessary. Clark asks Harlan to be at Fort Jefferson by December 1, 1779 (GRC Papers, I: 368-369).

11/04/79 Letter from Silas Harlan at Harrodsburg to George Rogers Clark at Falls. Plans to settle at the Iron Banks was approved by the Commissioners; Harlan believes it will also be approved by the Assembly (MHS: B1, F11).

01/01/80 Letter from Governor Jefferson to George Rogers Clark. Clark's Illinois Battalion is to be completed; 100 men will be stationed at the Mouth of Ohio under Major Slaughter. The battalion will go as early as the weather will allow. The battalion will march with Clark during the summer and in the fall will fortify the posts which are expected to be taken on the Ohio (Seineke 1981: 418).

01/29/80 Letter from Jefferson to George Rogers Clark. Encloses letters with his to Joseph Martin and Daniel Smith and Thomas Walker. Discusses new location for a fort at the Mouth of the Ohio. Jefferson is in agreement with building a fort at or near the Mouth of Ohio (Seineke 1981: 418-419).

01/29/80 Jefferson's letter to Thomas Walker and Daniel Smith. Jefferson requests either Walker or Smith with George Rogers Clark to travel to the Mouth of Ohio. The exact latitude of the fort is needed. Jefferson requests one "plat" of their work be returned to him and one to Col. Clark (GRC Papers, I: 392-393; Seineke 1981: 420).

03/00/80 Letter from George Rogers Clark at Louisville to Col. John Todd. Clark suggests that to maintain authority in Illinois, it may be necessary to evacuate the present posts and let the force center at the Mouth of Ohio. If militia families would station there, Clark feels they would be followed by two or three times their numbers of young men (Seineke 1981: 429).

04/04/80 Letter from George Rogers Clark in Louisville to William Fleming in Harrodsburg. Clark is very sorry for the great loss of blood and property by the Kentuckians. They have sent Clark several petitions wanting an expedition against the Shawnee Towns. Clark does not want to interfere with an expedition already planned by Governor Jefferson. The success of that expedition depends upon the Kentuckians, and it will give them immediate and permanent peace with the Savages. If the Kentuckians do not have peace by fall, Clark feels it will be their own fault (GRC Papers, I: 407).

04/08/80 Daniel Smith and Thomas Walker recruit a guard to accompany them to the Falls of the Ohio thinking they would meet with Col. Clark there to carry out Governor Jefferson's January 29, 1780 letter to them (Souissant 1915).

04/11/80 William Shannon received six land warrants from George Rogers Clark on this date, containing 560 acres each. Shannon promises to deliver one able bodied soldier per warrant (GRC Papers, I: 412).

04/12/80 William Shannon's deposition of August 25, 1781 states he received 39 land warrants containing 360 acres each from Clark to purchase provisions for the use of troops under Clark's command in the Illinois Department, valued at 8,771 pounds, 2 shillings, Virginia Currency (GRC Papers I: 593).

Fort Jefferson Personnel

04/12/80 Abraham Kellar and William Shannon sign they received from George Rogers Clark, four land warrants containing 560 acres each, for recruiting four soldiers during the war to serve in Col. Clark's regiment (GRC Papers, I: 413).

04/12/80 Edward Worthington and William Shannon sign they received from George Rogers Clark, 20 land warrants containing 560 acres each, for recruiting 20 soldiers during the war to serve in Clark's regiment (GRC Papers, I: 413).

04/14/80 George Rogers Clark left the Falls of Ohio on this date to go to the Iron Banks (Souissant 1915).

04/19/80 Thomas Jefferson in Richmond writes to George Rogers Clark answering Clark's letter of February 22, 1780, regarding the location of fort at Mouth of Ohio; Jefferson discusses several options within letter concerning a site for a new fort (GRC Papers, I: 414-416).

04/19/80 Valentine T. Dalton at Fort Patrick Henry writes George Rogers Clark at Mouth of Ohio, informing him of opposition to the building of a fort at the Mouth of Ohio by the English (MHS: B1, F16).

04/19/80 Thomas Jefferson at Richmond writes to George Rogers Clark regarding murders by the Indians between Fort Pitt and Kentucky. Jefferson suggests he should carry out an expedition against the Indians immediately (GRC Papers, I: 416-417).

04/20/80 George Rogers Clark at Mouth of Ohio writes to John Dodge stating he arrived at Mouth of Ohio yesterday; Dodge should send Clark's furniture, seeds for garden, and "beans the French plant to make shades." Clark states that Captain Bentley will give Dodge the news (GRC Papers, I: 418-419).

04/25/80 Captain Richard McCarty writes to George Rogers Clark congratulating him on his arrival at the Mouth of Ohio. McCarty speaks of expected attack on Cahokia, also states, "health good but pockets is low." Wishes George Rogers Clark was with him (MHS: B1, F16).

04/25/80 Col. John Montgomery at Fort Clark writes George Rogers Clark at Mouth of Ohio. Montgomery is pleased Clark has arrived. Montgomery states condition at Fort Clark [Kaskaskia], not good, but he will do all he can to bring Clark his goods (MHS: B1, F16).

04/27/80 Laurence Slaughter signed he received from George Rogers Clark, five land warrants containing 560 acres each. Slaughter promises to return five able bodied soldiers to serve in Clark's Battalion during the war (MHS: B1, F16).

04/29/80 Letter from Batisst, Chief of the Kaskaskia Indians, at Fort Clark to George Rogers Clark. Batisst states he has heard of Clark's arrival at the Mouth of the Ohio; Batisst plans to visit Clark with Montgomery (GRC Papers, I: 418).

04/29/80 Letter from McCarty at Fort Clark to George Rogers Clark. McCarty is sending something with Mr. Gratiot to Clark; Clark's presence is wished for at Fort Clark (MHS: B1, F16).

05/03/80 Walker and Smith meet in the evening with Col. Clark respecting their business (Souissant 1915).

05/06/80 George Rogers Clark received letter from Charles Gratiot in Kaskaskia; reference made to Col. Montgomery taking opinions of officers, military, and militia to determine if they should proceed with an expedition against the Indains. The vote was to proceed in order to scatter the enemy and strike terror in the Indians. Trip was cancelled. About 30 men will stay at Kaskaskia for its defense. Gratiot is leaving Kaskaskia for Cahokia to tell the inhabitants that the expedition had failed. Gratiot apologizes for not being able to send tafia to Clark. It is scarce in the town. He promises to send some from Cahokia. All the garden seeds were sent down by Mr. Lindsay and there are no more in Kaskaskia (MHS: B1, F17).

05/07/80 Letter from Col. Montgomery at Fort Clark to George Rogers Clark. Expedition planned will be delayed, because inhabitants won't furnish the needed supplies of flour and corn to feed his troops for two months. Gillepsie will deliver to Clark part of the artillery, some salt, and

Fort Jefferson Personnel

2,000 lbs lead; the balance of the provisions will be delivered by Col. Montgomery (MHS: B1, F17).

05/09/80 Letter from John Rogers at Kaskaskia to George Rogers Clark at Camp Jefferson. Rogers will be leaving May 10th for Kaskaskia with his company. Mr. Dodge has purchased horses for him. Rogers is asking for instructions in order for him to receive saddles, bear skins and clothing for his soldiers (MHS: B1, F18).

05/11/80 Letter from George Rogers Clark at Camp Jefferson to Oliver Pollock, New Orleans. Clark arrived at Fort Jefferson to execute orders for establishing a post for the convenience of trade and other purposes (GRC Papers, I: 418-419; Seineke 1981: 432-433).

05/15/80 Letter from Captain John Rogers at Fort Clark to George Rogers Clark. Rogers speaks of dirty conditions and need for repair of the fort at Cahokia [Fort Bowman], and his efforts to clean it. Rogers also tells that Col. Montgomery is on the Spanish side [of the Mississippi]. Clark told Rogers to remain at Cahokia (MHS: B1, F17; Seineke 1981: 434).

05/15/80 Letter from Col. Montgomery at Fort Bowman to Clark. Montgomery with his troops wish to join the Spanish forces, because of the approach of the enemy. They hope to prevent an attack on the village. Montgomery was furnished 100 men with artillery and ammunition. The expedition should take place in a couple days with about 250 men (MHS: B1, F17).

05/16/80 Letter from Captain Valentine T. Dalton at Fort Clark to George Rogers Clark. Dalton went to O'Post (Vincennes) from Fort Clark to obtain salt. Letter mentions Montbreuen and his latest actions at Ouia (Ouiatenon) (Seineke 1981: 435).

05/17/80 Letter from British Major de Peyster at Detroit to British Gen. Haldimand. Tells of several Indian tribes. DePeyster also states Clark has gone to Iron Mines on the Mississippi, below the Ohio to establish a fort (Seineke 1981: 435-436).

05/18/80 George Rogers Clark amends several entries of land deeds to include 73,962 acres of "drowned lands" from the mouth of the Tennessee River down Ohio to the Mississippi River (Draper Manuscripts: 5K3; MHS, B1, F17).

05/18/80 Captain Robert George at Fort Jefferson writes George Rogers Clark at Cahokia informing him that Captain Shannon and Doctor Smith's arrival at Fort Jefferson a few days ago; additionally, only 18 men including non-commissioned officers are present, but George is not worried as he expects no action. The doctor is short of medicines. Captain George is keeping the doctor at Fort Jefferson, but sending a letter with Shannon to Cahokia. George refers to the sickly season approaching (MHS: B1, F17).

05/20/80 Col. Daniel Broadhead at Fort Pitt writes George Rogers Clark. Broadhead wishes Clark would make an attack on the Shawnee. Broadhead feels an attack by himself would be impractical for want of resources. Major Slaughter and his 100 men will be joining Clark. Letter delivered by Slaughter (GRC Papers, I: 419-420).

05/20/80 Captain Edward Worthington at Falls of Ohio writes George Rogers Clark at Mouth of Ohio explaining why he did not accompany Col. Legras and Mr. Dejean from Williamsburg to Fort Jefferson. There are several dissatisfied people at the Falls of Ohio. Worthington mentions supplies being prepared by the Commissary which will be sent Clark (MHS:B1, F17).

05/22/80 Letter from James Robertson at New Orleans to George Rogers Clark. Robertson has just arrived in New Orleans and informs Clark of the Spanish plans in that location (Seineke 1981: 437).

05/25/80 Letter from Captain William Shannon at Kaskaskia to George Rogers Clark. Shannon arrived at Kaskaskia after an eight day trip from Clarksville. He plans to see Clark in two days if his horse can hold out. Indians are daily hostile with the inhabitants at the Falls; Clark's return is much wanted (MHS: B1, F17; Seineke 1981: 439).

06/03/80 Clark signed a document showing that Edward Taylor was paid one dollar per day and supplies for going express from Fort Patrick Henry to Fort

Fort Jefferson Personnel

Jefferson to Fort Clark and back to Fort Patrick Henry and taking 19 days to do so (VSA-11).

06/04/80 Captain Robert George writes from Fort Jefferson to George Rogers Clark. Letter delivered by Col. Legras who accompanied Mr. Dejean from Williamsburg. The trenches for Fort Jefferson are ready for the pickets, which the inhabitants are bringing. They hope to have the fort enclosed within the week. The inhabitants are not yet finished planting. Provisions are being spared and he is issuing single rations of corn. The present stock of corn is a little more than 100 bushels. Mr. Donne has tried to procure meat without success (MHS: B1, F19; Seineke 1981: 441).

06/05/80 George Rogers Clark at Kaskaskia requests of William Shannon, that he be issued five gallons of tafia to take to Fort Jefferson (VSA-11).

06/05/80 Clark left Kaskaskia for Fort Jefferson with a few men (GRC Papers, I: cxxxviii; VSA-11).

06/06/80 Letter from Captain John Rogers at Kaskaskia to George Rogers Clark at Fort Jefferson. Rogers wants to go on a dangerous expedition to learn more about the service and better serve his country (MHS: B1, F19; Seineke 1981: 442).

06/10/80 Issued to Georgr Rogers Clark the following list of items, by verbal orders, for use of his slaves while Clark's is on an expedition: one check linen handkerchief, seven yards osnaburg for two shirts for Negro man, five yards damaged linen for Wench, seven yards osnaburg for Wench and boy, 2 1/2 yards dark ground calico for Wench, three yards spotted flannel for Wench, one Indian handkerchief for Wench, one check linen handkerchief for Wench, four skeins thread, one scalping knife for Negro man, and 5 1/2 yards osnaburg for two pair trousers (VSA-48).

06/10/80 Issued to George Rogers Clark the following items for his use when going to the Falls of Ohio to make an expedition against the Indian towns: three ruffled shirts 3 1/4 each, 1 3/4 yards blue bath coating, 1 1/2 yards scarlet cloth, one yard blue cloth, 12 yards ribbon, two skeins silk, one clasp knife, one pr scissors, one pair ravelled gartering, one lb vermilion (VSA-48).

06/10/80 Issued to George Rogers Clark four lbs white sugar and one lb coffee (VSA-48).

06/10/80 Issued to George Rogers Clark, 18 check handkerchiefs to be paid to Lafont for 18 plates. [Two saltcellars were listed but had been crossed out] (VSA-48).

06/10/80 Issued one snaffle bridle by John Dodge to pay for two saltcellars for 18 plates (VSA-48).

06/10/80 Issued six gallons tafia to be sent to Fort Jefferson by Captain Brashears (VSA-48).

06/10/80 Issued to George Rogers Clark, 60 lbs peltry for one dozen China plates to be paid Gratiot (VSA-48).

06/12/80 Letter from Captain Valentine T. Dalton at Fort Patrick Henry to George Rogers Clark. Dalton tells Clark about activities at Vincennes (Seineke 1981: 442-443).

06/25/80 Letter from Captain Valentine T. Dalton at Fort Patrick Henry [Vincennes] to George Rogers Clark. They recently fought a battle with the enemy [between 80 and 100] and won (MHS: B1, F19).

07/11/80 Thomas Jefferson's letter, which was written 04/19/80 to George Rogers Clark, is received at the Falls on this date. Jefferson tells Clark about recruiting difficulties and problems with the Indians (GRC Papers, I: 416-417).

09/25/80 A listing of goods paid Don Leyba for an order drawn in his favor by Colonel Clark for sundries furnished the troops in this department. Amount 1,172 dollars and receipt dated 11 July 80 (VSA-48).

10/28/80 John Williams at Fort Jefferson writes George Rogers Clark to inform him that he arrived at Fort Jefferson 10/23 to take command by order of Col. John Montgomery. He described hunger at the fort as a result of an inability to receive supplies due to low water. He did not take command from Robert George due to circumstances (GRC Papers, I: 463).

Fort Jefferson Personnel

10/28/80 Robert George at Fort Jefferson writes to George Rogers Clark at the Falls of the Ohio. Fort Jefferson is reduced to a small number due to famine, dissertion, and death; Montgomery visited Fort Jefferson enroute to New Orleans; provisions are expected from New Orleans via Pollock any day; most Fort Jefferson civilians left down river, remainder very distressed; Lt. Dalton may go down river with Montgomery; Captain Williams arrived to take command, but George refused to relinquish it to him (GRC Papers, I: 461-462; Seineke 1981: 465-466).

12/05/80 Letter from John Donne at Fort Jefferson to George Rogers Clark. Donne writes to inform Clark of the situation at Fort Jefferson. Talks of attack made by Indians on August 27 and tells that three of Captain George's men left after the attack for the Falls. He states that the most useful inhabitants have deserted, being struck with panic. The Indians destroyed the cornfields and anything else they could. All that remains of the settlers are those who are sick and weak. The remains of the cornfields were appraised for use of the troops. A small part of the corn was stored. Mr. Harlan has been hunting for meat since the beginning of last month [November]. Donne states that Harlan had brought in 14 or 15,000 weight and the Kaskaskia Indians had brought in 1,000 to 3,000 weight to the fort. Eight thousand weight was eaten last month [November], and Captain Rogers has been ordered from the Illinois to reinforce Fort Jefferson, which will add 1,000 weight to the monthly issue. Donne believes that Captain George has done all in his power to issue the provisions with frugality to the inhabitants. The greatest difficulty is transporting the provisions from the Illinois to Fort Jefferson. The trip takes about 15 to 20 days. Dodge in Illinois fears there will be a revolt in the Illinois. Donne suggests that Col. Montgomery might have done more to save Fort Jefferson (MHS: B1, F23).

12/07/80 Letter from Captain Richard Harrison at the Falls to Col. Clark in Richmond. Harrison is planning to leave on the 9th to go to Fort Jefferson and is taking all of his artillery and "her stores" with him. Harrison hopes Fort Jefferson will soon be relieved of its distresses. Mentions Captain Worthington is at Harrodsburgh, but has no intention of going to Fort Jefferson during the winter. Harrison hopes to return to the Falls in February (GRC Papers, I: 468).

12/10/80 George Slaughter at the Falls of Ohio writes to George Rogers Clark in Richmond. Slaughter tells he has enclosed letters from the Mouth of Ohio which will give a full account of affairs in that quarter (MHS: B1, F23).

12/17/80 Letter from Col. John Gibson at Fort Pitt to George Rogers Clark at Louisville. Gibson had been asked to deliver a quantity of clothing to Captain Moore for the use of the troops on the Ohio. Gibson says he cannot comply with the order because his men are "quite naked" (GRC Papers, I: 474).

12/24/80 Letter from Robert George at Fort Jefferson to George Rogers Clark. George states he received letters from Oliver Pollock and Col. Montgomery. George says that the greatest part of the cargo sent to Clark for use of the State was lost in a hurricane. The remainder of Capt. Barbour's goods were purchased. Captain Harrison informed George that it is Clark's intent to evacuate Fort Jefferson and erect another fortification at the Iron Banks. George states that his "yellow locks" will turn grey if Clark does not arrive soon to clarify his intentions. George also tells that Captain Helm is of infinite service and comfort to George at Fort Jefferson (MHS: B1, F23; Seineke 1981: 468-469).

12/25/80 Jefferson's Christmas present to Clark, "Attack Detroit!" (GRC Papers, I: 485-490).

01/01/81-01/19/81 Sometime between these dates, a letter was written from John Donne at Fort Jefferson to George Rogers Clark at Richmond. Reference is made to a letter written by Donne to George Rogers Clark on December 5, 1780. In the December letter, Donne mentioned he would take a trip to Kaskaskia where he expected to obtain a large quantity of goods which had been purchased; instead they were unpaid. The quantity on hand in

Fort Jefferson Personnel

the Illinois consists of about 200 bushels of corn, but a large quantity of flour is said to have been purchased while Donne was away. Captain Barbour arrived from New Orleans with a quantity of goods, part of which Captain George intends to use for the purchase of provisions (MHS: B1, F23).

04/11/81 George Rogers Clark's letters to Fort Jefferson are being carried by Jacob Pyatt (MHS: B1, F15).

04/11/81 Letter from William Clark, who is in Louisville, writing to George Rogers Clark at Fort Pitt. William will be in Louisville for some time, and hopes to see George while he is there to discuss Fort Jefferson (MHS: B2, F15).

04/20/81 George Rogers Clark receives a letter from Captain Worthington. George Rogers Clark is at Fort Pitt; Worthington is at Fort Jefferson. Worthington writes of the poor situation at the fort, the low provisions, and soldiers deserting. Some officers and soldiers are willing to stay until they are down to their last hour's worth of provisions (MHS: B2, F2).

Clark, John (Bailey's Company)
07/26/80-11/30/81 Listed as a private in Captain John Bailey's Company of the Illinois Regiment (Harding 1981: 45-46).
09/15/80 Issued two lbs sugar with Edward Murray (VSA-13).
10/15/80 Issued cloth and trimmings to make one suit for enlisting (VSA-13).
10/15/80 Received seven yards blue cloth, six yards flannel, twelve skeins thread and ten dozen buttons (VSA-13).
10/16/80 Deserted (Harding 1981: 46).

Clark, John (George's Company)
06/04/79-12/03/81 Listed as matross [corporal] in Captain Robert George's Company of Artillery (Harding 1981: 29-30).

Clark, Richard (Lt.)
06/00/80 Recieved from Mr. William Clark, three yards flannel and three skeins thread (MHS: B1, F19).
07/11/80 Issued quota of clothing by order of Captain George at Fort Jefferson. Member of Captain Worthington's Company (VSA-12).
07/12/80 Issued to Lt. Clark, 1 1/2 yards scarlet cloth 7/4 wide, 1 1/2 yards brown cloth 7/4 wide, 2 3/4 yards shalloon for lining, issued for six vests, two yards calender, 1 3/4 yards spotted flannel, three yards gray cloth 7/8 wide, and 1 3/4 yards white casimir; issued for six breeches, 4 1/2 yards fustian, six yards check linen; 21 yards fine linen for six shirts, 3/4 yards fine holland for ruffling shirts, two yards muslin for six stocks, four yards coarse linen for lining(damaged), two pair thread hose, one silk handkerchief, one Indian handkerchief, four check linen handkerchiefs, 17 skeins thread, four skeins silk, one stick silk twist, one hat, two dozen large metal buttons, 1/2 dozen small metal buttons, and three yards blue cloth 7/4 wide (VSA-48).
08/01/80 Arrived with Captain Bailey 1400w flour, 25 bushels corn, and 28 men [possibly Richard] (Seineke 1981: 449).
08/02/80 Issued 14 plain shirts to Captain Worthington's Company; items issued to Lt. Clark (VSA-48).
08/04/80 Issued to Lt. Clark, one English blanket, two check linen handkerchiefs, two yards silk ferret, one leather ink pot, one fine comb, one coarse comb, seven skeins thread, five yards blue ferretting, four skeins silk per receipt of August 4, say September 11, issued to and overdrawn by Lt. Clark. The blanket, two yards silk ferret, one leather ink pot, one fine comb, one coarse comb, and five yards blue ferretting did not appear on the July 12 list of goods issued to Lt. Clark (VSA-48).
08/12/80 Issued for Captain Worthington's Company two plain shirts for David Allen per Lt. Clark's receipt (VSA-48).
08/16/80 Ammunition delivered to Lt. Richard Clark, 1/2 lb gunpowder, one lb lead, and one flint (VSA-50).

Fort Jefferson Personnel

08/17/80 Ammunition delivered to Lt. Richard Clark for a man in Captain Worthington's, 1/4 lb gunpowder and 1/2 lb lead (VSA-50).
08/19/80 Issued 14 weight coffee (VSA-48).
08/21/80 Arms delivered to Lt. Richard Clark for his use, one rifle (VSA-50).
08/24/80 Tobacco delivered to Lt. Richard Clark, for his own use, one carot weighing three lbs (VSA-50).
08/27/80 Lt. Clark commands the blockhouse (Seineke 1981: 459).
08/29/80 Was cited for bravery during Indian attack in letter from Captain Robert George, dated Sept. 2, 1780 (Seineke 1981: 459).
09/11/80 Issued seven yards linen for 14 days service as an engineer at Kaskaskia (VSA-48).
09/13/80 Issued for Captain Worthington's Company, eight blankets, 18 3/4 yards blue cloth, 15 1/2 yards white flannel, and thread and buttons (VSA-48).
09/16/80 Soap delivered to Lt. Richard Clark, two lbs (VSA-13; 50).
09/25/80 Issued five bags, 15 brass kettles (68 weight), seven large dressed deer skins, one cask sugar, and one case soap per receipt of Lt. Clark for use of the troops at Fort Jefferson (VSA-48).
09/25/80 Issued Clark five skeins thread for use of Captain Worthington's Company (VSA-13).
10/11/80 Soap delivered to Lt. Richard Clark for his own use, six lbs (VSA-13; 50).
10/28/80 Issued 20 lbs gunpowder from Martin Carney (VSA-13).
11/15/80 Brass kettles delivered to Lt. Richard Clark for Captain Worthington's Company, two kettles (VSA-50).
11/29/80 Ammunition delivered to Lt. Richard Clark in the Illinois Regiment, 1/2 lb gunpowder, one lb lead (VSA-50).
11/29/80 Stores issued to Lt. Clark, three tomahawks (VSA-50).
12/01/80 Sugar delivered to Lt. Richard Clark, for his use, six lbs (VSA-50: 28).
12/04/80 Issued two yards flannel (VSA-14).
12/31/80 Received one pair shoes (VSA-14).
01/12/81 Ammunition delivered to Lt. Richard Clark, 1/2 lb gunpowder, one lb lead, and two flints (VSA-50).
02/03/81 Ammunition delivered to Lt. Clark for his use, 1/2 lb gunpowder (VSA-50).
02/16/81 Ammunition delivered to Lt. Clark's Company, 3 3/4 lb gunpowder, 7 1/2 lbs lead (VSA-50).
03/28/81 Ammunition delivered to Lt. Richard Clark, 1/2 lbs gunpowder, one lb lead (VSA-50).
05/03/81 Per order from day book, three gallons and one quart rum (VSA-49).
05/05/81 Per order from day book, eight lbs sugar (VSA-49).
05/15/81 Ammunition delivered to Lt. Clark's blockhouse, 5 1/2 lbs gunpowder, 11 lbs lead (VSA-50).
05/25/81 Per orders from day book, one carot of tobacco and six lbs sugar (VSA-49).
06/05/81 Ammunition delivered to Lt. Clark, 1/2 lb gunpowder, one lb lead; t o three men of Lt. Clark's Company, 1 1/2 lbs gunpowder, three lbs lead (VSA-50).

<u>Clark, William Lt.</u> [also Mr.] Cousin to George Rogers Clark.
06/06/80-11/30/81 Listed as Lieutenant in Captain John Bailey's Company (Harding 1981: 45-46).
06/12/80 Issued to William Clark, secretary to Col. Clark, for three vests and three pair breeches, 5 1/4 yards fustian, five yards spotted velvet, 2 1/2 yards sycee, 9 3/4 yards linen for three shirts, and 3/8 yard cambric for ruffling shirts; one yard muslin for three stocks, two pair thread hose, one silk handkerchief, one check linen handkerchief, 13 skeins thread, four skeins silk, one stick silk twist, 2 1/2 yards linen for lining vests and breeches, and five yards toile gris for two pair trousers (VSA-48).
06/12/80 Issued linen for three shirts with ruffling, stuff for four summer vests, two pair breeches, two pair trousers with proper trimming, two pair thread stockings, and two handkerchiefs (VSA-11).

Fort Jefferson Personnel

06/15/80 Captain John Dodge wrote he received several goods from Lt. William Clark belonging to the State of Virginia, most of which was cloth with some brass buttons (VSA-11).
06/16/80 Lt. William Clark request payment in the form of 27 Spanish milled dollars in merchandise for the delivery of goods sent to John Dodge by orders of John Todd at the Falls (VSA-11).
06/16/80 Issued one pair 2 1/2 point blankets (15 1/2 dollars), one check linen handkerchief (one dollar), one brass ink pot (one dollar), one large clasp knife (1/2 dollar), and four yards ribbon (two dollars). Total order equals 20 dollars, paid in lieu of 20 Spanish milled dollars for his services in bringing a quantity of cloth to Fort Jefferson (VSA-11; 48).
06/17/80 One hat issued (VSA-48).
07/12/80 Issued one hat (VSA-12).
07/12/80 Received one hat from Captain Dodge (VSA-12).
07/28/80 Tobacco delivered to Mr. Clark, Secretary to Col. Clark, one carot and three lbs (VSA-50).
08/03/80 Issued 18 weight coffee (VSA-48).
09/11/80 Present at Fort Jefferson (VSA-13).
09/13/80 Listed as one "officer of the mess" and received a share of 60 lbs sugar (VSA-13).
09/13/80 With Leonard Helm, estimates corn that could have been raised by inhabitants of Clarksville had it not been destroyed by the Indians in their recent (Aug 27th) attack on Ft. Jefferson (Draper Manuscripts 1M8; VSA-20).
09/16/80 Soap delivered to Mr. William Clark (VSA-50).
10/14/80 William Clark attests that Monsieur Carbonveaux received from William Shannon, $10,880 in payment for 34 gallons tafia (VSA-13).
10/27/80 Robert George at Fort Jefferson writes to John Rogers at Kaskaskia to explain that Lt. Clark had been sent to acquire a boat, men, and provisions needed for Fort Jefferson; Fort Jefferson boat on dry land and immobile (GRC Papers, I: 462-463; Draper Manuscripts 50J72; Seineke 1981: 465).
10/27/80 Sent to Kaskaskia for supplies (GRC Papers, I: 462).
10/28/80 Account of ammunition delivered by Martin Carney by Col. Montgomery's orders, to Captain Rogers for the use of his men by Lt. Clark, 20 lbs gunpowder, 12 lbs lead [could be Richard and not William] (VSA-50).
11/26/80 Account of ammunition delivered by Martin Carney by order of Captain Robert George at Fort Jefferson, to Mr. William Clark for his use, one lb gunpowder (VSA-50).
11/29/80 Stores issued by order of Captain Robert George, to Lt. Clark, three tomahawks [could be Richard and not William] (VSA-50).
12/07/80 Robert George requests of Israel Dodge to issue and charge Mr. William Clark for four yards osnaburg for a hunting shirt (VSA-14).
12/07/80 William Clark signed that he received of Israel Dodge the within contents (VSA-14).
12/10/80 Account of soap delivered by Martin Carney by order of Captain George at Fort Jefferson: to Mr. William Clark, six lbs (VSA-50: 52).
12/13/80 William Clark, Secretery, requests of the quartermaster to send him one quart rum (VSA-14; misfile).
12/29/80 William Clark and Robert George sign request an issue of one lb sugar for Clark's own use (VSa- 14; misfile).
02/03/81 Account of ammunition delivered by Martin Carney by order of Captain Robert George at Fort Jefferson, to Lt. Clark for his use, 1/2 lb gunpowder [could be Richard and not William] (VSA-50).
02/16/81 Ammunition delivered by order of Captain George, to Lt. Clark's Company, 3 3/4 lbs gunpowder, 7 1/2 lbs lead [could be Richard and not William] (VSA-50).
02/26/81 Served on Board of Court of Inquiry at Fort Jefferson as Judge Advocate (Draper Manuscripts 56J27).
02/27/81-03/07/81 Served on board of Court of Inquiry and as acting Judge Advocate examining charges made against Captain Richard McCarty by

Fort Jefferson Personnel

Captain John Dodge. Proceedings at Fort Jefferson (Draper Manuscripts 56J29).
03/09/81 Served on Board of Court of Inquiry as acting Judge Advocate examining Captain John Rogers conduct while in command at Kaskaskia (Draper Manuscripts 56J45).
03/20/81 Served on Board of Court Martial proceedings at Fort Jefferson for David Allen and James Taylor (Draper Manuscripts 56J40).
03/22/81 Ammunition delivered by order of Captain George, to Mr. William Clark, 1/2 lb gunpowder, 2 1/2 lbs lead (VSA-50).
03/23/81 Left Fort Jefferson with Captain John Dodge, Dodge went to Lexington, Clark went to Louisville (MHS: B1, F15).
04/11/81 William Clark wrote a letter to George Rogers Clark at Fort Pitt, William Clark was in Louisville for several days, wanted to talk with George Rogers Clark. William tells of his meeting with Pyeatt who was carrying letters from Gen. Clark to Fort Jefferson (MHS: B2, F15).
05/27/81 Stores issued by order of Captain Robert George, to William Carr, soldier conductor to Lt. Clark, one musket or smoothed gun and one bayonet with belt [could be Richard and not William] (VSA-50).
06/05/81 Account of ammunition delivered by Martin Carney by order of Captain George and Col. Montgomery, to Lt. Clark, 1/2 lb gunpowder, one lb lead; to three men of Lt. Clark's Company, 1 1/2 lbs gunpowder, three lbs lead [could be Richard and not William] (VSA-50).

Coffy, Samuel
11/29/79 On a return signed by Robert George and dated 12/10/80, Samuel Coffy enlisted on this date for three years by Lt. Valentine T. Dalton into Captain Robert George's Company of Artillery. Coffy was not included in payroll because Dalton neglected to give account of what has become of him or when or how his time expired (MHS: B1, F23).

Coleman, Frank
09/12/80 Issued 2 1/2 ells spotted flannel paid Frank Coleman for ten flour casks by order Col. Montgomery (VSA-48).
09/25/80 Paid Frank Coleman for barrels, 20 dollars (VSA-48).

Connor, John
01/28/80 Enlisted as private in Captain John Bailey's Company of the Illinois Regiment in the Virginia State Service (Harding 1981: 45-46).
07/12/80 Among list of men receiving clothing issue at Fort Jefferson; received two shirts for being enlisted during the war (VSA-12).
11/15/81 Deserted (Harding 1981: 45-46).

Conors, Andrew [Konor]
06/04/79-12/03/81 Listed as Matross [Corporal] in Captain Robert George's Company of Artillery in Service of the Commonwealth of Virginia and Illinois Department. Pay Abstract (Harding 1981: 29-30).
03/20/80 On a reuturn signed by Robert George and dated 12/10/80, Andrew Conor enlisted on this date for three years by Lt. Valentine T. Dalton into Captain Robert George's Company of Artillery (MHS: B1, F23).
09/11/80 Issued two shirts for enlisting for three yrs or duration into Captain George's Company (VSA-13).
09/13/80 Valentine T. Dalton requests of John Dodge to issue two shirts to Andrew Conors for enlisting (VSA-13).
09/13/80 Valentine T. Dalton signs that the shirts were received for Andrew Conors (VSA-13).

Consola, Herman
06/05/80 Clark arrived at Fort Jefferson from Kaskaskia, later left with Major Harlan and Captain Consola for Harrodsburg (VSA-11; GRC Papers, I: cxxxviii).
06/09/80 Account of ammunition delivered by Martin Carney by order of Col. Clark, to Harman Consola at Camp Jefferson, 1/2 lb gunpowder (VSA-50).

Fort Jefferson Personnel

06/10/80 Accompanied Clark and Harlan from Fort Jefferson to Harrodsburg (GRC Papers, I: cxxxviii; Journal of Daniel Smith, Tennessee Hist. Mag., Vol. I, No.1, 1915: 64) [see G. Clark]

Cooper, Barny
05/09/79 Member Captain Kellar's Company (Harding 1981: 23).
10/04/79 Enlisted (Harding 1981: 23).
07/12/80 Among list of men receiving clothing at Fort Jefferson, as members of Captain Abraham Kellar's Company; Cooper having one year to serve (VSA-12).

Cooper, Joseph
05/09/79 Member Captain Kellar's Company (Harding 1981: 23).
10/04/79 Enlisted (Harding 1981: 23).
07/12/80 Among list of men receiving clothing at Fort Jefferson, as members of Captain Abraham Kellar's Company; Cooper having one year to serve (VSA-12).
04/12/81 Died (Harding 1981: 23).

Cooper, Samuel
05/01/80-12/21/80 Listed as private in Captain George Owens' Company of Militia of the District of Clarksville in the State of Virginia [Jefferson Company]. Pay Abstract (Harding 1981: 48-49).
07/07/80 A private in Captain George Owens' Company, Cooper advanced in rank. Field promotion [to] Lieutenant (Harding 1981: 48).
09/12/80 Moved. Ended his pay as Lieutenant on this date (Harding 1981: 49).

Cowen, John
04/21/80 William Bartholomew, John Breeding, George King, Bob Logan, William Bohman, John Deck, John Cowan, and Daniel Tyger are mentioned as being at Fort Clark, some are later at Fort Jefferson (VSA-10; Non-Fort Jefferson Document).
05/30/80 Enlisted as a private in Captain Brashears' Company (Harding 1981: 51-52).
07/12/80 Robert George requests of John Dodge by order of Col. Clark, that 36 shirts be issued for 18 men which they are entitled to by law. Cowen is among the list of 18 men who receive clothing (VSA-12).
09/18/80 Listed as one of five sick men of Captain Brashears' Company to receive a share of five lbs sugar by order of Captain George to Martin Carney (VSA-13).

Cox, John
06/03/80 Came from Fort Patrick Henry [Vincennes] with provisions for Fort Jefferson (VSA-12).
07/03/80 Patt. Kennedy signs that he sent Joseph Duncan, Samuel Watkins, and John Cox to Camp Jefferson with provisions and they were to be paid in linen for two shirts each. Captain Robert George requests an issuance of linen and thread enough to make each man two shirts (VSA-12).
07/03/80 Issued one lb gunpowder and two lbs lead balls along with Samuel Watkins and Joseph Duncan for their return trip (VSA-12; VSA-50).
07/03/80 Issued 16 1/4 yards white linen and 3 1/4 yards check linen per order Captain George and receipt of Joseph Duncan, Samuel Watkins, and John Cox for bringing provisions (VSA-48).

Cox, Thomas
07/15/80 Listed in Captain Worthington's Company (MHS B1, F20; VSA-12).

Craten, Robert
06/01/80-12/21/80 Listed as Private in Capt. George Owens' Co. of Militia of the District of Clarksville in the District of Virginia [Jefferson Co.]. Pay Abstract (GRC Papers, I: 465;; Harding 1981: 48-49).

Fort Jefferson Personnel

Crawley, John
10/15/79 Enlisted (Harding 1981: 24).
07/04/80 Enlisted in Capt. Kellar's Co. for three years or during the present war; witnessed by Harmon Eagle (MHS B1, F20).
07/12/80 Among list of men received his clothing issue at FJ, as members of Capt. Kellar's Co.; Crawley has one year to serve (VSA-12).
10/10/80 Died (Harding 1981: 24).

Creton, William
09/15/80 Account of sugar delivered by Martin Carney by order of Capt. George a Fort Jefferson, to William Creton of militia, one lb (VSA-50).
09/15/80 George Owens requests [Robert George signs] an issue of one lb sugar to William Creton (VSA-13).

Crump, Dan
Maybe father, brother, or same Crump [Wm] who is listed on Capt. Worthington's Co. (Greg Holm, personnel comm., 11/27/84).
10/28/80 Voucher receipt for ten cartridges for "use of 2# swivel belonging to the Blockhouse on the hill" Signed by R. George (VSA-13).

Crump, William [also Krump]
07/15/80 Listed in Capt. Worthington's Company (MHS B1, F20) (VSA-12).
09/19/80 Account of sugar delivered by Martin Carney by order of Capt. George at Fort Jefferson, to William Crump, a soldier in Worthington's Company, two lbs (VSA-50).
09/19/80 Robert George requests of the Quartermaster to issue two lbs of sugar to William Crump of Worthington's Company out of the public store (VSA-13).

Crutcher, Henry
10/03/80 Three India handkerchiefs, 1 1/2 ells camlet, five fine combs, six ells white linen, one romal handkerchief, two check linen handkerchiefs paid Henry Crutcher for 37 bushels corn per receipt (VSA-48).

Crutchfield, Commissary
10/09/80 Two shirts and three linen handkerchiefs issued by order Capt. Rogers to Commissary Crutchfield per receipt (VSA-48).

Curry, James
07/12/80 Jarrett Williams certifies that James Curry, William Elms, James Morris, William Bartholomew, James Dawson, James Elms, and John Elms are enlisted during the war (VSA-12).
07/12/80 Robert George requests of John Dodge, by order of Col. Clark, that full clothing be issued for Curry, W. Elms, Morris, Bartholomew, Dawson, J. Elms, and J. Elms of Capt. Brashears' Company (VSA-12).
07/12/80 Issued two shirts, three yds flannel, blue cloth, and button and thread to make up the shirts (VSA- 12).

Curry, Patrick
07/12/80 Robert George requests of John Dodge by order of Col. Clark that 36 shirts be issued for 18 of the men which they are entitled to by law; Curry is among the list of 18 men who receive clothing (VSA- 12).

Curtis, Rice
07/10/80 Member of Capt. John Rogers' Co. Among list of men who were issued two shirts and two stocks at FJ for having more than one year to serve per Capt. George's orders to Capt. John Dodge (VSA-12).

Dalton, Hannah
Probably married to VT Dalton (VSA-13).
10/24/80 Hannah Dalton requests payment of $325 [one silver dollar per day] for her services as Interpreter for the Walbash Indian district from October

Fort Jefferson Personnel

20, 1779 to date. J. Montgomery requests Olvier Pollock to pay her the above (VSA-16, misfiled).
10/24/80 Paid $325.00 as Indian interpreter (VSA-13).

Dalton, Valentine Thomas [Lt. and Deputy Conductor] [also Daltin]
06/04/79-12/03/81 Listed as Lieutenant in Capt. Robert George's Co. of Artillery in the Service of the Commonwealth of Virginia and Illinois Department. Pay Abstract (Harding 1981: 29-30).
11/18/79 Jeremiah Horn [also Hern] enlisted for three years or for the duratin of the war by Lt. V. T. Dalton into Capt. Robert George's Company of Artillery (MHS: B1, F23).
11/29/79 Thomas Laney, Patrick Marr, Samuel Coffy, and John Anderson enlisted for three years or during the war by LT. V. T. Dalton into Capt. Robert George's Company of Artillery. Coffy was not included on the payroll because Dalton neglected to give account of what has become of him or when and how his time expired (MHS: B1, F23).
12/11/79 Benjamin Lewis enlisted for three years or during the war by Lt. V. T. Dalton into Capt. Robert George's Company of Artillery (MHS: B1, F23).
01/01/80 Thomas Bolton enlisted for three years or during the war into Capt. Robert George's Company of Artillery by Lt. V. T. Dalton (MHS: B1, F23).
01/10/80 Paul Quibea enlisted for three years or during the war into Capt. Robert George's Company of Artillery by Lt. V.T. Dalton (MHS: B1, F23).
01/31/80 James McDonell enlisted for three years or during the war by Lt. V.T. Dalton into Capt. Robert George's Company of Artillery (MHS: B1, F23).
03/10/80 Patt Mcutly enlisted for three years or during the war by Lt. V.T. Dalton into Capt. Robert George's Company of Artillery. Was not included on payroll as Dalton neglected to give account of what has become of him or when and how his time expired (MHS: B1, F23).
03/20/80 Andrew Conor enlisted for three years or during the war by Lt. V.T. Dalton into Capt. Robert George's Company of Artillery (MHS: B1, F23).
03/28/80 John Hazzard enlisted for three years or during the war by Lt. V.T. Dalton into Capt. Robert George's Company of Artillery (MHS: B1, F23).
04/12/80 Francis Puccan enlisted for three years or during the war by Lt. V.T. Dalton into Capt. Robert George's Company of Artillery. Was not on payroll because Dalton neglected to give account of what has become of him or when or how his time expried (MHS: B1, F23).
04/19/80 V.T. Dalton at Fort Patrick Henry writes George Rogers Clark at Mouth of Ohio informing him of opposition to the building of a fort at the Mouth of the Ohio by the English (MHS: B1, F16).
04/20/80 Jacob Ditterin has enlisted for three years or during the war by Lt. V.T. Dalton into Capt. George's Company of Artillery (MHS: B1, F23).
04/20/80 John Bouden enlisted for three years or during the war by Lt. Valentine Thomas Dalton into Capt. Robert George's Company of artillery. Not on payroll because Dalton failed to give account of what has become of him or when and how his time expired (MHS: B1, F23).
05/16/80 Letter from Capt. V.T. Dalton at Fort Clark to George Rogers Clark. Dalton had gone to O Post from Ft. Clark to pick up salt. Letter mentions Montbreuen and his latest actions at Ouia (Seineke, 1981: 435).
05/18/80 Valentine Dalton signs request at Fort Clark to issue pork for the use of Capt. George's Company [George is at Fort Jefferson] (VSA-11).
06/09/80 V.T. Dalton writes from Ft. Patrick Henry that Monsr. Ambross sold a pirogue for 200 livres in peltry. Dalton notes that the pirogue measures 45' x 3'; can carry 5,000 lbs. The pirogue is employed to carry artillery stores to headquarters at Clarksville (VSA-11).
06/12/80 Letter from Dalton at Ft. Patrick Henry to GR Clark. Dalton tells Clark of the "goings on" there. Tells of Dodge being under arrest and Dodge is being sent to GRC for trial. He is on public service to GRC (Seineke, 1981: 442-443).
06/13/80 Jacob Ditteren enlisted for three years or during the war by Lt. V.T. Dalton into Capt. Robt. George's Co. of Artillery (MHS: B1, F23).

Fort Jefferson Personnel

06/18/80 Anthony Montroy enlisted for three years or during the war into Capt. Robert George's Company of Artillery by Lt. V.T. Dalton (MHS: B1, F23).

06/25/80 Capt. V. T. Dalton at Ft. Patrick Henry [Vincennes] wrote GRC. They recently fought a battle with the enemy [between 80 and 100] and won. Dalton feels prepared and confident of winning another battle if one should occur. Dalton is on public service for GRC who is Commander in Chief of the Illinois forces at Fort Jefferson or elsewhere (MHS:B1, F19; Seineke 1981: 443- 444).

07/02/80 Zephaniah Blackford and V.T. Dalton sign request at Ft. Clark, for an issuance of rations for 10 men for six days [July 2 - July 7] going from Fort Jefferson to get provisions for the Fort (VSA-13a, misfiled).

07/10/80 Capt. John Rogers and V.T. Dalton sign they received of John Dodge, two yds blue persian and one piece binding (VSA-12).

07/10/80 James Mulboy and Joseph Lonion enlisted for three years or during the war by Lt. V.T. Dalton into Capt. Robert George's Company of Artillery. They were not on the payroll because Dalton failed to give account of what had become of them or when or how their time expired (MHS: B1, F23).

09/09/80 Account of ammunition received by Martin Carney at this post Clarksville, May 1, 1780. Received of Lt. Dalton, powder and ball, 23 lbs powder and 15 lbs lead (VSA-50).

09/10/80 Issued clothing entitled to by law (VSA-13a).

09/10/80 Issued one blanket and four lbs coffee (VSA-13a).

09/10/80 Overdrawn by Lt. Val. Thos Dalton, four weight coffee and one English blanket per receipt and order of Lt. Col. John Montgomery (VSA-48).

09/11/80 Present at FJ (VSA-13a).

09/11/80 Issued to Lt. Dalton in part of the clothing allowed him by law, five yards cotton sachaque, four yards spotted flannel, 2 1/2 yds corded dimity, eight yds camlet, 13 skeins thread, 2 3/4 yds of cambric, 21 yds white linen (VSA-48).

09/13/80 Issued 12, 2 1/2 point blankets per order of Lt. Col. Montgomery and receipt of Lt. Dalton for use of the company (VSA-48).

09/13/80 Account of ammunition delivered by Martin Carney by Col. Montgomery's orders, to Lt. Dalton for two of his men, one lb powder, two lbs lead (VSA-50).

09/13/80 Account of sugar delivered by Martin Carney by order of Col. Montgomery at Fort Jefferson, to Lt. Dalton for his own use, 20 lbs (VSA-50).

10/02/80 J. Montgomery signs an abstract that indicates V. T. Dalton received a total of 40 lbs flour and 16 lbs pork [note: "Voyage to the post"] Between Sept. 2, 1779, and April 17, 1780, via verbal orders (VSA-13a).

10/06/80 Account of soap delivered by Martin Carney by order of Col. Montgomery and Capt. George at Fort Jefferson, to Lt. Dalton for his use, 5 1/2 lbs (VSA-50).

10/07/80 R. George requests of the Quartermaster to issue six lbs soap to Lt. Dal[ton?] (VSA-13a).

10/24/80 Account of ammunition delivered by Martin Carney by order of Capt. George, to Lt. Dalton for his journey to New Orleans, one lb powder, ten lbs lead (VSA-50).

10/24/80 J. Montgomery writes Oliver Pollock to pay V. T. Dalton $1860.00 + 1/6$ for all provisions (VSA-16b, misfiled).

10/24/80 Zephaniah Blackford writes of a quantity of beef delivered to V. T. Dalton (VSA-16a, misfiled)

10/24/80 Zephaniah Blackfoed writes that V. T. Dalton has received no money (VSA-16b, misfiled).

10/24/80 J. Montgomery [at FJ] writes one to pay 188 silver dollars to V. T. Dalton for within account (VSA-16a, misfiled).

10/24/80 The account is a list of goods dispensed by V. T. Dalton at Ft. Patrick Henry (VSA-16b, misfiled).

10/24/80 V. T. Dalton signs that he received the list of goods at New Orleans and O. Pollock attests in French (VSA-16a, misfiled).

Fort Jefferson Personnel

10/24/80 J. Montgomery requests of Israel Dodge to issue V. T. Dalton four yds of linen to make a hunting shirt and charge Dalton's account. V. T. Dalton signs he received the contents in full (VSA-13a).
10/24/80 J. Montgomery requests Israel Dodge to issue V. T. Dalton four yds white flannel and charge Dalton's account. V. T. Dalton signs he received the within of Israel Dodge. [Entire transaction subsequently crossed out] (VSA-13b).
10/24/80 V. T. Dalton requests payment of $650 for services as agent for Indian affairs for Wabash District [$2 in silver per day] from October 20, 1779 to Sept. 9, 1780. J. Montgomery requests Oliver Pollock to pay the above (VSA-16, misfiled).
10/27/80 R. George mentions in a letter to G. R. Clark that Dalton might go down river with Montgomery (GRC, I: 461-463) (Seineke 1981: 465-466).
10/28/80 Went down river with Montgomery to look for deserters (GRC, I: 462).
12/10/80 Robert George signs a return of men enlisted by Lt. Valentine T. Dalton for the artillery service from November 18, 1779, to December 10, 1780 for the term of three years or during the war:

Jeremiah Horn	November 18, 1779	Thomas Laney	November 29, 1779
Patrick Marr	November 29, 1779	Samuel Coffy	November 29, 1779
John Anderson	November 29, 1779	Benjamin Lewis	Dec 11, 1779
Thomas Bolton	January 1, 1780	Paul Quibea	January 10, 1780
James McDonnell	January 31, 1780	Patt McCulty	March 10, 1780
Andrew Canore	March 20, 1780	John Hazzard	March 28, 1780
Francis Puccan	April 12, 1780	John Bowden	April 20, 1780
Jacob Ditterin	June 13, 1780	Anthony Montroy	June 18, 1780
James Mulboy	July 10, 1780	Joseph Lonion	December 10, 1780

Six of the men are not included in George's payroll because Lt. Dalton neglected to give an account of what had become of them or when and how their time expired (MHS: B1, F23).
05/04/81 Per order brought from day book, one gallon rum (VSA-49).
05/11/81 Ammunition delivered by order of Capt. Robert George at Fort Jefferson, to Lt. Dalton, one lb lead (VSA-50).
05/14/81 Per order brought from day book, ten lbs sugar (VSA-49).
05/26/81 Per order brought from day book, six lbs sugar (VSA-49).
06/05/81 Per order brought from day book, 25 lbs sugar (VSA-49).

Damewood, Boston [also Dance, Bostin and Dainwood]
06/04/79-12/03/81 Listed as Matross [Corporal] in Capt. Robert George's Co. of Artillery in the Service of the Commonwealth of Virginia and Illinois Department. Pay Abstract (Harding 1981: 29-30).
06/12/80 Going on expedition with Capt. Harrison to Falls of Ohio; among list of men who are issued clothing for the trip (VSA-11).
03/03/81 Probably married to Mrs. Mary Damewood (VSA-17).

Damewood, Mrs. Boston [Mary] [also Danewood]
06/16/80 Issued 1 1/2 yds calico paid Mary Damewood for making three ruffled shirts, three yds calico paid Mary Damewood for making three plain shirts (VSA-48).
03/03/81 Paid 1/2 lb twine for making two shirts for Capt. Robert George's Co. at FJ (VSA-17).
03/20/81 Her name mentioned by Philip Hupp during David Allen/James Taylor Court Martial Proceedings as being the person who also took part in harassing Rachel Yeats by throwing bones at her through the window (DMS 56J41).

Datcherut
Paid for salt and flour per order Col. Montgomery 153 livres peltry, paid for salt and flour per order Col. Montgomery 2360 livres merchandise, paid for provisions per order Col. Montgomery 963. 15 livres peltry (VSA-48).
10/09/80 Paid Datcherut for Col. Montgomery's order 265 livres peltry, for sundries furnished by him for public use per his account and receipt charged J. Montgomery with (VSA-48).

Fort Jefferson Personnel

Daughterty, John
09/19/80 Has two very sick children at FJ. Issued two lbs of sugar for his sick children per Capt. George's orders to the Quartermaster (VSA-13).
09/19/80 Account of sugar delivered by Martin Carney by order of Capt. George at Fort Jefferson, to John Daughterty of Capt. George's Company, two lbs (VSA-50).
03/20/81 Provided testimony in defense of James Taylor at Court Martial proceedings at FJ, saying he was with Taylor throughout the "fray" (DMS 56J41).
06/06/81 Issued six lbs sugar for he and his children for their journey to the Falls of Ohio (VSA-20).

Davies, James [Davis]
10/12/79 Enlistment (Harding 1981: 24).
07/12/80 Among list of men who are members of Capt. Abraham Kellar's Co. at FJ and are receiving clothing issue; has one year to serve (VSA-12).
10/17/80 Died (Harding 1981: 24).

Davis, Robert
01/00/81-02/00/81 May have come to Fort Jefferson from Falls of Ohio with Miles, Calvit, and Capt. Worthington (DMS 56J28).
02/26/81 No rank or affiliation given, but he collaborated testimony of Sgt. Miles and Lt. Calvit at FJ during Board of Inquiry regarding Capt. Worthington (DMS 56J28).

Dawson, James
05/03/80 Enlisted on this date for three years in Isaac Taylor's Company (Harding 1981: 141).
06/12/80-07/14/80 Issued clothing at FJ as member of Ensign Williams' Company. Had already received two shirts (VSA-12).
07/12/80 Among list of men who are members of Ensign Williams' Co., receiving two shirts each at FJ which they are entitled to by law; has previously received clothing VSA-12).
07/12/80 Jarrett Williams certifies that James Curry, William Elms, James Morris, William Bartholomew, James Dawson, James Elms, and John Elms are enlisted during the war; George requests full clothing for the men (VSA-12).

Dean, James
04/26/80 Enlisted on this date as a private in Capt. Worthington's Company (Harding 1981: 47).
07/24/80 Deserted (Harding 1981: 47).

Deck, John
04/21/80 William Bartholomew, John Breeding, George King, Bob Logan, William Bohman, John Deck, John Cowan, and Daniel Tyger are mentioned as being at Ft. Clark, some are later at Fort Jefferson (VSA-10; Non-FJ Document).

Decker, Jacob [Dasker, Decart]
11/15/79 Enlisted as a private on this date in Capt. Kellar's Company (Harding 1981: 24).
06/02/80 Capt. A. Kellar listed 17 men who had served in his unit at one time during the war. Decker was one of these enlistments (MHS: B1, F19).
06/29/80 Capt. Robert George requests of John Dodge by Col. Clark's orders to issue eight shirts to James Thompson, Joseph Panther, John Shank, and Jacob Decker of Capt. Kellar's Company (VSA-11).
07/12/80 Among list of men who are members of Capt. Abraham Kellar's Co. at FJ and are receiving clothing issue; had already received two shirts; has one year to serve (VSA-12).
10/07/80 Died (Harding 1981: 24).

Fort Jefferson Personnel

Dejean, Mr. [?]
05/20/80 Capt. Ed. Worthington at Falls of Ohio in letter to George Rogers Clark at Mouth of Ohio explains why he did not accompany Col. Legras and Mr. Dejean from Williamsburg to Fort Jefferson (MHS: B1, F17).
06/04/80 Letter from Capt. Robt. George to GRC will be delivered by Col. Legras who is accompanied by Mr. Dejean from Williamsburg (Seineke, 1981: 441) (MHS: B1, F19).
03/21/81 Issued six lbs sugar from Quartermaster per Capt. George's orders at FJ (VSA-17).
03/21/81 Issued six gallons tafia per Capt. George's orders at FJ (VSA-17).
03/21/81 Referred to as "Prisoner of War" (VSA-17).

Deleale, Charles
08/23/80 Paid Charls Deleale for one quart vinegar (VSA-48).

Demore, Mary
09/09/80 Washerwoman for Capt. George's Company at Fort Jefferson (VSA-13).
09/09/80 Issued two lbs sugar at Fort Jefferson (VSA-13).
09/09/80 Account of sugar delivered by Martin Carney by order of Col. Montgomery at Fort Jefferson, to Mary Demore, a soldier's wife, two lbs (VSA-50).

Dewit, Henry [Dewitt]
07/15/80 Listed in Capt. Worthington's Company (MHS B1, F20; VSA-12).

Ditterin, Jacob [Dittering]
03/13/80 Enlisted on this date as a matross in Capt. Robert George's Company (Harding 1981: 32).
03/13/80-10/04/80 Listed on Pay Abstract (Harding 1981: 32).
04/20/80 On a return signed by Robert George and dated December 10, 1780, Jacob Ditterin enlisted on this date for three years or during the war by Lt. V. T. Dalton into Capt. George's Company of Artillery (MHS: B1, F23).
06/13/80 Jacob Ditteren enlisted for three years or during the war by Lt. V.T. Dalton into Capt. Robt. George's Company of Artillery (MHS: B1, F23).
09/09/80 Account of sugar delivered by Martin Carney by order of Col. Montgomery at Fort Jefferson, to Jacob Ditterin, one lb (VSA-50).
09/10/80 Issued one lb of sugar for being sick (VSA-13a).
09/11/80 Issued one blanket along with ten other men by order of Capt. George (VSA-13a).
09/11/80 Issued two shirts for enlisting three yrs. or duration into Capt. George's Co. (VSA-13a).
09/13/80 V.T. Dalton requests Capt. Dodge to issue two shirts to Jacob Ditterin for enlisting (VSA-13a).
09/13/80 V.T. Dalton signs that the shirts were received for Jacob Ditterin (VSA-13b).
09/15/80 Account of sugar delivered by Martin Carney by order of Capt. George at Fort Jefferson, to Jacob Ditterin of Artillery, one lb (VSA-50).
10/04/80 Killed (Harding 1981: 32).

Diveny
09/25/80 Fifteen ells linen paid Diveny for a hog for the troops per order Col. Montgomery (VSA-48).

Dodge, Israel [brother to John Dodge]
For sundry articles delivered to Israel Dodge Deputy Agent for the use of the troops: one piece blue cloth good, three remnants blue cloth 64 yds good, two remnants white cloth 2 3/4 yds good, eight remnants blue cloth 95 1/2 yds damaged, one remnant grey cloth 4 1/2yds damaged, five piece flannel, three remnants five yds flannel, nine piece linen, eight remnants linen containing 50 yds, one remnant fine linen 82 yds damaged, nine remnants linen 158 1/2 yds damaged, 20 3/4 yds toile gris, two yds brown holland damaged, 8 1/2 yds osnaburgs, eight paper pins, 30 weight thread, 35 weight twine, two boxes brass buttons, 131 dozen Capt.

Fort Jefferson Personnel

buttons, 30 looking glasses, 30 yds tinsel lace, 208 gunworms, 23 yds camlet, 1 1/2 yds calamanco, 3/4 yd camlet, four check handkerchiefs, two combs, two clasp knives, and six plain shirts (VSA-48).
2 1/2 yds toile gris, 1 1/4 yds calendry, one yd coarse white linen, one skein thread, one English blanket, one scalping knife issued to Israel Dodge in lieu of sundry articles lost by him in the Ohio the 27th March 1780 when accompanying Joseph Lindsay Esquire on public business (VSA-48).

06/02/80 Josesph Lindsay writes about his and Israel Dodge's trip to Illinois describing the losses they encountered as a result of a hurricane. Lindsay asks that the public make amends for I. Dodge's clothing lost because he was not paid for his trouble or time. Signed also at Ft. Jeff by Will. Shannon and Henry Smith (VSA-11a).

06/02/80 Arrived Fort Jefferson with Josesph Lindsey bringing quantity of goods for Falls; Henry Smith and Wm. Shannon attest the arrival and quantity of goods (VSA-11).

06/23/80 Issued to Israel Dodge, Deputy Agent, two yds brown cloth 7/4 wide, 3 1/2 yds blue bath coating, 2 1/2 yds shalloon, 4 1/4 doz metal buttons, two sticks silk twist, six skeins silk, one pair knee garters, issued for six vests and six pair breeches five yds cottonade, three yds chintz, two yds toile gris, 2 1/2 yds spotted velvet, 2 1/2 yds thickset, 4 1/4 yds casimir, and 2 1/2 yds chintz, issued four yds linen damaged for lining, 21 yds linen for six shirts, 3/4 yd fine holland for ruffling, two yds brittanca's for six stocks, one silk handkerchief, one Indian handkerchief, three linen check handkerchiefs, three pair thread hose and one hat (VSA-48).

07/13/80 The daughter of Mary Smith, no name given, had been badly paid by Israel and John Dodge for making shirts for them according to Mary Smith's testimony at FJ Court of Inquiry (DMS 56J22).

08/07/80 Israel Dodge swore before John Donne that the following list of sundry articles were lost by Dodge on his passage from the Falls of Ohio to post St. Vincent on public business in February: one of each of the following; broadcloth coat superfine, waistcoat superfine, nankeen waistcoat, black persian stock, a pair of silk stockings, pair of worsted stockings, piece yarn stockings, four point blanket, blanket coat, butcher knife and tomahawk, two pair fine cloth breeches, two shirts, two pieces thread stockings, five stocks one of cambric four of linen (VSA-48).

09/03/80 Issued to Patrick Henry, ten ells of blue stroud, ten ells of blue cloth, 20 ells of osnaburgs, eight, 2 1/2 point blankets, 4 3/8 ells of calico, 9 7/8 ells of linen, and seven checked hanckerchiefs to pay for $1000 of supplies to be sent from Fort Clark to Fort Jefferson (VSA-13).

10/24/80 J. Montgomery requests Israel Dodge to issue four yds linen to V. T. Dalton for a hunting shirt and charge Dalton's Account. V. T. Dalton signs that he received the contents in full (VSA-13a).

10/24/80 J. Montgomery requests Israel Dodge to issue V. T. Dalton with four yds white flannel and charge V. T. Dalton's account. V. T. Dalton signs he received the within from Israel Dodge [Entire transaction subsequently crossed out] (VSA-13b).

10/24/80 J. Montgomery orders Israel Dodge to pay $108 "at the Orleans price" for an order given by John Dodge (VSA-13a).

10/26/80 Account of ammunition delivered by Martin Carney by Col. Montgomery's orders to Israel Dodge upon Mr. Bentley's Account, 73 lbs powder (VSA-50).

10/26/80 Montgomery requests the Quartermaster to issue within quantity of pwdr to Israel Dodge; J. Dodge signs that the quantity of powder delivered on Bentley [Acct.?] (VSA-13b, misfiled).

10/26/80 Reverse: Montgomery requests 73 lbs powder to be issued to Quartermaster to T. Bentley (VSA-13a).

10/27/80 R. George requests Capt. Dodge to issue 1/2 yd stroud to Samuel Allen in part of payment for beef delivered; it is acknowledged that Allen has already received 12 yds of flannel (VSA-13a).

Fort Jefferson Personnel

10/27/80 Samuel Allen signs that he received the flannel from Israel Dodge (VSA-13b).

10/27/80 Israel Dodge signs that he received a delivery of goods [detailed on document] from John Dodge, attested by John Donne (VSA-13a).

10/31/80 Account of ammunition delivered by Martin Carney by order of Capt. George, to Israel Dodge, Deputy Agent, 1/2 lb powder, one lb lead (VSA-50).

11/27/80 Account of soap delivered by Martin Carney by order of Capt. George, to Mr. Israel Dodge, six lbs (VSA-50).

11/29/80 Account of sugar delivered by Martin Carney by orders of Capt. George, to Mr. Israel Dodge, Deputy Agent, four lbs (VSA-50).

12/02/80 Robert George signs request of Israel Dodge to pay Mary McAuley out of the public store, for making six soldier shirts for George's Company (VSA-14a).

12/02/80 Mary McAuley signs her "mark" that she received of Israel Dodge three yds of white flannel in full of her demands for making six shirts (VSA-14b).

12/03/81 Silas Harlan and Robert George sign request of Israel Dodge to issue to John McGarr eight yds of linen for hunting with Harlan one month (VSA-14a).

12/03/80 John McGarr signs his "mark" that he received of Israel Dodge the within contents (VSA-14b).

12/03/80 John Bailey and Robert George sign request of Israel Dodge to issue to Levi Theel of Bailey's Company, two yds damaged blue cloth for enlisting for three years or during the war (VSA-14).

12/04/80 Lt. Richard Clark and Robert George sign request of Israel Dodge to issue two yds flannel for Clark's use (VSA-14a).

12/04/80 Richard Clark signed that he received of Israel Dodge the within contents (VSA-14b).

12/07/80 Robert George requests of Israel Dodge to issue and charge Mr. William Clark for four yds osnaburg for a hunting shirt (VSA-14a).

12/07/80 Mr. William Clark signed that he received of Israel Dodge the within contents (VSA-14b).

12/07/80 Capt. Abraham Kellar and Robert George sign request of Israel Dodge to pay Mrs. Francis Bredin out of the public store for making four soldier coats for Kellar's Co. (VSA-14a).

12/07/80 Francis Bredin "marks" that she recieved of Israel Dodge eight yds white flannel in full of her demand for making the coats (VSA-14b).

12/07/80 Robert George requests of Israel Dodge to issue two ounces of thread fit to make a pair of leather breeches to Zephaniah Blackford and charge it to his account (VSA-14a).

12/07/80 Z. Blackford signed that he received of Israel Dodge six skeins of thread (VSA-14b).

12/09/80 Robert George requests of Israel Dodge to pay John Anderson out of the public store for making one suit of clothes for a soldier of George's Company (VSA-14a).

12/09/80 John Anderson signs that he received of Israel Dodge three yds flannel and a skein of thread in full of Anderson's demands for making a suit of clothes (VSA-14b).

12/09/80 Robert George requests of Israel Dodge to pay Elizabeth Jones for making four suits of soldier clothes for George's Company (VSA-14a).

12/09/80 Elizabeth Jones signs her mark that she received of Israel Dodge six yds white linen which is in full of her demands for making four suits of clothes (VSA-14b).

12/15/80 Robert George at Fort Jefferson certifies that the within is a true copy of the invoice delivered to Israel Dodge: one bail of cloth in different colors; 16 3/4 ells brown cloth; 15 3/4 ells brown cloth; 14 1/4 ells blue cloth; 18 ells pompedore; one piece of linen, 36 1/2 ells; two pieces of linen, 50 1/2 ells; four lbs vermillion; 29 1/2 ells white flannel; eight bunches of thread; 17 lbs thread in different colors; 8 skeins of silk; 24 dozen large buttons; 24 dozen small buttons; four dozen large [quilt?] buttons; 5 1/2 dozen small buttons; 104 skeins

Fort Jefferson Personnel

mohair; 105 pair of shoes;'15 ells of Topsell Duck [?]; eight small bags; 53 bunches of capwire; one brass ink stand; 16 [illeg.] needles; four paper of pins and one [illeg.] pins (VSA-14a,b).

12/15/80 Statement concerning Fort Jefferson in which Robert George had an inventory of a quantity of tafia delivered to Martin Carney and another for a quantity of broad cloth with a receipt signed by Israel Dodge and dated Fort Jefferson 12/15/80. It was witnessed by Capt. John Bailey and Leonard Helm (GRC Papers, II: 315).

12/18/80 Silas Harlan and Robert George sign request of Israel Dodge to issue to Thomas Snellock, Nicholas Tuttle, and Thomas Hays eight yds linen each for 31 days of assistance to Harlan on a hunting trip for Fort Jefferson (VSA-14a).

12/18/80 Thomas Snellock, Nicholas Tuttle, and Thomas Hays sign that they received of Israel Dodge the within contents (VSA-14b).

12/19/80 Abraham Kellar and Robert George sign request of Israel Dodge to issue Mrs. Nancy Hunter pay for making a coat, two waistcoats, and a pair of overalls for Kellar's Company (VSA-14a).

12/19/80 Nancy Hunter signs her "mark" that she received of Israel Dodge 3 3/4 yds white flannel in full of her demands for the within order (VSA-14b).

12/19/80 Robert George requests of Israel Dodge to issue to Silas Harlan cloth and trimmings for one suit of clothes, one pair of shoes, cloth for a cuppoe, and linen for two shirts (VSA-14a).

12/19/80 Silas Harlan signs that he received of Israel Dodge 3 1/2 yds superfine broadcloth; two dozen and seven large buttons; two dozen and four small buttons; one skein mohair; two yds of broadcloth for the cuppoe; one pair of shoes; six yds linen; and two yds flannel (VSA-14b).

12/20/80 Israel Dodge requests of Martin Carney to issue one gallon of "spirits" for Dodge's own use (VSA-14).

12/21/80 Capt. Richard Brashears and Robert George sign request of Israel Dodge to issue eight pair of shoes to eight men in Brashears' Company (VSA-14a).

12/21/80 Richard Brashears signs that he received of Israel Dodge the within contents (VSA-14b).

12/21/80 Richard Brashears and Robert George sign request of Israel Dodge to issue two shirts each to 13 men of Brashears' Company (VSA-14a).

12/21/80 Richard Brashears signs that he received of Israel Dodge 84 1/2 yds linen agreeable to the within order (VSA-14b).

12/21/80 Robert George requests of Israel Dodge to issue 40 pair of shoes for men of George's Company (VSA- 14a).

12/21/80 Richard Harison signed that he received of Israel Dodge the within contents for Capt. George's Company (VSA-14b).

12/21/80 Abraham Kellar and Robert George sign request of Israel Dodge to issue 11 pairs of shoes for 11 men in Kellar's Company (VSA-14a).

12/21/80 Abraham Kellar signed that he received of Israel Dodge the within contents (VSA-14b).

12/21/80 Robert George requests of Israel Dodge to issue two shirts each for 40 men of George's Company for the ensuing year (VSA-14a).

12/21/80 Richard Harrison signed that he received of Israel Dodge 260 yds of linen for the use of Capt. Robert George's Company of Artillery agreeable to the within order (VSA-14b).

12/21/80 Abraham Kellar and Robert George sign request of Israel Dodge to issue enough linen to make two shirts each for 11 men of Kellar's Company for the ensuing year (VSA-14a).

12/21/80 Abraham Kellar signed that he received of Israel Dodge 71 1/2 yds linen for the use of Kellar's Company agreeable to the within order (VSA-14b).

12/21/80 Robert George requests of Israel Dodge to issue 3/4 yd of cloth to Major Harlan for a waistcoat (VSA- 14a).

12/21/80 Silas Harlan signed that he received of Israel Dodge the within contents (VSA-14b).

12/23/80 Abraham Kellar and Robert George sign request of Israel Dodge to issue thread for making two shirts each for seven men of Kellar's Company (VSA-14a).

Fort Jefferson Personnel

12/23/80 Kellar signed that he received of Israel Dodge 22 skeins of thread (VSA-14b).

12/23/80 Benjamin Roberts signs that he received of Israel Dodge, two bags to carry necessities to Col. Slaughter at the Falls of Ohio (VSA-14a).

12/23/80 Robert George requests of Mr. Dodge to issue Capt. Roberts for the use of the troops and Col. Slaughter at the Falls: 157 3/4 yds linen, 23 1/2 yds fine linen, eight yds toile gris, two yds flannel, six skeins colored thread, 46 skeins white thread and two paper of pins (VSA-14).

12/23/80 Robert George requests of Israel Dodge to issue Capt. Roberts 1 1/2 yds blue cloth, two yds course flannel, four skeins thread, and one skein silk thread (VSA-14a).

12/23/80 Benjamin Roberts signed that he received of Israel Dodge the within contents (VSA-14b).

12/23/80 Robert George requests of Mr. Dodge [Israel] to issue to Capt. Roberts three dozen coat buttons and three dozen small buttons (VSA-14).

12/24/80 Robert George requests of Israel Dodge to issue William Freeman of George's Company a full suit of clothes which he is entitled to having enlisted during the present war (VSA-14a).

12/24/80 William Freeman signed his "mark" that he received of Israel Dodge the mentioned suit (VSA-14b).

12/24/80 John Bailey and Robert George sign request of Israel Dodge to issue enough linen to make two shirts each for 25 men of Bailey's Company for the ensuing year (VSA-14a).

12/24/80 John Bailey signed that he received of Israel Dodge 162 1/2 yds linen agreeable to the within order (VSA-14b).

12/26/80 Richard Harrison signed that he received of Israel Dodge 1 1/2 yds sky blue cloth, 38 large buttons, six small buttons, two skeins mohair, one skein silk, two yds white flannel, 3/4 yd linen, 1/8 yd pompedore and one skein white thread for a coat (VSA-14b).

12/26/80 Abraham Kellar and Robert George sign request of Israel Dodge to pay William Pritchet for making four suits of clothes for the use of Kellar's Company (VSA-14a).

12/26/80 William Pritchet signed that he received of Israel Dodge six yds toile gris which is in full of his demands for making the within suits (VSA-14b).

12/27/80 Robert George requests of Mr. Dodge to issue to Ensign Slaughter a set of buttons and mohair to make a suit of clothes (VSA-14a).

12/27/80 Slaughter signed that he received of Israel Dodge two dozen and eleven large buttons, 2 1/2 dozen small buttons and three skeins mohair (VSA-14b).

12/27/80 Richard Brashears and Robert George sign request of Israel Dodge to issue 12 needles to John Boiles for making clothes (VSA-14a).

12/27/80 John Boiles signs his "mark" that he received of Israel Dodge the within contents (VSA-14b).

12/29/80 John Bailey signed that he received two yds of flannel from Dodge [probably Israel; no record of John having returned to Fort Jefferson] (VSA-14).

12/31/80 Robert George requests of Mr. Dodge to issue Phillip Orbin of George's Company a coat, waistcoat, and pair of overalls for enlisting for three years or during the war (VSA-14a).

12/31/80 P. Orbin signed his "mark" that he received of Israel Dodge the within contents (VSA-14b).

12/31/80 Martin Carney signed that he received of Israel Dodge, three yds super fine broad cloth to complete an order given John Dodge to deliver to Martin Carney (VSA-14a).

12/31/80 Ensign Slaughter signed that he received of Israel Dodge, two pair of shoes upon a certificate given to Slaughter by John Dodge (VSA-14a).

12/31/80 Martin Carney signed that he received of Israel Dodge two pair of shoes upon an order given Carney by John Dodge (VSA-14a).

12/31/80 Leonard Helm signed that he received of Israel Dodge one pair of shoes upon a certificate given Helm by John Dodge (VSA-14b).

Fort Jefferson Personnel

12/31/80 Lt. John Girault signed that he received of Israel Dodge one pair of shoes upon a certificate given Girault by John Dodge (VSA-14b).
12/31/80 John Williams Helm signed that he received of Israel Dodge one pair of shoes upon a certificate given Williams by John Dodge (VSA-14b).
12/31/80 Jarrett Williams signed that he received of Israel Dodge one pair of shoes upon a certificate given Williams by John Dodge (VSA-14b).
12/31/80 Capt. Richard Brashears signed that he received of Israel Dodge one pair of shoes upon a certificate given Brashears by John Dodge (VSA-14b).
12/31/80 Richard Harrison signed that he received of Israel Dodge one pair of shoes upon a certificate given Harrison by John Dodge (VSA-14b).
12/31/80 Richard Clark signed that he received of Israel Dodge one pair of shoes upon a certificate given Clark by John Dodge (VSA-14b).
12/31/80 Capt. John Bailey signed that he received of Israel Dodge one pair of shoes upon a certificate given Bailey by John Dodge (VSA-14b).
03/22/81 Ammunition delivered by order of Capt. George, to Mr. Dodge, 1/2 lb powder, one lb lead [could be John and not Israel] (VSA-50).
05/03/81 Per orders brought from day book, three gallons and one quart rum and eight lbs sugar (VSA-49).
05/19/81 Per orders brought from day book, six lbs sugar (VSA-49).
05/29/81 Per orders brought from day book, ten lbs sugar (VSA-49).
06/04/81 Per orders brought from day book, ten lbs sugar (VSA-49).

Dodge, John

Undated One piece ribbon charged to J. Dodge (VSA-48).
03/23/80 Left Ft. Jefferson and travelled with William Clark. Clark went to Louisville and Dodge went to Lexington (MHS: B2, F15).
04/20/80 George Rogers Clark at Mouth of Ohio writes to John Dodge stating he arrived at Mouth of Ohio yesterday [4-19-80] and that Dodge should send Clark's furniture, seeds for garden, and "beans the French plant to make shades." Clark states that Capt. Bentley will give Dodge the news (GRC Papers, I: 417-418).
05/09/80 Letter from John Rogers at Kaskaskia to George Rogers Clark at Camp Jefferson. Rogers mentions the horses and instructions he received from Mr. Dodge. Asks to have instructions to receive bear skins, saddles, and reams of soldiers clothes from Dodge (MHS: B1, F18).
05/11/80 Col. John Montgomery signs request to John Dodge to except [accept] and pay the within contents. Gasper Butcher signs that he received the goods from Dodge [what contents are requested is not mentioned] (VSA-11a).
05/14/80 Account of ammunition received by Martin Carney at this post Clarksville, May 1, 1780: Received from Capt. Dodge, 21 piggs of lead said to be 1600 lbs lead (VSA-50: 5).
06/09/80 GRC requested and received for the use of the company department at Fort Jefferson, from John Dodge, two quire of writing paper (VSA-11a,b) (VSA-48).
06/09/80 GRC requests John Dodge issue two quire of paper to Capt. Robt. George. It was received by George (VSA-11a,b) (VSA-48).
06/09/80 GRC requests John Dodge, who's at Fort Jefferson, issue six quire of paper to troops and staff at Falls of Ohio. William Shannon received the six quire from John Dodge (VSA-11a,b).
06/09/80 Col. G.R. Clark requests of John Dodge to issue to Col. Walker and Maj. Smith, four pairs of cotton overalls, two pairs of linen drawers, six linen shirts, one osnaburg shirt, and one pair of scissors for them on their public service [Fort Jefferson] (VSA-11a).
06/10/80 Capt. Robt. George writes J. Dodge that GRC ordered the issuance of clothing to Capt. Lt. Harrison (VSA-11).
06/10/80 Issued to GRC, one snaffle bridle by John Dodge, Quartermaster at FJ to be paid for two saltcellars for 18 plates (VSA-48).
06/10/80 Samuel Smyth received from Virginia State Stores via John Dodge per Capt. George's order, one knife, one horn comb, 1 1/2 yds white half-thicks for leggings, one bath coating, breech cloth, four yds gartering,

Fort Jefferson Personnel

one ink stand, one pair blankets, one bridle for his use on expedition up the Ohio River to Falls (VSA-11).

06/11/80 Capt. Robt. George requests of J. Dodge to give M. Carney clothing as directed by Col. Clark [Fort Jefferson] (VSA-11a).

06/12/80 Capt. Robt. George requests of John Dodge to furnish Rich. Harrison with the following: [for 26 men of George's Co. going to Falls by Clark's orders] 26 yds of stroud for making leggings and breech cloths for 26 men, 52 shirts, 26 knives, one ink pot, one bridle, and thread to make leggings (VSA-11a).

06/12/80 Capt. Robt. George requests of J. Dodge to furnish Sam Smyth with: one knife, two combs [one horn and one ivory], 1 1/4 yd white half-thicks for leggings, bath coating, breech cloth, four yds gartering, one ink stand, one pair blankets, and one bridle for the use of the expedition to the Falls by Clark's orders (VSA-11a).

06/12/80 Capt Robt. George requests of J. Dodge to furnish Wm. Shannon with the following by Clark's orders: Chintz for two pr. trousers, cloth or other stuff for two waistecoats, two pr. breeches, one breech cloth, one bridle, one blanket, one ink stand, one knife, one course and one fine comb (VSA-11a).

06/12/80 Wm. Shannon received from J. Dodge, five yds check linen, 2 3/4 yds thickset, 1 1/2 yds course white linen, 1/2 yd blue bath coating, one stick mohair, one blanket, one snaffle bridle, one large knife, one ink stand, one course and one fine comb (VSA- 11b) (VSA-48).

06/12/80 Capt. Robert George requests of J. Dodge by Clark's orders to furnish Capt. Lt. Harrison with the following for the expedition to the Falls: three knives, three horn and one ivory comb, 1 1/2 yds white half-thicks for leggings, bath coating for breech cloth, four yds gartering, one pair blankets (VSA-11a).

06/12/80 Capt. Robt George requests of J. Dodge by Clark's orders to furnish Lt. Wm. Clark with the following: linen for three shirts with ruffling, stuff for four summer vests, two pair of breeches, two pair of trousers with proper trimming, two pair thread stockings, and two handkerchiefs (VSA-11a).

06/13/80 John Dodge signs invoice of goods he received for the use of the Illinois troops and other purposes (VSA-11a,b,c).

06/13/80 Capt. Robt. George requests of J. Dodge by Clark's orders to issue black calamanco to make a short gown for Mistress Flor (VSA-11a).

06/13/80 Capt. Robt. George requests of J. Dodge by Clark's orders to deliver the following for the use of George's Co., to the Falls: three blankets, 26 horn combs, 13 ivory combs, 2 1/2 yds blue bath coating, and thread (VSA-11a).

06/13/80 Capt. Robt. George requests of J. Dodge by Clark's orders to issue him four blankets for the use of his company on the trip to the falls (VSA-11a).

06/13/80 Capt. Robt. George requests of J. Dodge to furnish him with 24 yds of osnaburgs and thread to make up bags for the trip to the Falls (VSA-11a).

06/13/80 Capt. Robt. George requests of J. Dodge by Clark's orders to furnish Capt. Shannon with the following: 1/2 yd linen, 1/4 yd check, one Indian handkerchief, one pair small scissors, one silk handkerchief, one linen handkerchief, and six skeins brown thread (VSA-11a) (VSA-48).

06/14/80 Capt. Robt. George requests of J. Dodge to issue Wm. Shannon three yds of the best ribbon by order of Col. Clark. Wm. Shannon signed that he received the above (VSA-11a) (VSA-48).

06/14/80 Robt. George requests of J. Dodge to deliver to the bearer, two shirts, one blanket, and one hat for his use on expedition to the Falls of Ohio (VSA- 11a).

06/15/80 Capt. John Dodge writes that he received several goods of Lt. Wm. Clark belonging to the State of Virginia, most of which was cloth with some brass buttons (VSA-11a).

06/15/80 John Dodge writes again that he received the same as above from Lt. Wm. Clark (VSA-11a).

Fort Jefferson Personnel

06/16/80 Lt. Wm. Clark writes to State of Virginia [J. Dodge]. He wants payment in the form of 27 Spanish milled dollars in merchandise for the delivery of goods sent to J. Dodge by the orders of John Todd at the Falls (VSA-11a).

06/16/80 Capt. Robt. George requests of J. Dodge to deliver to M. Carney the following by orders of Col. Clark; one brass ink stand, one clasp knife, one small and one large tooth comb, six yds ferretting (VSA-11a).

06/16/80 Capt. Robt. George requests of John Dodge to deliver the following for use of the artillery; 2 1/2 yds flannel, twine, 2 1/2 yds osnaburg, one pair scissors, and two needles (VSA-11a).

06/18/80 Issued for own use, six yds brown broadcloth 7/4 wide, 2 1/2 yds shalloon, 5 5/12 dozen metal buttons, two sticks silk twist, six skeins silk, one pair knee garters, issued for six vests and six pair breeches six yds white cashmere, 2 1/2 yds corduroy, four yds chintz, 2 1/2 yds corduroy, 2 1/2 yds thickset, 1 1/4 yds spotted persian, and 4 1/2 yds cottonade, 21 yds linen for six shirts, 3/4 yd fine holland for ruffling, one yd fine holland and one yd cambric for six stocks, three pair thread hose, two silk handkerchiefs, one cotton red handkerchief, one India handkerchief, two linen handkerchiefs, one hat, two pair shoes, two pair silk hose (VSA-48).

06/19/80 Capt. Robt. George requests of John Dodge to issue two shirts each for the 23 men of his Artillery by order of Col. CLark (VSA-11a).

06/20/80 Capt. Robt. George requests of John Dodge to issue two shirts each to Joseph Thornton, John Sword, and Zachariah Williams of Capt. Worthington's Co. by order of Col. Clark (VSA-11a) (VSA-48).

06/20/80 Capt. Robt. George writes to John Dodge by Col. Clark's orders to ask him to deliver to Mr. Blackford 187 hard dollars worth of bread and such goods for the use use of Kaskaskia and its neighborhood (VSA-11a).

06/20/80 Capt. Robt. George requests of John Dodge to deliver to Mr. Donne, one leather ink pot and one fine and one cours comb for the use of Co. Dept. by Clark's orders (VSA-11a) (VSA-48).

06/20/80 Capt. Robt. George requests of John Dodge to issue Mr. Blackford [Commissary], linen for three shirts, stuff for three summer jackets and trousers, two pocket handkerchiefs with thread to make them, one ink pot, and stuff for three stocks by order of Col. Clark (VSA-11a).

06/20/80 Capt. Robt. George requests of John Dodge to issue Zephaniah Blackford with trimmings for three jackets by order of Col. Clark (VSA-11a).

06/20/80 Capt. Robt. George requests of John Dodge to pay Mrs. Smith 12 shillings and six pence, for making a suit of soldiers clothes for Jacob Wheat, by orders of Col. Clark (VSA-11a).

06/20/80 Mary Smith writes that she received from John Dodge two yds of white flannel [which was in full of her demand] (VSA-11b).

06/20/80 Capt. Robt. George requests of John Dodge to pay John Bryan 15 pounds four shillings, and six pence in goods for making clothing for Capt. George's Co. (VSA-11a).

06/22/80 Capt. Robert George requests of John Dodge to issue Andrew Clark truck [credit] for two pairs of trousers, check handerchief, small-tooth and large-tooth comb by order of Col. Clark (VSA-11b).

06/23/80 Capt. Robert George requests of John Dodge by order of Col. Clark, to issue 16 shirts to Reuben Kemp, Daniel Williams, Richard Bredin, Charles Evans, Andrew Johnston, Isaac Yates, and William Nelson who are members of Capt. Worthington's Co. (VSA-11) (VSA-48).

06/23/80 Capt. Robert George requests of John Dodge by Col. Clark's orders, to issue a brass ink stand to Sgt. Anderson (VSA-11a).

06/23/80 William Robeson is issued two shirts at FJ from John Dodge per Capt. George's orders; member of Worthington's Co. (VSA-11).

06/29/80 Capt. Robt. George requests of John Dodge by Col. Clark's orders to issue eight shirts to James Thompson, Joseph Panther, John Shank, and Jacob Decker of Capt. Kellar's Co. (VSA-11).

07/03/80 Capt. Robt. George requests of John Dodge by Col. Clark's orders, to issue two pairs of leggings of half-thicks to Sgt. Anderson and Michael Hacketon of his Co., going on command (VSA-12a).

Fort Jefferson Personnel

07/03/80 John Cox, Sam Watkins, and J. Duncan arrived at FJ from Ft. Patrick Henry and was issued linen and thread for two shirts per Capt. George's orders to Capt. John Dodge at FJ (VSA-12).

07/09/80 Baptist Daquoin signs his mark to Capt. Dodge that he needs help. He is trying to convince the enemy that he is an American but realizes that these are trying times for all men (VSA-12a).

07/10/80 Capt. Rogers and Capt. George sign request of John Dodge to issue 62 shirts and black stuff for as many stocks and thread or silk to make up the stocks for 31 men (VSA-12b).

07/10/80 Capt. George requests of John Dodge by order of Col. Clark, that Capt. Abraham Kellar be issued his quota of clothing allowed by law [passed in 1779] (VSA-12a).

07/10/80 Capt. Robert George requests of John Dodge by order of Col. Clark that two officers of Capt. Rogers' be issued their full quota of clothing which they are entitled to by law [passed in June, 1779] (VSA-12).

07/10/80 Capt. Robert George requests of John Dodge by Col. Clark's orders, that Capt. John Bailey and Ensign Slaughter be issued their full quota of clothing which they are entitled to by law (VSA-12a).

07/10/80 Capt. John Rogers and V.T. Dalton sign that they received of John Dodge, two yds blue persian and one piece of binding (VSA-12).

07/11/80 Lt. John Montgomery requests of John Dodge to pay at his leisure, Mrs. Ann Elms and her daughter a petticoat each (VSA-12).

07/11/80 Lt. Girault issued clothing to which he is entitled by law agreeable to Col. Clark's orders at FJ from Capt. John Dodge per Capt. George's orders (VSA-12).

07/11/80 Capt. George requests of John Dodge that Capt. Richard Brashears be issued his full quota of clothing which he is entitled to by law agreeable to Col. Clark's orders at FJ (VSA-12).

07/11/80 Capt. George requests of John Dodge that Major McCarty be issued the clothing he is entitled to by law by order of Col. Clark (VSA-12).

07/11/80 Capt. Robert George requests of John Dodge that Lt. Girault be issued the clothing which he is entitled to by law by order of Col. Clark at FJ (VSA-12).

07/11/80 Capt. Robert George requests of John Dodge that John Montgomery be issued the clothing he is entitled to by law by order of Col. Clark (VSA-12).

07/11/80 Col. Montgomery requests of John Dodge that Doctor Ray be issued his full complement of clothing as is allowed to officers by Act of Assembly agreeable to Col. Clark's orders (VSA-12).

07/11/80 Capt. Abraham Kellar issued one comb, one inkstand, and one scalping knife at Camp Jefferson by order of Col. Clark, from Capt. John Dodge per Capt. George's orders (VSA-12).

07/11/80 Capt. Kellar signs that he received the within contents from John Dodge (VSA-12).

07/11/80 Frederick Guion is issued one ink holder for the use of the Commissary Dept. at Fort Jefferson from Capt. John Dodge, Agent by order of Col. Rogers per Capt. George's order (VSA-12; 48).

07/12/80 Dodge issued to Lt. Col. John Montgomery a list of sundry goods in part of the clothing allowed Montgomery by law. Attested to by J. Donne (VSA-48).

07/12/80 Dodge issued list of sundry articles for Majr Richard McCarty. Majr John Williams signed in behalf of McCarty and J. Donne attested (VSA-48).

07/12/80 Dodge issued to Capt. Abrm Kellar, a list of sundry goods in part of the clothing allowed him by law. Attested by J. Donne (VSA-48).

07/12/80 Dodge issued list of sundry articles for Capt. John Bailey. Ensign Slaughter, Ill Battalion signed in behalf of Bailey and J. Donne attested (VSA-48).

07/12/80 Dodge issued list of goods for Capt. Brashears in part of the clothing allowed Brashears by law. Ensign Jarret Williams, Ill Regiment apparently signed in behalf of Capt. Brashears and J. Donne Attested (VSA-48).

Fort Jefferson Personnel

07/12/80 Dodge issued list of goods to Lt. Girault in part of the clothing allowed Girault by law. J. Donne attested (VSA-48).
07/12/80 Dodge issued goods for Lt. Merriwether in part of the clothing allowed him by law. Capt. John Rogers, V. L. Dragoons, signed in behalf of Lt. Merriwether and J. Donne attested (VSA-48).
07/12/80 Dodge issued goods in part of the clothing allowed Lt. Michael Perrault by law. A. Rey, Surgeon signed in behalf of Lt. Michael Perrault and J. Donne attested (VSA-48).
07/12/80 Dodge issued to Ensign Jarret Williams a list of goods in part of the clothing allowed him by law. J. Donne attested (VSA-48).
07/12/80 Dodge issued to Ensign Laurence Slaughter, Ill Regiment, a list of goods in part of the clothing allowed Slaughter by law. J. Donne attested (VSA-48).
07/12/80 Dodge issued goods in part of the clothing allowed Cornet Thruston by law. Capt. John Rogers, V. L. Dragoons signed in behalf of Thruston, J. Donne attested (VSA-48).
07/12/80 Dodge issued goods to A. Rey, Surgeon in part of the clothing allowed Rey by law. J. Donne attested (VSA-48).
07/12/80 Dodge issued goods to Lt. Timothe Montbreuen in part of the clothing allowed Montbreuen by law J. Donne attested (VSA-48).
07/12/80 Dodge issued a list of sundry articles to Majr. John Williams, Ill Battalion, in part of the clothing allowed Williams by law. J. Donne attested (VSA-48).
07/12/80 Dodge issued a list of sundry goods to Capt. John Rogers, V. L. D., in part of the clothing allowed Rogers by law. J. Donne attested (VSA-48).
07/12/80 Dodge issued a quantity of merchandise in part of an order drawn on him in Lt. Richard Clark's favor by order of Col. G. R. Clark, dated the 11th Inst. attested by J. Donne (VSA-48).
07/12/80 Capt. Robert George requests of John Dodge by Col. Clark's orders, that 23 men of Capt. Abraham Kellar's Company be issued full clothing (VSA-12).
07/12/80 Capt. Kellar signs that he received from John Dodge, 80 1/2 yds blue cloth, 69 yds white flannel, thread and buttons to make up the same, three ruffled shirts, 35 plain shirts for the use of Kellar's Co. (VSA-12).
07/12/80 Capt. Robert George requests of John Dodge by order of Col. Clark, that Joseph Momeral, Louis Lepaint, James Brown, and Jacke Rubedo, four soldiers of Capt. Williams' Company be issued cloth and trimmings for a complete suit of clothes each, also two shirts each, they being entitled to the same by law having more than one year to serve (VSA-12).
07/12/80 Capt. Robert George requests of John Dodge by order of Col. Clark, that full clothing be issued for three men enlisted during the war, who have never received any part thereof. Also for one man enlisted for one year. The men were recruited by Lt. Col. Montgomery whose names are as follows: William Buchanan, Robert Whitehead, William Whitehead, John Roberts. John Roberts enlisted for one year the others enlisted during the war (VSA- 12).
07/12/80 Capt. Robert George requests of John Dodge by order of Col. Clark, that John Donne be issued the same allowance of clothing as to the officers of the line (VSA-12).
07/12/80 Robert George requests of John Dodge by order of Col. Clark, that full clothing be issued for James Curry, William Elms, James Morris, William Barthalomew, James Dawson, James Elms, and John Elms, of Capt. Brashears' Company (VSA-12).
07/12/80 Jarrett Williams signs that the previous order was received from John Dodge agreeable to the within order. 14 shirts, 21 yds flannel, 24 1/4 yds blue cloth with thread and buttons tomake up the shirts. John Donne attests (VSA-12).
07/12/80 Capt. Robert George requests of John Dodge by order of Col. Clark, that Ensign Slaughter be given 44 shirts for 22 men of Capt. John Bailey's Co. which are enlisted during the present war (VSA-12a).

Fort Jefferson Personnel

07/12/80 Slaughter signs that he received of Capt. John Dodge the full contents agreeable to the above order (VSA-12a).

07/12/80 Capt. Robert George requests of John Dodge, by order of Col. Clark, that Frederick Guion, a sergeant enlisted during the war in George's Company of Artillery, be issued full clothing and scarlet cloth sufficient to face his coat, at FJ (VSA-12a).

07/12/80 John Montgomery requests of John Dodge that Qtrm James Finn be issued the same portion of clothing as other state officers in the service. This is the 2nd order of the same date, at Fort Jefferson (VSA-12).

07/12/80 Capt. Robert George requests of John Dodge by order of col. Clark, that Ensign Jarret Williams be issued his full quota of clothing which he is entitled to by law, at FJ (VSA-12).

07/12/80 Capt. Robert George requests of Capt. Dodge by order of Col. Clark, that Wm. Clark be issued one hat, at FJ (VSA-12a).

07/12/80 Wm. Clark signed that he received the hat from J. Dodge (VSA-12).

07/12/80 Robert George requests of John Dodge by order of Col. Clark, that 36 shirts be issued for 18 men, which they are entitled to by law (VSA-12).

07/13/80 Capt. Robert George, Commandant, requests of Capt. John Dodge at FJ to issue Major John Williams his full quota of clothing which he is entitled to by law and agreeable to Col. Clark's orders (VSA-12).

07/13/80 Lt. Col. John Montgomery requests of Capt. John Dodge to issue Major John Williams for the use of Batist LeQuang, two shrouds, two blankets, two pair leggings, four shirts as he is entitled to them for his good service to the state on an expedition with Montogmery (VSA-12).

07/13/80 John Montgomery requests of John Dodge to issue Montgomery 5 3/4 yds muslin, one snaffle bridle, one black ball, and 3 1/4 yds ribbon (VSA-12a).

07/13/80 Capt. John Rogers, VLD, requests of Capt. Dodge at FJ 18 yds of osnaburg for the purpose of padding saddles, one lb thread, and 1 1/2 dozen course needles for the use of Rogers' Company (VSA-12).

07/13/80 Lt. Montgomery requests of John Dodge to deliver to Major John Williams, one stroud [2 1/2 yds], and one shirt which he borrowed to bury an Indian which was killed by mistake by one of the Light Horse men; also one stroud and a shirt which Montgomery borrowed for a chief of the Sauk nation in Dodge's absence at Cahokia (VSA-12).

07/13/80 Lt. Montgomery requests of John Dodge to issue Shadrack Bond two shirts and as much course linen that will make a pair of trousers in part of an account Bond has against the state, for which he is to be paid from the country store (VSA-12).

07/13/80 Lt. Montgomery requests of Capt. Dodge by Col. Clark's orders, to issue James Brown, a Sgt. in Brashears' Company, one ink pot. James Brown signs that he received the within contents (VSA-12) (VSA- 48).

07/13/80 Subject of Court of Inquiry proceedings at Ft. Jefferson; regarding Dodge's disrespectful language against Capt. George. Dodge acquitted (DMS 56J22-24).

07/13/80 The daughter of Mary Smith, no name given, had been badly paid by Israel and John Dodge for making shirts for them according to Mary Smith's testimony at FJ Court of Inquiry (DMS 56J22).

07/14/80 Dodge issued list of goods for James Finn, Quartermaster by order of Lt. Col. John Montgomery and attested by J. Donne (VSA-48).

07/14/80 Finn signed that he received from John Dodge, Agent the mentioned goods by order of Lt. Col. John Montgomery and attested by J. Donne (VSA-48).

07/14/80 Dodge issued goods in part of an order drawn on him in J. Donne's, Deputy Conductor/Western Department, favor by order of Col. George Rogers Clark of the 12th Inst. attested by Leonard Helm (VSA-48).

07/14/80 John Montgomery requests of Capt. Dodge, that Major Williams be issued one English blanket for Montgomery's use and also one 2 1/2 point blanket and one snaffle bridle for Williams' use at FJ (VSA-12a).

07/14/80 Ensign Williams signed that he received the goods from Capt. Dodge (VSA-12b).

07/14/80 Capt. Rogers requests of John Dodge that his Company of Light Dragoons be issued 11 coarse combs, 11 fine combs, three ink stands, two rolls

Fort Jefferson Personnel

	black ball and 24 skeins fine thread to make the officers' shirts and two horse fleams and 1/2 lb of coarse thread, at FJ (VSA-12).
07/14/80	Capt. R. George requests of John dodge by order of Col. Clark that Frederick Guion be issued one coarse and one fine comb (VSA-12).
07/14/80	John Montgomery requests of John Dodge that 24 men be issued one shirt each (VSA-12a).
07/14/80	John Wilson signed that he received from Capt. John Dodge 24 shirts for self and others. John Donne attested (VSA-12b).
07/14/80	John Rogers requests of J. Dodge by order of Col. Clark, that 31 men of Capt. Rogers' company of Light Dragoons be issued 37 1/2 yds blue cloth and thread in order to make cloaks which they are entitled to by law, having more than one year to serve (VSA-12a).
07/14/80	John Montgomery requests of Dodge to issue to James Finn material to make coat and trimmings and one hat at FJ (VSA-12a).
07/14/80	John Dodge, Agent certifies that Lt. Girault is due for three pair silk hose, one pair of thread hose, two pair shoes, buttons for one suit of clothes. This was to complete an order drawn on Dodge in Girault's favor by GRC for the clothing allowed him by law (VSA-12).
07/14/80	John Montgomery requests of John Dodge that Lt. Thomas Wilson be issued as much linen as will make two shirts and two pair of trousers which will be part of his clothing if acquitted, if not Lt. Col. Montgomery will see them paid for as it is impossible to keep a prisoner naked (VSA-12).
07/14/80	Capt. Robert George requests of John Dodge, by order of Col. Clark, that Richard Sennet, Peter Freeman, James Ballenger, and Jacob Huffman be issued one shirt each or linen to make the same with thread. In payment for services performed when going to Kaskaskia for provisions for the troops (VSA-12).
07/16/80	Dodge issued goods in part of an order drawn on him in Leonard Helm's, Superintendant of Indian Affairs, favor by order of Col. George Rogers Clark, dated this day, attested by J. Donne (VSA-48).
07/17/80	Issued 8 1/2 yds coarse linen for sheets 6 3/4 ells at six pair [?] 5 - -- 6 (VSA-48).
07/20/80	Issued 4 1/2 yds white linen and one paper pins for washwoman, house expense (VSA-48).
08/01/80	Listed as Capt. Wrote to T. Jefferson from Ft. Jefferson (GRC Papers, I: 435).
09/06/80	Account of ammunition delivered by Martin Carney by Capt. George's odr to John Dodge, Agent for Indians, five lbs powder and ten lbs lead; also to John Dodge for a French Boat going to Pencore, 20 lbs lead (VSA-50).
09/08/80	Account of tobacco delivered by Martin Carney by order of Capt. George at Fort Jefferson, to Capt. John Dodge for Indians by Col. Montgomery's order, two carots weighing six lbs (VSA-50).
09/09/80	Received of Capt. John Dodge one pair steelyards for use of the Commissary Dept. by John Donne (VSA-13).
09/09/80	Paid Moses Henry, four ells black calamanco house expense, six yds ferretting, three skeins silk, one ivory comb, 1 1/2 weight sugar, one snaffle bridle, ten skeins silk, three ells ticken bot. of gratiot 45 livres peltry, 12 ells linen, ten weight soap [house expense] (VSA-48).
09/09/80	Account of ammunition delivered by Martin Carney by Col. Montgomery's orders, to John Dodge, Agent for Indians 100 lbs powder, 200 lbs lead (VSA-50).
09/10/80	Present at FJ (VSA-13a).
09/10/80	Account of ammunition delivered by Martin Carney by Col. Montgomery's orders, to John Dodge, Agent, ten lbs powder, 20 lbs lead (VSA-50).
09/12/80	Issued "the Old Barge by the Landing" for his use [going ?] to Kaskaskia for Public Benefit (VSA-13).
09/13/80	Account of sugar delivered by Martin Carney by order of Col. Montgomery at Fort Jefferson, to Capt. Dodge, Agent for his own use, four lbs; to Capt. Dodge's order by Frank Little, 5 1/2 lbs (VSA-50).
09/13/80	Issued one blanket to Major McCarty per request of J. Montgomery (VSA-13a).

Fort Jefferson Personnel

09/13/80 Robert George signs he received one blanket from J. Dodge (VSA-13b).
09/15/80 Rbt. George requests of John Dodge to pay Francis Bredin for clothing made, payment out of the public store (VSA-13a).
09/19/80 J. Montgomery writes instructions to John Dodge to purchase $10,000 worth of supplies for the troops at Ft. Jefferson; specifies salt, flour, corn, some furniture for Col. Clark, and blankets and shoes for the troops (VSA-13a).
09/19/80 Rbt. George requests of John Dodge, by order of Col. Clark, to issue 1/4 yd white cloth to John Vaughan to face a jacket (VSA-13a).
09/22/80 By order of Col. Clark, R. George requests of John Dodge "or his agent" to issue seven yds of linen and two skeins thread to Silas Harlan (VSA-13a).
09/23/80 By order of Col. Clark, R. George requests of John Dodge to issue 5/8 yd blue cloth for leggings to Silas Harlan (VSA-13a).
09/25/80 2,820 weight flour and 327 12/40 bushels corn by Dodge issued on the orders of Sundry Commanding Officers and sent per receipt for the relief of Fort Jefferson (VSA-48).
09/25/80 Richard Clark requests of John Dodge to issue five skeins of thread for use by Capt. Worthington's Company (VSA-13a).
09/28/80 T. Hutchings writes Col. Montgomery about [dispensed?] tafia, two quarts, one gal., one pint, and one half pint; Col. Montgomery requests John Dodge to replace these items (VSA-13a).
09/30/80 John Dodge requests by George, by order of Col. Clark, to issue four yds to "bury a soldier in" of Capt. Kellar's Company (VSA-13a).
10/01/80 J. Dodge requesed by J. Montgomery [at Kaskaskia?] to pay J. B. Lecroix for a perogue used to carry corn to Ft. Jefferson (VSA-13a).
10/03/80 J. Montgomery, from Kaskaskia requests of John Dodge to issue 230 lbs flour and two bags for the use of the troops at Ft. Jefferson (VSA-13a).
10/05/80 J. Montgomery, from Kaskaskia, requests of John Dodge to replace 61 lbs flour that Thomas Kirk loaned some troops who moved from Ft. Jefferson to Kaskaskia (VSA-13a).
10/06/80 By order of J. Montgomery, Maj. J. Williams requests of John Dodge to deliver to [Sgt. McClever?] for the use of Ft. Jefferson. 121 bushels of corn and 265 lbs flour and three bags (VSA-13a).
10/12/80 Someone signs that John Dodge received the within contents [Corn?] (VSA-13b).
10/12/80 [Mrs. Johnes?] writes [she?] received three yds flannel from Israel Dodge for making shirts (VSA-13b).
10/13/80 By order of Col. Clark, R. George requests of John Dodge to issue one yd flannel to J. Hazzard of George's Co. to loin a waistcoat (VSA-13a).
10/14/80 R. George requests of John Dodge to issue 12 yds flannel and six skeins of thread to Samuel Allen for payment for 496 lbs beef (VSA-13a).
10/15/80 By order of Col. Clark, George signs J. Bailey's request for J. Dodge to issue cloth and trimmings to produce one suit each for Levi Theel and John Clark (VSA-13a).
10/17/80 John Dodge signs that he received $2000 from John Rogers to purchase provisions for troops at Ft. Jefferson (VSA-13b).
10/18/80 J. Montgomery requests [from Kaskaskia], John Dodge to issue 300 lbs flour and 1/2 crock tafia for the use of the troops at Ft. Jefferson (VSA-13a).
10/18/80 J. Montgomery signs that he received tafia from J. Dodge (VSA-13b).
10/18/80 J. Montgomery [at Kaskaskia] requests of John Dodge to issue two bags for transporting flour for use of troops at Ft. Jefferson (VSA-13a).
10/20/80 Abraham Kellar signs that he received from John Dodge at Kaskaskia, one bushel of corn for the use of Kellar's Company and four lbs of sugar for Kellar's own use (VSA-13a, misfiled).
10/23/80 By order of Col. Clark, Robert George requests of John Dodge to issue cloth and trimmings to produce a suit of clothing each for enlsiting for nine men; John Anderson, Matthew Murray, William Fever, James Ramsey, William Posley, John Gilbert, Patrick Rogers, Francis Little, and Patrick Marr. William Posely to receive extra linen to make two shirts (VSA-13a).

Fort Jefferson Personnel

10/24/80 John Montgomery orders Israel Dodge to pay $108 "at the Orleans price" for an order given by John Dodge (VSA-13a).
10/26/80 John Dodge signs that a quantity of powder was received by Israel Dodge on Thomas Bentley's account (VSA-13b).
10/26/80 Indicated amount of 73 lbs powder on T. Bentley's account (VSA-13a).
10/26/80 George requests of Capt. Dodge to pay 25 shillings or equal amount in goods to Francis Bredin [Breeding] for making two shldier suits for Capt. McCarty's Company (VSA-13a).
10/27/80 George requests of Capt. Dodge to issue 1/2 yd stroud to Samuel Allen in part pay for beef delivered (VSA-13a).
10/27/80 Allen signs that he received within order of Israel Dodge (VSA-13b).
10/27/80 Israel Dodge signs that he received a delivery of goods [detailed in document] from John Dodge, attested by John Donne (VSA-13a).
10/27/80 John Dodge signs that an inventory [detailed in document] is a true copy of the original, John Donne attests (VSA-13b).
12/01/80 John Dodge and John Donne sign [Joseph Hunter attests] that they will see to it that the sheriff oc Clarksville, his successor or their assigns will be paid $554 continental currency within six months of this date for a debt owed by the deceased John Oiler (VSA-14a).
12/01/80 John Donne certifies that John Dodge paid money for corn, cornfields, and sundry other merchandise for the use of the savages (VSA-14b).
12/03/80 John Dodge certifies [from Kaskaskia] that the State of Virginia is indebted to an Indian one stroud blanket for cominig express from Fort Jefferson on public business (VSA-14a).
12/05/80 Letter from John Donne at Fort Jefferson to George Rogers clark. Tells that supplies come from Illinois and that John Dodge has been there for some time. The greatest difficulty is in transporting the provisions from Illinois to Fort Jefferson. The trip takes about 15 to 20 days. Dodge fears that there will be a revolt in the Illinois (MHS: B1, F23).
12/09/80 Sgt. John Giles signs his mark that he received of John Dodge the following: 150 lbs flour; 45 bushels of corn at 40 quarts per bushel; and 16 bags. The flour and corn are for the use of the troops at Fort Jefferson. The bags are to be returned to Giles. Five files and 15 lbs steel were received by Giles for the armourer (VSA-14).
12/20/80 John Dodge signs that 4 1/2 yds of cotton sacque and 2 1/2 yds scarlet calamanco were taken out of the store to bear Dodge's expenses (VSA-14).
12/23/80 John Dodge at Kaskaksia writes letter to Oliver Pollack. Letter does not speak of Fort Jefferson. Significant becase Dodge has not yet returned to Fort Jefferson (GRC, I: 475).
12/26/80 Robert George requests of John Dodge to issue Capt. Richard Harrison sky blue cloth and good trimmings for a coat, and pompedore broad cloth for facing and edging (VSA-14).
12/31/80 Martin Carney signed that he received of Israel Dodge, three yds super fine broad cloth to complete an order given John dodge to deliver to Martin Carney (VSA-14a).
12/31/80 Ensign Slaughter signed that he received of Israel Dodge, two pair of shoes upon a certificate given to Slaughter by John Dodge (VSA-14a).
12/31/80 Martin Carney signed that he received of Israel Dodge two pair of shoes upon an order given Carney by John Dodge (VSA-14a).
12/31/80 Leonard Helm signed that he received of Israel Dodge one pair of shoes upon a certificate given Helm by John Dodge (VSA-14b).
12/31/80 Lt. John Girault signed that he received of Israel Dodge one poar of shoes upon a certificate given Girault by John Dodge (VSA-14b).
12/31/80 John Williams signed that he received of Israel Dodge on pair of shoes upon a certificate given Williams by John Dodge (VSA-14b).
12/31/80 Jarrett Willisams signed that he received of Israel Dodge on pair of shoes upon a certificate given Williams by John Dodge (VSA-14c).
12/31/80 Capt. Richard Brashears signed that he received of Israel Dodge on pair of shoes upon a certificate given Brashears by John Dodge (VSA-14c).
12/31/80 Richard Harrison signed that he received of Israel Dodge one pair of shoes upon a certificate given Harrison by John Dodge (VSA-14c).

Fort Jefferson Personnel

12/31/80 Richard Clark signed that he recieved of Israel Dodge one pair of shoes upon a certificate given Clark by John Dodge (VSA-14c).

12/31/80 Capt. John Bailey signed that he received of Israel Dodge on pair of shoes upon a certificate given Bailey by John Dodge (VSA-14c).

Donne, John Sr. Deputy Commissary [also Donn and Downe] Listed as Major. A "survivor of Ft. Jefferson" (Louisville Directory 1832: 100-103). Paid sundry inhabitants at Kaskaskia for 5438 weight flour and 535 bushels corn, not yet delivered and whose obligations I have delivered to Mr. Donne Deputy Conductor per his receipt, three yds toile gris, one skein fine thread, five yds osnaburgs, and one stick twist paid J. Donne for assisting in public business with the accounts while hurried four bags - eight ells osnaburgs delivered to Deputy Conductor Donne per his receipt, 25 yds white flannel, one weight twine, 12 skeins thread, two paper pins, four skeins thread, one yard linen, one yard blue cloth paid John Donne for assisting in adjusting public accounts (VSA- 48).Received per receipt of John Donne, Deputy Conductor, 5,013 buffalo beef, 745 venison, 58c bear meat (VSA-48).

One piece steel yards bought of Mark Ker and delivered to John Donne for use of the Commissary Department, eight dollars (VSA-48). Thirty-seven bushels corn sent to Fort Jefferson per receipt John Donne, Deputy Conductor (VSA-48).

03/01/80 Account of arms received by Martin Carney in this department, the property of the Commonwealth of Virginia: received from Mr. Donne, Commissary at the Falls of Ohio, two rifles and three muskets (VSA-50: 16).

04/08/80 List of sundry disbursements from Commonwealth of Virginia from Nov. 1779 to April 8, 1780 [some for going to FJ] (VSA-10).

06/04/80 Robt. George writes from Ft. Jefferson to GR Clark. Letter will be delivered by Col. Legras and Mr. Dejean. Mentiones that Mr. Donne has tried to procure meat without success (Seineke, 1981: 441) (MHS: B1, F19).

06/10/80 Inventory of articles issued to Capt. Lt. Richard Harrison agreeable to his receipt taken in Receipt Book A, was certified by Donne (VSA-48).

06/12/80 Inventory of Articles issued to Secretary Clark as taken from Receipt Book A, agreeable to his receipt therein by Donne (VSA-48).

06/12/80 Inventory of articles issued to Samuel Smyth, Surgeon, agreeable to his receipt taken in receipt book A, certified by Donne (VSA-48).

06/14/80 Goods issued to Surgeon Smyth by order of Capt. Robert George Commandant agreeable to Col Clarks orders as per inventory and receipt taken from Receipt Book A by Donne (VSA-48).

06/14/80 Issued inventory list of the articles issued to Martin Carney, Deputy Quartermaster agreeable to his receipt taken from receipt book A by J. Donne (VSA-48).

06/14/80 Rich. Harrison writes a return to Wm. Shannon for 27 gallons of tafia for the use of his escort party [for Col. Walker] to the Falls [Ft. Jeff]. J. Donne signs that the above was delivered (VSA-11a).

06/14/80 J. Donne signs that the State of Virginia is indebted for tafia (VSA-11a).

06/20/80 One ink pot, one ivory comb, one horn comb per order and receipt John Donne for use of Co. Dept. (VSA-iia) (VSA-48).

06/20/80 Account of tobacco delivered by Martin Carney by order of Capt. Robert George at this place, to Mr. Donne, Commissary, one carot weighing three lbs (VSA-50).

06/20/80 Inventory of articles issued to Secretary Clark as taken from Receipt Book A, agreeable to his receipt therein by J. Donne (VSA-48).

06/21/80 Account of ammunition delivered by Martin Carney by Capt. Robert George's order at Camp Jefferson, to Mr. Donne, Commissary, one lb powder and two lbs lead (VSA-50).

Fort Jefferson Personnel

06/21/80 Capt. Robert George requests of Martin Carney to issue Mr. Donne one carot of tobacco and charge him the customary price of others in public service (VSA-11a).

06/21/80 J. Donne signs that he received the above (VSA- 11b).

07/03/80 One pair garters per order and receipt of John Donne (VSA-48).

07/11/80 Attested to the list of goods issued to Thomas Wilson by Henry Hutton on Jan. 5, 1780 [cloth, flannel, buttons, and thread] (MHS: B1, F14).

07/12/80 Attested to list of goods received from Capt. John Dodge in part of the clothing issued to Majr. John Williams, Ill Battalion (VSA-48).

07/12/80 Attested to list of sundry goods received from Capt. John Dodge in part of the clothing allowed Lt. Col. John Montgomery (VSA-48).

07/12/80 Attested to list of sundry articles received from Capt. John Dodge and signed for by Mjr. John Williams in behalf of Mjr. Richard McCarty (VSA-48).

07/12/80 Orders issued to Capt. Dodge for Donne to be issued the same allowance of clothing as the officers of the line (VSA-11).

07/12/80 Attested to list of sundry goods received from Capt. John Dodge, Agent for Capt. John Rogers in part of the clothing allowed him by law (VSA-48).

07/12/80 Attested to list of sundry goods received from Capt. John Dodge, Agent, and issued to Capt. Abrm Kellar, Ill Battalion, in part of the clothing allowed him by law (VSA-48).

07/12/80 Attested to list of sundry goods received from Capt. John Dodge, Agent, and signed for by Ensign Slaughter in behalf of Capt. Bailey in part of the clothing allowed Bailey by law (VSA-48).

07/12/80 Attested to list of goods received from Capt. John Dodge, Agent, and signed for by Capt. John Rogers, V. L. Dragoons, in behalf of Lt. James Merriwether in part of the clothing allowed Merriwether by law (VSA-48).

07/12/80 Attested to list of goods received from Capt. John Dodge, Agent, and apparently signed for by Ensign Williams in behalf of Capt. Brashears in part of the clothing allowed Brashears by law (VSA-48).

07/12/80 Attested to list of goods issued to Lt. Girault and received from Capt. John Dodge Agent (VSA-48).

07/12/80 Attested to list of goods received from Capt. John Dodge, Agent, and signed for by A. Rey, Surgeon in behalf of Lt. Michael Perrault (VSA-48).

07/12/80 Attested to list of goods received from Capt. John Dodge, Agent, and issued to Ensign Jarret Williams in part of the clothing allowed Williams by law (VSA-48).

07/12/80 Attested to list of goods received from Capt. John Dodge, Agent, and issued to Ensign Laurence Slaughter as part of the clothing allowed Slaughter by law (VSA-48).

07/12/80 Attested to list of goods received from Capt. John Dodge, Agent, and signed for by Capt. John Rogers, V. L. Dragoons in behalf of Cornet Thruston (VSA-48).

07/12/80 Attested to list of goods received from Capt. John Dodge, Agent, and issued to A. Rey, Surgeon in part of the clothing allowed Rey by law (VSA-48).

07/12/80 Issued to Mr. John Donne, Deputy Conductor, 1 3/4 yds blue bath coating 7/4 wide, three yds grey cloth 7/8 wide in lieu of 1 1/2 yds of 7/4 wide, three yds coarse linen for lining, 5 1/4 yds coarse linen for lining in lieu of 2 1/2 yds shalloon, 21 yds linen for six shirts, two yds cambric for six stocks, 3/4 yds cambric for ruffling six shirts, issued for six pr breeches five yds spotted velvet, 2 1/2 yds thickset, 2 1/2 yds check linen, five yds white linen, issued for six vests 1 1/2 yds blue persian, 3 3/4 yds sycee and five yds linen, one silk handkerchief, one romal handkerchief, four check linen handkerchiefs, 26 skeins thread, four skeins silk, two sticks twist, two pair knee garters, 6 1/2 yds ferretting, one hat, 2 3/4 uds white cloth (VSA-48).

07/12/80 Attested to list of goods received from Capt. John Dodge, Agent in part of the clothing allowed Lt. Timothe Montbreuen by law (VSA-48).

Fort Jefferson Personnel

07/12/80 Attested to list of merchandise received from Capt. John Dodge, Agent in part of an order drawn on Dodge in Lt. Richard Clark's favor by order of Col. George Rogers Clark dated the 11th inst (VSA-48).

07/12/80 Attested to receipt by Jarret Williams from Capt. John Dodge for 14 shirts, 21 yds flannel, 24 1/4 yds blue cloth with thread and buttons to make up shirts (VSA-12).

07/14/80 Present at FJ (VSA-12).

07/14/80 Attested for goods received from Capt. John Dodge, Agent by order of Lt. Col. John Montgomery for James Finn, Quartermaster (VSA-48).

07/14/80 J. Donne, Deputy Conductor WD, received from Capt. John Dodge Agent, the within mentioned quantity of goods in part of an order drawn on him in Donne's favor by order of Col. George Rogers Clark of the 12th Inst. Attested by Leonard Helm (VSA-48).

07/14/80 Attested to John Wilson's receipt from John Dodge of 24 shirts for Wilson and other men of Montgomery's Co. (VSA-12).

07/14/80 Attests to Richard Sennet's receipt of one shirt or linen to make the shirt with thread for Sennet, Peter Freeman, James Ballenger, and Jacob Huffman who are being paid for services performed when going to Kaskaskia for provisions for the troops (VSA-12).

07/16/80 Attested to list of goods received from Capt. John Dodge, Agent in part of an order drawn on Dodge in Leonard Helm's favor by order of Col. George Rogers Clark dated this day (VSA-12).

07/29/80 With family at FJ (VSA-12).

07/29/80 Received six lbs coffee for family by order of Capt. George (VSA-12).

08/03/80 Six weight coffee per order and receipt of John Donne (VSA-48).

08/07/80 Israel Dodge swore before John Donne that sundry articles were lost by Dodge on his passage from the Falls of Ohio to post St. Vincent on public business in February (VSA-48).

09/05/80 Present at FJ (VSA-13a).

09/09/80 Present at FJ (VSA-13).

09/09/80 Account of sugar delivered by Martin Carney by order of Col. Montgomery at Fort Jefferson, to Mr. Donne, Commissary, four lbs (VSA-50).

09/09/80 Issued four lbs of soap by Carney per order of Rbt. Montgomery (VSA-13a).

09/11/80 Issued one blanket to John Donne (VSA-13a).

09/11/80 One English blanket per receipt and order of Lt. Col. Montgomery issued to and overdrawn by J. Donne, Deputy Conductor. Blanket does not appear on the July 12 list of goods issued to Donne (VSA-48).

09/12/80 Attested for articles and goods received by Martin Carney from John Dodge (VSA-13).

09/13/80 Issued three lbs soap (VSA-13).

09/13/80 Received the beef cow [heifer] weighing 278 lbs for the use of the troops at FJ from McCarty (VSA-13).

09/13/80 Account of soap delivered by Martin Carney by order of Col. Montgomery and Capt. George at Fort Jefferson, to Mr. Donne, Commissary, three lbs (VSA-50).

09/19/80 Account of sugar delivered by Martin Carney by order of Capt. George at Fort Jefferson, to Mr. Donne, Commissary, for his family, four lbs (VSA-50).

09/25/80 One pair blue stroud leggings and one pair breach cloth paid Joseph Hunter for a sheep per certificate of J. Donne, Deputy Conductor (VSA-48).

09/25/80 Eleven bags, 2 1/4 quarts delivered the Commissary Department for the use of transporting provisions and lost by the troops per receipt of J. Donne (VSA-48).

10/09/80 Account of soap delivered by Martin Carney by order of Col. Montgomery and Capt. George at Fort Jefferson, to Mr. Donne, Commissary for his use, four lbs (VSA-50).

10/10/80 John Donne signs that he received 496 lbs beef from Samuel Allen, to be paid for at the current rate (VSA-13a).

10/25/80 John Donne attests that Abraham Kellar received $1000 from J. Montgomery for his service in recruiting (VSA-13a).

Fort Jefferson Personnel

10/27/80 Israel Dodge signs that he received a delivery of goods [detailed in document] of John Dodge, attested by John Donne (VSA-13a).

10/27/80 John Dodge signs that an inventory of goods [detailed in document] is a true copy of the original; John Donne attests (VSA-13b).

11/26/80 Account of sugar delivered by Martin Carney by orders of Capt. George, to Mr. Donne, Commissary, six lbs (VSA-50).

11/27/80 Account of soap delivered by Martin Carney by order of Capt. George at Fort Jefferson, to Mr. Donne, Commissary, six lbs (VSA-50).

11/29/80 Account of ammunition delivered by Martin Carney by order of Capt. Robert George at Fort Jefferson, to Mr. Donne, Commissary, for his use, one lb powder, three lbs lead (VSA-50).

12/01/80 John Dodge and John Donne sign [Joseph Hunter attests] that they will see to it that the sheriff of Clarksville, his successor, or their assigns will be paid $554 continental currency within six months of this date for debt owed by the deceased John Oiler (VSA-14a).

12/01/80 John Donne certifies that John Dodge paid money for corn, cornfields, and sundry other merchandise for the use of the Savages (VSA-14).

12/05/80 Letter from J. Donne at Fort Jefferson to George Rogers Clark. Donne writes to inform Clark of the situation at Fort Jefferson. Talks of attack made by Indians on August 27 and tells that three of Capt. George's men left after the attack for the Falls. Tells that the most useful inhabitants have deserted, being struck with panic. The Indians destroyed the cornfields and anything else that they could. All that remains of the settlers are those who are sick and weak. The remains of the cornfields were appraised for use of the troops. A small part of the corn was stored. Speaks of Mr. Harlan hunting for meat at the beginning of last month [November]. Tells that he had brought in 14 and 15,000 weight and the Kaskaskia Indians had brought 3,000 weight and 1,000 weight was also brought to the Fort. Tells that 8,000 weight was eaten last month [November]. Capt. Rogers has been ordered from Illinois to reinforce Fort Jefferson and will add 1,000 weight to the monthly issue. Donne belives that Capt. George has done all in his power to issue the provisions with frugality to the inhabitants. Tells that supplies come from the Illinois and that John Dodge has been there for some time. The greatest difficulty is in transporting the provisions from Illinois to Fort Jefferson. The trip takes about 15 to 20 days. Dodge fears that there will be a revolt in the Illinois. Mr. Blackford arrived after Clark's departure and will be attending to the issues in Donne's absence. Donne suggests that Col. Montgomery might have done more to save Fort Jefferson before Major Harlan departs for the Falls (MHS: B1, F23).

12/05/80 With wife and family at FJ (VSA-14).

01/01/81 Received of Capt. John Dodge Agent for the State of Virginia, three quarts tafia for use of the Commissary Department, also two quarts spirits for use of a fatigue party on command going for provisions which he has purchased from Mr. Thomas Bentley at J. Donne's desire. In the form of a letter and signed by J. Donne, Deputy Conductor WD. (VSA-48).

01/01/81-01/19/81 Letter written sometime between these days from John Donne at Ft. Jefferson, to GRC at Richmond. Reference is made to the letter written by Donne to GRC on Dec. 5. In the Jan. 5 letter, Donne had mentioned that he would be taking a trip to Kaskaskia. He had expected to obtain a large quantity of goods which had been purchased but found instead a quantity unpaid. The quantity on hand in the Illinois consists of about 200 bushels of corn in stow, but a large quantity of flour is said to have been purchased. While Donne was away, Capt. Barbour arrived from New Orleans with a quantity of goods, part of which Capt. George intends to use for the purchase of provisions (MHS: B1, F23).

01/19/81 Stores issued by order of Capt. Robert George, to Mr. Donne, Commissary, two muskets, two bayonettes with belts, and one sword (VSA-50).

03/28/81 Ammunition delivered by order of Capt. George to Mr. Donne, 1/2 lb powder (VSA-50).

Fort Jefferson Personnel

04/13/81 Tobacco issued to sundry persons per order of Capt. George, Commandant to John Donne, three lbs (VSA-50).
04/17/81 Issued fishing line for "use of his family in these scarce times" (VSA-18).
05/03/81 Per orders brought from day book, three gallons rum (VSA-49).
06/07/81 Per orders brought from day book, 12 lbs sugar and one carot of tobacco (VSA-49).
09/10/81 At Falls of the Ohio, writes to GRC requesting three quire of paper, two for abstract books, one for a sundry of uses (MHS: B1, F7).

Donne, Mrs. John [probably Mrs. Martha Donne]
A "survivor of Ft. Jefferson" (Louisville Directory1832: 100-103).
Martha (History of Louisville/ Yater 1979).

Donne, John Jr.
A "survivor of Ft. Jefferson" (Louisville Directory 1832: 100-103).

Dorrely, John
06/18/80 Listed as member of Capt. George's Co. at FJ and issued two shirts by order of Capt. George for being enlisted during the war (VSA-11).

Dossey, Leaving
06/02/80 Capt. A. Kellar listed 17 men who had served in his unit at one time or another during the war. Leaving Dossey was one of those listed. [NOTE: There is no further information about Dossey at Ft. Jefferson] (MHS: B1, F19).

Dragoon, Ephraim
01/20/80-11/30/81 Enlistment. Listed as Private in Capt. John Bailey's Co. of the Illinois Regiment in the Virginia State Service. Payroll (Harding 1981: 45-46).
04/19/80 Deserted on this date from Capt. John Bailey's Company (Harding 1981: 46).

Duff, John
05/26/80 Account of ammunition delivered by Martin Carney by order of Col. Clark: to John Duff spy at Cahokia 1/4 powder and 1/2 lb lead (VSA-50).

Duly, Haymore
07/12/80 Among list of men who are Members of Capt. Abraham Kellar's Co. ar FJ receiving clothing issue; has one year to serve (VSA-12).

Duly, Phillip
7/12/80 Among list of men who are members of Capt. Abrham Kellar's Co. at FJ receiving clothing issue; has one year to serve (VSA-12).

Duncan, Joseph
06/03/80 Came from Fort Patrick Henry [Vincennes] with provisions for FJ (VSA-12).
07/03/80 Arrived at FJ from Fort Patrick Henry and issued linen and thread for two shirts per Capt. George's orders to Capt. John Dodge ar FJ [traveled to FJ with Sam. Watkins and John Cox] (VSA-12).
07/03/80 Issued 16 1/4 yds white linen, 3 1/4 yds check linen, per order Capt. George and receipt of Joseph Duncan, Samuel Watkins, and John Cox for bringing provisions (VSA-12).

Duplasse [Displase, Duplassi]
Paid Duplasse part of Col. Montgomery's order for a cow and calf eighty pounds peltry, paid for 171 weight pork 171 livres hard money, paid for 85 weight pork 85 livres peltry (VSA-48).

Fort Jefferson Personnel

08/28/80 Issued in the Indian Department, paid Duplasse his account for bread and tobacco 24..0..0 (VSA-48).
09/25/80 One clasp knife paid Duplasse for a lock for the store (VSA-48).

Eagle, Harmon
07/04/80 John Crawley's enlistment voucher, witnessed by Harmon Eagle, for enlisting three years with Capt. Abraham Kellar's Co. (MHS: B1, F20).
07/12/80 Among list of men who are members of Capt. Abraham Kellar's Co. at FJ receiving clothing issue; has more that one year to serve (VSA-12).

Elms, Mrs. Ann [also Ellams]
07/11/80 Lt. Col. John Montgomery at FJ writes that Ann Elms attended the sick in the hospital at Ft. Clark from 10 February until 5 June and that she is entitled to receive the same pay as anyone else employed for the same purpose; she is to be paid out of the country store at FJ. Lt. Col. John Montgomery signing as FJ Commandant, writes to Capt. John Dodge, Agent, stating that Capt. Dodge should, at his leisure, pay Mrs. Ann Elms and her daughter a petticoat each. Payment via goods needed at FJ 7/15/80 (VSA-12).
07/15/80 Seven yds calico, per order Col. MOntgomery for Anne Elms Nurse in the Hospital per her receipt (VSA-48).
08/22/80 Two linen handkerchiefs and one coarse comb paid Anne Elms for making one hunting shirt and three plain shirts (VSA-48).
09/19/80 Present at FJ (VSA-13a).
09/19/80 Robert George requests the Quartermaster to issue two lbs sugar to Mrs. Elms for her sick children (VSA-13a).
01/18/81 Present at FJ (VSA-15).
03/10/81 Present at FJ (VSA-17).

Daughter of Mrs. Ann Elms [no first name given]
07/11/80 Present at FJ (VSA-12)

Elms, James
05/30/80-11/30/81 Listed as Private on Capt. Richard Brashears' payroll in the Illinois Regiment (Harding 1981: 51-52).
06/12/80-07/14/80 Issued clothing at FJ as member of Ensign Williams' Company-had already received two shirts (VSA-12).
07/12/80 Received flannel, blue cloth, and thread and buttons along with James Curry, William Elms, James Morris, William Bartholomew, James Dawson, and John Elms who are all enlisted during the war in Capt. Brashears' Company (VSA-12).
07/12/80 Capt. Robert George requests of John Dodge by order of Col. Clark, that 36 shirts be issued for 18 men which they are entitled to by law; James Elms is among the list of 18 men; also noted that he has previously received clothing (VSA-12).

Elms, John
05/30/80-11/30/81 Listed as Private on Capt. Richard Brashears' payroll in the Illinois Regiment (Harding 1981: 51-52).
06/12/80-07/14/80 Issued clothing at FJ as member of Ensign Williams' Company-had already received two shirts (VSA-12).
07/12/80 Received flannel, blue cloth, and thread and buttons along with James Curry, William Elms, James Morris, William Bartholomew, James Dawson, and James Elms who are all enlisted during the war in Capt. Brashears' Company (VSA-12).
07/12/80 Capt. Robert George requests of John Dodge by order of Col. Clark, that 36 shirts be issued for 18 men which they are entitled to by law; John Elms is among the list of 18 men; also noted that he has previously received clothing (VSA-12).

Fort Jefferson Personnel

Elms, William
05/30/80-11/30/81 Listed as Sergeant on Capt. Richard Brashears' payroll in the Illinois Regiment (Harding 1981: 51-52).
06/12/80-07/14/80 Issued clothing at FJ as member of Ensign Williams' Company-had already received two shirts (VSA-12).
07/12/80 Received flannel, blue cloth, and thread and buttons along with James Curry, James Morris, William Bartholomew, James Dawson, James Elms, and John Elms; these men are enlisted during the war in Capt. Brashears' Company (VSA-12).
07/12/80 Robert George requests of John Dodge by order of Col. Clark, for 36 shirts to be issued to 18 men, which they are entitled to by law; William Elms is among the list of 18 men; also noted that Elms has previously received clothes (VSA-12).
07/27/80 Issued one carot of tobacco with Cagy [Micajah] Mayfield by order of Capt. George (VSA-12).
08/03/80 Account of tobacco delivered by Martin Carney by order of Capt. Robert George at this place, to Sgt. Elms for Brashears' Company, one carot weighing three lbs (VSA-50).
10/16/80 Account of ammuntiton delivered by Martin Carney by order of Capt. George, to Sgt. Elms of Capt. Brashears' Company, 1/2 lb powder, one lb lead (VSA-50).

Estis, James [Estes] [Private]
05/03/80 Enlisted (Harding 1981: 47).
06/02/80 Killed[?] (Harding 1981: 53).
07/15/80 Listed in Capt. Worthington's Company (MHS B1, F20) (VSA-12).
07/24/80 Deserted (Harding 1981: 53).

Etheridge, Abner
[Do not know from which company he was discharged]
07/14/80 Among list of men being issued one shirt each per Col. Montgomery's orders at FJ (VSA-12).
07/14/80 Discharged at FJ (VSA-12).

Evans, Charles
06/23/80 Capt. Robert George requests of John Dodge by order of Col. Clark, to issue 16 shirts to Reuben Kemp, Daniel Williams, Richard Bredin, Charles Evans, Andrew Johnston, Issac Yates, and William Nelson who are members of Capt. Worthington's Co. (VSA- 11) (VSA-48).
07/15/80 Listed on Capt. Worthington's Company (MHS B1, F20) (VSA-12).
09/09/80 Account of sugar delivered by Martin Carney by order of Col. Montgomery at Fort Jefferson, to Charles Evans, a soldier in Capt. Worthington's Company, one lb (VSA-50).
09/11/80 Issued one lb sugar for being sick (VSA-13a).

Eyler, Mr.
06/10/80 Issued to Col. George Rogers Clark, four lbs white sugar and one lb coffee to be paid Mr. Eyler for a mortar (VSA-48).
06/13/80 Four yds black calamanco per order and receipt of Mark Eyler (VSA-48).

Fair, Edmund
06/04/79-12/03/81 Listed as matross [corporal] in Capt. Robert George's Co. of Artillery in the Service of the Commonwealth of Virginia and Illinois Department. Pay Abstract (Harding 1981: 29-30).
04/10/80 - 09/04/80 Actual time of service (Harding 1981: 31).
05/10/80 Enlisted (Harding 1981: 32).
06/12/80 Going on expedition with Capt. Harrison to the Falls of Ohio; among list of men receiving clothing issue for the trip (VSA-11).
09/04/80 Died (Harding 1981: 31 & 32).

Fort Jefferson Personnel

Fever, William [also Fabers]
06/04/79-12/03/81 Listed as matross [corporal] is Capt. Robert George's Co. of Artillery in the Service of the Commonwealth of Virginia and Illinois Department. Muster Roll (Harding 1981: 32).
03/28/80 Enlisted (Harding 1981: 32).
06/19/80 Listed as member of Capt. George's Co. at Ft. Jefferson and issued two shirts by order of Capt. George for being enlisted during the war (VSA-11).
10/23/80 By order of Col. Clark, George requests John Dodge to issue cloth and trimmings for one suit each to nine men for enlisting, William Fever listed as one of the nine men (VSA-13a).
01/15/81 Killed (Harding 1981: 32).

Finn, James
07/12/80 Issued to Mr. James Finn, Quartermaster, 9 3/4 yds white linen for three shirts, six yds toile gris for three breeches, four yds check linen and 2 1/4 yds toile gris for three trousers, one yd fine holland for three stocks, three yds chintz for three vests, three yds damaged linen for lining, ten skeins thread, one silk handkerchief, one linen handkerchief, one ink holder, 4 1/4 uds camlet for a coat, one hat, 2 1/2 yds toile gris, one skein silk and two skeins thread for trimmings to his coat (VSA-48).
07/12/80 John Montgomery requests of John Dodge that Qtrm James Finn be issued the same portion of clothing as other state officers in the service. This is the 2nd order of the same date, at FJ (VSA-12).
07/13/80 Account of ammunition delivered by Martin Carney by Col. Montgomery's orders to James Finn, Quartermaster, Illinois Regiment, 20 lbs powder, 40 lbs lead (VSA-12) (VSA-50).
07/14/80 John Montgomery requests of Dodge to issue James Finn material [no quantity stated] to make a coat and trimmings and one hat at FJ (VSA-12).
07/14/80 Dodge issued list of goods for James Finn, Quartermaster by order of Lt. Col. John Montgomery and attested by J. Donne (VSA-48).
07/14/80 Finn signed that he received from John Dodge, Agent the mentioned goods by order of Lt. Col. John Montgomery and attested by J. Donne (VSA-48).
09/19/81-04/07/81 Sometime between these dates, tobacco is issued to sundry persons per order Capt. George, Commandant: to James Finn, three lbs (VSA-50: 13).
03/01/81 Gave testimony at FJ during Court of Inquiry regarding Capt. Richard McCarty (DMS 56J31).
04/13/81 Ammunition delivered by order of Capt. Robert George at Fort Jefferson, to Mr. Finn, Commissary, 1/2 lb powder, one lb lead (VSA-50).
05/03/81 Per orders brought from day book, two gallons, three quarts, and one pint rum (VSA-49).
05/08/81 Per orders brought from day book, for purchasing provisions for the use of the troops at Fort Jefferson 17 gallons and one quart rum (VSA-49).
05/10/81 Per orders brought from day book for use of Finn, eight lbs sugar and one carot of tobacco (VSA-49).
05/10/81 Tobacco issued by order of Capt. George, Commander, to James Finn, three lbs (VSA-50).
05/19/81 Per orders brought from day book, ten lbs sugar (VSA-49).
06/01/80 Omitted, per orders brought from day book, ten lbs sugar (VSA-49).
06/06/81 Account of ammunition delivered by Martin Carney by order of Capt. Robert George and Col. Montgomery, to Mr. Finn, 1/2 lb powder (VSA-50).
06/07/81 Per orders brought from day book, one carot of tobacco (VSA-49).

Fitzhigh, John
06/04/79-12/03/81 Listed as matross [corporal] in Capt. Robert George's Co. of Artillery in the Service of the Commonwealth of Virginia and Illinois Department. Pay Abstract (Harding 1981: 29-30).
05/10/80 Deserted on this date from Capt. George's Company (Harding 1981: 31).

Fort Jefferson Personnel

Flanerry, Daniel
05/31/80 Account of ammunition delivered by Martin Carney by order of Col. Clark: to Daniel Flanerry at Cahokia, five lbs powder (VSA-50: 8).

Flarry, James [may be James Harry]
06/12/80-07/14/80 Issued clothing at FJ as member of Ensign Williams' Company (VSA-12).

Fleure d epec
09/11/80 Issued in the Indian Department, paid Fleure d epec for repairs on Indian arms, 40 (VSA-48).

Flor, Mistress Mary
06/13/80 Capt. Robert George requests of John Dodge by Col. Clark's orders, to issue four yds of black calamanco for a short gown, at FJ (VSA-11a).
06/13/80 Mistress Flor signed that she received the above four yds (VSA-11b).

Floyd, Isam
06/04/79-12/03/81 Listed as corporal in Capt. Robert George's Co. of Artillery in the Service of the Commonwealth of Virginia and Illinois Department. Pay Abstract (Harding 1981: 29-30).
06/12/80 Going on expedition with Capt. Harrison to Falls of Ohio; among list of men receiving clothing for the trip (VSA-11).

Foley, Mark
06/04/79-12/03/81 Listed as matross [corporal] in Capt. Robert George's Co. of Artillery in the Service of the Commonwealth of Virginia and Illinois Department (Harding 1981: 30).
05/29/80 Discharged on this date from Capt. Robert George's Company (Harding 1981: 30).
05/30/80 Enlisted on this date as a private in Capt. Brashears' Company (Harding 1981: 51-52).
09/11/80 Issued as a soldier in Capt. Brashears' Company, one pair breeches, two shirts, one jacket, and one coat (VSA-13a).
10/02/80 Deserted Brashears' Co. (Harding 1981: 51-52).

Ford, Esther
One Indian handkerchief, one linen handkerchief, one coarse handkerchief paid E. Ford for making six plain shirts (VSA-48).

Two linen handkerchiefs and 2 3/4 uds ribbon paid Esther Ford for making six plain shirts per receipt (VSA-48).

Ford, John
05/01/80-09/12/80 Listed as Private in Capt. George Owens Co. of Militia of the District of Clarksville [Jefferson Co.] in the State of Virginia. Pay Abstract (Harding 1981: 48-49).
09/12/80 Moved (Harding 1981: 48).

Ford, Joseph
05/01/80-12/21/80 Listed as Private in Capt. George Owens' Co. of Militia of the District of Clarksville in the State of Virginia [Jefferson Co.]. Pay Abstract (Harding 1981: 48-49).
09/01/80[?] Farmed four acres; would have produced 100 bushels had Indians not burned it (DMS 1M8).
09/12/80 Moved (Harding 1981: 48).

Ford, R.
06/19/80 Two India handkerchiefs paid R. Ford for making six shirts plain (VSA-48).

Fort Jefferson Personnel

Ford, Robert [also Foard]
05/01/80-12/21/80 Listed as private in Capt. George Owens' Co. of Militia of the District of Clarksville of the State of Virginia [Jefferson Co.]. Pay Abstract (Harding 1981: 48-49).
09/01/80[?] Farmed 3 1/2 acres and est. 87 1/2 bushels (DMS 1M8).
09/09/80 Received seven lbs sugar and one pint tafia by order of Col. John Montgomery from Quartermaster stores at FJ. Referred to as "an Inhabitant of this place." Paid one pound, 13 shillings for goods (VSA-13).
09/12/80 Moved (Harding 1981: 48).
09/13/80 Account of sugar delivered by Martin Carney by order of Col. Montgomery at Fort Jefferson, to Robert Ford, a militia man, for 57 lbs beef for public use, seven lbs (VSA-50).

Freeman, Eliasha
04/06/80 Articles purchased by Martin Carney for the state of Virginia by order of Col. Clark: Purchased one bateau for 275 pounds to be paid to Eliasha Freeman (VSA-50: 2).

Freeman, Peter
02/18/79-07/14/80 Listed as private in Capt. Isaac Taylors Co. of volunteers in the Illinois Regiment Commanded by Col. John Montgomery (Harding 1981: 13).
07/14/80 Payroll reflects Freeman discharged (Harding 1981: 13).
07/14/80 Received either one shirt or linen to make shirt from Capt. John Dodge per Capt. George's orders at FJ for having gone to Kaskaskia for provisions for FJ [accompanied by Richard Sennet, James Ballenger, and Jacob Huffman] (VSA-12).
07/14/80 Among list of men being issued one each shirt per Col. Montgomery's orders at FJ (VSA-12).

Freeman, William
06/04/79-12/03/81 Listed as matross [corporal] in Capt. Robert George's Co. of Artillery in the Service of Virginia and Illinois Department. Pay Abstract (Harding 1981: 29-30).
03/20/80-12/03/81 Actual time of service (Harding 1981: 31).
06/12/80 Going on expedition with Capt. Harrison to the Falls of Ohio; among list of men receiving clothing issue for the trip (VSA-11).
12/24/80 Robert George requests of Israel Dodge to issue William Freeman of George's Co. of full suit of clothes which he is entitled to having enlisted during the present war (VSA-14a).
12/24/80 William Freeman signed his "mark" that he received of Israel Dodge the mentioned suit (VSA-14b).

Frogget, William
07/10/80 Member of Capt. John Roger's Co. Among list of men who have more than one year to serve and are issued two shirts and two stocks each at FJ per Capt. George's orders to Capt. John Dodge (VSA-12).
11/03/80 Paid Frogget for thrashing per receipt two gals tafia and four lb sugar (VSA-48).

Gage, Ensign [?]
08/27/80 Helped dig well in fort with Matthew Jones and Abraham Lockart (VSA-12).

Gagnia, Louis [also Gagne']
05/30/78-06/02/81 Private in Capt. McCarty's Co. (Harding 1981: 27).
09/10/80 Issued full clothing for enlisting into McCarty's Co. (VSA-13a).
03/03/81 Gave testimony in Capt. Richard McCarty's Court of Inquiry at FJ (DMS 56J35).

Fort Jefferson Personnel

Gagnus, Jacque [also Gagnier]
03/08/79-05/31/79 Corporal in Capt. Richard McCarty's Co. (Harding 1981: 21).
09/10/80 Issued full clothing for enlisting into Capt. Richard McCarty's Co. (VSA-13).

Gamlin, Francis
09/09/80 Received 2 1/2 lbs sugar, one quart tafia valued at 18 shillings, six pence from Quartermaster by orders of Col. John Montgomery (VSA-13).
09/09/80 Referred to as an "inhabitant of this place" (VSA- 13).
09/09/80 Account of sugar delivered by Martin Carney by order of Col. Montgomery at Fort Jefferson, to Francis Gamlin, a militia man, 2 1/2 lbs (VSA-50).

Gamlin, Pierre
09/04/80 Issued in the Indian Department, five ells linen paid Pierre Gamlin for tafia (VSA-48).

Garr, John
11/08/80 Account of soap delivered by Martin Carney by order of Col. Montgomery and Capt. George at Fort Jefferson, to Mr. John Garr, a soldier in Capt. George's Company, one lb (VSA-50).

George, Robert (Captain and Fort Commandant)
Issued three lbs soap to three men of Capt. George's Company per Col. Montgomery's order, two dressed deer skins for Capt. George's Company per Col. Montgomery's order, one quart tafia to two of Capt. George's Company per order Col. Montgomery (VSA-48).

Called upon by Western Commissioner to elucidate on cost of Capt. Barbour's cargo for Ft. Jeff (GRC Papers, II: 307-311).

In command when Archer furnished Ft. Jeff with meat (GRC Papers, II: 34).
General information regarding Capt. George's career (GRC, Papers II: 77).

06/04/79-12/03/81 Listed as Captain. Pay Abstract (Harding 1981: 29-30).
06/04/79-12/03/81 Refers to Capt. George's Pay Abstract for his Company of Artillery (GRC, Papers II: 394).
06/04/79 Henry Haul enlisted on this date in Capt. Robert George's Company as a Sergeant (Harding 1981: 30).
06/04/79 Joseph Anderson enlisted on this date as a sergeant in Capt. Robert George's Company (Harding 1981: 29-30).
06/04/79 George Armstrong enlisted on this date as matross (corporal) in Capt. Robert George's Company (Harding 1981: 29-30).
06/04/79 John Ash enlisted on this date as matross in Capt. Robert George's Company (Harding 1981: 29-30).
06/04/79 Valentine Balsinger enlisted on this date as sergeant in Capt. Robert George's Company (Harding 1981: 29-30).
09/25/79 Richard Turpin enlisted on this date as a matross in Capt. George's Company (Harding, 1981: 32).
11/18/79 Jeremiah Horn [also Hern] enlisted for three years or for the duration of the war by Lt. V. T. Dalton into Capt. Robert George's Company of Artillery (MHS: B1, F23).
11/29/79 Thomas Laney, Patrick Marr, Samuel Coffy, and John Anderson enlisted for three years or during the war by Lt. V. T. Dalton into Capt. Robert George's Company of Artillery. Samuel Coffy was not included in the payroll because Dalton neglected to give account of what has become of him or when and how his time expried (MHS: B1, F23).
12/11/79 Benjamin Lewis enlisted for three years or during the war by Lt. V. T. Dalton into Capt. Robert George's Company of Artillery (MHS: B1, F23).
01/01/80 Thomas Bolton enlisted for three years or during the war into Capt. Robert George's Company of Artillery by Lt. V. T. Dalton (MHS: B1, F23).

Fort Jefferson Personnel

01/06/80 George Smith enlisted on this date as a matross in Capt. George's Company (Harding, 1981: 32).
01/10/80 Paul Quibea enlisted for three years or during the war into Capt. George's Company of Artillery by Lt. V.T. Dalton (MHS: B1, F23).
01/31/80 James McDonell enlisted for three years or during the war by Lt. V.T. Dalton into Capt. Robert George's Company of Artillery (MHS: B1, F23).
02/03/80 Daniel Baber enlisted on this date as matross in Capt. Robert George's Company (Harding 1981: 29- 31).
03/10/80 Patt Mcutly enlisted for three years or during the war by Lt. V.T. Dalton into Capt. Robert George's Company of Artillery. Was not included on payroll as Dalton neglected to give account of what has become of him or when and how his time expired (MHS: B1, F23).
03/13/80 Jacob Ditterin enlisted on this date as a matross in Capt. George's Company (Harding, 1981: 32).
03/20/80 Andrew Conor enlisted for three years or during the war by Lt. V.T.Dalton into Capt. Robert George's Company of Artillery (MHS: B1, F23).
03/28/80 John Hazzard enlisted for three years or during the war by Lt. V.T.Dalton into Capt. Robert George's Company of Artillery (MHS: B1, F23).
04/05/80 Joshua Pruitt enlisted on this date as a matross in Capt. Robert George's Company (Harding, 1891: 31).
04/10/80 William Purcell enlisted on this date as a matross in Capt. Robert George's Company (Harding, 1981: 31-33).
04/12/80 Francis Puccan enlisted for three years or during the war by Lt. V.T. Dalton into Capt. Robert George's Company of Artillery. Was not on the payroll because Dalton neglected to give account of what has become of him or when or how his time expired (MHS: B1, F23).
04/12/80 Account of arms delivered by Martin Carney to Capt. George's Company of Artillery of the Illinois Virignia Regiment: delivered to Sgt. Walker, two rifle guns (VSA-50: 3).
04/14/80 William Pursley enlisted in Capt. Robert George's Company of Artillery (Harding, 1981: 140, 156, 203).
04/17/80 Tobacco issued to sundry persons per order of Capt. George, Commandant, to Jacob Pyatte, three lbs (VSA-50).
04/20/80 John Bouden enlisted for three years or during the war by Lt. V.T. Dalton into Capt. Robert George's Company of Artillery. Not on payroll because Dalton failed to give account of what has become of him or when and how his time expired (MHS: B1, F23).
04/20/80 Jacob Ditterin has enlisted for three years of during the wat by Lt. Valentine Dalton into Capt. George's Company of Artillery (MHS: B1, F23).
04/26/80 Account of arms delivered by Martin Carney to Capt. George's Company of Artillery of the Illinois Virginia Regiment: delivered to Capt. George, one rifle gun (VSA-50: 3).
05/01/80 Buckner Pittman enlisted on this date as a sergeant in Capt. George's Company (Harding, 1981: 31-33).
05/02/80 Account of arms delivered by Martin Carney to Capt. George's Company of Artillery of the Illinois Virginia Regiment: delivered to Capt. Lt. Harrison, four muskets and three carabins (VSA-50: 3) (VSA-11).
05/10/80-06/08/81 Commandant of Fort Jefferson (Harding 1981: 29-30).
05/10/80 Matross John Fitzhugh, Matross Adam Payne and Matross Christopher Lowerback deserted on this date from Capt. George's Company (Harding, 1981: 30-31).
05/14/80 Account of ammunition received by Martin Carney at this post Clarksville: from Capt. George by Col. Clark's verbal orders, three kegs gun powder none of them full [Document did state that the kegs were said to contain 100 weight each, but had been crossed out] equals 200 lbs powder (VSA-50: 5).
05/17/80 Capt. Edward Worthington and Robert George sign request to Martin Carney for three pints of tafia for Worthington's use (VSA-11).

Fort Jefferson Personnel

05/18/80 Valentine Dalton signs request at Fort Clark to issue pork for the use of Capt. George's Company [George is at Fort Jefferson] (VSA-11a).

05/18/80 Capt. Robert George at Fort Jefferson writes to George Rogers Clark at Cahokia informing him of Capt. Shannon and Doctor Smith's [i.e., the surgeon?] arrival at Fort Jefferson a few days ago; additionally only 18 men including non-commissioned officers are present, but George is not worried as he expects no action. Doctor is short of medicines. Capt. George is keeping the doctor at Fort Jefferson, but sending a letter with Shannon to Cahokia. George refers to the sickly season approaching (MHS: B1, F17).

05/18/80 Three lbs of tobacco issued at Fort Jefferson, by order of Capt. George, Commandant, to Martin Carney (VSA-50).

05/29/80 Matross Mark Foley, Matross Thomas Snellock, and Sergeant David Wallace were all discharged on this date from Capt. George's Company (Harding, 1981: 30).

06/00/80 Fred Guion received one lb lead to kill meat for garrison at FJ per Capt. George's orders [Date not legible] (VSA-11: Misc. Doc.).

06/03/80 Matross John March is listed as "died." He was a member of Capt. George's Company (Harding, 1981: 32).

06/04/80 Capt. Robert George writes from Ft. Jefferson to G.R. Clark. Letter will be delivered by Col. LeGras who is accompanied by Mr. Dejean from Williamsburg. The trenches are ready for the pickets which the inhabitants are bringing. The inhabitants are not yet finished planting. Hope to have the fort enclosed within the week. Provisions are being spared; issuing single rations of corn. Mr. Donne has tried to procure meat without success. Present stock of corn is a little more than 100 bushels (Seineke, 1981: 441) (MHS: B1, F19).

06/09/80 GR Clark requests of John Dodge to issue two quire of paper to Capt. Robt. George. George signed that he recieved the contents (VSA-11a,b) (VSA-48).

06/09/80 Appointed Commander of Ft. Jeff [Day before Clark leaves for Louisville] (VSA-June 1782).

06/09/80 Col. GRC at FJ requests of Capt. George to allow Quartermaster Carney the same clothing privileges as an officer of the regiment (VSA-11a).

06/10/80 Sundry merchandise drawn out of the public store more than George's quota for which in part no returns or receipts have been issued or passed: 26 yds blue stroud, 32 ruffled shirts, 20 plain shirts, 26 butcher knives, one ink holder, one bridle, 26 skeins thread per order, issued to Capt. Harrison, no receipt (VSA-48).

06/10/80 Account of ammunition delivered by Martin Carney by Capt. Robert George's order at Camp Jefferson, to Capt. Lt. Richard R. Harrison, 1 1/2 lbs lead and 40 flints (VSA-50).

06/10/80 Capt. Robt. George writes to J. Dodge that G.R. Clark ordered the issuance of clohting to Capt. Lt. Harrison (VSA-11).

06/10/80 Capt. Robt. George requests of M. Carney to deliver 1 1/2 lbs lead to Capt. Harrison for his use of his expedition to the Falls of Ohio; also issue 40 flints according to (VSA-50) (VSA-11).

06/10/80 Samuel Smyth received from VSS via John Dodge per Capt. George's order one knife, one horn comb, one ivory comb, 1 1/4 yds white half-thicks for leggings, one bath coating, breech cloth, four yds gartering, one ink stand, one pair blankets, one bridle for his use on expedition up Ohio River to Falls (VSA-11).

06/11/80 Capt. Robt. George requests of J. Dodge to give M. Carney clothing as directed by Col. Clark [Ft. Jefferson] (VSA-11a).

06/12/80 Capt. Robt. George requests of J. Dodge to furnish Richard Harrison with the following for 26 men of George's Co. going to the Falls by Clark's orders: 26 yds of stroud for making leggings and breech clohts for 26 men, 52 shirts, 26 knives, one ink pot, one bridle, and thread to make leggings (VSA- 11a).

06/12/80 Capt. George submits list of enlisted soldiers: J. Walker, Wm. Moore, L. Ryan, L. Keinan, P. Hup, P. Long, J. Taylor, Wm. White, B. Damewood, M. Hacketon, D. Kennedy, D. Baber, M. Tinklee, V. Balsinger, J. Oakly,

Fort Jefferson Personnel

I. Floyd, E. Fair, J. Megarr, P. Marr, P. McCalley, A. Miller, Wm. Freeman, G. Smith, D. Bush, J. Wheat, and J. Bush (VSA-11b).

06/12/80 Capt. Robt. George requests of J. Dodge to furnish Sam Smyth with: one knife, two combs [one horn, one ivory], 1 1/4 yd white half-thicks for leggings, bath coating, breech cloth, for yds gartering, one ink stand, one pair blankets, and one bridle for the use of the expedition to the Falls by Clark's orders (VSA-11a).

06/12/80 Capt. Robt. George requests of J. Dodge to furnish WM. Shannon with the following per Clark's orders: chintz for two pr trousers, cloth or other stuff for two waistcoats, two pr breeches, one breech cloth, one bridle, one blanket, one ink stand, one knife, one course and one fine comb (VSA-11a).

06/12/80 List of goods received by Capt. William Shannon, Conductor General, from J. Dodge; five yds check linen, 2 3/4 yds thickset, 1 1/2 yds course white linen, 1/2 yd blue bath coating, one stick mohair, one blanket, one snaffle bridle, one large knife, one ink stand, one course and one fine comb (VSA- 11b) (VSA-48).

06/12/80 Capt. Robt. George requests of J. Dodge by Clarks order to furnish Sgt. Walker with: two pair stockings, as much cottonade to make two trousers, and 12 yds red tape (VSA-11a).

06/12/80 Capt. Robt. George requests of J. Dodge by Clark's orders to furnish Capt. Lt. Harrison with the following for the expedition to the Falls: three knives, three horn and one ivory comb, 1 1/2 yds white half-thicks for leggings, bath coating for breech cloth, four yds gartering, one pair blankets (VSA-11a).

06/12/80 Capt. Robt. George requests of J. Dodge by Clark's orders to furnish Lt. Wm. Clark with the following; linen for three shirts with ruffling, stuff for four summer vests, two pair of breeches, two pair of trousers with proper trimmings, two pair thread stockings, and two handkerchiefs (VSA-11a).

06/12/80 Capt. Robert George certifies that M. Carney did everything in his power to preserve the boat, that was delivered to him by Col. Clark, which sunk unavoidably and became lost [Ft. Jeff] (VSA-11a).

06/12/80 Sundry merchandise drawn out of the public store more than George's quota for which in part no returns or receipts have been issued or passed: 1 1/2 yds white half-thicks, 1/2 yd blue bath coating, four yds gartering, two 2 1/2 point blankets, one leather ink pot per order, delivered to Capt. Harrison per receipt (VSA-48).

06/12/80 Sundry merchandise drawn out of the public store more than his quota for which in part no returns or receipts have been issued or passed: two pair thread hose, 5 1/4 yds cottonade, 12 yds ferret per order, delivered to Sgt. Walker per receipt (VSA-48).

06/12/80 List of goods issued to Capt. William Shannone, Conductor General, by orders of Capt. George, Commandant per Capt. Shannon's receipts on said orders (VSA-48).

06/13/80 Account of ammunition delivered by Martin Carney by Capt. Robert George's order at Camp Jefferson, to Josiah Phelps and John Montgomery, one lb powder and two lbs lead; to Capt. Harrison, 1/2 lb lead; to Capt. Harrison to take to the Falls of Ohio, 500 lbs powder and 1000 lbs lead; to Capt. George for the use of the troops, 3/4 lb powder and 1 1/2 lbs lead (VSA-50).

06/13/80 Account of tobacco delivered by Martin Carney by order of Capt. Robert George at this place, to Capt. Lt. Harrison going up Ohio, six carots weighing 18 lbs (VSA-50).

06/13/80 Capt. Robt. George requests of J. Dodge by COl. Clark's orders to issue black calamanco to make a short gown for Mistress Flor (VSA-11a).

06/13/80 Capt. Robt. George orders M. Carney to purchase tobacco from Mr. Lindsay for the use of the troops in this dept [Ft. Jeff] (VSA-11a).

06/13/80 Capt. Robt. George requests of J. Dodge by Clark's orders to deliver the following for use of George's Co. to the Falls: three blankets, 26 horn combs, 13 ivory combs, 2 1/2 yds blue bath coating, and thread (VSA-11a).

Fort Jefferson Personnel

06/13/80 R. Harrison and R. George request of the Quartermaster, 1/2 lb lead for use on expediton to Falls (VSA-11) (VSA-50).

06/13/80 Capt. Robt. George requests of J. Dodge by Clark's orders to issue him four blankets for the use of his company on the trip to the Falls (VSA-11a).

06/13/80 Capt. Robt. George requests of J. Dodge to furnish him with 24 yds of osnaburg and thread to make up bags for the trip to the falls (VSA-11a).

06/13/80 Capt. Robt. George requests of M. Carney to deliver to him six carots of tobacco for his company's use on the trip to the falls (VSA-11a).

06/13/80 Capt. Robt. George requests of J. Dodge by Clark's orders to furnish Capt. Shannon with the following: 1/2 yd linen, 1/4 yd check [linen], one Indian handkerchief, one linen handkerchief, and six skeins brown thread (VSA-11a) (VSA-48).

06/13/80 Jacob Ditteren enlisted for three years or during the war by Lt. V.T. Dalton into Capt. Robert George's Company of Artillery (MHS: B1, F23).

06/14/80 Issued to Surgeon Smyth by order of George agreeable to Col. Clark's orders as per inventory and receipt taken from receipt book A by J. Donne (VSA-48).

06/14/80 Account of ammunition delivered by Martin Carney by Capt. Robert George's order at Camp Jefferson, to Capt. George's men going to the Falls of Ohio, two lbs powder (VSA-50).

06/14/80 Capt. Robt. George requests of John Dodge to issue Wm. Shannon three yds of the best ribbon by order of Col. Clark. Wm. Shannon signed that he received the above (VSA-11a) (VSA-48).

06/14/80 Capt. Robert George requests that 3 1/4 lbs powder and 1 1/2 lbs lead be delivered for the use of the Ft. Jefferson garrison by order of Col. Clark (VSA- 11).

06/14/80 Capt. Robert George requests of j. Dodge to deliver to the bearer: two shirts, one blanket, and one hat for his use on expedition to the Falls of Ohio (VSA-11a).

06/15/80 Issued 2 1/8 yds superfine grey cloth 7/4 wide and four yds brown cloth 7/4 wide, 1/4 yd overdrawn, taken from list of sundry articles taken out of the public store for which no return or receipt has been passed (VSA-48).

06/15/80 For sundry merchandise drawn out of the public store more than his quota for which in part no returns or receipts have been issued or passed: 1/4 yd superfine broad cloth 7/4 wide, 1 1/8 yds chintz, 2 1/2 yds shalloon, 1 3/4 yds linen, one pair scissors, six skeins fine white tread, six skeins coarse white thread, one snaffle bridle, one ruffled shirts, 3 1/2 yds osnaburgs, one skein thread, two metal buttons (VSA-48).

06/16/80 Issued 2 1/2 yds white flannel, 2 1/2 yds osnaburgs one pair scissors, eight skeins twine, two needles, per order Capt. George and receipt of Daniel Bolton to make cartridges for the cannon (VSA-48).

06/16/80 Capt. Robt. George requests of J. Dodge to deliver to M. Carney the following by orders of Col. Clark, one brass ink stand, one clasp knife, one small and one large tooth comb, six yds ferretting (VSA-11a).

06/16/80 Capt. Robt. George requests of J. Dodge to deliver the following for use of the artillery, 2 1/2 yds flannel, twien, 2 1/2 yds osnaburg, one pair scissors, and two needles (VSA-11a).

06/16/80 Daniel Bolton delivered munition supplies to Lawrence Keinan in Capt. George's Co. (VSA-11).

06/18/80 Anthony Montroy enlisted for three years or during the war into Capt. Robt. George's Company of Artillery by Lt. V.T. Dalton (MHS: B1, F23).

06/19/80 Capt. Robt. George requests of John Dodge to issue two shirts each for the 23 men of his Artillery Co. by orders of Col. Clark (VSA-11a).

06/19/80 Capt. George signs that the men are enlisted during the war except one who had one year to serve: Joseph Anderson, John Smothers, Richard Hopkins, Matthew Jones, James McDaniel, Charles Bush, John Ash, Isaac Pruit, Ceasar, George Venshiner, Thomas Win, John Hacker, Richard Turpin Matthew Murray, Lazarus Kening, Peter Wagoner, Andrew Clark, Daniel

Fort Jefferson Personnel

Bolton, Francis Little, John Bryan, William Fever, John Dorrely, and William Posten (VSA-11b).
06/19/80 Twenty-three ruffled shirts and 23 plain shirts per order issued to Capt. George no receipt (VSA-48).
06/20/80 List of goods issued by Capt. Robert George's orders as per Mr. Z. Blackford's receipt on said orders (VSA-48).
06/20/80 Four yds flannel per order Capt. George and receipt of Mary Smith for making one suit of soldiers clothes (VSA-48).
06/20/80 One pair damask 5 1/8 yds, one pair flowered lawn 13 yds, five ells ribbon, one dozen check linen handkerchiefs, one piece chintz no. 12, one piece chintz no. six, one piece chintz no. ten issued to Zeph. Blackford by order Capt. George to purchase provisions and disposed of agreeable to the return made for 187 hard dollars (VSA-48).
06/20/80 Account of arms delivered by Martin Carney to Capt. George's Company of Artillery of the Illinois Virginia Regiment, delivered to Capt. George at Camp Jefferson, one rifle gun and one musket (VSA-50) (VSA-11).
06/20/80 Capt. Robt. George writes to John Dodge by Col. CLark's orders to ask him to deliver to Mr. Blackford 187 hard dollars worth of bread and such goods for the use of Kaskaskia and its neighborhood (VSA-11a).
06/20/80 Three ruffled and three plain shirts per order Capt. George and receipt Reuben Kemp, issued for Capt. Worthington's Company (VSA-48).
06/20/80 Account of tobacco delivered by Martin Carney by order of Capt. George at this place, to Mr. Donne, Commissary, one carot weighing three lbs (VSA-50).
06/20/80 Capt. Robt. George requests of John Dodge to issue two shirts each to Joseph Thornton, John Sword, and Zachariah Williams of Capt. Worthington's Co. by order of Col. Clark (VSA-11a) (VSA-48).
06/20/80 Capt. Robt. George requests of John Dodge to deliver to Mr. Donne, one leather ink pot and one fine and one course comb for the use of Co. Dept. by Clark's orders (VSA-11a) (VSA-48).
06/20/80 Capt. Robt. George requests of John Dodge to issue Mr. Blackford [Commissary], linen for three shirts, stuff for three summer jackets and trousers, two pocket handkerchiefs with thread to make them, one ink pot, and stuff for three stocks by order of Col. Clark (VSA-11a).
06/20/80 Capt. Robt. George asks of John Dodge to issue Zephaniah Blackford with trimmings for three jackets by order of Col. Clark (VSA-11a).
06/20/80 Capt. Robert George requests of John Dodge to pay Mrs. Smith 12 shillings and six pence, for making a suit of soldiers clothes for Jacob Wheat, by order of Col. Clark (VSA-11a).
06/20/80 Capt. Robt. George requests of John Dodge to pay John Bryan 15 pounds four shillings, and six pence in goods for making clothing for Capt. George's Co. (VSA-11a).
06/21/80 One pair chintz no. 23, 6 3/4 yds white linen, one paper pins, two silk handkerchiefs, 1 1/2 yds ribbon per order of Capt. George and receipt of John Bryan for making up soldiers clothing (VSA-48).
06/21/80 Account of ammunition delivered by Martin Carney by Capt. Robert George's order at Camp Jefferson, to Mr. Donne, commissary, one lb powder and two lbs lead; to Lt. Thomas Wilson, two lbs powder and four lbs lead; to Capt. George for the troops at Camp Jefferson, 2 1/4 lbs powder and 4 1/2 lbs lead; to Indians going to Kaskaskia, one lb powder, two lbs lead, and six flints (VSA-50).
06/21/80 Capt. Robert George requests of Martin Carney to issue Mr. Donne one carot of tobacco and charge him the cusomary price of others in public service (VSA-11a).
06/22/80 Capt. Robert George requests of John Dodge by order of Col. Clark, to issue Andrew Clark truck [credit] for two pairs of trousers, check handkerchief, small and large tooth comb (VSA-11).
06/23/80 Four ruffled shirts per order for soldiers going for provisions drawn out of the public store more than George's quota for which in part no returns or receipts have been issued or passed (VSA-48).
06/23/80 Account of ammunition delivered by Martin Carney by Capt. Robert George's order at Camp Jefferson, to Capt. George for the troops at this

Fort Jefferson Personnel

	place, 3/4 lb powder and 1 1/2 lbs lead; to Sgt. Anderson, 1/2 lb lead and one flint (VSA-50).
06/23/80	Fifteen plain and one ruffled shirt per order Capt. George and receipt of Reuben Kemp issued for Reuben Kemp, Daniel Williams, Richard Bredin, Charles Evans, Andrew Johnston, Isaac Yates, and Williams Nelson of Capt. Worthington's Company (VSA-11) (VSA-48).
06/23/80	Capt. Robert George requests of John Dodge by Col. Clark's orders to issue a brass ink stand to Sgt. Anderson (VSA-11).
06/23/80	Account of ammunition delivered by Martin Carney by Capt. Robert George's order at Camp Jefferson, to Sgt. Anderson for use of the garrison, 4 1/2 lbs powder, nine lbs lead, and eight flints (VSA-50).
06/23/80	William Robeson is issued two shirts at FJ from John Dodge per Capt. George's orders; member of Worthington's Company (VSA-11).
06/29/80	Capt. Robert George requests of John Dodge by Col. Clark's orders to issue eight shirts to James Thompson, Joseph Panther, John Shank, and Jacob Decker of Capt. Kellar's Co. (VSA-11).
06/29/80	Account of ammunition delivered by Martin Carney by Capt. Robert George's order at Camp Jefferson, to Daniel Bolton, Gunner, 15 lbs powder (VSA-50).
06/30/80	Eight plain shirts listed per order of Capt. George and receipt of James Thompson (VSA-48).
06/30/80	Account of ammunition delivered by Martin Carney by Capt. Robert George's order at Camp Jefferson, to Lt. Wilson for a party of men going hunting; to Michael Hacketon a soldier in Capt. George's Command, one lb lead; to Sgt. Anderson for the use of the garrison, 4 1/2 lbs powder, nine lbs lead, and eight flints (VSA-50).
06/30/80	Five yds cottonade per self drawn out of the public store more than George's quota of which in part no returns or receipts have been issued or passed (VSA-48).
06/30/80	Account of ammunition delivered by Martin Carney by order of Capt. Robert George at Camp Jefferson, to Sgt. Anderson, 1/2 lb lead and one flint (VSA-50).
07/03/80	Fifteen skeins thread issued by order of George per Pattrick Kennedy's receipt (VSA-48).
07/03/80	Issued 16 1/4 yds white linen, 3 1/4 yds check linen, per order Capt. George and receipt of Joseph Duncan, Samual Watkins, and John Cox for bringing provisions (VSA-48).
07/03/80	Account of ammunition delivered by Martin Carney by Capt. Robert George's order at Camp Jefferson, to Mr. Kennedy, Conductor, one lb powder and two lbs lead (VSA-50).
07/03/80	Capt. Robt. George requests of John Dodge to issue two pairs of leggings of half-thicks to Sgt. Anderson and Michael Hacketon of his Co. going on command by Col. Clark's orders (VSA-12a).
07/03/80	Capt. Robert George requests of Martin Carney to issue Pat Kennedy, Joseph Duncan, Samuel Watkins, and John Cox, one lb powder and two lbs ball [lead] for their return trip to Illinois (VSA-12) (VSA- 50).
07/03/80	List of goods issued to Patrick Kennedy by order of Capt. Robert George per Kennedy's receipt on said orders (VSa-48).
07/05/80	Sundry articles taken out of the public store for which no return or receipt has been passed: 1/8 yd scarlet cloth 7/4 wide, for six vests and six breeches four yds white casimir fine, 3 3/4 yds sycee, and 8 3/4 yds chintz, 21 yds fine white linen for six shirts, 3/4 yd fine holland for ruffling shirts, two yds holland for six stocks, three silk handkerchiefs, three red silk and cotton handkerchiefs, 2 1/2 yds white linen for lining, 2 1/2 yds shalloon for lining, 5 7/12 dozen metal buttons, 2/12 dozen overdrawn, five skeins silk, two skeins silk twist, 12 skeins fine white thread and 12 skeins coarse thread a skein of each overdrawn (VSA-48).
07/05/80	Account of ammunition delivered by Martin Carney by Capt. Robert George's order at Camp Jefferson, to the militia at this place, 1 3/4 lbs powder and 3 1/2 lbs lead and 46 flints (VSA-50).

Fort Jefferson Personnel

07/08/80 Account of ammunition delivered by Martin Carney by Capt. Robert George's order at Camp Jefferson, to Lt. Wilson going on command, 1 1/4 lbs powder and 2 1/2 lbs lead [only issue for powder in (VSA-12)] (VSA-50).

07/10/80 Capt. Rogers and Capt. George sign request of John Dodge to issue 62 shirts and black stuff for as many stocks and thread or silk to make up the stocks for 31 men (VSA-12).

07/10/80 Capt. George requests by order of Col. Clark, that John Dodge issue Capt. Kellar his quota of clothing allowed by law [passed in 1779] (VSA-12).

07/10/80 Capt. George requests by order of Col. Clark, that John Dodge issue to Capt. John Rogers and his two officers their full quota of clothing which they are entitled to by law passed in June, 1779 (VSA- 12).

07/10/80 Capt. Robert George requests by order of Col. Clark, that John Dodge issue Capt. John Bailey and Ensign Slaughter their full quota of clothing which they are entitled to by law (VSA-12).

07/10/80 James Mulboy and Joseph Lonion enlisted for three years or during the war by Lt. V.T. Dalton into Capt. Robert George's Company of Artillery. They were not on the payroll because Dalton failed to give account of what had become of them or when or how their time expired (MHS: B1, F23).

07/11/80 Lt. Girault issued clothing to which he is entitled by law agreeable to Col. Clark's orders at FJ from Capt. John Dodge per Capt. George's orders (VSA- 12).

07/11/80 Capt. George requests of John Dodge that Capt. Richard Brashears be issued his full quota of clothing which he is entitled to by law agreeable to Col. Clark's orders at FJ (VSA-12).

07/11/80 Capt. George requests of John Dodge that Major McCarty be issued the clothing he is entitled to by law by order of Col. Clark at FJ (VSA-12).

07/11/80 Capt. George requests of John Dodge that Lt. Girault be issued the clothing which he is entitled to by law by order of Col. Clark at FJ (VSA-12).

07/11/80 Capt. George requests of John Dodge that Col. John Montgomery be issued the clothing which he is entitled to by law by order of Col. Clark at FJ (VSA-12).

07/11/80 Capt. Abraham Kellar issued one comb, one inkstand, and one scalping knife at Camp Jefferson by order of Col. Clark, from Capt. John Dodge per Capt. George's orders (VSA-12).

07/11/80 Mr. Frederick Guion issued one ink holder for use of the Commissary Department at FJ from Capt. John Dodge by order of Col. Rogers per Capt. George's order (VSA-12) (VSA-48).

07/12/80 Account of ammunition delivered by Martin Carney by Capt. Robert George's order at Camp Jefferson, to Capt. Abraham Kellar going to Cahokia, 1/2 lb powder and one lb lead (VSA-50).

07/12/80 Capt. George requests of John Dodge by order of Col. Clark that Joseph Momeral, Louis Lepaint, James Brown, and Jacke Rubedo, four soldiers of Capt. Williams' Company be issued cloth and trimmings for a complete suit of clothes each, also two shirts each, they being entitled to the same by law having more than one year to serve (VSA-12).

07/12/80 Capt. Robert George requests of John Dodge by order of Col. Clark, that full clothing be issued for three men enlisted during the war, who have never received any part thereof. Also for one man enlisted for one year. The men were recruited by Lt. Col. Montgomery and names are as follows: William Buchanan, Robert Whitehead, William Whitehead, John Roberts. Roberts enlisted for one year and the others during the war (VSA-12a).

07/12/80 Capt. Robert George requests of John Dodge by order of Col. Clark, that Deputy Conductor John Donne be issued the same allowance of clothing as to the officers of the line (VSA-12).

07/12/80 Robert George requests of John Dodge by order of Col. Clark, that full clothing be issued for James Curry, William Elms, James Morris, William

Fort Jefferson Personnel

Bartholomew, James Dawson, James Elms and John Elms of Capt. Brashears' Company which the law allows (VSA-12).

07/12/80 Capt. Robert George requests of John Dodge, by order of Col. Clark, that Ensign Slaughter be given 44 shirts for 22 men of Capt. John Bailey's Co., which are enlisted during the present war (VSA-12).

07/12/80 Capt. Robert George requests of John Dodge, by order of Col. Clark, that Frederick Guion, a Sergeant enlisted during the war in George's Company of Artillery be issued full clothing and scarlet cloth sufficient to face his coat (VSA-12).

07/12/80 Capt. Robert George requests that four enlisted men be issued to serve all during the war full clothing by Lt. Girault. The four men being: Francis Villier, Charles M. Laughlin, John LaRichardy, Francis Bennoit. Lt. Girault certifies that the men are all enlisted during the war (VSA-12).

07/12/80 John Rogers and Robert George sign request of M. Carney that four men of Capt. Rogers' Company be issued one lb powder and one lb lead (VSA-12).

07/12/80 Capt. Robert George requests of John Dodge by order of Col. Clark, that Ensign Jarrett Williams be issued his full quota of clothing which he is entitled to by law (VSA-12).

07/12/80 Capt. R. George requests of M. Carney that Capt. Kellar be issued one lb of powder and one lb of lead at FJ for his own use (VSA-12).

07/12/80 Capt. Robert George requests of Capt. Dodge by order of Col. Clark, that Wm. Clark be issued one hat (VSA-12).

07/12/80 Capt. Robert George requests of John Dodge, by order of Col. Clark, that 36 shirts be issued for 18 men which they are netitled to by law (VSA-12).

07/13/80 Participant in court proceedings at Ft. Jefferson. Brought case against John Dodge for speaking disrespectful against Capt. George and making other accusations (DMS 56J22-24).

07/13/80 Capt. Robert George requests of John Dodge to issue Major John Williams his full quota of clothing which he is entitled to by law and agreeable to Col. Clark's order (VSA-12).

07/14/80 Account of ammunition delivered by Martin Carney by Capt. Robert George's order at Camp Jefferson, to Capt. John Rogers going to Cahokia, one lb powder and one lb lead (VSA-50).

07/14/80 Capt. R. George requests of John Dodge by order of Col. Clark, that Frederick Guion be issued one coarse and one fine comb at FJ (VSA-12a).

07/14/80 Capt. Robert George requests of John dodge by order of Col. Clark, that Richard Sennet, Peter Freeman, James Ballenger, and Jacob Huffman be issued one shirt each or linen to make the same with thread. In payment of services performed when going to Kaskaskia for provisions for the troops (VSA-12a).

07/15/80 Account of arms delivered by Martin Carney to Capt. George's Company of Artillery of the Illinois Virginia Regiment, delivered to Sgt. Anderson, five muskets and five carabins (VSA-50).

07/15/80 Account of ammunition delivered by Martin Carney by Capt. Robert George's order at Camp Jefferson, to Martin Carney, Quartermaster, in given lue of meat, one lb powder (VSA-50).

07/16/80 A list of goods was issued to James Sherlock, Indian and French Interpreter by order of Capt. Robert George, Commandant (VSA-48).

07/17/80 Account of ammunition delivered by Martin Carney by Capt. Robert George's order at Camp Jefferson, to Sgt. Anderson for the defense of this place, 22 lbs powder and 104 lbs lead (VSA-50).

07/21/80 Account of tobacco delivered by Martin Carney by order of Capt. George at this place, to Lawrence Keinan by Capt. George's order, 2/3 carot of tobacco weighing two lbs (VSA-50).

07/25/80 Account of tobacco delivered by Martin Carney by order of Capt. George at this place, to Thorntons, a soldier in Capt. Worthington's Co. by Capt. George's order, 1/3 carot of tobacco weighing one lb (VSA-50).

07/28/80 Account of tobacco delivered by Martin Carney by order of Capt. George at this place, to Sgt. Anderson in Capt. George's Company, three carots

Fort Jefferson Personnel

	weighing nine lbs; to Sgt. Mains in Capt. Worthington's Company, two carots weighing six lbs; to Mr. Clark, Secretary to Col. Clark, one carot and three lbs; to Andrew Clark, Artificer, 1/2 carot weighing 1 1/2 lbs (VSA-50).
07/29/80	Account of ammunition delivered by Martin Carney by Capt. Robert George's order at Camp Jefferson, to one of the militia soldiers at this place, 1/2 lb powder and one lb lead (VSA-50).
08/01/80	Account of ammunition delivered by Martin Carney by Capt. Robert George's order at Camp Jefferson to Frances Little a soldier at this place, 1/2 lb powder and one lb lead; to Sgt. Vaughan of Capt. Bailey's Company, seven lbs powder and 14 lbs lead; to James Sherlock, Interpreter for the Kaskaskia Indians, ten lbs powder and 20 lbs lead; to Mr. Jacob Pyatte on his way to the Falls of Ohio, 1/2 lb powder and one lb lead (VSA-50).
08/02/80	Fourteen plain shirts issued for Capt. Worthington's Company by order Capt. George and issued to Lt. Clark (VSA-48).
08/03/80	Account of ammunition delivered by Martin Carney by Capt. George's order, to Sgt. Anderson for the use of some of the soldiers, one lb powder and two lbs lead (VSA-50).
08/03/80	Account of tobacco delivered by Martin Carney by order of Capt. George at this place, to Sgt. Anderson, 1 1/2 carots weighing 4 1/2 lbs; to Mr. Sherlock, Interpretar to the Indians, two carots weighing six lbs; to Sgt. Elms for Capt. Brashears' Company, one carot and three lbs; to Mr. Sherlock, Interpretar to the Kaskaskia Indians, one carot and three lbs (VSA-50).
08/04/80	Account of tobacco delivered by Martin Carney by Capt. George's order at this place, to Mathew Murray, a soldier in Capt. Abraham Kellar's Company, 1/2 carot weighing 1 1/2 lbs (VSA-50).
08/05/80	Account of tobacco delivered by Martin Carney by Capt. George's order at this place, to Sgt. Vaughan of Capt. Bailey's Company, 3 1/3 carots weighing ten lbs; to Frances Little for taking care of the state boats, one carot and three lbs (VSA-50).
08/08/80	Account of tobacco delivered by Martin Carney by Capt. George's order at this place, to Martin Carney, Quartermaster for his own use, one carot weighing three lbs; to Capt. Leonard Helms, for his own use, one carot weighing three lbs (VSA-50).
08/09/80	Three yds white flannel per order Capt. George and receipt Lawrence Keinan for making cannon cartridges (VSA-48).
08/09/80	Account of ammunition delivered by Martin Carney by Capt. George's order, to Capt. George Owens' Company of Militia, 11 1/2 lbs powder and 46 lbs lead (VSA-50).
08/12/80	Two plain shirts for David Allen per Lt. Clark's receipt and Capt. George's order issued for Capt. Worthington's Company (VSA-48).
08/12/80	Four plain shirts per order and receipt of Capt. George (VSA-48).
08/14/80	Account of ammunition delivered by Martin Carney by Capt. George's order to Sgt. Anderson for a hunter at this place, 1/2 lb powder and one lb lead; to Lawrence Keinan, Gunner at this place, 13 1/2 lbs powder and 2 1/2 yds flannel (VSA-50).
08/14/80	Stores issued by order of Capt. Robert George to the Indians, three tomahawks (VSA-50).
08/16/80	Account of ammunition delivered by Martin Carney by Capt. George's order to Lt. Richard Clark, 1/2 lb powder, one lb lead, and one flint (VSA-50).
08/17/80	Account of arms delivered by Martin Carney to Capt. George's Company of Artillery of the Illinois Virginia Regiment, delivered to Sgt. Anderson for Sailor Worthington, one rifle gun (VSA-50).
08/17/80	Account of ammunition delivered by Martin Carney by Capt. George's order to Lt. Richard Clark for a man of Capt. Worthington's 1/4 lb powder and 1/2 lb lead (VSA-50).
08/19/80	Twenty-one yds blue cloth, 18 yds white flannel, and thread and buttons per order and receipt of R. George (VSA-48).

Fort Jefferson Personnel

08/21/80 Account of ammunition delivered by Martin Carney by Capt. George's order, to Capt. Leonard Helm for his own use, 1/2 lb powder and one lb lead; to a French man in Capt. George's Company, 1/4 lb powder (VSA-50).

08/21/80 Account of arms delivered by Martin Carney by order of Capt. Robert George, to individuals, to Capt. Leonard Helm for his use, one rifle; to Lt. Richard Clark, for his use, one rifle (VSA-50).

08/24/80 Account of ammunition delivered by Martin Carney by Capt. George's order, to a man of Capt. Bailey's company, 1/4 lb powder and 1/2 lb lead; to a soldier of Capt. George's Company, 1/4 lb powder and 1/2 lb lead (VSA-50).

08/24/80 Account of tobacco delivered by Martin Carney by order of Capt. George at this place, to Sgt. Reuben Kemp of Worthington's Company, one carot weighing three lbs; to Thornton, a soldier in Capt. Worthington's Company, one carot weighing three lbs; to Lt. Richard Clark, for his own use, one carot weighing three lbs (VSA-50).

08/26/80 Account of ammunition delivered by Martin Carney by Capt. George's order, to Thomas Leny Gunner at the blockhouse, one lb powder and two lbs lead (VSA-50).

08/26/80 Account of tobacco delivered by Martin Carney by order of Capt. George at this place, to Sgt. Joseph Anderson for his own use, 1/2 carot weighing 1 1/2 lbs (VSA-50).

08/27/80 Account of ammunition delivered by Martin Carney by Capt. George's order, to the soldiery and inhabitants at this place, 22 lbs powder and 44 lbs lead; to the artillery men at this place, 25 lbs powder and 50 lbs lead (VSA-50).

08/28/80 Account of tobacco delivered by Martin Carney by order of Capt. George at this place, to Mr. Sherlock, Interpreter for Indians, one carot and three lbs (VSA-50).

09/01/80 Account of tobacco delivered by Martin Carney by order of Capt. George at this place, to John Grimshaw, Gunner, 1/2 carot weighing 1 1/2 lbs (VSA-50).

09/02/80 Ten yds white linen and two linen handkerchiefs per order R. George paid for transporting provisions from Illinois per receipt of M. Carney (VSA-48).

09/02/80 Account of tobacco delivered by Martin Carney by order of Capt. George at this place, to Richard Hopkins for corking and paying public boats, two carots weighing six lbs (VSA-50).

09/02/80 Capt. Robert George writes a letter to Lt. Col. John Montgomery "commanding at Illiniois" about details of Indian attack on Ft. Jefferson, on the 27th of August. George describes low morale of men after destruction of corn crop by Indians and George requests additional men and supplies; expresses his fear that men might evacuate the fort (Seineke 1981: 457-459).

09/03/80 Account of tobacco delivered by Martin Carney by order of Sgt. Vaughan for Capt. Bailey's Company, five carots weighing 16 lbs (VSA-50).

09/03/80 Account of tobacco delivered by Martin Carney by order of Capt. George at Fort Jefferson, to Sgt. Anderson for Capt. George's Company, 5 1/2 carots weighing 16 lbs (VSA-50).

09/06/80 Account of ammunition delivered by Martin Carney by Capt. George's order, to John Dodge agent for Indians, five lbs powder and ten lbs lead; also to John Dodge, for a French boat going to Pencore, 20 lbs lead (VSA-50).

09/08/80 Account of tobacco delivered by Martin Carney by order of Capt. George at Fort Jefferson, to Capt. John Dodge for Indians, by Col. Montgomery's order, two carots weighing six lbs (VSA-50).

09/08/80 Account of sugar delivered by Martin Carney by order of Col. Montgomery at Fort Jefferson, to two men in Capt. George's Company, four lbs (VSA-50).

09/09/80 Account of sugar delivered by Martin Carney by order of Col. Montgomery at Fort Jefferson, to Matthew Jones, a soldier in Capt. George's Company, two lbs; to John Bryan of Capt. George's Company, three lbs (VSA-50).

Fort Jefferson Personnel

09/09/80 Account of soap delivered by Martin Carney by order of Col. Montgomery and Capt. George at Fort Jefferson, to Fredrick Guion, two lbs (VSA-50).

09/10/80 Issued one barrel of tafia, one case of sugar, one case of soap, one fish seine, one large cross-cut saw, 166 lb bull and what other articles in John Dodge's Quartermaster, to the troops in garrison at FJ (VSA-13a).

09/11/80 Present at FJ (VSA-13a).

09/11/80 Account of ammunition delivered by Martin Carney by Col. Montgomery's orders to one man of Capt. George's Company, 1/2 lbs powder, one lb lead (VSA-50).

09/11/80 Account of soap delivered by Martin Carney by order of Col. Montgomery and Capt. George at Fort Jefferson, to Zephaniah Blackford, one lb; to Ensign Slaughter, two lbs (VSA-50).

09/12/80 Account of sugar delivered by Martin Carney by order of Col. Montgomery at Fort Jefferson, to John Smithers in Capt. George's Company, one lb (VSA-50).

09/13/80 Account of sugar delivered by Martin Carney by order of Capt. George at Fort Jefferson, to Sgt. Anderson of Capt. George's Company, two lbs; to Phelps of Militia, six lbs (VSA-50).

09/13/80 Account of soap delivered by Martin Carney by order of Col. Montgomery and Capt. George at Fort Jefferson, to Capt. Bailey's Company, 12 lbs; to Capt. Robert George's Company, 16 lbs; to Capt. Edward Worthington's Company, 9 1/2 lbs; to Capt. Brashears' Company, 8 1/2 lbs; to Mr. Donne, Commissary, three lbs; to Capt. McCarty's Company, 15 lbs; to Lt. Williams for his use, one lb; to Capt. Brashears and Doctor Ray, one lb (VSA-50).

09/13/80 Issued one, 2 1/2 point blanket per order and receipt, part of sundry merchandise drawn out of the public store more than George's quota for which in part no returns or receipts have been issued or passed also listed were, ten shirts for your company per order, ten shirts plain per order, 11 2 1/2 point blankets per order (VSA-48).

09/13/80 Account of sugar delivered by Martin Carney by order of Col. Montgomery at Fort Jefferson, to Frank Little of Capt. George's Company, two lbs (VSA-50).

09/13/80 Capt. Robert George is listed as one officer of the mess who received a share of 60 lbs of sugar (VSA-13b).

09/13/80 Robert George requests an issue of one blanket for his own use (VSA-13a).

09/13/80 Robert George signs that he received one blanket from John Dodge (VSA-13b).

09/14/80 Account of sugar delivered by Martin Carney by order of Capt. George a Fort Jefferson, to James Thomson, a soldier in Capt. Kellar's Company, one lb; to two sick soldiers in Capt. Kellar's Company, two lbs; to Joseph Hunter of militia, three lbs (VSA-50).

09/14/80 Robert George requests M. Carney to issue two lbs sugar to James Brown and Sam Allen who are sick (VSA-13).

09/14/80 Robert George requests an issue of two lbs sugar to Francis Little, being sick (VSA-13).

09/14/80 Robert George requests the Quartermaster to issue two lbs sugar to Mr. Burks from the public store. Robert George signs as "commd." (VSA-13).

09/14/80 Robert George signs Owens' request for six lbs of sugar for sick family of George Phelps (VSA-13).

09/15/80 Eight yds white flannel per order for sundry merchandise drawn out of the public store more than George's quota for which in part no returns or receipts have been issued or passed (VSA-48).

09/15/80 Account of ammunition delivered by Martin Carney by Capt. George's order, to Capt. Bailey's Company, 5 1/2 lbs powder and 11 lbs lead; to John Hazard of Artillery, 1/4 lb powder, 1/2 lb lead, and two flints; to two men of Capt. McCarty's Company, one lb powder and two lbs lead; to the artillery at this place, 16 lbs powder, 32 lbs lead and six yds of flannel (VSA-50).

Fort Jefferson Personnel

09/15/80 Account of sugar delivered by Martin Carney by order of Capt. George at Fort Jefferson, to John Hazard of Capt. George's Company, one lb; to William Creton of militia, one lb; to Paul Quivis of Capt. George's Company, one lb; to William McCauly of militia, one lb; to John Johnston of militia, one lb; to Jacob Ditterin of Artillery, one lb; to John Reed of militia, one lb; to Zacharaih Williams, soldier in Worthington's Company, one lb; to John Grimshaw and Mr. Mullens of George's Company, two lbs; to Edward Murray, a soldier in Capt. Bailey's Company, two lbs (VSA-50).

09/15/80 Robert George requests of M. Carney to issue three lbs of sugar to Joseph Hunter. Robert George calls Ft. Jefferson "Clarks vale" (VSA-13).

09/15/80 Robert George requests of the Quartermaster to issue one lb of sugar to sick Jacob Ditterin (VSA-13).

09/15/80 Robert George requests of John Dodge to pay Francis Bredin for clothes making out of the public store (VSA-13a).

09/15/80 Robert George requests of the Quartermaster to issue one lb of sugar to John Hazzard (VSA-13).

09/15/80 Robert George requests [Quartermaster?] to issue one lb sugar to Billy [?] who is sick (VSA-13).

09/15/80 Robert George requests of the Quartermaster to issue two lbs of sugar to Edward Murray and John Clark (VSA-13a).

09/15/80 Robert George signs a request by George Owens for issue of one lb sugar for William Creton (VSA-13).

09/15/80 Robert George signs return written by John Bailey for five lbs powder and [thirty?]-two lbs lead for use of ten men of Bailey's Company (VSA-13a).

09/15/80 Robert George signs request by John Bailey for five lbs powder and eleven lbs lead for use of Bailey's Company (VSA-13b).

09/15/80 Robert George signs a request for the Quartermaster to issue one lb sugar to John Johnston, Paul Quibea, and John Reid for being sick (VSA-13a).

09/16/80 Account of sugar delivered by Martin Carney by order of Capt. George at Fort Jefferson, to Andrew Clark, Artificer at public work, two lbs; to Joseph Panther a soldier in Capt. Kellar's Company, one lb; to Petter Helebrand, a militia man, two lbs; to four men of Capt. John Bailey's Company, two lbs (VSA-50).

09/16/80 Account of soap delivered by Martin Carney by order of Col. Montgomery and Capt. George at Fort Jefferson, to Mr. William Clark, one lb; to Capt. Abraham Kellar's Company, six lbs; to Mr. Lt. Richard Clark, two lbs (VSA-50).

09/16/80 Robert George signs Abram Kellar's request for six lbs soap for twelve men of Kellar's Company (VSA-13a).

09/16/80 Robert George requests of Quartermaster M. Carney to issue one lb soap to Mr. William Clark (VSA-13).

09/16/80 Robert George signs J. Bailey's request to Quartermaster to issue two lbs sugar to four sick men of J. Bailey's Company (VSA-13a).

09/16/80 Robert George signs A. Kellar requests of Quartermaster M. Carney to issue one lb sugar to J. Panther a sick soldier of Kellar's Co. (VSA-13).

09/16/80 Robert George signs G. Owens' request for M. Carney to issue two lbs sugar to P. Hellebrant for sickness (VSA-13).

09/16/80 Robert George requests of Quartermaster to issue 16 lbs powder, 32 lbs lead, and six yds flannel for cartridge manufacture to the "artillery at post" (VSA-13a).

09/16/80 Robert George requests the Quartermaster to issue two lbs sugar to Andrew Clark, Artificer (VSA-13).

09/18/80 Account of sugar delivered by Martin Carney by order of Capt. George at Fort Jefferson, to Andrew Johnston of Worthington's Company, one lb; to five men of Capt. Brashears' Company, five lbs (VSA-50).

09/18/80 Robert George signs Lt. Richard Clark's request for one lb sugar issue to Andrew Johnson of Worhtinton's Company, for sickness (VSA-13a).

Fort Jefferson Personnel

09/18/80 Robert George requests M. Carney to issue five lbs sugar to five sick men of Capt. Brashears' Company (VSA-13).

09/19/80 1/4 yd white cloth per order part of list of sundry merchandise drawn out of the public store more than George's quota for which in part no returns or receipts have been issued or passed (VSA-48).

09/19/80 Account of tobacco delivered by Martin Carney by order of Capt. George at Fort Jefferson, to Capt. George for his own use, three carots weighing nine lbs (VSA-50).

09/19/80 Account of sugar delivered by Martin Carney by order of Capt. George at Fort Jefferson, to Mr. Donne, Commissary, for his family, four lbs; to James Thomson, a soldier in Capt. Kellar's Company, one lb; to Matthew Jones of Capt. George's Company, one lb; to John Daughterty of Capt. George's Company, two lbs; to Bredin of Worthington's Company, two lbs; to Helms a soldier, two lbs; to Edward Johnston, a soldier in Worthington's Company, one lb; to William Crump a soldier in Worthington's Company, two lbs (VSA-50).

09/19/80 George requests of the Quartermaster to issue two lbs sugar to Bredin and family "a soldier in Capt. Worthinton's Company being sick" (VSA-13).

09/19/80 George requests of the Quartermaster to issue two lbs sugar to Edward Johnson of Worthington's Company (VSA-13).

09/19/80 George requests of the Quartermaster to issue two lbs sugar to William Crump of Worthington's Company out of the public store (VSA-13).

09/19/80 Robert George requests of the Quartermaster to issue two lbs sugar to Mrs. Elms and sick children (VSA-13a).

09/19/80 Robert George requests Quartermaster issue two lbs sugar to John Daughterty and his two sick children (VSA-13a).

09/19/80 Robert George requests of the Quartermaster to issue three carots tobacco for his own use out of the public store (VSA-13a).

09/19/80 Robert George requests of the Quartermaster to issue one lb sugar to Matthew Jones for sick family (VSA-13a).

09/19/80 Robert George requests of John Dodge, by order of Col. Clark, to issue 1/4 yd white cloth to John Vaughan to face a jacket (VSA-13a).

09/19/80-04/07/81 Sometime between these dates, tobacco is issued to sundry persons per order of Capt. George, Commandant: to William Clark, Secretary, three lbs; to Martin Carney, two lbs; to Leonard Helm, ten lbs; to Edward Worthington, 3 1/2 lbs; to John Girault, two lbs; to James Finn, three lbs; to Philip Barbour, four lbs; and to John Harris, Armourer, two lbs (VSA-50: 13).

09/22/80 Seven yds linen per order and two skeins thread per order for sundry merchandise drawn out of the public store more than George's quota for which in part no returns or receipts have been issued or passed (VSA-48).

09/22/80 Robert George requests, by order of Col. Clark, of John Dodge [or his agent] to issue seven yds of linen and two skeins of thread to Silas Harlan (VSA-13a).

09/23/80 Robert George requests an issue of one lb sugar to Francis Little for sickness (VSA-13a).

09/23/80 Account of sugar delivered by Martin Carney by order of Capt. George at Fort Jefferson, to Frances Little of Capt. George's Company, one lb (VSA-50).

09/24/80 Issued 5/8 yd blue cloth per order for sundry merchandise drawn out of the public store more than George's quota for which in part no returns or receipts have been given or passed (VSA-48).

09/24/80 Robert George, by order of Col. Clark, requests John Dodge to issue 5/8 yd blue cloth to Silas Harlan for leggings (VSA-13a).

09/25/80 Five skeins thread per order for sundry merchandise drawn out of the public store more than George's quota for which in part no returns or receipts have been issued or passed (VSA-48).

09/25/80 Account of soap delivered by Martin Carney by order of Col. Montgomery and Capt. George at Fort Jefferson, to Sgt. Moore of Capt. George's Company, 7 1/2 lbs (VSA-50).

Fort Jefferson Personnel

09/26/80 Account of ammunition delivered by Martin Carney by Capt. George's order, to Sgt. Anderson of Capt. George's Company, one lb powder and two lbs lead; to two men of Capt. Bailey's company, one lbs powder and two lbs lead (VSA-50).

09/26/80 Robert George requests the Quartermaster to issue one lb powder and two lbs lead to Sgt. Anderson (VSA-13a).

09/26/80 Robert George signs J. Bailey's request for one lb powder, two lbs lead to issue to two men of Bailey's Company "from the Illinois" (VSA-13a).

09/27/80 Account of ammunition delivered by Martin Carney by Capt. George's order, to two men of Capt. Brashears' Company, one lb powder and two lbs lead; to a man of Capt. George's company, 1/4 lb powder and 1/2 lb lead (VSA-50).

09/27/80 Account of sugar delivered by Martin Carney by order of Capt. George at Fort Jefferson, to two men of Capt. John Bailey's Company, one lb (VSA-50).

09/27/80 Lt. Richard Clark requests [George signs] 1/2 lb sugar issue to R. Underwood, a sick soldier in Capt. Worthington's Company (VSA-13a).

09/27/80 Robert George requests of Quartermaster M. Carney to issue one lb powder and two lbs lead to two men of Bailey's Company (VSA-13a).

09/27/80 Robert George signs J. Bailey's request of the Quartermaster to issue one lb sugar for two sick men of Bailey's Company (VSA-13a).

09/28/80 Account of sugar delivered by Martin Carney by order of Capt. George at Fort Jefferson, to one man of Capt. Worthington's Company, 1/2 lb (VSA-50).

09/28/80 George signs A. Kellar's request for an issue of two lbs sugar for Kellar's own use (VSA-13a).

09/30/80 Four yds white flannel per order for sundry merchandise drawn out of the public store more than George's quota for which in part no returns or receipts have been issued or passed (VSA-48).

09/30/80 Robert George requests of J. Dodge to issue four yds flannel "to bury a soldier in, belonging to" Capt. A. Kellar's Company (VSA-13a).

10/01/80 Account of sugar delivered by Martin Carney by order of Capt. George at Fort Jefferson, to Capt. Kellar for his own use, two lbs; to Edward Murray, a soldier in Capt. Bailey's Company, 1/2 lb (VSA-50).

10/02/80 Account of ammunition delivered by Martin Carney by Capt. George's order to Sgt. Hazard of Capt. George's Company, 3/4 lb powder and 1 1/2 lbs lead; to Capt. Kellar, 1/2 lb powder and one lb lead (VSA-50).

10/02/80 Robert George requests of M. Carney to issue 3/4 lb powder to three men of Robert George's Company (VSA-13a).

10/02/80 Robert George signs A. Kellar's request for M. Carney to issue 1/2 lb powder and one lb lead for Abraham Kellar's trip to Cahokia (VSA-13a).

10/04/80 Account of ammunition delivered by Martin Carney by Capt. George's order to three men of Capt. Worthington's Company, 3/4 lb powder and 1 1/2 lbs lead (VSA-50).

10/04/80 Account of ammunition delivered by Martin Carney by order of Capt. George, to Sgt. Pitmen of Capt. McCarty's Company, 1/2 lb powder, one lb lead (VSA-50).

10/05/80 Account of ammunition delivered by Martin Carney by order of Capt. George, to the militia at this place, five lbs powder, ten lbs lead; to eight men of Capt. George's Company, four lbs powder, eight lbs lead (VSA-50).

10/06/80 Account of sugar delivered by Martin Carney by order of Capt. George at Fort Jefferson, to William Carr of Capt. Bailey's Company, 1/2 lb (VSA-50).

10/06/80 Account of soap delivered by Martin Carney by order of Col. Montgomery and Capt. George at Fort Jefferson, to Lt. Dalton for his use, 5 1/2 lbs; to Capt. Leonard Helm for his use, two lbs (VSA-50).

10/06/80 Account of sugar delivered by Martin Carney by orders of Capt. George, to Wagoner, a soldier in Capt. George's Company, 1/2 lb (VSA-50).

10/06/80 J. Bailey requests [R. George signs] of the Quartermaster to issue 1/2 lb sugar to Edward Murray (VSA-13a).

Fort Jefferson Personnel

10/06/80 J. Bailey requests [Robert George signs] of the Quartermaster to issue 1/2 lb sugar to a man of Bailey's Company "long sick" (VSA-13a).

10/06/80 Robert George requests the Quartermaster to issue 1/2 lb sugar to Peter Wagoner of Robert George's Company (VSA-13a).

10/07/80 Robert George requests of the Quartermaster to issue six lbs soap to Lt. [Dalton?] (VSA-13a).

10/07/80 Robert George signs Leonard Helm's, "supt. of Indian Affairs," request for the Quartermaster to issue two lbs sugar and two lbs soap for Leonard Helm's use (VSA-13a).

10/09/80 One quart tafia to two of Capt. George's Company per order Col. Montgomery (VSA-48).

10/09/80 Account of soap delivered by Martin Carney by order of Col. Montgomery and Capt. George at Fort Jefferson, to Capt. George for his own use, 12 lbs; to Capt. Bailey for his own use, eight lbs; to Mr. Donne, Commissary for his own use, four lbs; to Carney for his use, eight lbs (VSA-50).

10/09/80 Robert George signs J. Bailey's request for the Quartermaster to issue eight lbs soap to John Bailey from the public store (VSA-13a).

10/09/80 Robert George requests of the Quartermaster to issue 12 lbs soap for Robert George's own use from the public store (VSA-13a).

10/11/80 Six shirts per order for sundry merchandise drawn out of the public store more than George's quota for which in part no returns or receipts have been issued or passed (VSA-48).

10/11/80 Account of ammunition delivered by Martin Carney by order of Capt. George, to Major Harlan for his own use, 1/4 lb powder, 1/2 lb lead; to John Ash a soldier in Capt. George's Company, 1/4 lb powder, 1/2 lb lead (VSA-50).

10/11/80 Account of soap delivered by Martin Carney by order of Col. Montgomery and Capt. George at Fort Jefferson, to Lt. Richard Clark for his own use, six lbs (VSA-50).

10/11/80 Robert George requests of the Quartermaster to issue to Lt. Richard Clark, six lbs soap (VSA-13a).

10/11/80 Robert George signs that he received the "within mentioned shirts" (VSA-13a).

10/12/80 Robert George requests the Quartermaster to issue one lb soap to Francis Little (VSA-13a).

10/12/80 Robert George requests of M. Carney to issue one lb soap to John Ash (VSA-13).

10/12/80 Robert George signs J. Bailey's message that [Mrs. Johnes?] made five shirts for the men of Bailey's Company and is to be paid in goods from the public store (VSA-13a).

10/13/80 One yard flannel per order for sundry merchandise drawn out of the public store more than George's quota for which in part no returns or receipts have been issued or passed (VSA-48).

10/13/80 Account of soap delivered by Martin Carney by order of Col. Montgomery and Capt. George at Fort Jefferson, to Capt. Leonard Helm for his use, six lbs; to Ensign Jarret Williams, four lbs (VSA-50).

10/13/80 Robert George requests of the Quartermaster to issue four lbs soap to Ensign J. Williams (VSA-13a).

10/13/80 Robert George signs L. Helm's request of the Quartermaster to issue L. Helm six lbs soap (VSA-13a).

10/13/80 Robert George requests, by order of Col. Clark, J. Dodge to issue one yd flannel to J. Hazard of George's Company to loin a waistcoat (VSA-13a).

10/14/80 Issued 12 yards flannel and six skeins thread per order for sundry merchandise drawn out of the public store more than George's quota for which in part no returns or receipts have been issued or passed (VSA-48).

10/14/80 Account of ammunition delivered by Martin Carney by order of Capt. George, to Sgt. Allen of Capt. Brashears' Company, 1 1/2 lbs powder, three lbs lead (VSA-50).

Fort Jefferson Personnel

10/14/80 Robert George requests of J. Dodge to pay Samuel Allen twelve yds flannel and six skeins thread for 496 lbs beef (VSA-13a).

10/15/80 Seven yds blue cloth, six yds flannel, and 12 skeins thread per order for sundry merchandise drawn out of the public store more than George's quota for which in part no returns or receipts have been issued or passed (VSA-48).

10/15/80 By order of Col. Clark, George signs J. Bailey's request for J. Dodge to issue cloth and trimmings to produce one suit each for Levi Theel and John Clark (VSA-13a).

10/16/80 Account of ammunition delivered by Martin Carney by order of Capt. George, to Frank Little of Capt. George's Company, 1/4 lb powder, 1/2 lb lead; to Sgt. Elms of Capt. Brashears' Company, 1/2 lb powder, one lb lead (VSA-50).

10/18/80 Account of ammunition delivered by Martin Carney by order of Capt. George, to two men of Capt. Bailey's Company, 1 1/2 lbs powder, one lb lead (VSA-50).

10/19/80 Account of ammunition delivered by Martin Carney by order of Capt. George, to Sgt. Moore of Capt. George's Company, 2 1/2 lbs powder, five lbs lead (VSA-50).

10/20/80 Account of ammunition delivered by Martin Carney by order of Capt. George, to Bryan, a soldier in Capt. Worthington's Company, 1/4 lb powder, 1/2 lb lead; to four men of Capt. Bailey's Company, one lb powder, two lbs lead (VSA-50).

10/22/80 Account of soap delivered by Martin Carney by order of Col. Montgomery and Capt. George at Fort Jefferson, to Frank Little, a soldier in Capt. George's Company, one lb; to John Ash, a soldier in Capt. George's Company, one lb (VSA-50).

10/23/80 By order of Col. Clark, Robert George requests of J. Dodge to issue cloth and trimmings to produce one suit each for enlisting for nine men: John Anderson, Matthew Murray, William Fever[s], James Ramsey, William Posley, John Gilbert, Patrick Rogers, Francis Little, and Patrick Marr. William Posley to receive extra linen for two shirts (VSA-13a).

10/23/80 Rbt. George signed he received for the nine men mentioned, 31 1/2 yds cloth, 27 yds flannel, 58 skeins thread, 45 dozen buttons, 6 1/2 yds linen (VSA-13b).

10/24/80 Account of ammunition delivered by Martin Carney by order of Capt. George, to Lt. Dalton for his journey to New Orleans, one lb powder, ten lbs lead (VSA-50).

10/25/80 Account of soap delivered by Martin Carney by order of Col. Montgomery and Capt. George at Fort Jefferson, to Capt. Abraham Kellar, two lbs (VSA-50).

10/25/80 Robert George signs A. Kellar's request for M. Carney to issue two lbs soap for Kellar's use (VSA-13a).

10/27/80 Account of ammunition delivered by Martin Carney by order of Capt. George, to Ensign Slaughter for his own use, 1/2 lb powder, one lb lead; to Capt. Abraham Kellar for his own use, two lbs lead (VSA-50).

10/27/80 Robert George at Ft. Jefferson writes to John Rogers at Kaskaskia about Lt. Clark [Wm.] need for supplies at Ft. Jefferson; supplies should be sent by boat with enough men to return boat to Kaskaskia; Ft. Jefferson boat is on dry land and immobile (GRC, I: 462-463) (Seineke, 1981: 465) (DMS 50J72).

10/27/80 Richard Brashears requests, R. George signs, that two skeins of thread by issued to Mayfield to repair his clothes (VSA-13).

10/27/80 Robert George requests of Capt. Dodge to issue 1/2 yd stroud to Samuel Allen in part pay for beef delivered, Allen already received 12 yds flannel (VSA-13a).

10/28/80 Writes to GRC stating: "numbers daily dying." (VSA-13).

10/28/80 Account of ammunition delivered by Martin Carney by order of Capt. George, to Sgt. Vaughan of Capt. Bailey's Company, 1/4 lb powder and 1/2 lb lead; to Anderson going express to the Falls of Ohio, 1 1/4 lbs powder, three lbs lead (VSA-50).

Fort Jefferson Personnel

10/28/80 John Williams at Ft. Jefferson writes GRC: Wms arrived at Ft. Jefferson to take command by order of John Montgomery; described hunger at Fort due to inability to receive supplies because of low water; did not take command; will take command after arrival of G.R. Clark (GRC Papers, I: 463).

10/28/80 Robert George at Ft. Jefferson writes to GRC at Falls of Ohio and states that: 1) Ft. Jefferson reduced to small number by famine, death, and desertion; 2)Montgomery visited Ft. Jefferson enroute to Orleans; 3)expects provisions any day from Pollock; 4) most of Ft. Jefferson gone down river and remainder in a distressed state; 5)mention made of arrival of Montgomery [maybe]; 6) mention made of arrival of Capt. Williams and Robert George's refusal to give up command (GRC, I: 461-462) (Seineke 1981: 465-466).

10/28/80 R. George requests ten cartridges to be issued to Dan Crump for use of two lbs swivel belonging to the blockhouse on the hill (VSA-13).

10/29/80 Leo. Helm writes to Slaughter about hardships at Ft. Jefferson; is sitting at Robert George's fire with two buffalo ribs (GRC Papers, I: 466).

10/31/80 Account of ammunition delivered by Martin Carney by order of Capt. George, to Capt. John Williams, one lb powder, two lbs lead; to Israel Dodge, Deputy Agent, 1/2 lb powder, one lb lead (VSA-50).

11/02/80 Account of ammunition delivered by Martin Carney by order of Capt. George to Mr. Sherlock for the use of the Kaskaskia Indians, 80 lbs powder, 89 lbs lead; to Capt. Helm for his own use, two lbs powder, two lbs lead; to three men of Capt. Brashears' Company 1 1/2 lbs powder, three lbs lead (VSA-50).

11/03/80 Account of ammunition delivered by Martin Carney by order of Capt. George, to one man of Capt. Brashears' Company, 1/2 lb powder, one lb lead (VSA-50).

11/05/80 Account of ammunition delivered by Martin Carney by order of Capt. George, to Simon Burney in lue of 380 lbs of beef, six lbs powder; to Major Harlan for hunting, one lb powder, two lbs lead (VSA-50).

11/06/80 Account of ammunition delivered by Martin Carney by order of Capt. George, to two men of Capt. George's Company, one lbs powder, two lbs lead (VSA-50).

11/08/80 Account of soap delivered by Martin Carney by order of Col. Montgomery and Capt. George at Fort Jefferson, to John Garr, a soldier in Capt. George's Company, one lb; to Joseph Thornton, Artificer for public works, two lbs (VSA-50).

11/09/80 Account of ammunition delivered by Martin Carney by order of Capt. George, to two men of Capt. Bailey's Company, one lb powder, two lbs lead; to two men of Capt. Brashears' Company, one lb powder, two lbs lead; to two men of Capt. Kellar's Company, one lb powder, two lbs lead (VSA-50).

11/14/80 Account of sugar delivered by Martin Carney by orders of Capt. George, to three men for carrying the sugar, three lbs (VSA-50).

11/15/80 Account of sugar delivered by Martin Carney by orders of Capt. George, to Nelly Lewis, a soldier's widow, one lb; to five sick men of Capt. Bailey's Company, five lbs; to 11 men of Capt. George's Company, 11 lbs; to a sick woman of Capt. Bailey's Company, one lb (VSA-50).

11/15/80 Account of brass kettles delivered by Martin Carney by order of Capt. George at Fort Jefferson, to Capt. Robert George and Company, three kettles; to Capt. Leonard Helm for his use, one kettle; to Capt. Abraham Kellar and Company, two kettles; to Majr. John Williams for his use, one kettle, to Lt. Richard Clark for Capt. Worthington's Company, two kettles; to Ensign Lawrence Slaughter for Capt. Bailey's Company, two kettles; to Capt. Richard Brashears, one kettle; to John Harry, Armourer at this place, one kettle; for Carney's own use, one kettle (VSA-50).

11/16/80 Account of sugar delivered by Martin Carney by orders of Capt. George, to a sick man of Capt. Worthington's Company, one lb; to Joseph Thornton Artificer, two lbs (VSA-50).

Fort Jefferson Personnel

11/17/80 Account of sugar delivered by Martin Carney by orders of Capt. George, to Andrew Johnston and family of Capt. Worthington's Company, 1 1/2 lbs; to a soldier of Capt. Bailey's Company, one lb; to two men of Capt. Brashears' Company, two lbs; to a sick woman and child of Brashears' Company, two lbs (VSA-50).

11/18/80 Account of sugar delivered by Martin Carney by orders of Capt. George, to George Owens, Capt. of Militia, three lbs; to Capt. Kellar for his own use, two lbs (VSA-50).

11/18/80 Account of soap delivered by Martin Carney by order of Col. Montgomery and Capt. George at Fort Jefferson, to Mr. Blackford, Commissary, three lbs (VSA-50).

11/18/80 Account of soap delivered by Martin Carney by order of Capt. George at Fort Jefferson, to eight men of Capt. Worthington's Company, eight lbs; to Sgt. Morgan for Capt. George's Company, 15 lbs (VSA-50).

11/19/80 Account of ammunition delivered by Martin Carney by order of Capt. George, to four men of Capt. Kellar's Company, one lb powder, two lbs lead (VSA-50).

11/19/80 Account of sugar delivered by Martin Carney by orders of Capt. George, to John Burks, sick militia man, one lb (VSA-50).

11/19/80 Account of soap delivered by Martin Carney by order of Capt. George at Fort Jefferson, to Capt. Brashears' Company, 4 1/2 lbs; to Capt. Bailey's Company, 12 lbs; to Capt. McCarty's Company, 1 1/2 lbs (VSA-50).

11/20/80 Account of sugar delivered by Martin Carney by orders of Capt. George, to three men of Capt. George's Company, three lbs; to two men of Capt. George's Company, two lbs; to Col. Clark's Negro, sick, one lb (VSA-50).

11/21/80 Account of ammunition delivered by Martin Carney by order of Capt. George, to Major Harlan for hunting, 2 1/4 lbs powder, 4 1/2 lbs lead (VSA-50).

11/21/80 Account of sugar delivered by Martin Carney by orders of Capt. George, to Mr. Phelps for his sick family, two lbs; to Mr. Hughs, a widow of militia, two lbs; to myself for my use, six lbs; to John Wilson, Capt. Worthington's servant, one lb (VSA-50).

11/22/80 Account of ammunition delivered by Martin Carney by order of Capt. George, to eight men going hunting with Harlan, three lbs powder, six lbs lead (VSA-50).

11/22/80 Account of soap delivered by Martin Carney by order of Capt. George at Fort Jefferson, to Capt. Abraham Kellar's Company, six lbs (VSA-50).

11/23/80 Account of soap delivered by Martin Carney by order of Capt. George at Fort Jefferson, to Major Harlan for his own use, three lbs; to James Sherlock, Interpreter for his use, six lbs (VSA-50).

11/23/80 Account of sugar delivered by Martin Carney by orders of Capt. George, to Capt. George's Mess, three lbs; to a soldier of Worthington's, one lb (VSA-50).

11/25/80 Account of sugar delivered by Martin Carney by orders of Capt. George, to a sick woman of Capt. George's Company, one lb; to Joshua Archer of militia, one lb (VSA-50).

11/26/80 Account of sugar delivered by Martin Carney by orders of Capt. George, to Mr. Donne, Commissary, six lbs (VSA-50).

11/26/80 Account of ammunition delivered by Martin Carney by order of Capt. Robert George at Fort Jefferson, to Jessee Piner for two dressed deerskins for the use of the soldiers at this post, 1 1/4 lb powder, two lbs lead; to Mr. William Clark for his use, one lb; to Mr. Archer, a militia man, one lb (VSA-50).

11/27/80 Account of sugar delivered by Martin Carney by orders of Capt. George, to Mr. Lunsford and family, sick, five lbs; to the widow Meredith's family, sick, three lbs (VSA-50).

11/27/80 Account of soap delivered by Martin Carney by order of Capt. George at Fort Jefferson, to Mr. Donne, Commissary, six lbs; to Mr. Israel Dodge, six lbs (VSA-50).

11/29/80 Account of sugar delivered by Martin Carney by orders of Capt. George, to Capt. Bailey and Mr. Slaughter, 12 lbs (VSA-50).

Fort Jefferson Personnel

11/29/80 Account of sugar delivered by Martin Carney by orders of Capt. George, to Mr. Israel Dodge, Deputy Agent, four lbs; to Joseph Hunter's family, two lbs; to Capt. Brashears for his use, six lbs (VSA-50).

11/29/80 Account of sugar delivered by Martin Carney by order of Capt. George at Fort Jefferson, to Major Williams for his own use, six lbs (VSA-50).

11/29/80 Account of ammunition delivered by Martin Carney by order of Capt. Robert George at Fort Jefferson, to Mr. Donne, Commissary, for his own use, one lb powder, three lbs lead; to Richard Clark, Lt. in the Illinois Regiment, 1/2 lb powder, one lb lead; to two men of Capt. Bailey's Company, 1/2 lb powder, one lb lead; to 11 men going on Command to the Illinois, 2 3/4 lbs powder, 5 1/2 lbs lead (VSA-50).

11/29/80 Account of soap delivered by Martin Carney by order of Capt. George at Fort Jefferson, to Capt. Brashears for his own use, six lbs; to Major Williams for his own use, six lbs (VSA-50).

11/29/80 Stores issued by order of Capt. Robert George, to Lt. Clark, three tomahawks (VSA-50).

11/30/80 Account of sugar delivered by Martin Carney by order of Capt. George at Fort Jefferson, to a woman and two children of Worthington's Company, two lbs; to Capt. Abraham Kellar for his use, two lbs (VSA-50).

12/01/80 Stores issued by order of Capt. Robert George: to Capt. Brashears' Company, two tomahawks (VSA-50: 40).

12/01/80 Account of sugar delivered by Martin Carney by order of Capt. George at Fort Jefferson: to Lt. Richard Clark for his use, six lbs; to Capt. Leonard Helm for his use, six lbs; to Ensign Williams and Major Harlan, 12 lbs; to Mr. Harris, Armourer at this place, two lbs (VSA-50: 28).

12/01/80 Lt. Richard Clark and Robert George sign request of the Quartermaster to issue to Clark, ten lbs sugar for Clark's own use out of the public store (VSA- 14).

12/02/80 Robert George requests of Israel Dodge to pay Mary McAuley out of the public store for making six soldier shirts for George's Company (VSA-14).

12/02/80 Stores issued by order of Capt. Robert George: to Capt. Helm, one tomahawk (VSA-50: 40).

12/03/80 Silas Harlan and Robert George sign request of Israel Dodge to issue John McGarr eight yds linen for hunting with Harlan for one month (VSA-14).

12/03/80 John Bailey and Robert George sign request of Israel Dodge to issue to Levi Theel of Bailey's Company two yds damaged blue cloth for enlisting for three years or during the war (VSA-14).

12/03/80 Account of soap delivered by Martin Carney by order of Capt. George at Fort Jefferson: to John Hazard of Capt. George's Company, one lb (VSA-50: 52).

12/04/80 Lt. Richard Clark and Robert George sign request of Israel Dodge to issue two yds flannel for Clark's use (VSA-14a).

12/04/80 Robert George requests of Martin Carney to issue four lbs powder and eight lbs lead to Major Harlan and his hunting party as they are going to hunt meat for Fort Jefferson (VSA-14).

12/04/80 Account of soap delivered by Martin Carney by order of Capt. George at Fort Jefferson: to Capt. Helm for his use, six lbs (VSA-50: 52).

12/04/80 Account of ammunition delivered by Martin Carney by order of Capt. Robert George at Fort Jefferson: to Major Harlan's hunting party, four lbs powder, eight lbs lead; to the soldiers going with Major Harlan, two lbs powder, four lbs lead (VSA-50: 29).

12/04/80 Stores issued by order of Capt. Robert George: to Capt. McCarty's Company, one tomahawk (VSA-50: 40).

12/05/80 Account of ammunition delivered by Martin Carney by order of Capt. Robert George at Fort Jefferson: to the soldiers going with Major Harlan, two lbs powder and four lbs lead (VSA-50: 29).

12/05/80 Account of soap delivered by Martin Carney by order of Capt. George at Fort Jefferson: to a man of Capt. McCarty's company, 1/2 lb [amount assumed due to manuscript being torn]; to a man of Capt. George's Company, one lb (VSA-50: 52).

Fort Jefferson Personnel

12/05/80 Robert George requests of the Quartermaster to issue two lbs powder and four lbs lead for the party going out with Major Harlan because yesterday's draw was insufficient (VSA-14).

12/05/80 Letter from John Donne at Fort Jefferson to George Rogers Clark. Donne talks of attack made by Indians on August 27 and tells that three of Capt. George's men left after the attack for the Falls. Donne believes that Capt. George has done all in his power to issue the provisions with frugality to the inhabitants (MHS: B1, F23).

12/06/80 Account of soap delivered by Martin Carney by order of Capt. George at Fort Jefferson: to Mr. Harris, Armourer at this place, two lbs (VSA-50: 52).

12/07/80 Account of soap delivered by Martin Carney by order of Capt. George at Fort Jefferson: to Ensign Slaughter for his use, six lbs (VSA-50: 52).

12/07/80 Account of ammunition delivered by Martin Carney by order of Capt. Robert George at Fort Jefferson: to one man of Capt. John Bailey's Company, 1/4 lb powder and 1/2 lb lead; to two men of Capt. Bailey's Company, 1/2 lb powder and two lbs lead (VSA-50: 29).

12/07/80 Stores issued by order of Capt. Robert George: to Capt. George, one sword (VSA-50: 40).

12/07/80 Stores issued by order of Capt. Robert George: to Capt. Kellar, one axe (VSA-50: 37).

12/07/80 Robert George requests of Israel Dodge to issue and charge Mr. William Clark for four yds osnaburg for a hunting shirt (VSA-14a).

12/07/80 Capt. Abraham Kellar and Robert George sign request of Israel Dodge to pay Mrs. Francis Bredin out of the public store for making four soldier coats for Kellar's Company (VSA-14).

12/07/80 Robert George requests of Israel Dodge to issue two ounces of thread fit to make a pair of leather breeches to Zephaniah Blackford and charge it to his account (VSA-14).

12/09/80 Robert George requests of Israel Dodge to pay John Anderson out of the public store for making one suit of clothes for a soldier of George's Company (VSA-14).

12/09/80 Robert George requests of Israel Dodge to pay Elizabeth Jones for making four suits of clothes for George's Company (VSA-14).

12/09/80 Stores issued by order of Capt. Robert George: to Capt. Brashears' Company, two tomahawks (VSA-50: 37).

12/10/80 Account of soap delivered by Martin Carney by order of Capt. George at Fort Jefferson: to Capt. George for his use, 15 lbs; to Negro Ceasar, Artificer, 1 1/2 lbs; to Mr. William Clark, six lbs; to Ensign Williams, six lbs; to Mr. Carney, Quartermaster, six lbs; dried away and wasted, 13 lbs (VSA-50: 52).

12/10/80 Robert George signs a return of men enlisted by Lt. Valentine Thomas Dalton for the artillery service from November 18, 1779, to December 10, 1780 for the term of three years or during the war: Jeremiah Horn 11/18/79, Thomas Laney 11/29/79, Patrick Marr 11/29/79, Samuel Coffy (x) 11/29/79, John Anderson 11/29/79, Benjamin Lewis 12/11/79, Thomas Bolton 01/01/80, Paul Quibea 01/10/80, James McDonald 01/31/80, Patt McCulty (x) 03/10/80, Andrew Conore 03/20/80, John Hazzard 03/28/80, Francis Puccan (x) 04/12/80, John Bowden (x) 04/20/80, Jacob Ditterin 06/13/80, Anthony Montroy 06/18/80, James Mulboy (x) 07/10/80, Joseph Lonion (x) 12/10/80. The above six men marked "x" are not included on George's payroll because Lt. Dalton neglected to give an account of what had become of them or when and how their time expired (MHS: B1, F23).

12/15/80 Someone wrote from Fort Jefferson [no signature] that the within merchandise was received of Robert George for the use of the troops in the Illinois Department belonging to the state of Virginia. Robert George at Fort Jefferson certifies that the within is a true copy of the invoice delivered to Israel Dodge: one bail of cloth in different colors; 16 3/4 ells brown cloth; 15 3/4 ells brown cloth; 14 1/4 ells blue cloth; 18 ells pompedore; one piece of linen, 36 1/2 ells; two pieces of linen, 50 1/2 ells; four lbs vermillion; 29 1/2 ells white

Fort Jefferson Personnel

flannel; eight bushels of thread; 17 lbs of thread in different colors; 34 skeins of silk; 24 dozen large buttons; 24 dozen small buttons; four dozen large [quilt?] buttons; 5 1/2 dozen small buttons; 104 skeins mohair; 105 pair shoes; 15 ells of Topsell Duck[?]; eight small bags; 53 bunches of capwire; one brass ink stand; 16 [illeg.] needles; four paper of pins and one [illeg.] pins (VSA-14a, b).

12/15/80 Statement concerning Fort JEfferson in which Capt. George had an inventory of a quantity of tafia delivered to Martin Carney and another for a quantity of broad cloth with a receipt signed by Israel Dodge and dated Fort Jefferson 12/15/80. It was witnessed by Capt. Bailey and Leonard Helm (GRC, Papers I: 315).

12/18/80 Account of ammunition delivered by Martin Carney by order of Capt. Robert George at Fort Jefferson: to Capt. Bailey, 1/2 lb powder and one lb lead (VSA- 50: 29).

12/18/80 Silas Harlan and Robert George sign request of Israel Dodge to issue to Thomas Snellock, Nicholas Tuttle, and Thomas Hays eight yds linen each for 31 days of assistance to Harlan on a hunting trip for Fort Jefferson (VSA-14).

12/19/80 Abraham Kellar and Robert George sign request of Israel Dodge to issue Mrs. Nancy Hunter pay for making a coat, waistcoat, and a pair of overalls for Kellar's Company (VSA-14).

12/19/80 Robert George requests of Israel Dodge to issue to Silas Harlan cloth and trimmings for one suit of clothes, one pair of shoes, cloth for a copote, and linen for two shirts (VSA-14).

12/19/80 Account of ammunition delivered by Martin Carney by order of Capt. Robert George at Fort Jefferson: to Abraham Taylor, a militia man, 1/4 lb powder and 1/2 lb lead (VSA-50: 29).

12/20/80 Account of ammunition expended by the artillery at sundry times by order of Capt. R. George, Commandant at Fort Jefferson: at Capt. Harrison and Capt. Roberts' arrival from the Falls of Ohio per verbal order, six lbs powder, two lbs lead, and one yd flannel (VSA-50: 33).

12/20/80 Robert George requests of the Agent to issue Capt. Benjamin Roberts his full quota of clothing as allowed by law by order of Col. Clark (VSA-14).

12/21/80 Capt. Richard Brashears and Robert George sign request of Israel Dodge to issue eight pair of shoes to eight men of Brashears' Company (VSA-14).

12/21/80 Richard Brashears and Robert George sign request of Israel Dodge to issue two shirts each for 13 men of Brashears' Company (VSA-14a).

12/21/80 Robert George requests of Israel Dodge to issue 40 pair of shoes for men of George's Company (VSA-14).

12/21/80 Richard Harrison signed that he received of Israel Dodge the within contents (VSA-14).

12/21/80 Abraham Kellar and Robert George sign request of Israel Dodge to issue 11 pairs of shoes for 11 men in Kellar's Company (VSA-14).

12/21/80 Robert George requests of Israel Dodge to issue two shirts each for 40 men of George's for the ensuing year (VSA-14a).

12/21/80 Richard Harrison signed that he received of Israel Dodge 260 yds linen for the use of Capt. Robert George's Company of Artillery agreeable to the within order (VSA-14b).

12/21/80 Abraham Kellar and Robert George sign request of Israel Dodge to issue enough linen to make two shirts each for 11 men in Kellar's Company for the ensuing year (VSA-14).

12/21/80 Robert George requests of Israel Dodge to issue 3/4 yd cloth to Major Harlan for a waistcoat (VSA-14).

12/22/80 Stores issued by order of Capt. Robert George: to Capt. Benjamin Roberts, two tents or oil cloths (VSA-50: 39).

12/22/80 John Williams and Robert George sign request of the Quartermaster to issue three lbs loaf sugar (VSA- 14).

12/22/80 Silas Harlan and Robert George sign request of the Quartermaster to issue Abraham Taylor, Hugh Montgomery, John Levrig, and John Wilson 1/2 lb powder and one lb lead for each man (VSA-14).

Fort Jefferson Personnel

12/23/80 Account of ammunition delivered by Martin Carney by order of Capt. Robert George at Fort Jefferson: to four militia men, two lbs powder and four lbs lead (VSA-50: 29).

12/23/80 Abraham Kellar and Robert George sign request of Israel Dodge to issue thread for making two shirts each for seven men of Kellar's Company (VSA-14).

12/23/80 Robert George requests an issuance of two bags to Capt. Benjamin Roberts to carry necessities to Col. Slaughter at the Falls of Ohio (VSA-14).

12/23/80 Robert George requests of the Quartermaster to issue to Major Silas Harlan one barrell rum, three lbs coffee, and six lbs sugar (VSA-14).

12/23/80 Robert George requests of Mr. Dodge to issue Capt. Roberts for the use of the troops and Col. Slaughter at the Falls: 157 3/4 yds linen; eight yds toile gris; two yds flannel; six skeins colored thread; 23 1/2 yds fine linen; 46 skeins white thread and two papers of pin (VSA-14).

12/23/80 Robert George requests of Israel Dodge to issue to Capt. Roberts: 1 1/2 yds blue cloth, two yds coarse flannel, four skeins thread, and one skein silk thread (VSA-14).

12/23/80 Robert George requests of Mr. Dodge to issue to Capt. Roberts three dozen coat buttons and three dozen small buttons (VSA-14).

12/24/80 Account of ammunition delivered by Martin Carney by order of Capt. Robert George at Fort Jefferson: to Capt. Benjamin Roberts, 24 flints (VSA-50: 31).

12/24/80 Letter from Capt. Robert George at Fort Jefferson to George Rogers Clark. George states that he received letters from Oliver Pollock and Col. Montgomery. George states that the greatest part of the cargo sent to Clark for use of the state was lost in a hurricane. The remainder of Capt. Phillip Barbour's goods were purchased as a result. Capt. Harrison informed George that it is Clark's intent to evacuate Fort Jefferson and erect another fortification at the Iron Banks. George states that his "yellow locks" will turn grey if Clark does not clarify his intentions. George also tells that Capt. Helm is of infinite service and comfort to George at Fort Jefferson (MHS: B1, F23) (Seineke, 1981: 468-469).

12/24/80 Robert George requests of Israel Dodge to issue William Freeman of George's Company a full suit of clothes which he is entitled to having enlisted during the present war (VSA-14).

12/24/80 John Bailey and Robert George sign request of Israel Dodge to issue enough linen to make two shirts each for 25 men of Bailey's Company for the ensuing year (VSA-14).

12/25/80 Account of ammunition delivered by Martin Carney by order of Capt. Robert George at Fort Jefferson: to Capt. Bailey's Company, six lbs powder and 12 lbs lead (VSA-50: 29).

12/25/80 Account of ammunition expended by the artillery at sundry times by order of Capt. Robert George, Commandant at Fort Jefferson: by five swivals and one four pounder both in town and garrison per verbal orders, 60 lbs powder, seven lbs lead, and six yds flannel (VSA-50: 33).

12/25/80 Joshua Archer should be paid ten shillings and four pence for buffalo and bear meat funished Capt. George's troops (GRC, II: 334).

12/26/80 Robert George requests of John Dodge to issue Capt. Richard Harrison sky blue cloth and good trimmings for a coat and pompedore broad cloth for facing and edging (VSA-14a).

12/26/80 Jeremiah Horn is listed on Capt. Robert George's pay abstract as having died on this date (Harding, 1981: 29-30, 32).

12/27/80 Account of ammunition delivered by Martin Carney by order of Capt. Robert George at Fort Jefferson: to Capt. George's Company, ten lbs powder and 20 lbs lead (VSA-50: 31).

12/27/80 Robert George requests of Mr. Dodge to issue to Ensign Slaughter a set of buttons and mohair to make a suit of clothes (VSA-14).

12/27/80 Richard Brashears and Robert George sign request of Israel Dodge to issue 12 needles to John Boiles for making clothes (VSA-14).

12/28/80 Stores issued by order of Capt. Robert George: to three men of Capt. Worthington's Company, one rifle and two muskets (VSA-50: 37).

Fort Jefferson Personnel

12/28/80 Account of ammunition delivered by Martin Carney by order of Capt. Robert George at Fort Jefferson: to Ensign Williams and his hunting party, 22 flints; to Capt. George's Company, 28 men, two flints each, 56 flints (VSA-50: 31).

12/29/80 Stores issued by order of Capt. Robert George: to two men of Capt. Bailey's Company, two muskets (VSA-50: 37).

12/29/80 Account of ammunition delivered by Martin Carney by order of Capt. Robert George at Fort Jefferson: to Capt. Brashears' Company, 20 flints; to Capt. Worthingtons' Company, 32 flints; to Capt. Bailey's Company, 36 flints (VSA-50: 31).

12/29/80 William Clark and Robert George sign request for an issuance of one lb sugar for Clark's own use (VSA- 14; misfiled).

12/29/80 John Bailey and Robert George sign request for an issuance of two yds flannel for Bailey's own use (VSA-14).

12/30/80 Account of ammunition delivered by Martin Carney by order of Capt. Robert George at Fort Jefferson, to two men of Capt. Brashears' Company, one lb powder and two lbs lead; to Capt. Roberts [document read of Col. Slaughter's Company, 100 lbs powder and 200 lbs lead but had been crossed out]; to Capt. Brashears, one lb powder and four lbs lead; to two men of Capt. Rogers' Company, 1/2 lb powder and one lb lead; to Capt. Harrison, four lbs powder and eight lbs lead (VSA-50: 30).

12/30/80 Stores issued by order of Capt. Robert George: to Capt. Bailey's Company, one kettle (VSA-50: 37) (VSA-14; misfiled).

12/31/80 Stores issued by order of Capt. Robert George: to Capt. Harrison, one tent or oil cloth; to Capt. Brashears one tent or oil cloth (VSA-50: 37).

12/31/80 Account of ammunition delivered by Martin Carney by order of Capt. Robert George at Fort Jefferson, to Capt. Kellar's Blockhouse, eight lbs powder and five lbs lead (VSA-50: 30).

12/31/80 Robert George requests of Mr. Dodge to issue to Phillip Orbin of George's Company, a coat, waistcoat, and pair of overalls for enlisting for three years or during the war (VSA-14).

01/01/81 Capt. Robert George at Ft. Jefferson writes to Oliver Pollock at New Orleans. Letter sent with two sets of exchange for $237,320 in favor of Capt. Philip Barbour who furnished a large cargo of liquors and dry goods which George says has saved the post. George states that he called a council and consulted them about the sum. The council and George felt it was a reasonable amount considering the difficulties Barbour encountered in getting the cargo to Fort Jefferson. George begs Pollock to pay for the cargo in gold or silver coin so that Barbour can supply Fort Jefferson in the future (GRC, I: 496-497).

01/01/81 Robert George requests of Oliver Pollock [Agent at New Orleans] to pay Capt. Philip Barbour 5000 Spanish milled dollars for liquor and clothing furnished George for use of the troops of the Illinois Department (VSA-15; misfiled).

01/01/81 Leonard Helm and Robert George sign request of the Quartermaster to issue to each of 25 Indians going to war against the Chickasaws, 1/2 lb powder, one lb lead, and two flints each (VSA-15).

01/01/81 Buckner Pittman and Robert George sign request of the Quartermaster to issue tafia for 16 men on fatigue (VSA-15).

01/01/81 Richard Brashears and Robert George sign request of the Quartermaster to issue two pairs overalls for two men of Brashears' Company who enlisted for three years or during the war going down river on a purigee [pirogue] (VSA-15a).

01/01/81-01/19/81 Sometime between these dates, a letter was written from John Donne at Fort Jefferson to George Rogers Clark in Richmond. John Donne had been gone to Kaskaskia. WHile he was away, Capt. Barbour arrived from New Orleans with a quantity of goods part of which Capt. George intends to use for the purchase of provisions (MHS: B1, F23; filed as Misc. FJ Doc.).

01/02/81 Stores issued by order of Capt. Robert George, to three men of Capt. George's Company, three muskets (VSA-50).

Fort Jefferson Personnel

01/03/81 Stores issued by order of Capt. Robert George, to B. Pitman, boat master, one axe (VSA-50).

01/04/81 Ordered by George Slaughter at Louisville to send 100 lbs gunpowder and 400 lbs lead to Kaskaskia (GRC, I: 493).

01/04/81 Account of ammunition delivered by Martin Carney by order of Capt. Robert George at Fort Jefferson, to Mr. Hunter, a militia man, 1/4 lb powder, one lb lead (VSA-50).

01/08/81 Account of ammunition delivered by Martin Carney by order of Capt. Robert George at Fort Jefferson, to three men of Capt. Bailey's Company, one lb powder, two lbs lead; to friendly Indians going to war, 12 1/2 lbs powder, 25 lbs lead, and 50 flints; to Capt. Bailey's and Owens going express to the falls, 1 1/2 lbs powder, four lbs lead; to Capt. Rogers' Company, three lbs powder, six lbs lead (VSA-50).

01/10/81 Account of ammunition delivered by Martin Carney by order of Capt. Robert George at Fort Jefferson, to Capt. George's Company, going on Command to Illinois, four lbs powder, eight lbs lead (VSA-50).

01/10/81 Stores issued by order of Capt. Robert George, to Patrick Kennedy, one musket and one bayonet with belt (VSA-50).

01/11/81 Stores issued by order of Capt. Robert George, to a soldier of Capt. Bailey's Company, one musket and one bayonet with belt; to Major Williams, eight tents or oil cloths [amount may have been crossed out]; to Major Williams, one swivel (VSA-50).

01/11/81 Account of ammunition expended by the artillery at sundry times by order of Capt. Robert George, Commandant at Fort Jefferson, expended at other different times, 17 lbs powder, 3 1/2 yds flannel; issued Capt. Bailey for the use of the artillery at Opost, three yds flannel (VSA-50).

01/12/81 Stores issued by order of Capt. Robert George, to Capt. Bailey's Company, 23 swords; to Capt. Worthington's Company, 17 swords; to Mr. Hunter of the Militia, one lb sword; to James Sherlock, one sword; to Capt. George's Company, one kettle (VSA-50).

01/12/81 Account of ammunition delivered by Martin Carney by order of Capt. Robert George at Fort Jefferson, to Lt. Richard Clark, 1/2 lb powder, one lb lead, and two flints; to Majr. Williams, six cartridges of swivel, four lbs powder, six lbs lead; to Capt. Bailey's Company, six flints (VSA-50).

01/16/81 Stores issued by order of Capt. Robert George, to Capt. George's Company, 32 swords (VSA-50).

01/18/81 Stores issued by order of Capt. Robert George, to Capt. George's Company, one musket and one kettle (VSA-50).

01/19/81 Stores issued by order of Capt. Robert George, to Mr. Donne, Commissary, two muskets, two bayonets, and one sword (VSA-50).

01/19/81 Account of ammunition delivered by Martin Carney by order of Capt. Robert George at Fort Jefferson, to three men of Capt. Worthington's Company, 1 1/2 lbs powder, three lbs lead (VSA-50).

01/24/81 Account of ammunition delivered by Martin Carney by order of Capt. Robert George at Fort Jefferson, to two men of Capt. George's Company, 1/4 lb powder [one lb lead had been written but was crossed out] (VSA-50).

01/25/81 Stores issued by order of Capt. Robert George, to Capt. Brashears' Company, ten swords (VSA-50).

01/27/81 Account of ammunition delivered by Martin Carney by order of Capt. Robert George at Fort Jefferson, to two men of Capt. George's Company, 1/2 lb powder, one lb lead (VSA-50).

01/27/81 Stores issued by order of Capt. Robert George, to Lt. Calvit, one kettle (VSA-50).

02/01/81 Account of ammunition delivered by Martin Carney by order of Capt. Robert George at Fort Jefferson, to two men of Capt. Kellar's Company, 1/2 lb powder, one lb lead (VSA-50).

02/03/81 Account of ammunition delivered by Martin Carney by order of Capt. Robert George at Fort Jefferson, to Lt. Clark for his use, 1/2 lb powder; to Lt. Calvit for his use, 1/2 lb powder, one lb lead (VSA-50).

Fort Jefferson Personnel

02/03/81 Stores issued by order of Capt. Robert George, to Lt. Calvit, three swords and two axes (VSA-50).

02/04/81 Account of ammunition delivered by Martin Carney by order of Capt. Robert George at Fort Jefferson, to two men of Capt. Worthington's Company, 1/2 lb powder, one lb lead (VSA-50).

02/04/81 Stores issued by order of Capt. Robert Goerge, to a soldier of Capt. Bailey's Company, one musket and one bayonet (VSA-50).

02/05/81 Account of ammunition delivered by Martin Carney by order of Capt. Robert George at Fort Jefferson, to Abraham Taylor, a militia man at this post, 1/4 lb powder and 1/2 lb lead (VSA-50).

02/06/81 Account of ammunition delivered by Martin Carney by order of Capt. Robert George at Fort Jefferson, to two men of Capt. George's Company, one lb powder, two lbs lead (VSA-50).

02/07/81 Account of ammunition delivered by Martin Carney by order of Capt. Robert George at Fort Jefferson, to three men of Capt. George's Company, 3/4 lb powder, 1 1/2 lbs lead; to the Kickapoo Indians, seven lbs powder, four lbs lead; to two militia men going to the Falls, two lbs powder, one lb lead (VSA-50).

02/08/81 Account of ammunition delivered by Martin Carney by order of Capt. Robert George at Fort Jefferson, to Capt. Bailey's hunting party, 12 lbs powder, 24 lbs lead (VSA-50).

02/12/81 Account of ammunition delivered by Martin Carney by order of Capt. Robert George at Fort Jefferson, to Z. Blackford, 1/4 lb powder, 1/2 lb lead (VSA-50).

02/13/81 Stores issued by order of Capt. Robert George, to a soldier of Capt. Brashears, one musket and one bayonet with belt; to Capt. Bailey, one axe; to Peorian Indians, seven swords; to Buckner Pittman, Boat master, one kettle; to Capt. Worthington's Company, two muskets; to Capt. Worthington for his use, one kettle (VSA-50).

02/14/81 Account of ammunition delivered by Martin Carney by order of Capt. Robert George at Fort Jefferson, to B. Scarcy, express, 2 1/2 lbs powder, five lbs lead (VSA-50).

02/15/81 Writes back to George Slaughter from Ft. Jeff (GRC, I: 506).

02/15/81 Account of ammunition delivered by Martin Carney by order of Capt. Robert George at Fort Jefferson, to Capt. Roberts' Company, going on command, 2 1/4 lbs powder (VSA-50).

02/15/81 Ammunition delivered by order of Capt. George, to Ensign Slaughter, 1/2 lb powder, one lb lead (VSA-50).

02/16/81 Ammunition delivered by order of Capt. George, to Capt. Bailey for the defence of the Opost, 150 lbs powder, 100 lbs lead, and 100 flints; to Major Linctot for the Indian Department, 400 lbs powder, 212 lbs lead, and 300 flints; to Lt. Calvit, 1/2 lb powder; to Lt. Clark's Company, 3 3/4 lbs powder, 7 1/2 lbs lead (VSA-50).

02/16/81 Account of ammunition expended by the artillery at sundry times by order of Capt. Robert George, Commandant at Fort Jefferson, expended at the arrival and setting off of some French Batus, five lbs powder and 1/2 yd flannel (VSA-50).

02/19/81 Ammunition delivered by order of Capt. George, to Lt. Williams' hunting party, one lb powder, two lbs lead (VSA-50).

02/22/81 Ammunition delivered by order of Capt. George, to Peorian Indians, 30 lbs powder, 30 lbs lead, and 80 flints; to two men going with Majr. Harlan to the Falls of Ohio, 1 1/2 lbs powder, three lbs lead; to Buckner Pittman, boat master, 1/2 lb powder, one lb lead; to Mr. Kennedy, one lb powder, to three men of Capt. Bailey's Company, 1 1/2 lbs powder, three lbs lead (VSA-50).

02/26/81 Capt. R. George orders Court of Inquiry into allegations against Capt. Edward Worthington at FJ by Major Slaughter (DMS 56J27).

02/28/81-03/07/81 Ordered Court of Inquiry at FJ examining charges brought against Capt. McCarty by Capt. John Dodge (DMS 56J29).

03/02/81 Stores issued by order of Capt. Robert George, to Capt. Brashears' Company, three muskets or smoothed guns; to Capt. Robert George's

Fort Jefferson Personnel

Company, one musket or smoothed gun; to Capt. Robert George's company, no voucher, one kettle (VSA-50).

03/06/81 Ammunition delivered by order of Capt. George, to three men of Capt. Bailey's Company, six flints (VSA-50).

03/08/81 Ammunition delivered by order of Capt. George, to Ensign Williams' hunting party, one lb powder, two lbs lead (VSA-50).

03/09/81 Orders Court of Inquiry at FJ to examine Capt. John Rogers' conduct while in command at Kaskaskia as requested by Capt. John Rogers. Allegations dismissed (DMS 56J45).

03/09/81 Ammunition delivered by order of Capt. George, to Lt. Calvit, command to the Illinois, 3 3/4 lbs powder, 7 1/2 lbs lead; to Capt. McCarty for his use, one lb powder; to Patrick Kennedy for the inhabitants of the Illinois, 100 lbs powder, to Patrick Kennedy for his use 1/2 lb powder, one lb lead; to John Burks, Militia man, 1/4 lb powder (VSA-50).

03/10/81 Ammunition delivered by order of Capt. George, to Capt. Kellar for hunting, 1/4 lb powder, 1/2 lb lead; to Kaskaskia Indians, 20 lbs powder, 40 lbs lead, and 50 flints (VSA-50).

03/10/81 Stores issued by order of Capt. Robert George, to Lt. Calvit's Command, four tents or oil cloths (VSA-50).

03/13/81 Stores issued by order of Capt. Robert George, to Kaskaskia Indians, two swords (VSA-50).

03/16/81 Stores issued by order of Capt. Robert George, to Mr. Kennedy, one tent or oil cloth (VSA-50).

03/19/81 Ammunition delivered by order of Capt. George, to the Kaskaskia Indians, 1 1/2 lbs powder, three lbs lead; to Capt. Rogers going to the Falls of Ohio, 25 lbs powder, 20 lbs lead; to the Regiment, 10 3/4 lbs powder, 21 1/2 lbs lead (VSA-50).

03/19/81 Stores issued by order of Capt. Robert George, to Mr. Miles, Quartermaster Sgt., one musket or smoothed gun; to Capt. Rogers going to Falls of Ohio, two muskets or smoothed guns and five tents or oil cloths; to the Kaskaskia Indians, two swords (VSA-50).

03/20/81 Orders Court Martial proceedings for David Allen and James Taylor at FJ at 10 am (DMS 56J40).

03/22/81 Ammunition delivered by order of Capt. George, to Mr. Dodge, 1/2 lb powder, one lb lead; to Mr. William Clark, 1/2 lb powder, 2 1/2 lbs lead (VSA-50).

03/23/81 Ammunition delivered by order of Capt. George, to Mr. Archer, 1/2 lb powder; to Ensign Williams' hunting party, 1 1/2 lbs powder, three lbs lead (VSA-50).

03/24/81 Ammunition delivered by order of Capt. George, to one man of Capt. George's Company, 1/4 lb powder, 1/2 lb lead (VSA-50).

03/27/81 Ammunition delivered by order of Capt. George, to Sgt. Walker, 1/2 lb powder, one lb lead (VSA-50).

03/28/81 Ammunition delivered by order of Capt. George, to Lt. Richard Clark, 1/2 lb powder, one lb lead; to Militia at Clarksville, 2 1/2 lbs powder, five lbs lead; to Mr. Donne, 1/2 lb powder, to Lt. Girault, 1/2 lb powder, one lb lead (VSA-50).

03/28/81 Ammunition delivered by order of Capt. Robert George at Fort Jefferson, to Lt. Calvit and bowman, one lb powder (VSA-50).

04/13/81 Ammunition delivered by order of Capt. Robert George at Fort Jefferson, to Capt. Owens of militia, one lb powder; to Mr. Finn, Commissary, 1/2 lb powder, one lb lead (VSA-50).

04/17/81 Ammunition delivered by order of Capt. Robert George at Fort Jefferson, to Capt. Robert George's Company, one lb powder, two lbs lead (VSA-50).

04/20/81 Mentioned by Hunter (GRC Papers, I: 539).

04/21/81 Ammunition delivered by order of Capt. Robert George at Fort Jefferson, to express from Falls of Ohio, two lbs powder, four lbs lead; to Capt. George's Company, 2 1/2 lbs powder, five lbs lead; to Capt. Worthington's Company, 1/2 lb powder, one lb lead (VSA-50).

04/23/81 Omitted, per order brought from day book, three lbs tobacco (VSA-49).

04/23/81 Ammunition delivered by order of Capt. Robert George at Fort Jefferson, to Mr. Pyatt going on command to the Falls, 12 flints (VSA-50).

Fort Jefferson Personnel

04/24/81 Stores issued by order of Capt. Robert George, to Buckner Pittman, Boat master, two tents or oil cloths (VSA-50).

05/02/81 Ammunition delivered by order of Capt. Robert George at Fort Jefferson, to Capt. Kellar's hunting party, two lbs powder, four lbs lead; to six men on command, 1 1/2 lbs powder, three lbs lead (VSA-50).

05/03/81 Omitted, per order to four men of Capt. George's Company, eight lbs sugar (VSA-49).

05/06/81 Ammunition delivered by order of Capt. George at Fort Jefferson, to one man of Capt. George's, 1/2 lb powder, one lb lead; to two men of Capt. George's, one lb powder, 1/2 lb lead, and eight flints (VSA-50).

05/10/81 Tobacco issued by order of Capt. George, Commandant, to James Finn, three lbs (VSA-50).

05/10/81 Ammunition delivered by order of Capt. George at Fort Jefferson, to one man of Capt. George's Company, 1/4 lb powder, 1/2 lb lead (VSA-50).

05/11/81 Ammunition delivered by order of Capt. Robert George at Fort Jefferson, to Lt. Dalton, one lb lead; to one man of Capt. Worthington's, 1/2 lb powder, one lb lead (VSA-50).

05/14/80 Tobacco issued by order of Capt. George, Commander, to Illinois Regiment, 27 lbs (VSA-50).

05/14/81 Ammunition delivered by order of Capt. Robert George at Fort Jefferson, to Capt. Owens of Militia, 1/2 lb powder; to Capt. Kellar, 1/2 lb powder, one lb lead; to Lt. Calvit, 1/2 lb powder, one lb lead (VSA-50).

05/15/81 Ammunition delivered by order of Capt. Robert George at Fort Jefferson, to Ensign Williams, 1/2 lb powder, one lb lead; to Capt. Brahsears, 1/2 lb powder, 1/2 lb lead; to Col. Montgomery, 1/2 lb powder, one lb lead; to Lt. Clark's Blockhouse, 5 1/2 lbs powder, 11 lbs lead; to the Regiment, 113 lbs powder, 23 lbs lead (VSA-50).

05/17/80 Tobacco issued by order of Capt. George, Commander, to Capt. Worthington, three lbs (VSA-50).

05/18/80 Tobacco issued by order of Capt. George, Commander, to Martin Carney, three lbs (VSA-50).

05/21/80 Tobacco issued by order of Capt. George, Commander, to Mr. Hunter, three lbs (VSA-50).

05/23/81 Per order to Mrs. Burks for making shirts for Capt. George's Company, five lbs sugar (VSA-49).

05/23/80 Tobacco issued by order of Capt. George, Commander, to Capt. Helm, three lbs (VSA-50).

05/25/81 Per orders brought from day book, five gallons, two quarts, and one pint of rum (VSA-49).

05/27/81 Stores issued by order of Capt. Robert George, to William Carr, soldier Conductor, Lt. Clark, one musket or smoothed gun and one bayonet with belt (VSA-50).

05/30/81 Per orders brought from day book, 24 lbs sugar (VSA-49).

06/01/81 Per order to one man of George's Company, three lbs sugar (VSA-49).

06/01/81 Account of ammunition delivered by Martin Carney by order of Capt. Robert George, to Major Williams, one lb powder; to Lt. Girault, one lb powder, two lbs lead (VSA-50).

06/02/80 Tobacco issued by order of Capt. George, Commander, to Illinois Regiment, 28 lbs (VSA-50).

06/05/81 Per order to three men of George's Company, three lbs sugar (VSA-49).

06/05/81 Account of ammunition delivered by Martin Carney by order of Capt. Robert George, to Capt. Kellar for the use of hunting for the troops going to the Falls, one lb powder, two lbs lead; to Mr. Archer, one lb powder, one lb lead; to Lt. Clark, 1/2 lb powder, one lb lead; to three men of Capt. Worthington's Company, 3/4 lb powder, 1 1/2 lbs lead; to three men of Lt. Clark's, 1 1/2 lbs powder, three lbs lead; to Mr. Kennedy for his voyage to the falls, one lb powder, two lbs lead, and six flints (VSA-50).

06/06/81 Per orders brought from day book, 150 lbs sugar (VSA-49).

06/06/81 Account of ammunition delivered by Martin Carney by order of Capt. Robert George, to Col. Montgomery, one lb powder, two lbs lead, and two

Fort Jefferson Personnel

flints; to Capt. Owens militia, four lbs powder, eight lbs lead; to Mr. Finn, 1/2 lb powder (VSA-50).
06/06/81 Stores issued by order of Capt. Robert George, to Ensign Williams, one kettle; to Col. Montgomery, one kettle (VSA-50).
06/07/81 Per orders brought from day book, 12 lbs sugar (VSA-49).
06/07/81 Per order for hospital or sick accounts to one man and two children of Capt. George's Company, six lbs sugar; per order one man and woman of Capt. George's Company, three lbs sugar; per order to one man of Capt. George, two lbs sugar (VSA-49).
06/07/81 Per order to a man of Capt. Georges, three lbs sugar (VSA-49).
06/07/81 Account of ammunition delivered by Martin Carney by order of Capt. Robert George, to six men going to the Falls by land, three lbs powder, six lbs lead; to Patrick Callahan, one lb powder, two lbs lead; to Dapiae Whitegar, one lb powder, two lbs lead (VSA-50).

Gest, John
Paid John Gest for 600 weight bacon by order of Lt. Col. Montgomery at six dollars per the order (VSA-48).

Gilbert, John
10/23/80 Member of Robert George's Company of Artillery; by order of Col. Clark, R. George requests J. Dodge to issue John Gilbert cloth and trimmings to produce one suit, due for enlisting; John Gilbert listed as one of nine men (VSA-13a).

Gillaspey, Mr.
05/07/80 Letter from Col. Montgomery at Ft. Clark to George Rogers Clark. Mentioned a Mr. Gillaspey who is to make a voyage with a party of men. He will deliver to Clark part of the artillery, some salt, 2000 lbs of lead and other provisions will then be brought by Col. Montgomery (MHS: B1, F17) (Seineke, 1981: 431-432).

Gilmore, George
05/01/80 Enlisted (Harding 1981: 47).
06/02/80 Killed (Harding 1981: 47).
06/18/80 Deserted (Harding 1981: 53).
07/15/80 Listed in Capt. Worthington's Company (MHS B1, F20) (VSA-12).

Gils, John
09/30/80 Issued to Ensign Jarret Williams for men of Capt. Richard Brashears' Company, ten lbs soap per order Brashears and receipt of John Gils (VSA-48).
12/09/80 Sgt. John Giles signs his "mark" that he received of John Dodge the following: 150 lbs flour; 45 bushels corn at 40 quts per bushel; and 16 bags. The corn and flour are for the use of the troops at Fort Jefferson. The bags are to be returned to Giles. Five files and 15 lbs steel were received by Giles for the Armourer (VSA-14).

Girault, John [also Jeraue], Lieut.
05/19/80 Account of ammunition delivered by Martin Carney by order of Col. Clark: to Doctor and Lt. Girault of regulars at Kaskaskia, one lb powder and two lbs lead (VSA-50: 8).
06/20/80 Issued 1 1/2 yds shalloon, one ink pot, one ivory comb, one horn comb, three yds ribbon paid to Mr. John Girault in lieu of his charge for assisting in Translating in Public Business (VSA-48).
07/11/80 Lt. John Girault issued clothing to which he was entitled by law agreeable to Col. Clark's orders at FJ from Capt. John dodge per Capt. George's orders (VSA-12).
07/11/80 Lt. Girault received part of the contents of the within as appears by the receipt he had signed of this date wherein the articles are mentioned at FJ (VSA-12).

Fort Jefferson Personnel

07/11/80 Capt. George requests of John Dodge that Lt. Girault be issued the clothing which he is entitled to by law by order of Col. Clark at FJ (VSA-12).

07/12/80 Issued to Girault, 1 1/2 yds brown broadcloth 7/4 wide, 2 1/2 yds brown broadcloth damaged, three yds gray cloth 7/8 wide, 2 1/2 yds shalloon, four skeins silk, one stick silk twist, two yds calender for two vests or breeches, four yds camlet for two vests or breeches, 2 1/2 yds dimity for one vest or breeches, two yds chintz for two vests or breeches, four yards toile gris for two vests or breeches, six yds calamanco 1/2 yd wide for two vests or breeches, 1 1/2 yds shalloon -- error, 3 1/2 coarse linen for lining, one silk handkerchief, one Indian handkerchief, four check linen handkerchiefs, two yds muslin for six stocks, 19 1/2 yds white linen for six shirts, 3/4 yard fine holland for ruffling, 12 skeins white thread, two pairs thread hose, one pair knee garters and 1 1/2 yds blue cloth, one hat, 2 1/4 yds calamanco 1/2 yd wide for one vest or breeches (VSA-48).

07/12/80 Girault signed that he received from Capt. John Dodge, Agent a list of goods in part of the clothing allowed Girault by law. J. Donne attested (VSA-48).

07/12/80 Capt. Robert George requests that four enlisted men be issued to serve all during the war full clothing by Lt. Girault. The four men being: Francis Villier, Charles M.Laughlan, John LaRichardy, Francis Bennoit. Lt. Girault certifies that the above mentioned are all enlisted to serve during the war (VSA-12).

07/12/80 Issued to Lt. John Girault for four men of Majr. Richard McCarty's company, 14 yds blue cloth, 12 yds white flannel, four shirts, 13 yds linen for four shirts (VSA-48).

07/13/80 Present for Court of Inquiry at Ft. Jeff, served as Acting Judge Advocate (DMS 56J26).

07/14/80 Account of ammunition delivered by Martin Carney by Col. Montgomery's orders, to Lt. Girault, Illinois Regiment, 1/4 lb powder, 1/2 lb lead (VSA-50).

07/14/80 John Dodge, Agent certifies that Lt. Girault is due for three pair silk hose, one pair thread hose, two pair shoes, buttons for one suit of clothes. This was to complete an order drawn on Dodge in Girault's favor by George Rogers Clark for the clothing allowed him by law (VSA-12a).

07/14/80 Lt. Girault signs request to let Lt. Clark have the within or part thereof (VSA-12b).

09/09/80 One English blanket per order Lt. Col. Montgomery, issued to and overdrawn by Lt. Girault. The blanket is not included in Girault's July 12th list of goods issued to him (VSA-13a) (VSA-48).

09/11/80 Issued one lb powder, two lbs lead to Lt. Girault (VSA-13a).

09/11/80 Account of ammunition delivered by Martin Carney by Col. Montgomery's orders to Lt. Girault, one lb powder, two lbs lead (VSA-50).

09/11/80 Account of sugar delivered by Martin Carney by order of Col. Montgomery at Fort Jefferson, to Lt. Girault for his own use, one lb (VSA-50).

09/12/80 Issued one lb sugar for his own use (VSA-13).

09/19/80-04/07/81 Sometime between these dates, tobacco is issued to sundry persons per order of Capt. George, Commandant: to John Girault, two lbs (VSA-50: 13).

12/31/80 Lt. John Girault signed that he received of Israel Dodge one pair of shoes upon a certificate given Girault by John Dodge (VSA-14b).

02/26/81 Served on Court of Inquiry Board at FJ (DMS 56J27).

02/27/81-03/07/81 Served on Court of Inquiry Board at FJ regarding Capt. Dodge's charges against Capt. McCarty (DMS 56J29).

03/09/81 Served on Court of Inquiry proceedings at FJ regarding Capt. John Rogers conduct while in command at Kaskaskia (DMS 56J45).

03/20/81 Served on Court Martial Proceedings Board at FJ for David Allen and James Taylor; was acting Judge Advocate (DMS 56J40).

03/28/81 Ammunition delivered by order of Capt. George, to Lt. Girault, 1/2 lb powder, one lb lead (VSA-50).

Fort Jefferson Personnel

05/03/81 Per order brought from day book, one gallon, one quart, and one pint rum (VSA-49).
05/05/81 Per order brought from day book, two lbs sugar (VSA-49).
06/01/81 Account of ammunition delivered by Martin Carney by order of Capt. Robert George and Col. Montgomery, to Lt. Girault, one lb powder, two lbs lead (VSA-50).
06/02/81 Per order brought from day book, ten lbs sugar (VSA-49).
06/05/81 Per order brought from day book, five lbs sugar (VSA-49).
06/07/81 Per order brought from day book, two carots of tobacco and three lbs sugar (VSA-49).

Glass, Mikiel
07/10/80 Member of Capt. John Rogers' Co. Among list of men being issued two shirts and two stocks at FJ per Capt. George's orders to Capt. John Dodge for having more than one year to serve (VSA-12).

Glen, David
Two lbs soap to David Glen express per order Col. Montgomery (VSA-48).

Godin
09/25/80 Issued 7 1/4 ells osnaburgs and 2 1/2 ells calico paid Godin for 62 weight pork for the troops per order Lt. Col. Montgomery (VSA-48).
10/09/80 Paid Godin for three gallons wine for the sick 18 weight peltry (VSA-48).

Goodwin, William
07/10/80 Member of Capt. John Roger's Co. Among list of men being issued two shirts and two stocks at FJ per Capt. George's orders to Capt. John Dodge for having more than one year to serve (VSA-12).

Goyles, John
09/25/80 Two bags to John Goyles to transport four to Fort Jefferson per order of Capt. Rogers. 16 bags to John Goyles, five files and 15 weight steel to John Goyles per order Capt. Rogers and sent to Fort Jefferson (VSA-48).

Graffen, Daniel
05/01/80-12/21/80 Listed as Private in Capt. George Owens' Co. of Militia of the District of Clarksville in the State of Virginia. Pay Abstract (Harding 1981: 48-49).
09/01/80[?] Farmed 16 acres with eight others from Clarksville, totalling 320 bushels had Indians not burned crop (DMS 1M8).
09/07/80 D. Graffen signs that he received one rifle gun with mold and wipers and seven yds white linen for a milk cow [six years old with "4" branded on each rump] (VSA-13a).
09/12/80 Moved (Harding 1981: 49).
09/13/80 Account of sugar delivered by Martin Carney by order of Col. Montgomery at Fort Jefferson, to Mr. Graffen for a handmill for public use, six lbs (VSA-50).
09/25/80 One rifle gun and wipers and seven yds linen paid Daniel Graffen for a milk cow. These included in another where the cattle are charged (VSA-48).

Gratiot, Charles
Under account of house expenses, Gratiot was paid for 70 weight sugar, 105 livres peltry (VSA-48). Paid Gratiot for 3,876 weight lead at 12 is 2325,18. peltry, paid for 89 1/4 weight gunpowder, 1785 livres peltry (VSA-48). Paid for ferriage of light horses, 40 livres peltry (VSA-48). By Dodge's obligation in favor of Chas. Gratiot, 452 livres (VSA-48).
04/29/80 Letter from McCarty at Fort Clark to George Rogers Clark. McCarty sent something with Mr. Gratiot to Clark; Clark's presence is wished for at Fort Clark (MHS: B1, F16).

Fort Jefferson Personnel

05/06/80 Letter to George Rogers Clark from Charles Gratiot in Kaskaskia, reference is made to Col. Montgomery taking the opinions of the officers, military, and militia to determine whether they wish to proceed with the expedition [Gratiot had previously mentioned this expedition to Clark]. The vote was to proceed in order to scatter the enemy and strike terror in the Indians. About 30 men will stay at Kaskaskia for its defense. Gratiot is leaving Kaskaskia and going to Cahokia to tell the inhabitants that the expedition had failed [are there two expeditions --one previously failed and the other to begin?]. Gratiot apologizes for not being able to send tafia to Clark. It is scarce in the town. He promises to send some from Cahokia. Gratiot hopes that there is some tafia left from what he had reserved for his own use and will divide it with Clark. Gratiot asks that his respects be given to all the gentlemen and for Clark to tell them that all the garden seeds were sent down by Mr. Lindsay and there are no more in Kaskaskia (MHS: B1, F17).
06/10/80 Paid 60 lbs Peltry for one dozen China plates by Col. George Rogers Clark (VSA-48).
09/04/80 Issued in the Indian Department, paid Gratiot for tafia, 45 livres peltry, paid Gratiot for 2 1/2 weight tobacco, seven livres peltry, ten shillings, paid Gratiot for five weight vermilion 100 livres peltry, paid Gratiot for three ells ticken given for tobacco for Indians, 45 livres peltry (VSA-48).
09/10/80 Issued 15 ells of linen to fulfill his demands (VSA-13a).
09/25/80 Paid Charles Gratiot for a perogue by order Lt. Col. Montgomery 15 ells linen (VSA-48).

Grimshaw, John [also Gramshaw]
08/12/80 Enlisted (Harding 1981: 31-33).
08/19/80 Issued one suit of clothes and one blanket by order of Capt. George (VSA-12a).
08/25/80 Issued two shirts with James McMullan, Charles Morgan, and Thomas Laney (VSA-12a).
09/01/80 Account of tobacco delivered by Martin Carney by order of Capt. George at this place, to John Grimshaw, Gunner, 1/2 carot weighing 1 1/2 lbs (VSA-50).
09/11/80 Issued one blanket with ten others by order of Capt. George (VSA-13a).
09/15/80 Account of sugar delivered by Martin Carney by order of Capt. George at Fort Jefferson, to John Grimshaw and Mr. Mullens of George's Company, two lbs (VSA-50).
04/28/81-12/00/81 Listed as matross in Capt. Robert George's Co. of Artillery in the Service of the Commonwealth of Virginia and the Illinois Department. Pay Abstract. Based on incomplete list (Harding 1981: 29-30).
11/04/81 Deserted (Harding 1981: 33).

Groats, Jacob
05/01/80-12/21/80 Listed as Private in Capt. George Owens' Co. of Militia of the District of Clarksville in the State of Virginia [Jefferson Co.]. Pay Abstract (Harding 1981: 48-49).
09/01/80[?] Farmed 16 acres with eight others from Clarksville; totalling 320 bushels had Indians not burned crop (DMS 1M8).
09/13/80 Moved (Harding 1981: 49).

Groats, Mary (probably Mrs. Jacob Groats)
06/16/80 Five yards calico paid Mary Groats for making six ruffled and six plain shirts per receipt (VSA-48).
06/27/80 One ivory comb, one pair scissors, and one paper pins paid Mary Groats for making three plain shirts (VSA-48).

Fort Jefferson Personnel

Grolet, Francis [PVT]
[also Pere; he is the father; his son is in the same company]
09/10/80 Member of Capt. Richard McCarty's Company (VSA-13).
09/10/80 Issued full clothing for enlisting (VSA-13).

Grolet, Francis, Jr. [son] [PVT]
'[also "Fils" = son]
09/10/80 Member of Capt. Richard McCarty's Company (VSA-13).
09/10/80 Issued full clothing for enlisting (VSA-13).

Gruin, William
07/10/80 Member of Capt. John Rogers' Co. Among list of men being issued two shirts and two stocks at FJ per Capt. George's orders to Capt. John Dodge for having more than one year to serve (VSA-12).

Guire, M.
1 1/2 weight soap paid for threshing corn to M. Guire (VSA-48).

Guion, Fred S. [also Guyon]
06/04/79-12/03/81 Listed as matross [corporal] in Capt. Robert George's Co. of Artillery in the Service of the Commonwealth of Virginia and Illinois Department. Pay Abstract (Harding 1981: 29-30).
06/00/80 Fred Guion received on lb lead to kill meat for the garrison at FJ per Capt. George's orders [Date not legible] (VSA-11: Misc. Doc.).
07/03/80 Issued 3 1/2 yds blue cloth, three yds white flannel, two ruffled shirts, thread and buttons for clothes per order and receipt of Frederick Guion (VSA-48).
07/11/80 One ink pot (ommitted 11 July) per order and receipt of F. Guion for use of the Commissary Department at FJ (VSA-12) (VSA-48).
07/12/80 Robert George requests of John dodge, by order of Col. CLark, that Frederick Guion a sergeant enlisted during the war in George's Company of Artillery be issued full clothing and scarlet cloth sufficient to face his coat (VSA-12a).
07/12/80 Frederick Guion signs that he received 3 1/2 yds of blue cloth, three yds of white flannel, two ruffled shirts, thread and buttons (VSA-12b).
07/14/80 Capt. R. George requests of John Dodge by order of Col. Clark, that Frederick Guion be issued one coarse and one fine comb at FJ (VSA-12).
07/14/80 One ivory comb and one horn comb per order and receipt Fred Guion (VSA-48).
09/09/80 List of Dealings made from Fred Guion "Of what I have laid out
One rifled gun 1000 Dr.
09/10/80 $250 for side saddle and collar
09/10/80 $80 for four sickels
09/10/80 $20 for collar
09/10/80 $200 for saddle
09/11/80 Fifty-five weight iron at five dollars per pound
09/11/80 $600 for two spinning wheels
09/12/80 Account for one wagon and one rifled gun
09/12/80 Account for two ells of blue cloth
09/12/80 Account for ten pounds of tobacco
Borrowed from Ryly different times 500-200-50 dollars (VSA-13).
09/09/80 Account of ammunition delivered by Martin Carney by Col. Montgomery's orders, to Frederick Guion, 1/2 lb powder, one lb lead (VSA-50).
09/09/80 Account of soap delivered by Martin Carney by order of Col. Montgomery and Capt. George at Fort Jefferson, to Fred Guion, two lbs (VSA-50).
09/09/80 Col. Montgomery signs an order by Robert Young to Quartermaster to issue 1/2 lb powder and two lb lead to Fred Guion (VSA-13a).
09/10/80 Discharged (Harding 1981: 30).
09/25/80 Paid Fred S. Guion for tafia for the troops per order Lt. Col. Montgomery 275 dollars (VSA-48).
03/05/81 Fred Guion gave testimony at FJ at Capt. R. McCarty's Court of Inquiry; he was Issuing Commissary at Kaskaskia in Sept. 1780 (DMS 56J37).

Fort Jefferson Personnel

Hacketon, Michael [also Hasheton]
06/04/79-12/03/81 Listed as matross [corporal] in Capt. Robert George's Co. of Artillery in the Service of the Commonwealth of Virginia and Illinois Department. Pay Abstract (Harding 1981: 29-30).
06/00/80 Received one lb lead to kill meat for garrison at FJ per Capt. George's orders [Date not legible] (VSA-11: Misc. Doc).
06/12/80 Going on expedition with Capt. Harrison to the Falls of Ohio; among list of men receiving clothing for the trip (VSA-11).
06/30/80 Account of ammunition delivered by Martin Carney by Capt. Robert George's order at Camp Jefferson, to Michael Hacketon, a soldier in Capt. George's Company, one lb lead (VSA-50).
07/03/80 Capt. Robert George requests of Capt. John Dodge by Col. Clark's orders, to issue at FJ, two pair of leggings of half-thicks for Michael Hacketon and Sgt. Anderson (VSA-11).
08/24/80 Issued 1/4 lb of powder, 1/2 lb of lead (VSA-12a).
09/20/80 Deserted (Harding 1981: 31).

Hacker, John
06/04/79-12/03/81 Listed as matross [corporal] in Capt. Robert George's Co. of Artillery in the Service of the Commonwealth of Virginia and Illinois Department. Pay Abstract (Harding 1981: 29-30).
06/19/80 Issued two shirts by order of Capt. George; among list of men enlisted during the war (VSA-11).

Hall, William
01/13/79-06/00/80 Actual time of service (Harding 1981: 12).
12/20/79-06/17/80 Listed in Capt. Robert Todd's Company of Foot of the Illinois Battalion (Harding 1981: 11-12).
07/14/80 Among list of men being issued one shirt per Col. Montgomery's orders at FJ (VSA-12).

Hammit, James
07/10/80 Member of Capt. John Rogers' Co. Among list of men being issued two shirts and two stocks at FJ per Capt. George's orders to Capt. John Dodge for having more than one year to serve (VSA-12).

Hansler, Charles.
10/09/80 Paid Charles Hansler for three days work nine livres cash [hard] (VSA-48).

Hardin, Francis
02/02/80-11/30/81 Enlistment. Listed as Private in Capt. John Bailey's Co. of the Illinois Regiment in the Virginia State Service. Payroll (Harding 1981: 45-46).
07/12/80 Capt. Robert George requests of John Dodge, by order of Col. Clark, that 44 shirts be issued for 22 men of Capt. John Bailey's Company. Hardin is among the list of 22 men enlisted during the present war (VSA-12).
10/14/80 Died (Harding 1981: 46).

Hargis, John
07/15/80 Listed in Capt. Worthington's Company (MHS B1, F20) (VSA-12).

Harlan, Josiah (otherwise known as Silas)
Commanded 36 men at Clarksville (GRC Papers, II: 390) (DMS 26JA9).
06/05/80 Clark "with a few men" left Kaskaskia by boat to go to Fort Jefferson. Clark later left Ft. Jefferson with Major Harlan and Capt. Consola for Harrodsburg (VSA-11) (GRC Papers, I: cxxxviii).
06/10/80 Col. GR Clark leaves Fort Jefferson with J. Harlan and H. Consola for Harrdosburg (GRC Papers, I: cxxxviii) (Journal of Daniel Smith, *Tennessee Historical Magazine*, Vol. 1, No. 1: 64).
09/00/80 Relieved Ft. Jeff. Accompanied Clark and Consola to Harrodsburg (GRC Papers, I: cxxxviii).

Fort Jefferson Personnel

10/28/80 Out hunting without horses at Ft. Jeff (GRC Papers, I: 462).
11/23/80 Account of soap delivered by Martin Carney by order of Capt. George at Fort Jefferson, to Major Harlan for his own use, three lbs (VSA-50).
12/01/80 Account of sugar delivered by Martin Carney by order of Capt. George a Fort Jefferson: to Ensign Williams and Major Harlan, 12 lbs (VSA-50: 28).
12/04/80 Account of ammunition delivered by Martin Carney by order of Capt. Robert George at Fort Jefferson: to Major Harlan's hunting party, four lbs powder and eight lbs lead; to the soldiers going with Major Harlan, two lbs powder and four lbs lead (VSA-50: 29).
12/05/80 Account of ammunition delivered by Martin Carney by order of Capt. Robert George at Fort Jefferson: to the soldiers going with Major Harlan, two lbs powder and four lbs lead (VSA-50: 29).
02/15/81 Listed as Major. Sent to Louisville by Capt. George with letter (GRC Papers, I: 506, 462).
02/15/81 Ammunition delivered by Martin Carney by order of Capt. George, to two men going with Major Harlan to the Falls of Ohio, 1 1/2 lbs powder, three lbs lead (VSA-50).

Harlan, Silas [Major]
Note: Overall Commander of Jefferson Co. Militia including Capt. Owens' Co. of Militia at FJ (GRC Papers, I: 390).
Note: Was appointed Maj. of Jefferson Co. Militia and commanded same, including George Owens' Co. while Harlan was at FJ; however, commissioners state he was "not necessary" (GRC Papers, I: 390).
09/30/79 Letter from George Rogers Clark to Silas Harlan. Clark states that a fort will be built near the Mouth of Ohio "immediately." Clark orders Harlan to raise settlers to live at the post. The settlers will be paid as militia for as long as necessary. Clark asks Harlan to be at Fort Jefferson by December 1, 1779 (GRC Papers, I: 368-369) (VSA-; September 1779 file)
11/04/79 Letter from Silas Harlan at Harrodsburg to GRC at Falls of the Ohio. Their design of setting off to the Iron Banks was approved by the Commissioners, Harlan believes it will also be approved by the Assembly. Harlan is going on an expedition soon for cattle and horses (MHS: B1, F11).
03/12/80 Silas Harlan signed at "Camp Jefferson" that he received of George Rogers Clark, 3440 dollars for goods delivered to Falls. Attested by William Clark (VSA-10).
05/19/80 Account of ammunition delivered by Martin Carney by order of Col. Clark, to Major Harlan of militia, three lbs powder and six lbs lead (VSA-50: 8).
06/08/80 At Clarksborough. Sign issue of ammunition for Capt. Owens' Company of Militia (VSA-11).
06/08/80 Issued 2 1/4 yds blue cloth and three scalping knives issued to a Major Harlan for expresses per order Col. Clark (VSA-48).
06/08/80 Account of ammunition delivered by Martin Carney by order of Col. Clark, to Major Harlan at Camp Jefferson, 13 lbs powder, 26 lbs lead (VSA-50).
06/09/80 Camp Jefferson. Issued two pairs of leggings and two knives for the express to the Falls of Ohio from FJ (VSA-11).
09/21/80 Silas Harlan was rejected pay for the period Mar 27 - Sept 21, being "not necessary" and should not have been appointed because of the presence of Capt. Owens (VSA-13).
09/22/80 By order of Col. Clark, Robert George reugests of J. Dodge or agent to issue five yds linen and two skeins thread to Silas Harlan (VSA-13a).
09/22/80 Silas Harlan signs that he received the linen and thread (VSA-13b).
09/23/80 Robert George, by order of Col. Clark, requests J. Dodge to issue 5/8 yd blue cloth to Silas Harlan for leggings (VSA-13a).
09/23/80 Silas Harlan signs that he received cloth (VSA-13b).
10/11/80 Account of ammunition delivered by Martin Carney by order of Capt. George, to Major Harlan of Militia for his own use, 1/4 lb powder, 1/2 lb lead (VSA-50).

Fort Jefferson Personnel

10/28/80 Mentioned as hunting for Ft. Jefferson (Seineke, 1981: 466).
11/05/80 Account of ammunition delivered by Martin Carney by order of Capt. George, to Major Harlan for hunting, one lb powder, two lbs lead (VSA-50).
11/21/80 Account of ammunition delivered by Martin Carney by order of Capt. George, to Major Harlan for hunting, 2 1/4 lbs powder, 4 1/2 lbs lead (VSA-50).
11/22/80 Account of ammunition delivered by Martin Carney by order of Capt. George, to eight men going hunting with Harlan, three lbs powder, six lbs lead (VSA-50).
11/23/80 Account of soap delivered by Martin Carney by order of Capt. George at Fort Jefferson, to Major Harlan for his own use, three lbs (VSA-50).
12/01/80 Account of sugar delivered by Martin Carney by order of Capt. George at Fort Jefferson: to Ensign Williams and Major Harlan, 12 lbs (VSA-50: 28).
12/01/80 Silas Harlan [sheriff] signs with Leonard Helm as witness that he will assign a bond to Capt. James Piggot (VSA-14).
12/03/80 Silas Harlan and Robert George sign request of Israel Dodge to issue to John McGarr eight yds of linen for hunting with Harlan for one month (VSA- 14).
12/04/80 Robert George requests of Martin Carney to issue four lbs powder and eight lbs lead to Major Harlan and his hunting party as they are going to hunt mead for Ft. Jefferson (VSA-14a).
12/04/80 Capt. Leonard Helm signed in favor of Major Harlan (VSA-14b).
12/05/80 Robert George requests of the Quartermaster to issue two lbs powder and four lbs lead for the party going out with Major Harlan because yesterday's draw was insufficient (VSA-14).
12/05/80 Letter from John Donne at Fort Jefferson to George Rogers Clark. Speaks of Mr. Harlan hunting for meat at the beginning of last month [November]. Tells that he had brought in 14 and 15,000 weight and the Kaskaskia Indians had brought 3,000 weight and 1,000 weight was also brought to the fort. Donne hopes to return to Fort Jefferson before Major Harlan departs for the falls (MHS: B1, F23).
12/18/80 Silas Harlan and Robert George sign request of Israel Dodge to issue Thomas Snellock, Nicholas Tutle, and Thomas Hays eight yds linen each for 31 days of assistance to Harlan on a hunting trip for Fort Jefferson (VSA-14).
12/19/80 Robert George requests of Israel Dodge to issue to Silas Harlan cloth and trimmings for one suit of clothes, one pair of shoes, cloth for a capote, and linen for two shirts (VSA-14a).
12/19/80 Silas Harlan signs that he received of Israel Dodge 3 1/2 yds superfine broad cloth, two dozen and seven large buttons, two dozen and four small butoons, one skein of mohair, two yds of broad cloth for the cuppot, one pair of shoes and six yds linen and two yds flannel (VSA-14b).
12/21/80 Robert George requests of Israel Dodge to issue 3/4 yd of cloth to Major Harlan for a waistcoat (VSA- 14a).
12/21/80 Silas Harlan signed that he received of Israel Dodge the within contents (VSA-14b).
12/22/80 Silas Harlan and Robert George sign request of the Quartermaster to issue: Abraham Taylor, Hugh Montgomery, John Levrig, and John Wilson 1/2 lb powder and one lb lead for each man (VSA-14).
12/23/80 Robert George requests of the Quartermaster to issue to Major Silas Harlan one barrel rum, three lbs coffee, and six lbs sugar (VSA-14a).
12/23/80 Silas Harlan signed that he received the within contents from M. Carney (VSA-14b).
02/22/81 Ammunition delivered by order of Capt. George, to two men going with Major Harlan to the Falls of Ohio, 1 1/2 lbs powder, three lbs lead (VSA-50).

Harris, Francis
07/15/80 Listed in Capt. Worthington's Company (MHS B1, F20) (VSA-12).

Harris, John
(not known if Harris was civilian, militia, or member of state forces)
09/19/80-04/07/81 Sometime between these dates, tobacco is issued to sundry persons per order Capt. George, Commandant, to John Harris, armourer, two lbs (VSA- 50: 13).
12/01/80 Account of sugar delivered by Martin Carney by order of Capt. George at Fort Jefferson, to Mr. Harris, Armourer at this place, two lbs (VSA-50).
12/06/80 Account of soap delivered by Martin Carney by order of Capt. George at Fort Jefferson, to Mr. Harris, Armourer at this place, two lbs (VSA-50).
05/14/81 Mrs. Mary Hellebrant referred to a "Harry the Smith" probably referring to John Harris/Harry being nickname from Harris (VSA-19).
06/08/81 Named as armourer [blacksmith ?] at Ft. Jefferson; his bellows were left at FJ during evaction (VSA-20).

Harrison, James [Gunner]
09/10/80 Member of Capt. Richard McCarty's Co. (VSA-13).
09/10/80 Issued full clothing for enlisting (VSA-13).

Harrison, Richard
06/04/79-12/03/81 Listed as Captain Lieutenant in Capt. Robert George's Co. of Artillery in the Service of the Commonwealth of Virginia and Illinois Department. Pay Abstract (Harding 1981: 29-30).
05/01/80 R. Harrison authorized by GRC and cosigned by Wm. Clark to have 48 yds flannel at Ft. Jefferson for Harrison's troops (MHS: B1, F17).
05/01/80 Richard Harrison and George Rogers Clark sign request to William Clark to deliver the bearer 48 yds flannel for the use of the troops under Harrison's command (MHS: B1, F17).
05/01/80 Richard Harrison requests to William Clark to deliver 48 yds flannel for the use of the troops under Harrison's command (MHS: B1, F17).
05/02/80 Account of arms delivered by Martin Carney to Capt. George's Company 6 Artillery of the Illinois Virginia Regiment: delivered to Capt. Lt. Harrison, four muskets and three carabins (VSA-50: 3) (VSA-11).
05/19/80 Account of ammunition delivered by Martin Carney by order of Col. Clark: to Capt. Richard Harrison at Kaskaskia, 23 1/2 lbs lead (VSA-50: 8).
05/26/80 Account of ammunition delivered by Martin Carney by order of Col. Clark: to Capt. Richard Harrison at Cahokia, 136 lbs powder, to Harrison at Cahokia, 21 lbs lead (VSA-50: 8).
06/10/80 Issued to Capt. Lt. Richard Harrison, six yds superfine broadcloth, 2 1/2 yds shalloon, issued for six vests and six pair breeches eight yds casimir, ten yds thickset, 7 1/2 yds corduroy, one yd spotted persian, 2 1/2 yds linen, 19 1/2 yds linen for six shirts, 2 3/4 yds cambric for ruffling six shirts and making six stocks, one silk handkerchief, one romal handkerchief, two cotton handkerchiefs, two linen handkerchiefs, three pair thread hose, 5 1/4 dozen metal buttons, two sticks silk twist, six skeins silk, 12 skeins thread, one fine hat (VSA-48).
06/10/80 The articles issued to Captain Lt. Richard Harrison, agreeable to his receipt taken in Receipt Book A, certified by John Donne (VSA-48).
06/10/80 Sundry merchandise drawn out of the public store more than Capt. Robert George's quota for which in part no returns or receipts have been issued or passed: 26 yds blue stroud, 32 ruffled shirts, 20 plain shirts, 26 butcher knives, one ink holder, one bridle, 26 skeins thread per order, issued to Capt. Harrison, no receipt (VSA-48).
06/10/80 Account of ammunition delivered by Martin Carney by Capt. Robert George's order at Camp Jefferson, to Capt. Lt. Richard R. Harrison, 1 1/2 lbs lead and 40 flints (VSA-50) (VSA-11).
06/11/80 Lt. Rich. Harrison writes that he received from M. Carney, 24 yds of osnaburg made into bags to carry corn for the troops on their trip to Falls of Ohio from Camp Jefferson (VSA-11a).
06/12/80 Sundry merchandise drawn out of the public store more than Capt. Robert George's quota for which in part no returns or receipts have been issued or passed: three clasp knives, two horn combs, one ivory comb, 1 1/2 yds white half-thicks, 1/2 yd blue bath coating, four yds gartering, two

Fort Jefferson Personnel

2 1/2 point blankets, one leather ink pot per order, delivered to Capt. Harrison per receipt (VSA-48).

06/12/80 Capt. Robt. George requests of J. Dodge by Clark's orders to furnish Capt. Lt. Harrison with the following for the expedition to the Falls: three knives, three horn and one ivory comb; 1 1/2 yds white half-thicks for leggings, bath coating for breech cloth, four yds gartering, one pair blankets (VSA-11a).

06/12/80 Harrison signed that he received the above (VSA-11b).

06/12/80 Issued three, 2 1/2 point blankets, 26 horn combs, 13 ivory combs, 2 1/2 yds blue bath coating, per order, issued to Capt. Harrison per his receipt (VSA-48).

06/12/80 Capt. Robt. George requests of John Dodge to furnish Rich. Harrison with the following for 26 men of George's Co. going to the falls by Clark's orders: 26 yds of stroud for making leggings and breech cloths for 26 men, 52 shirts, 26 knives, one ink pot, one bridle, and thread to make leggings (VSA-11a).

06/12/80 John Bailey is going on expedition with Harrison to the Falls of Ohio (VSA-11).

06/13/80 Account of ammunition delivered by Martin Carney by Capt. Robert George's order at Camp Jefferson, to Capt. Harrison, 1/2 lb lead; to Capt. Harrison to take to the Falls of Ohio 500 lbs powder and 1000 lbs lead (VSA-50) (VSA-11a).

06/13/80 Account of tobacco delivered by Martin Carney by order of Capt. Robert George at this place, to Capt. Lt. Harrison going up Ohio, six carots weighing 18 lbs (VSA-50).

06/13/80 Richard Harrison signed that he recieved for use of George's Co., three blankets, 26 horn combs, 13 ivory combs, 2 1/2 yds blue bath coating, and thread (VSA-11a).

06/13/80 Richard Harrison signs that he received from M. Carney by Col. Clark's orders, the following: one large barge, one small canoe, 28 oars, 13 fathom cable, one grapling [hook] (VSA-11).

06/14/80 Richard Harrison writes a return to Wm. Shannon for 27 gallons of tafia for the use of his escort party [for Col. Walker] to the Falls [Ft. Jeff]. J. Donne signs that the above was delivered (VSA- 11a).

12/07/80 Letter from Capt. Richard Harrison at the Falls of Ohio to Col. Clark in Richmond or "elsewhere." Harrison is planning to leave on the 9th to go to Fort Jefferson and is taking all his artillery and "her stores". He mentions that Capt. Shannon is taking a quantity of corn with him. Harrison hopes that fort Jefferson will soon be relieved of their distresses. Mentions that Capt. Barbour is expected to bring a very large cargo. Harrison mentions that Capt. Worthington is at Harrodsburgh and feels he has no intention of going to Fort Jefferson during the winter. Harrison hopes to return to the falls in February (GRC Papers, I: 468).

12/20/80 Account of ammunition expended by the Artillery at sundry times by order of Capt. Robert George, Commandant at Fort Jefferson: upon Capt. Harrison and Capt. Roberts' arrival from the Falls of Ohio, per verbal orders, six lbs powder, two lbs lead, and one yd flannel (VSA-50: 33).

12/21/80 Richard Harrison signed that he received 40 pairs of shoes from Israel Dodge for Capt. George's Company (VSA-14).

12/21/80 Richard Harrison signed that he received of Israel Dodge 260 yds of linen for the use of Capt. Robert George's Company of Artillery agreeable to the within order (VSA-14).

12/24/80 Letter from Robert George at Fort Jefferson to George Rogers Clark. George tells Clark that Capt. Harrison had informed George that it is Clark's intent to evacuate Fort Jefferson and erect another fortification at the Iron Banks. George tells that his "yellow locks" will turn grey if Clark does not arrive soon to clarify his intentions (MHS: B1, F23) (Seineke, 1981: 468-469).

12/26/80 Robert George requests of John Dodge to issue Capt. Richard Harrison sky blue cloth and good trimmings for a coat and pompedore broad cloth for facing and edging (VSA-14a).

12/26/80 Richard Harrison signs that he received of Israel Dodge 1 1/2 yds sky blue cloth, 38 large buttons, six small buttons, two skeins mohair, one skein silk, two yds white flannel, 3/4 yd linen, 1/8 yd pompedore, and one skein white thread (VSA-14b).
12/30/80 Account of ammunition delivered by Martin Carney by order of Capt. Robert George at Fort Jefferson: to Capt. Harrison, four lbs powder and eight lbs lead (VSA-50: 30).
12/31/80 Stores issued by order of Capt. Robert George: to Capt. Harrison, one tent or oil cloth (VSA-50: 37).
12/31/80 Richard Harrision signed that he received of Israel Dodge one pair of shoes upon a certificate given Harrison by John Dodge (VSA-14c).

Harrison, Richard
05/30/80 Enlisted on this date as a private in Capt. Brashears' Company (Harding 1981: 51).
11/02/80 Deceased (Harding 1981: 51).

Hart, Miles
06/05/81 To Miles Hart, Militia of Clarksville, per orders, 12 lbs sugar (VSA-49).

Harry, James
05/30/80 Enlisted in Capt. Richard Brashears' Company of the Illinois Regiment (Harding, 1981: 51).
06/20/80 Deserted from Capt. Richard Brashears' Company (Harding, 1981: 51).
07/12/80 Robert George requests of John Dodge by order of Col. Clark, that 36 shirts be issued for 18 of the men which they are entitled to by law. James Harry is among the list of men receiving clothes (VSA- 12).
(note discrepancy in date of desertion and date of clothing issue)

Harry, John
11/15/80 Account of brass kettles delivered by Martin Carney by order of Capt. George at Fort Jefferson, to John Harry, Armourer at this place, one kettle (VSA-50).

Hatten, Christopher [Hatton]
04/26/80 Enlisted (Harding 1981: 47).
07/15/80 Listed in Capt. Worthington's Co. (MHS B1, F20) (VSA-12).
07/15/80 Killed (Harding 1981: 53).
08/27/80 Died (Harding 1981: 47).

Haul, Henry
06/04/79 Enlisted on this date in Capt. Robert George's Company as a Sergeant (Harding 1981: 30).
06/04/79-12/03/81 Listed as Sergeant [Gunner] in Capt. Robert George's Co. of Artillery in the Service of the Commonwealth of Virginia and Illinois Department. Pay Abstract (Harding 1981: 29-30).
06/08/80 Document #22 says he was killed on this date (Harding 1981: 31).
06/20/80 Killed (Harding 1981: 30).

Hays, James
03/26/80 Enlisted on this date as Private in Capt. John Bailey's Company of Illinois Regiment in the Virginia State Service (Harding 1981: 45-46).
07/12/80 Capt. Robert George requests of John Dodge by order of Col. Clark, to issue 44 shirts for 22 men of Capt. John Bailey's Company. Hays is among the list of 22 men who are enlisted during the present war (VSA-12).
09/13/80 Deserted (Harding 1981: 46).

Hays, Thomas
07/12/80 Among list of men who are members of Capt. Abraham Kellar's Co. at FJ receiving clothing issue for having more than one year to serve (VSA-12).

Fort Jefferson Personnel

12/18/80 Silas Harlan and Robert George sign request of Israel Dodge to issue to Thomas Snellock, Nicholas Tuttle, and Thomas Hayes eight yds of linen each for 31 days of assistance to Harlan on a hunting trip for Fort Jefferson (VSA-14a).

12/18/80 Thomas Snellock, Nicholas Tuttle, and Thomas Hays signed that they received of Israel Dodge the within contents (VSA-14b).

Hazard, John [also Hazzard]

06/04/79-12/03/81 Listed as matross [corporal] in Capt. Robert George's Co. of Artillery in the Service of the Commonwealth of Virginia and Illinois Department. Pay Abstract (Harding 1981: 29-30).

03/28/80 On a return signed by Robert George and dated 12/10/80, John Hazard enlisted for three years or during the war by Lt. V. T. Dalton into Capt. Robert George's Company of Artillery (MHS: B1, F23).

03/28/80 Enlisted (Harding 1981: 31).

09/11/80 Issued one blanket with ten others by order of Capt. George (VSA-13a).

09/11/80 Issued two shirts for enlisting for three years or duration into Capt. George's Co. (VSA-13).

09/13/80 V.T. Dalton requests of John Dodge to issue two shirts for John Hazard for enlisting (VSA-13a).

09/13/80 V.T. Dalton signs that the shirts were received for John Hazard (VSA-13b).

09/15/80 Account of ammunition delivered by Martin Carney by Capt. George's order to John Hazard of artillery, 1/4 lb powder and 1/2 lb lead (VSA-50).

09/15/80 Account of sugar delivered by Martin Carney by order of Capt. George at Fort Jefferson, to John Hazard of Capt. George's Company, one lb (VSA-50).

09/15/80 Request signed by George for one lb sugar to be issued to John Hazard "in the artillery" (VSA-13).

10/02/80 Account of ammunition delivered by Martin Carney by Capt. George's order to Sgt. Hazard of Capt. George's Company, 3/4 lb powder and 1 1/2 lbs lead (VSA-50).

10/13/80 By order of Col. Clark, Robert George requests J. Dodge to issue one yd flannel to John Hazard to loin a waistcoat (VSA-13a).

10/13/80 John Hazard signs that he received one yd of flannel (VSA-13b).

12/03/80 Account of soap delivered by Martin Carney by order of Capt. George at Fort Jefferson: to John Hazard of Capt. George's Company, one lb (VSA-50: 52).

Hellebrant, Peter [also Hellebrand]

05/01/80-12/21/80 [25] Listed as Private in Capt. George Owens' Co. of Militia of the District of Clarksville in the State of Virginia [Jefferson Co.]. Pay Abstract (Harding 1981: 48-49) (GRC, I: 465).

09/16/80 Account of sugar delivered by Martin Carney by order of Capt. George at Fort Jefferson, to Peter Hellebrant, a militia man, two lbs (VSA-50).

09/16/80 George Owens "marks" request [George signs] for M. Carney to issue Peter Hellebrant two lbs sugar for being sick (VSA-13).

05/14/81 Probably married to Mary Hellebrant[d] (VSA-19).

Hellebrant, Mrs. Mary [Hellebrand]

05/14/81 Probably married to Peter Hellebrant of Capt. George Owens Co. of Militia; sought four lbs sugar for "Harry the Smith" (VSA-19).

05/14/81 Mrs. Hellebrant per orders, four lbs sugar (VSA-49).

06/05/81 Mrs. Hellebrant per orders, three lbs sugar (VSA-49).

Helms, Ann

06/28/80 One paper pins paid Ann Helms for making one plain shirt (VSA-48).

Helm, Leonard [Leo]

Clark's reference to Helm as being past "meridian" of life and is Commander at Vincennes 1779 (GRC Papers, I: 240).

07/13/80 Issued in the Indian Department, 7 2/3 yds blue stroud, six plain shirts, 2 1/2 yds half-thicks, five yds ribbon - five ells, two, 2 1/2

Fort Jefferson Personnel 109

point blankets delivered to Capt. Williams by Col. Montgomery's orders (VSA-48).
07/14/80 Helm attested to list of goods received from Capt. John Dodge, Agent in part of an order drawn on Dodge in J. Donne's, Deputy Conductor WD, favor by order of Col. George Rogers Clark of the 12th Inst. (VSA-48).
07/14/80 Issued in the Indian Department, three yds blue persian at four dollars = 12 dollars, 1/2 yd fine cambric at 12 dollars = six dollars, 7 1/2 yds ribbon at one dollar = 7 1/2 dollars, thread = one dollar, one ivory comb, two horn combs, 7 1/2 yds calamanco at 2 1/2 dollars = 18 3/4 dollars. Total order 47 1/4 paid Major John Williams for liquor furnished for the savages in lieu of 120 lbs peltry per receipt (VSA-48).
07/16/80 Issued to Helm, Superintendant of Indian Affairs, two yds brown cloth 7/4 wide, 2 1/2 yds shalloon, 1 3/4 yds blue bath coating 7/4 wide, 2 1/4 yds white cloth 7/4 wide, issued for six vests 3 1/2 yds brown camblet, 2 1/4 yds chintz, 2 1/2 yds cottonade, and one yd chintz, issued for six pr breeches 8 1/4 yds toile gris, 2 3/4 yds thickset, and one yd chintz, 3 1/2 yds damaged linen for lining, 20 3/4 yds linen for six shirts, 3/4 yd fine holland for ruffling, two yds cambric for six stocks, one silk handkerchief, one Indian handcheif, four linen handkerchiefs, two pr thread hose, 16 skeins thread, one stick silk twist, four skeins silk, one hat, one pr knee garters. Two yds toile gris was also listed but had been crossed out (VSA-48).
07/16/80 Helm signed that he received from Capt. John Dodge the quantity of goods in part of an order drawn on Dodge in Helm's favor by order of Col. George Rogers Clark dated this day attested by J. Donne (VSA-48).
07/20/80 Issued to a party of friendly Kaskaskia Indians sent to hunt and scout for the garrison while it was weak, and delivered by approt. orders to Col. Montgomery. 13 3/4 yds blue strouds for blankets and breech cloths, 6 1/4 yds white half-thicks for leggings, 12 yds white linen for shirts, two yds dark ground calico for shirts, three scalping knives, two horn combs, eight skeins thread, one bolt ravelled gartering, three linen handkerchiefs, 5 1/2 yds ribbon, one piece of ribbon, one pair blue stroud leggings, one plain shirt, two scalping knives (VSA-48).
07/30/80 Issued in the Indian Department, 31 linen handkerchiefs to wear as tokens, 23 yds blue cloth damaged, 13 3/4 yds white half-thicks, 45 yds blue stroud, 15 1/2 yds blue stroud, 29 plain shirts, two prs ravelled gartering, one lb vermilion, 1 1/2 u. thread, 32 scalping knives, 1 3/4 yds blue cloth, three ruffled shirts, 15 plain shirts, one small shirt - - 1 3/4 yds, 12 piece ribbon, nine, 2 1/2 point blankets, six yds ribbon, one silk handkerchief, one ruffled shirt, one plain shirt, one pr leggings of half-thicks, three yds ribbon, one linen check handkerchief, one pair blue stroud leggings, one coarse hat bought for 20 dollars paper cury, four yds white flannel, two linen check handkerchiefs, two pair garters, four scalping knives, two yds ribbon, and eight yds white flannel for hunting shirts (VSA-48).
08/08/80 Account of tobacco delivered by Martin Carney by order of Capt. Robert George at this place, to Capt. Leonard Helm for his own use, one carot weighing three lbs (VSA-50).
08/21/80 Account of ammunition delivered by Martin Carney by Capt. George's odr to Capt. Leonard Helms for his own use, 1/2 lb powder and one lb lead (VSA-50).
08/21/80 Account of arms delivered by Martin Carney by order of Capt. Robert George, to individuals, to Capt. Leonard Helms, for his use, one rifle (VSA-50).
08/23/80 Paid Tourangean for tafia for Indians, 100, paid Tourangean for tafia for Indians, 30, four yds flannel for a hunting shirt made, two lbs vermillion, one ruffled shirt (VSA-48).
08/28/80 Issued in the Indian Department, paid Duplasse his account for bread and tobacco 24..0..0, paid Joneast his account of bread and pork, 145 (VSA-48).

Fort Jefferson Personnel

08/29/80 Paid Nichs. Canada for his account of Smith work per receipt 40 (VSA-48).
09/01/80-10/25/80 Wrote with Lt. Clark a summary of individuals listing their crops destroyed for Col. John Montgomery (DMS 1M8).
09/04/80 Issued in Indian Department, two ruffled shirts, four plain shirts, nine yds blue cloth damaged, 3 3/4 yds blue stroud, three yds blue cloth, one English blanket, one, 2 1/2 point blanket, 1 1/2 yds blue cloth for a stroud, 5/8 yd for leggings, two yds flannel, one ruffled shirt, six plain shirts, four pairs containing 200 yds linen, 145 yds white flannel, 50 scalping knives, one, 2 1/2 point blanket, one stroud 1 3/4 yds, 1 1/4 yds stroud, two linen shirts, four calico shirts, two pieces ribbon, eight gallons tafia, 5/8 yd stroud for leggings, 1/2 yd stroud for breech cloth, 15 weight flour, one, 2 1/2 point blanket, three gallons tafia, 17 scalping knives, 5/8 yd stroud for leggings, two yds ribbon, four gallons tafia, six check handkerchiefs, 1 1/4 yd blue stroud for two pair leggings, three calico shirts, 3 1/4 yds blue stroud, six yds white linen for two shirts, two white blankets, 2 1/2 points, 16 weight tobacco, one English blanket, 15 bushels corn, one hundred weight of flour, six yds ribbon, six linen shirts, three calico shirts, 24 bushels corn, one hundred weight of flour, six weight sugar paid for ferriage to Missouri, five ells linen paid Pierre Gamlin for tafia, six gallons tafia, four bushels corn, ten weight brown sugar, 50 weight flour, 20 weight tobacco, 15 combs, 16 scalping knives, two pair ravelled gartering, six weight coffee, five weight brown sugar, one hat, three gallons tafia, two shirts plain, ten bushels corn, 60 weight flour, three bags six ells each, ten weight tobacco, five bushels corn, 15 weight flour, 33 weight bread, five gallons tafia, 12 weight soap, six weight brown sugar, three bushels corn, six check handkerchiefs, two pieces ribbon, two dozen fine combs, one dozen coarse combs, 100 weight flour, four gallons tafia, 17 weight lead, 20 weight lead, one bushel salt, 1/2 bushel salt, ten weight lead, 1/2 bushel salt, 15 weight tobacco, 1/2 bushel salt, four bushels corn, four looking glasses, four yds gitt lace, two quarts tafia, two weight vermilion, peltry paid for tafia and tobacco to Isaac Levy 35 livres and ten dollars, paid I. Camp for medicine for the interpreter 16 livres peltry, paid I Camp for a keg for the savages 12 livres peltry, paid for 20 1/2 gallons tafia and cask to Isaac Levy per receipt 193 livres peltry, paid Capt. Joneast for sundries for Indians at different times 675: ten in cash per receipt, paid Lafortaine for interpreting ten days ten dollars cash per receipt, paid Canada for repairing Indian Arms and 200 flour per reciept 120 livres peltry, paid Gratiot for tafia 45 livres peltry, paid Gratiot for 2 1/2 weight tobacco ten shillings, seven livres peltry, paid Gratiot for five weight vermilion 100 livres peltry, paid Gratiot for three ells ticken given for tobacco for Indians 45 peltry, four ells cotton of 16 Sachaque given Major Bosson for assisting me in the Indian Department at Opost, three check handkerchiefs to Chapeau for carrying a speech to the savages, issued for a coat and jacket for a friendly Indian Chief eight yds red calamanco, 1/2 yd casimir, three yds linen (VSA-48).
09/09/80 Paid Thomas Bentley for his account ..93 paid Tourangean for tafia for Indians.. 100 (VSA-48).
09/11/80 Paid Fleure d epec for repairs on Indian arms ..40 (VSA-48).
09/13/80 Issued four lbs sugar for his own use (VSA-13).
09/13/80 Account of sugar delivered by Martin Carney by order of Col. Montgomery at Fort Jefferson, to Capt. Helm for his use, four lbs (VSA-50).
09/13/80 Issued five lbs coffee for his own use (VSA-13).
09/13/80 Five weight coffee per order and receipt, one English blanket and 1 1/2 yds ribbon issued to and overdrawn by Capt. Helm. Articles did not appear on the July 16 list of goods issued to Capt. Helm (VSA-48).
09/13/80 With Wm. Clark, estimates that amount of corn that could have been raised by the inhabitants of Clarksville was 190 bushels (VSA-20, misfiled).
09/19/80 Account of sugar delivered by Martin Carney by order of Capt. George at Fort Jefferson, to Helm, a soldier, two lbs (VSA-50).

Fort Jefferson Personnel

09/19/80-04/07/81 Sometime between these dates, tobacco is issued to sundry persons per order Capt. George, Commandant: to Leonard Helm, ten lbs (VSA-50: 13).

09/20/80 Issued in the Indian Department, four shirts issued to Major Williams, Commandant at Cahokia per his order for the Potowatomee chiefs, 13 yds linen, issued to the friendly Indians three clasp knives and six pair scissors, paid Tourangean for pork and tafia 35 livres peltry, paid the sheriff for corn and two corn fields for the use of the friendly savages who came to our assistance in time of danger 554 dollars continental, 11 yds cloth say blue cloth, nine yds white flannel, 3 1/2 yds linen, one yd toile gris, 30 skeins thread, four carots of tobacco, 1 3/4 yds cloth, one check handkerchief (VSA-48).

10/02/80 J. Montgomery signs a provision abstract that indicates Leonard Helm received a total of 12 lbs meal, 80 lbs flour, 80 lbs pork, and 95 lbs fresh beef via verbal orders during the period of 2 Sept. 1779, and 17 April 1780 (VSA-13a).

10/06/80 Account of soap delivered by Martin Carney by order of Col. Montgomery and Capt. George at Fort Jefferson, to Capt. Leonard Helm for his use, two lbs (VSA-50).

10/07/80 R. George signs Leonard Helm's request to the Quartermaster for issue of two lbs sugar and two lbs soap for Leonard Helm's use. Leonard Helm signs self "Suprnnt. of Indian Afair" (VSA-13a).

10/13/80 Account of soap delivered by Martin Carney by order of Col. Montgomery and Capt. George at Fort Jefferson, to Capt. Leonard Helm for his use, six lbs (VSA-50).

10/13/80 R. George signs Leonard Helm's request of the Quartermaster to issue six lbs soap to Leonard Helm (VSA-13a).

10/29/80 Leonard Helm writes to Slaughter of hardships at Ft. Jefferson; mentions is sitting at Capt. George's fire with two buffalo ribs (GRC, I: 466).

11/02/80 Account of ammunition delivered by Martin Carney by order of Capt. George, to Capt. Helm for his own use, two lbs powder, two lbs lead (VSA-50).

11/15/80 Account of brass kettles delivered by Martin Carney by order of Capt. George at Fort Jefferson, to Capt. Leonard Helm for his use, one kettle (VSA-50).

11/29/80 Writes to George Slaughter from Ft. Jefferson while sitting by Capt. George's fire and eating buffalo ribs (GRC, I: 466).

12/01/80 Account of sugar delivered by Martin Carney by order of Capt. George at Fort Jefferson: to Capt. Leonard Helm for his use, six lbs (VSA-50: 28).

12/01/80 Silas Harlan [sheriff] signs with Leonard Helm as witness that he will assign a bond to Capt. James Piggot (VSA-14).

12/02/80 Stores issued by order of Capt. Robert George: to Capt. Helm, one tomahawk (VSA-50: 40).

12/04/80 Account of soap delivered by Martin Carney by order of Capt. George at Fort Jefferson: to Capt. Helm for his use, six lbs (VSA-50: 52).

12/15/80 Statement concerning Robert George in which George had an inventory of a quantity of tafia delivered to Martin Carney and another for a quantity of broadcloth with a receipt signed by Israel Dodge and dated Fort Jefferson 12/15/80. It was witnessed by Capt. Bailey and Leonard Helm (GRC Papers, II: 315).

12/24/80 Letter from Capt. Robert George at Fort Jefferson to George Rogers Clark. George tells Clark that Capt. Helm is of infinite service and comfort to George at Fort Jefferson (MHS: B1, F23) (Seineke, 1981: 468-469).

12/31/80 Leonard Helm signed that he received of Israel Dodge one pair of shoes upon a certificate given Helm by John Dodge (VSA-14b).

01/01/81 Leonard Helm and Robert George sign request of the Quartermaster to issue to each of 25 Indians going to war against the Chickasaws, 1/2 lb powder, one lb lead, and two flints each (VSA-15).

04/10/81 Tobacco issued to sundry persons per order Capt. George, Commandant, to Capt. Helm, three lbs (VSA-50).

Fort Jefferson Personnel

05/03/81 Per orders brought from day book, three gallons, one quart, and one pint rum (VSA-49).
05/05/81 Per orders brought from day book, eight lbs sugar (VSA-49).
05/23/80 Tobacco issued by order of Capt. George, Commander, to Capt. Helm, three lbs (VSA-50).
05/25/81 Per orders brought from day book, eight lbs sugar and one carot tobacco (VSA-49).
06/07/81 Per orders brought from day book, 12 lbs sugar (VSA-49).

Henry, Moses
09/09/80 Issued to Capt. John Dodge for his own use, four ells black calamancoe [House expense] paid Moses Henry (VSA-48).

Hois, George [also Hoit, Hoyt or Hite]
06/02/80 Capt. A. Kellar listed 17 men who had served in his unit at one time during the war, Hite was one of these enlistments (MHS: B1, F19).
07/12/80 Among list of men who are members of Capt. Abraham Kellar's Co. at FJ receiving clothing issue for being enlisted during the war (VSA-12).
10/15/80 Deserted (Harding 1981: 23).

Hollis, Joshua
07/13/80 Member of Capt. Jesse Evans' Co. and discharged at FJ (Harding 1981:14).
07/14/80 Among list of men being issued one shirt per Col. Montgomery's orders at FJ (VSA-12).

Honfloy, Charles
09/25/80 Paid Charles Honfloy for five days work per order Lt. Col. Montgomery 15/- (VSA-48).

Holloway, John
10/03/80 Thirty ells osnaburgs, 16 ells black calamanco ten ells white linen, and five check linen handkerchiefs paid John Holloway for 110 bushels of corn (VSA-48).
10/03/80 Four paper pins and two ells camlet paid John Holloway for 110 bushels of corn (VSA-48).

Horn, Jeremiah [also Hern]
06/04/79-12/03/81 Listed as matross [corporal] in Capt. Robert George's Co. of Artillery in the Service of the Commonwealth of Virginia and Illinois Department. Pay Abstract (Harding 1981: 29-30).
09/18/79 Enlisted (Harding 1981: 32).
11/18/79 On a return signed by Robert George and dated 12/15/80, Jeremiah Horn enlisted for three years or during the war by Lt. V. T. Dalton into Capt. Robert George's Company of Artillery (MHS: B1, F23).
08/12/80 Issued two shirts for enlisting for duration of the war (VSA-12).
12/26/80 According to Capt. Robert George's Pay Abstract, Jeremiah Horn died on this date (Harding 1981: 29- 30 & 32).

Hopkins, Richard
06/04/79-12/03/81 Listed as matross [corporal] in Capt. Robert George's Co. of Artillery in the Service of the Commonwealth of Virginia and Illinois Department. Pay Abstract (Harding 1981: 29-30).
06/19/80 Issued two shirts from VSS by order of Capt. George; among list of men who are enlisted during the war (VSA-11).
07/26/80 Issued 1/2 carot of tobacco [three carots issued to six men] (VSA-12).
08/10/80 Issued one knife by order of Capt. George (VSA-12a).
08/10/80 One scalping knife per order and receipt of Richard Hopkins (VSA-48).
08/15/80 Furnished with one blanket out of the public store (VSA-12a).
08/15/80 One English blanket per order and receipt of Richard Hopkins (VSA-48).
09/02/80 Account of tobacco delivered by Martin Carney by order of Capt. Robert George at this place, to Richard Hopkins, for corking and paying public boats, two carots weighing six lbs (VSA-50).

12/14/80 Matross Richard Hopkins deserted on this date from Capt. Robert George's Company of Artillery (Harding 1981: 30).

Howell, Peter
06/12/80 Among list of men being issued clothing at FJ as members of Ensign Williams' Company (VSA-12).

Huffman, Jacob [also Hofman]
04/01/79-07/13/80 Listed as private on payroll of Capt. Jesse Evans' Company of Infantry Commanded by Col. John Montgomery of the Illinois Regiment (VSA-12) (Harding 1981: 14).
06/23/80 Issued shirt at FJ to go to Illinois for provisions; was formerly a member of Capt. Jesse Evans' Company of Infantry under Col. John Montgomery (VSA-11).
07/13/80 Payroll reflects Huffman discharged; formerly a member of Capt. Jesse Evans' Co. and is discharged at FJ (VSA-12) (Harding 1981: 14).
07/14/80 Received either one shirt or linen to make shirt from Capt. John Dodge per Capt. George's orders at FJ for having gone to Kaskaskia for provisions for FJ [accompanied by Richard Sennet, Peter Freeman, and James Ballanger] (VSA-12).
07/14/80 Issued one shirt for services performed in going to the Kaskaskias for provisions for the troops by order of Capt. George (VSA-12).
07/14/80 Among list of men being issued one shirt each by Col. Montgomery's orders (VSA-12).

Hughes, Mrs. Martha and family
Not dated. One paper pins paid Martha Hughes for making a shirt (VSA-48).
09/09/80 Account of sugar delivered by Martin Carney by order of Col. Montgomery at Fort Jefferson, to the Widow Hughes of Militia, three lbs (VSA-50).
09/10/80 Issued unto Widow Hughes three lbs of sugar for her sick family (VSA-13a).
10/28/80 Articles purchased by Martin Carney for the state of Virginia by order of Col. Clark. Purchased of the Widow Hughs hard money price to one iron pick for keeping the hand mills in order. Valued at 1/2 pound (VSA-50).
11/21/80 Account of sugar delivered by Martin Carney by orders of Capt. George, to Mrs. Hughes, a widow of militia, two lbs (VSA-50).
01/12/81 Received unspecified payment for making eight shirts for Capt. Benj. Roberts' Co. [Missing Reverse] from Mr. Dodge per Capt. George's orders (VSA-15).
03/10/81 Received two small looking glasses and two papers of pins for altering soldiers clothing (VSA-17).

Humble, David
07/12/80 Among list of men who are members of Capt. Abraham Kellar's Co. at FJ receiving clothing issue for having more than one year to serve (VSA-12).

Hunter, Joseph [Magistrate of Clarksville]
Not Dated Furnished beef, corn to Ft. Jefferson (GRC Papers, II: 362).
05/01/80-12/21/80 Listed as sergeant in Capt. George Owens' Co. of Militia of the District of Clarksville in the State of Virginia [Jefferson Co.]. Pay Abstract (Harding 1981: 48-49).
05/13/80 James Pigot, Ezekiel Johnson, Henry Smith, Joseph Hunter, and Mark Iles write a petition as trustees of Ft. Jefferson. They are making requests of circumstances within the settlement (GRC Papers, I: 425- 426).
06/13/80 James Pigot, Ezekiel Johnson, Henry Smith, Joseph Hunter, and Mark Iles write a petition as trustees of Ft. Jefferson. They are making requests of circumstances within the settlement (GRC Papers, I: 425- 426).
07/13/80 Participant in court of inquiry at Ft. Jeff (DMS 56J22-24).
09/01/80[?] Farmed 1 3/4 acres with Joshua Archer; would have yielded 45 bushels had Indians not burned it (DMS 1M8).

Fort Jefferson Personnel

09/09/80 Received three lbs sugar from Quartermaster by order of Col. John Montgomery; goods valued at 15 shillings (VSA-13).
09/09/80 Referred to as an "inhabitant of this place" (VSA-13).
09/09/80 Account of sugar delivered by Martin Carney by order of Col. Montgomery at Fort Jefferson, to Joseph Hunter, a militia man, three lbs (VSA-50).
09/14/80 Account of sugar delivered by Martin Carney by order of Capt. George at Fort Jefferson, to Joseph Hunter of Militia, three lbs (VSA-50).
09/25/80 One pair blue stroud leggings and one pair breech cloth paid Joseph Hunter for a sheep per certificate of J. Donne, Deputy Conductor (VSA-48).
11/29/80 Account of sugar delivered by Martin Carney by orders of Capt. George, to Joseph Hunter's family, two lbs (VSA-50).
12/01/80 John Dodge and John Donne sign [Joseph Hunter attests] that they will see to it that the sheriff of Clarksville, his successor or their assigns will be paid $554 Continental currency within six months of this date for a debt owed by the deceased John Oiler (VSA-14a).
12/21/80 Pay Abstract of a company of Militia commanded by Capt. George Owens of the district of Clarksville in the state of Virginia. Service ended on this date for Sgt. Joseph Hunter (GRC Papers, I: 464-465).
01/04/81 Account of ammunition delivered by Martin Carney by order of Capt. Robert George at Fort Jefferson, to Mr. Hunter, a militia man, 1/4 lb powder, one lb lead (VSA-50).
01/12/81 Stores issued by order of Capt. Robert George, to Mr. Hunter of the militia, one sword (VSA-50).
4/20/81 Wrote GRC from Ft. Jeff (GRC Papers, I: 539).
04/20/81 Wrote to GRC from Ft. Jeff [discusses distress at Ft. Jeff-he lost his stock and grain] (GRC Papers, I: 539).
05/21/81 Tobacco issued by order of Capt. George, Commander, to Mr. Hunter, three lbs (VSA-50).
06/05/81 Joseph Hunter, militia of Clarksville, per orders, 12 lbs sugar (VSA-49).

Hunter, Mrs. Nancy [also Miss] [probably Joseph's daughter]
06/15/80 One silk handkerchief and one Indian handkerchief paid N Hunter per receipt for making six ruffled shirts (VSA-48).
07/15/80 Seven yds calico paid N. Hunter for making ten plain and three ruffled shirts (VSA-48).
12/19/80 Abraham Kellar and Robert George sign request of Israel Dodge to issue Nancy Hunter pay for making a coat, two waistcoats, and one pair of overalls for Capt. Abraham Kellar's company (VSA-14a).
12/19/80 Nancy Hunter signs her mark that she received of Israel Dodge, 3 3/4 yds of white flannel in full of her demands for the within order (VSA-14b).

Hunter, Miss Marah [probably Joseph's wife]
02/02/81 Paid five yds of osnaburgs and two bunches of cap wire from I. Dodge, Deputy for making four soldier shirts at FJ per Capt. George's orders and Lt. Richard Clark's authorization (VSA-15).

Hunter, Mary
Four yds flannel and one pair garters per receipt of Mary Hunter paid for doubling and twisting twine for a net for the garrison (VSA-48).

Hupp, Philip
06/04/79-12/03/81 Listed as matross [corporal] in Capt. Robert George's Co. of Artillery in the Service of the Commonwealth of Virginia and Illinois Department (Harding 1981: 29-30).
06/12/80 Going on expedition with Capt. Harrison to Falls of Ohio; among list of men receiving clothing issue for the trip (VSA-11).
03/20/81 Gave testimony at FJ during Court Martial Proceedings of David Allen and James Taylor, saying he saw Boston Damewood make darts and shoot them through a window at Rachel Yeats (DMS 56J40).
09/03/81 Discharged (Harding 1981: 29-30).

Fort Jefferson Personnel 115

Hutchins, Thomas
Not Dated. Issued 2 1/2 gallons and 1 1/2 pints tafia to Thos. Hutchins per order of Lt. Col. Montgomery (VSA-48).
09/28/80 Thomas Hutchins writes to Col. Montgomery a list of goods [dispensed?], total of tafia from Aug. 7 to Sept. 28 = two gallons, two quarts, one pint, one halfpint; Montgomery requests Dodge to replace the goods (VSA-13a).
09/28/80 Thomas Hutchins signs that he received the above (VSA-13b).

Hutsil, John
05/01/80 Enlisted on this date as Private in Capt. George Owens' Company of Militia of the District of Clarksville in the State of Virginia (Harding 1981: 48-49).
05/01/80 Enlisted as a private in Capt. George Owens' Co. of Militia (Harding 1981: 49).
08/27/80 Killed (Harding 1981: 49) (GRC Papers, I: 465).
09/01/80 [?] Farmed two acres that would have yielded 50 bushels total had Indians not burned it (DMS 1M8).

Hutsel, Madam and family [also Hutsil] [widow John Hutsil]
09/08/80 Issued three lbs sugar for use of her sick children (VSA-13).

Hutsil, William
05/01/80-12/21/80 Listed as Private in Capt. George Owens' Co. of Militia of the District of Clarksville in the State of Virginia [Jefferson Co.]. Pay Abstract (Harding 1981: 48-49).
09/12/80 Moved (Harding 1981: 49) (GRC Papers, I: 465).

Hutton, Henry
Not Dated. Discharged not known from what company.
01/05/80 Henry Hutton, under the direction of G.R. Clark, issued 200 yds of flannel, 225 yds of cloth [blue and white], 277 dozen buttons, and 320 skeins of thread to Thomas Wilson at the Falls of the Ohio (MHS: B1,F14).
07/11/80 Attested to the list of articles that Thomas Wilson received from Henry Hutton at the Falls of Ohio on January 5, 1780. The quantity of cloth received by Thomas Wilson was the same as what John Wilson measured. Articles included flannel, cloth, button, and thread (MHS: B1, F14).
07/14/80 Among list of men being issued one shirt each per Col. Montgomery's orders (VSA-12).

Iles, Mark [Magistrate of Clarksville]
05/13/80 James Pigot, Ezekiel Johnson, Henry Smith, Joseph Hunter, and Mark Iles write a petition as trustees of Ft. Jefferson. They are making requests of circumstances within the settlement (GRC Papers, I: 425- 426).
06/13/80 Wrote and signed a petition to George Rogers Clark (GRC Papers, I: 426).
06/13/80 Four yds black calamanco per order and receipt of Mark Eyler (VSA-48).
09/12/80 Issued four pounds of sugar to pay for a morter for Col. Clark (VSA 13).

Irwin, Joseph
07/10/80 Member of Capt. John Rogers' Co. Among list of men being issued two shirts and two stocks at FJ per Capt. George's orders to Capt. John Dodge for having more than one year to serve (VSA-12).

Jarrell, James
01/04/80 Enlisted (Harding 1981: 46).
01/24/80-11/30/81 Listed as private in Capt. John Bailey's Co. of the Illinois Regiment in the Virginia State Service. Payroll (Harding 1981: 45-46).
07/12/80 Capt. Robert George requests of John Dodge by order of Col. Clark, that Ensign Slaughter be issued 44 shirts for 22 men of Capt. John Bailey's Company which are enlisted during the present war. James Jarrell is among the list of 22 men (VSA-12).
08/27/80 Taken prisoner (Harding 1981: 46).

Fort Jefferson Personnel

Jewel, John [also Jewell]
07/15/80 Listed in Capt. Worthington's Co. (MHS B1, F20) (VSA-12).

Jewell, John
11/18/79-11/30/81 Listed as private in Capt. John Bailey's Co. of the Illinois Regiment in the Virginia State Service. Payroll (Harding 1981: 45-46).

Johns, John A.
04/10/80 Articles purchased by Martin Carney for the state of Virginia by order of Col. Clark: purchased one large bateau to be paid to John Johns per receipt, 1000 pounds (VSA-50: 2).

Johnson, Edward
07/15/80 Listed as corporal in Capt. Worthington's Company (MHS B1, F20) (VSA-12).
09/19/80 Account of sugar delivered by Martin Carney by order of Capt. George at Fort Jefferson, to Edward Johnson, a soldier in Worthington's Company, one lb (VSA-50).
09/19/80 Rbt. George requests of the Quartermaster to issue one lb sugar to Edward Johnston of Worthington's Company (VSA-13).

Johnson, Ezekiel [Magistrate of Clarksville]
Not Dated. To cash paid Ezekiel Johnson for sundry articles delivered to Quartermaster Carney for the use of Fort Jefferson per receipt, 13.17 livres hard money, and 3,040 continental dollars (VSA-48). Paid Ezekiel Johnson for one horse, 2,000 continental dollars drowned in the Ohio by the soldiers (VSA-48).

Not Dated. Possibly married (VSA-13).
05/13/80 James Pigot, Ezekiel Johnson, Henry Smith, Joseph Hunter, and Mark Iles write a petition as trustees of Ft. Jefferson. They are making requests of circumstances within the settlement (GRC Papers, I: 425- 426).
07/13/80 Participant in Court of Inquiry at Ft. Jefferson (DMS 56J22-24).
09/09/80 Account of sugar delivered by Martin Carney by order of Col. Montgomery at Fort Jefferson, to Ezekial Johnston, a militia man, four lbs (VSA-50).
09/25/80 Issued 9 1/2 weight sugar for iron per order Col. Montgomery (VSA-48).

Johnston, Andrew [also Johnson]
Not Dated. One linen handkerchief paid A. Johnston for a dressed deer skin for use of an express in time of attack (VSA-48).
Not Dated. Issued two yds cottonade for two dressed skins for moccasins for an express in time of danger (VSA-48).
06/23/80 Capt. Robert George requests of John Dodge by order of Col. Clark, to issue 16 shirts to Reuben Kemp, Daniel Williams, Richard Bredin, Charles Evans, Andrew Johnston, Isaac Yeates, and William Nelson who are members of Worthington's Co (VSA-11) (VSA-48).
07/15/80 Listed as drummer in Capt. Worthington's Company (MHS B1, F20) (VSA-12).
09/18/80 Lt. R. Clark requests, George signs, one lb sugar to be issued to Andrew Johnson for sickness (VSA-13a).
09/18/80 Account of sugar delivered by Martin Carney by order of Capt. George, to Andrew Johnston of Worthington's Company, one lb (VSA-50).
11/17/80 Account of sugar delivered by Martin Carney by orders of Capt. George, to Andrew Johnston and family of Capt. Worthington's Company, 1 1/2 lbs (VSA-50).

Johnson, E.
06/17/80 Five yds calico paid for making six ruffled shirts and 12 plain shirts to E. Johnson (VSA-48).
09/25/80 Five weight sugar paid E. Johnson for a funnell (VSA-48).

Johnston, Mrs. Ezecal [also Ezekiel] Possibly Ann (D80).
06/16/80 Issued 11 1/4 yds calico paid Ann Johnson for making 12 ruffled and 24 plain shirts (VSA-48).
09/09/80 Wife of E. Johnston [also Johnson]? (VSA-13).
09/09/80 Received four lbs sugar, one quart Tafia from Quartermaster stores by order of Col. John Montgomery (VSA-13a).
09/09/80 Cost of supplies, t1,s6 (VSA-13).
09/09/80 Referred to as an inhabitant (VSA-13).

Johnston, John [also Johnson]
05/01/80-12/21/80 Listed as private in Capt. George Owens' Co. of Militia of the District of Clarksville in the State of Virginia [Jefferson Co.]. Pay Abstract (Harding 1981: 48-49).
06/28/80 Eight plain shirts per order and receipt of John Johnson (VSA-48).
09/01/80[?] Farmed 1 1/2 acres that would have produced 37 1/2 bushels had Indians not burned it (DMS 1M8).
09/15/80 Account of sugar delivered by Martin Carney by order of Capt. George at Fort Jefferson, to John Johnston of Militia, one lb (VSA-50).
10/25/80 Moved (Harding 1981: 49; GRC Papers, I: 465).

Johnston, John
11/15/79-11/30/81 Listed as private in Capt. John Bailey's Co. of the Illinois Regiment in the Virginia State Service. Payroll (Harding 1981: 45-46).
09/09/80 Issued [along with William Brauley] one pint of tafia and one lb sugar for being "very sick." Identified as a member of "Capt. John Bailey's Company" (VSA-13).
09/15/80 Rbt. George requests issue one lb sugar for John Johnston, Paul Quibea, and John Reid for being sick (VSA-13a).

Johnston, Samuel [Johnson]
01/20/79 Enlisted as a member of Capt. Robert Todd's Company [Time of enlistment when expired June 1780] Discharged at Fort Jefferson (Harding 1981: 12).
07/14/80 Among list of men being issued one shirt each per Col. Montgomery's orders at FJ (VSA-12).

Joins, John
07/12/80 Among list of men being issued clothing at FJ as members of Ensign Williams' Company which they are entitled to by law (VSA-12).

Joneast
Not Dated. Paid Capt. Joneast for 200 flour for the troops 100 livres in money (VSA-48).
08/28/80 Issued in the Indian Department, paid Joneast his account of bread and pork, 145 (VSA-48).
09/04/80 Issued in the Indian Department, paid Capt. Joneast for sundries for Indians at different times 645: ten in cash per receipt (VSA-48).

Jones, Elizabeth [also Johnes?] Probably wife of Matthew Jones
10/12/80 J. Bailey writes, George signs, that Mrs. Jones made five shirts for the men of Bailey's Company and is paid in goods from the public store (VSA-13a).
10/12/80 Mrs. Jones writes that [she?] received three yds flannel from Israel Dodge for making shirts (VSA-13b).
11/14/80 Received of Israel Dodge three yds of white flannel for making one suit of clothes per Capt. Abraham Kellar's orders to Israel Dodge and attested by Capt. George (VSA-14).
12/09/80 Robert George requests Israel Dodge to pay Elizabeth Jones for making four suits of soldier clothes for George's Company (VSA-14a).
12/09/80 Elizabeth Jones signs her "mark" that she received of Israel Dodge six yds white linen which is in full of her demands for making four suits of clothes (VSA-14b).

Fort Jefferson Personnel

Jones, John
07/10/80 Member of Capt. John Rogers' Co. Among list of men being issued two shirts and two stocks at FJ per Capt. George's orders to Capt. John Dodge for having more than one year to serve (VSA-12).

Jones, Matthew
Probably married to Mrs. Elizabeth Jones
06/04/79-12/03/81 Listed as matross [corporal] in Capt. Robert George's Co. of Artillery in the Service of the Commonwealth of Virginia and Illinois Department. Pay Abstract (Harding 1981: 29-30).
06/19/80 Issued two shirts by order of Capt. George; among list of men who are enlisted during the war (VSA- 11).
07/26/80 Issued three carots of tobacco for six men (VSA-12).
08/27/80 Helped dig well in fort with Abraham Lockard (VSA-12).
09/09/80 Received two lbs sugar and one pint tafia for one sick person in family (VSA-13).
09/09/80 Account of sugar delivered by Martin Carney by order of Col. Montgomery at Fort Jefferson, to Matthew Jones, a soldier in Capt. George's Company, two lbs (VSA-50).
09/11/80 Issued one blanket with ten others by order of Capt. George (VSA-13a).
09/19/80 Received one lb sugar for his sick family (VSA-13).

Jones [possibly Matthew, but no first name given]
03/20/81 Mentioned as having a lodge [house?] during the testimony of Elizabeth Watkins at the Court Martial proceedings at FJ. Mr. and Mrs. Watkins and James Taylor stayed at Jones' lodge (DMS 56J41).

Kearns, James
07/12/80 Among list of men who are members of Capt. Abraham Kellar's Co. at FJ receiving clothing issue for having over one year to serve (VSA-12).

Keesees, W. Sgt.
10/06/80 Issued 121 bushels corn at 40 qts per bushel 265 weight flour and three bags = six ells osnaburgs sent to Fort Jefferson by order of Col. Montgomery per Sgt. W. Keesees who deserted with the same (VSA-48).

Keinan, Lawrence [also Keening and Kenon]
06/04/79-12/03/81 Listed as sergeant in Capt. Robert George's Co. of Artillery in the Service of the Commonwealth of Virginia and Illinois Department. Pay Abstract (Harding 1981: 29-30).
06/12/80 Going on expedition with Capt. Harrison to the Falls of Ohio; among list of men receiving clothing issue for the trip (VSA-11).
06/16/80 Was to receive munition supplies from Capt. John Dodge per Capt. George's orders at FJ which were delivered to him by Daniel Boblarot. Capt. George's Co.: 2 1/2 yds flannel; 2 1/2 yds osnaburg, one pair scissors, two needles, and "some" twine (VSA-11).
06/19/80 Receives two shirts as part of a list of men in Capt. Robt. George's Co. who are enlisted during the war (VSA-11b).
07/20/80 Issued one pair leggings, one breech cloth, one handkerchief for being employed as expresses with dispactes to Col. Montgomery by order of Capt. George (VSA-12).
07/21/80 Issued 1/2 carot of tobacco by order of Capt. George (VSA-12).
07/21/80 Account of tobacco delivered by Martin Carney by order of Capt. Robert George at this place, to Lawrence Keinan, by Capt. George's order, 2/3 carot weighing two lbs (VSA-50).
08/09/80 Issued three yds of flannel for making cartridges by order of Capt. George (VSA-12).
08/09/80 Three yds white flannel per order Capt. George and receipt Lawrence Keinan for making cannon cartridges (VSA-48).
08/14/80 Furnished Lawrence Keinan to a swivel in Mr. Joseph Ford's house and 13 1/2 lbs of powder in defense of this place (VSA-12).

08/14/80 Account of ammunition delivered by Martin Carney by Capt. George's order to Lawrence Keinan, Gunner at this place, 13 1/2 lbs powder and 2 1/2 yds flannel (VSA-50).
12/14/80 Lawrence Keinan deserted on this date from Capt. Robert George's Company of Artillery (Harding 1981: 30).

Kellar, Abraham [also Kallar, Keller, Killer] Captain

Not Dated. One bottle tafia for Capt. Kellar's Company per order Col. Montgomery (VSA-48).
Not Dated. One dressed deer skin and five weight soap for Capt. Kellar's Company per receipt and order of Col. Montgomery, two dressed deer skins for Capt. Kellar's Company per order of Col. Montgomery, one weight soap for one of Capt. Kellar's Company, two weight coffee and four weight sugar for two sick of Capt. Kellar's Company (VSA-48).
11/15/79 Jacob Decker enlisted on this date as a private in Capt. Kellar's Company (Harding, 1981: 24).
12/08/79 James Thompson enlisted on this date as a private in Capt. Kellar's Co. (Harding, 1981: 24).
04/12/80 Abraham Kellar and William Shannon sign that they received of Col. George Rogers Clark four land warrants containing 560 acres each, for recruiting four soldiers during the war to serve in Col. Clark's regiment (GRC Papers, I: 413).
04/14/80 George Rogers Clark left the Falls of the Ohio on April 14, 1780 to go to the Iron Banks, informed by Capt. Kellar on April 25, 1780 (Journal of Daniel Smith, Tennessee Historical Magazine Vol. 1, No. 1: 63).
04/25/80 Went with Daniel Smith and T. Walker from Louisville to Col. Clark at Ft. Jeff "as he was just going there." Capt. Kellar was part of Clark's corps (Journal of Daniel Smith, Tennessee Historical Magazine Vol. 1, No. 1, March 1915).
04/26/80 Actually left [embarked] from Falls of Ohio for the Iron Banks (Journal of Daniel Smith, Tennessee Historical Magazine Vol. 1, #1, March 1915).
05/03/80 Reached Clark's encampment (Journal of Daniel Smith, Tennessee Historical Magazine Vol. 1, #1, March 1915).
05/03/80 "This morning at break of day opposite old Fort Massac. This afternoon at five o'clock got to the Mouth of Ohio; then down the Mississippi about five miles to Col. Clark's encampment, who we saw this evening and had some conversation with respecting our business." Capt. Kellar and untold number of individuals in party also arrives (Journal of Daniel Smith, Tennessee Historical Magazine, Vol. 1, No. 1: 64).
06/02/80 Capt. A. Kellar lists 17 men who had served in his unit during the war. The following men are known to have been at Ft. Jefferson: J a m e s Thompson, Abram M.Faggin, Leaving Dossey, John Williams George Hoit, John Chappel, Petter Boofry, Petter Belfau, Anthony Montroy, Baptist Raper, Wm Montgomery, James Macintos, Franway Larose, John Shank, Joseph Panther, Jacob Decker (MHS: B1, F19).
06/29/80 Capt. Robert George requests of John Dodge by order of Col. Clark, to issue eight shirts to James Thompson, Joseph Panther, John Shank, and Jacob Decker of Capt. Kellar's Co. (VSA-11).
07/04/80 John Crawley's enlistment voucher, witnessed by Harman Eagle, for enlisting three years with Capt. Abraham Kellar's Company [probably at Ft. Jefferson, but not stated] (MHS: B1, F20).
07/10/80 Capt. George requests by order of Col. Clark, that John Dodge issue Capt. Abraham Kellar his quota of clothing allowed by law [passed in 1779] (VSA-12a).
07/11/80 Capt. Abraham Kellar issued one comb, one inkstand, and one scalping knife at Camp Jefferson by order of Col. Clark from Capt. John Dodge per Capt. George's orders (VSA-12).
07/11/80 Capt. Kellar signs that he received the within contents the same day from Capt. Dodge (VSA-12).
07/12/80 List of sundries issued to Capt. Kellar: 1 1/2 yds brown broadcloth 7/4 wide, 1 1/2 scarlet broadcloth 7/4 wide, 2 1/2 yds of shalloon, one stick silk twist, 1 1/4 yds sycee for one vest and breeches, six skeins

Fort Jefferson Personnel

silk, 2 1/2 yds calender for one vest and breeches, two yds toile gris for two vests or breeches, 2 1/2 thickset for one pr breeches, 2 1/2 yds corded dimity for one pr breeches, 3 1/2 yds chintz for three vests, 14 yds white linen for four shirts, two yds muslin for six stocks, 1/2 yd fine holland for ruffling, seven skeins white thread, one silk handkerchief, one Indian handkerchief, four linen handkercheifs, two pair thread hose, one fine hat -- returned, 3 1/2 yds coarse linen for lining, one pair knee garters, three yds broadcloth 7/4 wide, 5 1/2 yds white linen for two shirts (VSA-48).

07/12/80 Capt. Abrm Kellar, Ill Battalion, signed he received from Capt. John Dodge Agent, a list of sundry goods in part of the clothing allowed Kellar by law. Attested by J. Donne (VSA-48).

07/12/80 Account of ammunition delivered by Martin Carney by Capt. Robert George's order at Camp Jefferson, to Capt. Abraham Kellar, going to Cahokia, 1/2 lb powder and one lb lead (VSA-50).

07/12/80 Capt. Robert George requests of John Dodge by Col. Clark's order, that 23 men of Capt. Abraham Kellar's Company be issued full clothing. The first six enlisted during the war, the others have over one year to serve:

1. John Chappel
2. George Hoit
3. Baptist Raper
4. Francis Laycore
5. Anthony Montrey
6. James Thompson
7. James Pritchet
8. Harman Eagle
9. Thomas Hays
10. George Smith
11. John Crawley
12. Joseph Cooper
13. Barny Cooper
14. John Kellar
15. David Russill
16. David Humble
17. James Davis
18. John Kearnes
19. Philip Duly
20. Haymore Duly
21. John Shank
22. Joseph Panther
23. Jacob Decker

Four of the above mentioned men James Thompson, John Shank, Joseph Panther, and Jacob Decker have received two shirts each in part of their clothing. Abraham Kellar signs to certify that the first six of the above mentioned men are enlisted during the war, and all the rest have more than one year to serve (VSA-12a).

07/12/80 Abraham Kellar signed that he received at FJ from Capt. John Dodge 80 1/2 yds blue cloth, 69 yds white flannel, thread and buttons to make up the same, three ruffled shirts, 35 plain shirts for the use of Capt. Abraham Kellar's Company of the Illinois Regiment agreeable to the within order (VSA-12b).

07/12/80 Capt. R. George requests of M. Carney that Capt. Kellar be issued one lb of powder and one lb of lead at Fj for his own use (VSA-12).

07/13/80 Issued to Capt. Kellar for his company per his receipt, 80 1/2 yds cloth, 69 yds white flannel, thread and buttons, three ruffled shirts, 24 plain shirts and eleven shirts. 35 3/4 yds linen for 11 shirts was listed but had been crossed out (VSA-48).

07/13/80 Served on Court of Inquiry board at FJ (DMS 56J22).

07/13/80 One horn comb, one scalping knife, one ink stand per order and receipt of Capt. Abrm Kellar (VSA-48).

09/02/80 Abraham Kellar receives pay voucher for bounty of men (VSA-13a).

09/08/80 Account of sugar delivered by Martin Carney by order of Col. Montgomery at Fort Jefferson, to Matthew Murray and family in Capt. Kellar's Company, two lbs (VSA-50).

09/09/80 Account of sugar delivered by Martin Carney by order of Col. Montgomery at Fort Jefferson, to Capt. Kellar for his own use, four lbs (VSA-50).

09/10/80 Account of ammunition delivered by Martin Carney by Col. Montgomery's orders, to Capt. Kellar's Company, four lbs powder, eight lbs lead (VSA-50).

09/10/80 Abraham Kellar receives four lbs sugar and four lbs coffee from Quartermaster Carney. Lt. Col. Montgomery cosigns Kellar's request (VSA-13).

Fort Jefferson Personnel 121

09/11/80 One blanket per order and receipt of Col. Montgomery, issued to and overdrawn by Capt. Kellar. Blanket not listed on July 12th list of sundry goods issued to Capt. Kellar (VSA-48).
09/11/80 Issues one blanket for his own use (VSA-13a).
09/12/80 Present at FJ (VSA-13).
09/12/80 Account of sugar delivered by Martin Carney by order of Col. Montgomery at Fort Jefferson, to two men of Capt. Abraham Kellar's Company, one lb (VSA-50).
09/13/80 Issued 1 1/2 lbs powder and three lbs lead to three men [one being Kellar] of Kellar's Co. (VSA-13).
09/13/80 Issued four weight coffee for his own use (VSA-13).
09/13/80 Four weight of coffee per order and receipt of Col. Montgomery, four weight of sugar per receipt, three weight of sugar per receipt, 1/2 weight of coffee per order Col. Montgomery, and two quarts tafia per order Col. Montgomery, issued to and overdrawn by Capt. Abrm Kellar. None of these articles appeared on the July 12th list of sundry goods issued to Capt. Kellar (VSA-48).
09/13/80 Account of ammunition delivered by Martin Carney by Col. Montgomery's orders, to Capt. Kellar's Company, 1 1/2 lbs powder, three lbs lead (VSA-50).
09/14/80 Account of sugar delivered by Martin Carney by order of Capt. George at Fort Jefferson, to James Thomson, a soldier in Capt. Kellar's Company, one lb; to two sick soldiers in Capt. Kellar's Company, two lbs (VSA-50).
09/14/80 Abraham Kellar requests an issue of one lb [sugar?] to James Thomson for being sick, R. George signs (VSA-13a).
09/14/80 Abraham Kellar requests, George signs, two lbs sugar be issued for two sick men of his Company (VSA-13).
09/16/80 Account of sugar delivered by Martin Carney by order of Capt. George at Fort Jefferson, to Joseph Panther, a soldier in Capt. Kellar's Company, one lb (VSA-50).
09/16/80 Account of soap delivered by Martin Carney by order of Col. Montgomery and Capt. George at Fort Jefferson, to Capt. Abraham Kellar's Company, six lbs (VSA-50).
09/16/80 Abraham Kellar requests, George signs, the Quartermaster to issue six lbs soap for twelve men of Kellar's Company (VSA-13a).
09/16/80 Abraham Kellar requests, George signs, Quartermaster Martin Carney to issue one lb sugar to J. Panther, a sick soldier of Kellar's Company (VSA-13).
09/19/80 Account of sugar delivered by Martin Carney by order of Capt. George at Fort Jefferson, to James Thomson, a soldier in Capt. Kellar's Company, one lb (VSA-50).
09/28/80 Abraham Kellar requests [George signs] an issue of two lbs sugar for own use (VSA-13a).
09/30/80 One unnamed soldier of Kellar's Co. dies (VSA-13).
09/30/80 Abraham Kellar signs that he received four yds of flannel to "bury a soldier in" (VSA-13a) (VSA-13b).
10/01/80 Account of sugar delivered by Martin Carney by order of Capt. George at Fort Jefferson, to Capt. Kellar for his own use, two lbs (VSA-50).
10/02/80 Account of ammunition delivered by Martin Carney by Capt. George's order to Capt. Kellar, 1/2 lb powder and one lb lead (VSA-50).
10/02/80 Abraham Kellar requests [George signs] of M. Carney to issue Abraham Kellar 1/2 lb powder and one lb lead for his trip to Cahokia (VSA-13a).
10/20/80 Abraham Kellar signs that he received from John Dodge at Kaskaskia one bushel of corn for Abraham Kellar's Company and four lbs sugar for Abraham Kellar's own use (VSA-13a, misfiled).
10/25/80 Account of soap delivered by Martin Carney by order of Col. Montgomery and Capt. George at Fort Jefferson, to Capt. Abraham Kellar, two lbs (VSA-50).
10/25/80 Robert George signs Abraham Kellar's request for M. Carney to issue two lbs soap for Abraham Kellars use (VSA-13a).

Fort Jefferson Personnel

10/25/80	J. Montgomery requests of Oliver Pollock to pay $2000 to Abraham Kellar, that being the sum borrowed from Abraham Kellar by Montgomery for public purposes; this is second request (VSA-13a).
10/27/80	Account of ammunition delivered by Martin Carney by order of Capt. George, to Capt. Abraham Kellar for his own use, two lbs lead (VSA-50).
10/28/80	John Donne attests that Abraham Kellar received $1000 from J. Montgomery for recruiting work (VSA-13a).
11/09/80	Account of ammunition delivered by Martin Carney by order of Capt. George, to two men of Capt. Kellar's Company, one lb powder, two lbs lead (VSA-50).
11/15/80	Account of brass kettles delivered by Martin Carney by order of Capt. George at Fort Jefferson, to Capt. Abraham Kellar and Company, two kettles (VSA-50).
11/18/80	Account of sugar delivered by Martin Carney by orders of Capt. George, to Capt. Kellar for his own use, two lbs (VSA-50).
11/22/80	Account of soap delivered by Martin Carney by order of Capt. George at Fort Jefferson, to Capt. Abraham Kellar's Company, six lbs (VSA-50).
11/30/80	Account of sugar delivered by Martin Carney by order of Capt. George at Fort Jefferson, to Capt. Abraham Kellar for his use, two lbs (VSA-50).
12/07/80	Stores issued by order of Capt. Robert George: to Capt. Kellar, one axe (VSA-50: 37).
12/07/80	Signed a request to pay Mrs. Francis Bredin for making four soldier coats for his company (VSA-14).
12/19/80	Signed a request to issue Nancy Hunter to pay her for making a coat, two waistcoats, and a pair of overalls for Kellar's Company (VSA-14).
12/21/80	Issued 11 pair shoes for 11 men in Kellar's Company (VSA-14).
12/21/80	Issued 71, 1/2 yards linen to make two shirts each for 11 men of Kellar's Company for the ensuing year (VSA-14).
12/23/80	Issued 22 skeins thread for making two shirts each for seven men of Kellar's Company (VSA-14).
12/26/80	Paid William Pritchet for making four suits of clothes (VSA-14).
12/31/80	Ammunition delivered to Captain Kellar's blockhouse, eight lbs gunpowder and five lbs lead (VSA-30; 50).
02/01/81	Ammunition delivered to two men of Captain Kellar's Company, 1/2 lb gunpowder, one lb lead (VSA-50).
02/26/81	Served on Court of Inquiry Board at Fort Jefferson for allegations made against Captain Worthington (Draper Manuscripts 56J27).
02/27/81-03/07/81	Served on Court of Inquiry Board at Fort Jeffrson examining charges Captain John Dodge brought against Captain Richard McCarty (Draper Manuscripts 56J29).
03/03/81	Gave testimony at Fort Jefferson during Richard McCarty Court of Inquiry (Draper Manuscritps 56J34)
03/09/81	Served as President of Court of Inquiry at Fort Jefferson examining Captain John Rogers conduct while in command at Kaskaskia (Draper Manucripts 56J45).
03/10/81	Ammunition delivered to Captain Kellar for hunting, 1/4 lb gunpowder, 1/2 lb lead (VSA-50).
03/20/81	Served as President of Court Martial proceedings of David Allen and James Taylor at FJ (DMS 56J40).
04/17/81	Tobacco issued to sundry persons per order Capt. George, Commandant, to Capt. Kellar's Company, two lbs (VSA-50).
05/02/81	Ammunition delivered by order of Capt. Robert George at Fort Jefferson, to Capt. Kellar's hunting party, two lbs powder, four lbs lead (VSA-50).
05/03/81	Per orders brought from day book, three gallons, two quarts, and one pint rum (VSA-49).
05/03/81	Per orders brought from day book, three lbs sugar (VSA-49).
05/21/81	Per orders brought from day book, four lbs sugar (VSA-49).
06/05/81	Per orders brought from day book, 24 lbs sugar (VSA-49).
06/05/81	Account of ammunition delivered by Martin Carney by order of Capt. Robert George and Col. Montgomery, to Capt. Kellar for the use of hunting for the troops going to the falls, one lb powder, two lbs lead (VSA-50).

1779   The Commonwealth of Virginia in account with Abraham Kellar: to cash paid soldiers for their bounty as per account and receipts, 234 (VSA-19; filed as May 10, 1781).

Kellar, John
07/12/80 Among list of men who are members of Capt. Abraham Kellar's Co. at FJ receiving clothing issue for having over one year to serve (VSA-12).

Kemp, Reuben [Sergeant] [also Camp]
06/20/80 Issued for Capt. Worthington's Company, three ruffled and three plain shirts per order Capt. George and receipt of Kemp (VSA-48).
06/23/80 Issued for Reuben Kemp, Daniel Williams, Richard Bredin, Charles Evans, Andrew Johnston, Isaac Yeates, and William Nelson of Capt. Worthington's Company, 15 plain and one ruffled shirt per order Capt. George and receipt of Kemp (VSA-48).
07/15/80 Listed as Sgt. in Capt. Worthington's Company (MHS B1, F20) (VSA-12).
08/24/80 One scalping knife per order and receipt of R. Camp (VSA-48).

08/24/80 Account of tobacco delivered by Martin Carney by order of Capt. Robert George at this place, to Sgt. Reuben Kemp, of Wothington's, 1/2 carot and 1 1/2 lbs (VSA-50).
09/13/80 Issued two lbs sugar to Reuben Kemp, a sick soldier of Capt. Worthington's Co. (VSA-13).
09/13/80 Account of sugar delivered by Martin Carney by order of Col. Montgomery at Fort Jefferson, to Reuben Kemp of Sgt. Worthington's Company, one lb (VSA-50).

Kening, Lazarous
06/19/80 Listed as member of Capt. George's Co. at FJ and issued two shirts by order of Capt. George (VSA-11).

Kennedy, David [also Kennada]
06/04/79-12/03/81 Listed as matross [corporal] in Capt. Robert George's Co. of Artillery in the Service of the Commonwealth of Virginia and Illinois Department. Pay Abstract (Harding 1981: 29-30).
06/12/80 Going on expedition with Capt. Harrison to the Falls of Ohio; among list of men receiving clothing issue for the trip (VSA-11).
10/22/81 Deserted (Harding 1981: 29-30).

Kennedy, Patrick Assistant Conductor

Not dated. Issued 519 weight lead, agdv., 17 1/2 bushels salt, and one pickle cask 30 continental dollars delivered to Patt. Kennedy, Assistant Conductor per his receipt (VSA-48).
06/05/80 Patt. Kennedy writes to certify that Col. Walker and son lived at Mr. Charlesvilles for 20 days at the rate of $2 per person per day [May 17 through June 5, 1780] (VSA-11).
07/03/80 Issued to Patrick Kennedy Assistant Conductor of Stores 9 3/4 yds linen for three shirts, 1 5/8 yds fine holland for three stocks and ruffling three shirts, 3 3/4 yds calender for three vests, 4 5/8 yds check linen for three pair trousers, 3 1/4 yds toile gris, 2 1/2 yds corded dimity for three pair breeches, 4 1/4 yds linen for lining, one ink pot, one ivory comb, one horn comb, one pair garters, 15 skeins thread issued by order of Capt. Robert George per Patrick Kennedy's receipt on said orders, six check handkerchiefs per order Capt. Rogers (VSA-48).
07/03/80 Account of ammunition delivered by Martin Carney by Capt. Robert George's order at Camp Jefferson, to Mr. Kennedy, Conductor, Joseph Duncan, Samuel Watkins, and John Cox one lb powder and two lbs lead for return trip to Illinois (VSA-12) (VSA-50).
07/03/80 Account of ammunition delivered by Martin Carney by Capt. Robert George's order at Camp Jefferson, to Mr. Kennedy, Conductor, one lb powder and two lbs lead (VSA-50).

Fort Jefferson Personnel

07/03/80 Patt Kennedy signs that he sent Joseph Duncan, Samuel Watkins, and John Cox to Camp Jefferson with provisions and they were to be paid in linen for two shirts each. Capt. Robt. George requests an issuance of linen and thread enough to make each man two shirts (VSA-12a).
07/03/80 Fifteen skeins thread issued by order of George per Pattrick Kennedy's receipt (VSA-48).
07/03/80 Six check handkerchiefs per order of Capt. Rogers issued to Patrick Kennedy Assistant Conductor of Stores (VSA-49).
09/03/80 Ten ells blue stroud, ten ells blue cloth, 20 ells osnaburgs, eight 2 1/2 point blankets, 4 3/8 ells fine linen, 24 ells 2d linen, eight ells flowered muslin, six ells spotted flannel, 12 ells calico, 9 7/8 ells linen and seven check handkerchiefs delivered to Patrick Kennedy Esqr Deputy Conductor per his receipt and Lt. Col. Montgomery's orders to purchase provisions for the relief of Fort Jefferson (VSA-48).
01/10/81 Stores issued by order of Capt. Robert George, to Patrick Kennedy, one musket and one bayonet with belt (VSA-50).
02/22/81 Ammunition delivered by order of Capt. George, to Mr. Kennedy, one lb (VSA-50).
02/25/81 Account of ammunitions received by Martin Carney at this post Clarksville, May 1, 1780. Received from Patt. Kennedy, 340 lbs lead (VSA-50).
03/05/81 Presented testimony at Capt. Richard McCarty's court of Inquiry at Ft. Jefferson (DMS 56J35).
03/09/81 Ammunition delivered by order of Capt. George, to Patrick Kennedy for the inhabitants of the Illinois, 100 lbs powder; to Patrick Kennedy for his use, 1/2 lb powder, one lb lead (VSA-50).
03/16/81 Stores issued by order of Capt. Robert George, to Mr. Kennedy, one tent or oil cloth (VSA-50).
06/05/81 Per order brought from day book, 12 lbs sugar (VSA-49).
06/05/81 Account of ammunition delivered by Martin Carney by order of Capt. Robert George, to Mr. Kennedy for his voyage to the falls, one lb powder, two lbs lead (VSA-50).
06/07/81 Per order brought from day book, 20 lbs sugar and two carots of tobacco (VSA-49).

Kennedy, Rachel
06/23/80 One silk handkerchief paid R. Kennedy for making four plain shirts (VSA-48).
07/06/80 One Indian handkerchief and one linen handkerchief paid for making five plain shirts to R. Kennedy (VSA-48).
01/18/81 Paid 1/2 yd of toile grey and two papers of pins and 12 skeins of thread for making seven shirts for Capt. John Bailey's Company as attested by Capt. George to Mr. Israel Dodge, Deputy Agent (VSA-15).
03/20/81 Gave testimony at FJ during Court Martial proceedings regarding derogatory language about Major Williams stated by either David Allen or James Taylor or both (DMS 56J40).

Ker, Conrad [also Ilor]
05/01/80 Enlisted on this date as a Private in Capt. George Owens' Company (Harding 1981: 48; GRC Papers, I: 464).
06/07/80 Killed; member of Capt. Owens' militia (Harding 1981: 48).

Ker, Henry [also Ilor]
05/01/80 Enlisted on this date as private in Capt. George Owens' Company (Harding 1981: 48; GRC Papers, I: 464).
06/07/80 Killed; member of Capt. Owens' militia (Harding 1981: 48).

Ker, Jonas [also Ilor]
05/01/80 Enlisted on this date as Private in Capt. George Owens' Company (Harding 1981: 48; GRC Papers, I: 464).
09/12/80 Moved (Harding 1981: 48).

Ker, Mark [also Ilor]
One piece steelyards bought of Mark Ker and delivered to John Donne for use of the Commissary Department, eight dollars (VSA-48).
05/01/80 Enlisted on this date as 1st Lieutenant in Capt. George Owens' Company of Militia of the District of Clarksville in the State of Virginia (GRC, I: 464; Harding 1981: 48-49).
06/07/80 Killed; member of Capt. Owens' militia (Harding 1981: 48).

Kerkely, James
07/15/80 Listed in Capt. Worthington's Company (MHS B1, F20) (VSA-12).

Key, George
07/10/80 Member of Capt. John Rogers' Co. Among list of men being issued two shirts and two stocks at FJ per Capt. George's orders to Capt. John Dodge for having more than one year to serve (VSA-12).

Key, Thomas
07/10/80 Member of Capt. John Rogers' Co. Among list of men being issued two shirts and two stocks at FJ per Capt. George's orders to Capt. John Dodge for having more than one year to serve (VSA-12).

Kimly, Charlotte [also Kimley]
06/23/80 Issued 1 1/4 yds calico and one Indian handkerchief paid Charlotte Kimly for making three ruffled and three plain shirts (VSA-48).
08/16/80 One linen handkerchief for making two hunting shirts paid to Charlotte Kimly (VSA-48).

Kincade, James
11/12/78-06/01/79 Member of Capt. Edward Worthington's Co. (Harding 1981: 6).
07/08/80-08/21/80 Member of Capt. Prather's Co. of Militia, on Shawnee Expedition (Harding 1981: 57).
07/14/80 Among list of men being issued one shirt per Col. Montgomery's orders at FJ (VSA-12).
07/14/80 Discharged at FJ but do not know from who's company (VSA-12).

Kindall, William
07/10/80 Member of Capt. John Rogers' Co. Among list of men being issued two shirts and two stocks at FJ per Capt. George's orders to Capt. John Dodge for having more than one year to serve (VSA-12).

King, B.
06/16/80 Five yds calico paid B. King, for making six ruffled and six plain shirts per receipt (VSA-48).

King, Charles
05/01/80-12/21/80 Listed as private in Capt. George Owens' Co. of Militia of the District of Clarksville in the State of Virginia [Jefferson Co.]. Pay Abstract (Harding 1981: 48-49; GRC Papers, I: 465).
09/01/80[?] Farmed total of 16 acres with eight others at Clarksville; would have yielded 320 bushels had Indians not burned it (DMS 1M8).
09/12/80 Moved (Harding 1981: 48-49).

King, Charlott
06/16/80 Issued 1 1/2 yds calico and two linen handkerchiefs to Charlott King for making six ruffled shirts (VSA-48).
06/29/80 One India handkerchief and one yd ribbon paid Charlott King for making four plain shirts (VSA-48).

Fort Jefferson Personnel

King, James
05/01/80-12/21/80 Listed as Private in Capt. George Owens' Co. of Militia
 (Harding 1981:48-49; GRC Papers, I: 465).
09/01/80 Farmed total of 16 acres with eight others at Clarksville (DMS 1M8).
09/12/80 Moved (Harding 1981: 48-49).
09/13/80 Given seven lbs sugar for trip on flat bottomed boat (VSA-50).

King, Judy
06/05/80 Three yds white flannel paid for making six plain shirts (VSA-48).

Kirk, Thomas
06/00/80 Came to FJ with Col. Montgomery (VSA-13a).
09/09/80 Account of sugar delivered by Martin Carney by order of Col. Montgomery
 at Fort Jefferson, to Thomas Kirk, one lb; to Thomas Kirk, two lbs (VSA-50).
09/10/80 Issued one shirt as serving 20 months in the service (VSA-13a).
09/10/80 Three plain shirts per order for Th. Kirk, Gasper Butcher and Stephensen
 issued to Col. Montgomery for part of clothing for four men of Capt.
Quirks Company (VSA-48).
09/10/80 Issued two lbs sugar for "Thom. Kirk a volunteer" (VSA-13a).
09/10/80 Two lbs sugar for one sick man and two children signed by Montgomery [on
 reverse for Thomas Kirk] (VSA-13b).
10/05/80 J. Montgomery [at Kaskaskia?] requests of J. Dodge to replace 61 lbs
 flour lent by Thomas Kirk to troops moving from Ft. Jefferson to
Kaskaskia (VSA-13a).
10/05/80 Thomas Kirk "marks" that he received flour (VSA-13b).

Lacroix [Jon Batest]
09/25/80 Paid for tobacco 110 livres in peltry per order Lt. Montgomery or 14
 ells check, 15 ells linen paid Lacroix per order Lt. Montgomery for a pirogue
(VSA-48).
10/01/80 J. Montgomery at Kaskaskia requests of J. Dodge to pay Jon Batest
Lacroix for a perogue used to haul corn to Ft. Jefferson (VSA-13a).
10/01/80 Jon Batest Lacroix signs that he received 15 ells of linen in payment
 (VSA-13b).

Lafont
06/10/80 Issued to Col. George Rogers Clark 18 check handkerchiefs to be paid
 Lafont. Two saltcellars were also listed but had been crossed out (VSA-48).
09/25/80 Three check handkerchiefs paid Lafont for three quire paper for public
 use. Six check handkerchiefs, four ells spotted flannel, two pieces
 ribbon, and 14 fine combs paid for two account books for public use to
 Monsr. Lafont (VSA-48).

Laform. Private (may be Charles Lavoine, see Harding 1981: 18).
09/10/80 Member of Capt. Richard McCarty's Company (VSA-13). (Harding 1981: 27).
09/10/80 Issued full clothing for enlisting (VSA-13a).

Lafortaine
09/04/80 Issued in the Indian Department, paid Lafortaine for interpreting ten
 days, ten dollars cash per receipt (VSA-48).

Fort Jefferson Personnel

Lamarine, John
05/30/79-06/02/81 Listed as a private in Captain Richard McCarty's Company (Harding 1981: 27).
09/10/80 Issued full clothing for enlisting (VSA-13).
11/20/80 Deserted (Harding 1981: 27).

Laney, Thomas [also Delany, Leney]
06/04/79-12/03/81 Listed as a matross [corporal] in Captain Robert George's Company of Artillery (Harding 1981:29-30).
08/19/80 Issued one suit of clothes and one blanket by order of Captain (VSA-12).
08/25/80 Issued two shirts at Fort Jefferson (VSA-12).
08/26/80 Ammunition delivered to Thomas Laney, gunner at the blockhouse, one lb gunpowder and two lbs lead (VSA-50).
08/27/80 Received one lb gunpowder, two lbs lead for four men in Captain George's Company (VSA-12).
08/28/80 Killed at Fort Jefferson (Harding 1981: 30; VSA-12).

Larishardie, Alexis [also Lainshardy, LaRichardy, John]
05/30/79-06/02/81 Listed as a private in Captain Richard McCarty's Company (Harding 1981: 27).
07/12/80 Issued full clothing (VSA-12).
11/20/80 Deserted (Harding 1981: 27).

Lastly, John [also Lasley]
07/13/80 Discharged at Fort Jefferson; member, Captain Jesse Evans' Company (Harding 1981: 14).
07/14/80 Issued one shirt (VSA-12).

Layarous, Ryan
06/12/80 Member, Captain George's Company going on expedition with Captain Harrison to the Falls of Ohio; received clothing for the trip (VSA-11).

Laycore, Francis
07/12/80 Member, Captain Abraham Kellar's Company at Fort Jefferson received clothing issue for enlisting during the war (VSA-12).

Leer, William
07/10/80 Member, Captain John Rogers' Company; received two shirts and two neckstocks at Fort Jefferson (VSA-12).

L'Enfant, Francois
09/10/80 Member, Captain McCarty's Company (VSA-13).
09/10/80 Issued, as a corporal, full clothing for enlisting (VSA-13).

Le Chaunce
09/25/80 Pd. six scalping knives for three lbs oakum to repair boats (VSA-48).

Legras, Col.
05/20/80 Captain Edward Worthington at Falls of Ohio wrote to George Rogers Clark at Mouth of the Ohio explaining why he did not accompany Col. Legras and Mr. Dejean from Williamsburg to Fort Jefferson (MHS: B1, F17).
06/04/80 Captain Robert George wrote from Fort Jefferson to George Rogers Clark. Letter was delivered to Clark by Col. Legras (MHS: B1, F19; Seineke 1981: 441).

LePaint, Louis
07/12/80 Issued cloth and trimmings for a complete suit of clothes and two shirts having more than one year to serve (VSA-12).

Fort Jefferson Personnel

Le Quang, Batist
07/13/80 Issued two strouds, two blankets, two pair leggings, and four shirts as he is entitled to them for his good service to the State on an expedition with Montgomery (VSA-12).

Leviston, George
07/15/80 Member, Captain Worthington's Company (MHS B1, F20; VSA-12).

Levrig, John
12/22/80 Issued 1/2 lb gunpowder, and one lb lead (VSA-14).

Lewis, Benjamin
12/11/79 Enlisted for three years by Lt. Valentine T. Dalton into Captain Robert George's Company of Artillery (MHS: B1, F23).

Lewis, Nelly
09/09/80 Issued two lbs of sugar as she is sick (VSA-13).
09/09/80 Sugar delivered to Nelly Lewis, a soldier's widow, two lbs (VSA-50).
11/15/80 Sugar delivered to Nelly Lewis, a soldier's widow, one lb (VSA-50).

Linctot, Geoffrey [also Linetot]
02/16/81 Ammunition delivered to Major Linctot for the Indian Department, 400 lbs gunpowder, 212 lbs lead, and 300 flints (VSA-50).

Lindsay, Joseph
05/06/80 In a letter to George Rogers Clark from Charles Gratiot, reference is made to all the garden seeds which were sent to Fort Jefferson from Kaskaskia with Mr. Lindsay (MHS: B1, F17).
06/02/80 Wrote about his and Israel Dodge's trip from the Illinois, describing their loses as a result of a hurricane. Lindsay asked that the Public make amends for Israel Dodge's clothing loss, because he was not paid for this trouble or time (VSA-11).
06/02/80 Israel Dodge and Joseph Lindsay arrived at Fort Jefferson bringing a quantity of goods from Kaskaskia (VSA-11).
06/13/80 Captain George requests Martin Carney to purchase tobacco from Mr. Lindsay for the use of the troops at Fort Jefferson (VSA-11).
06/13/80 John Lindsay recieved of Martin Carney, a receipt for 161 lbs tobacco, equal to 240.50 livres in peltry (VSA- 11;   50).

Linnett, Richard [probably Sinnett]
07/14/80 Issued one shirt at Fort Jefferson; discharged at Fort Jefferson (VSA-12).
07/14/80 Issued one shirt for going to Kaskaskia for provisions (VSA-12).

Little, Francis [also Litle; also Frank]
06/04/79-12/03/81 Listed as a matross [corporal] in Captain Robert George's Company of Artillery (Harding 1981: 29-30).
06/19/80 Issued two shirts for being enlisted during the war (VSA-11).
07/29/80 Issued 1/2 lb of gunpowder, one lb lead (VSA-12).
08/01/80 Ammunition delivered to Francis Little a soldier at this place, 1/2 lb gunpowder and one lb lead (VSA-50).
08/05/80 Tobacco delivered to Francis Little, for taking care of the state boats, one carot weighing three lbs (VSA-50).
08/18/80 Paid one pair blue stroud leggings for opening and drying public cloths (VSA-48).
09/13/80 Sugar delivered to Francis Little of Captain George's Company, two lbs; by Captain Dodge's order by Francis Little, 5 1/2 lbs (VSA-50).
09/14/80 Issued two lbs sugar for sickness (VSA-13).
09/23/80 Issued one lb sugar for sickness at the request of Robert George (VSA-13; 50).
10/12/80 Issued Francis Little one lb soap (VSA-13).

Fort Jefferson Personnel   129

10/16/80 Ammunition delivered to Frank Little of Captain George's Company,
          1/4 lb gunpowder, 1/2 lb lead (VSA-50).
10/22/80 Soap delivered to Francis Little, a soldier in Captain George's
          Company, one lb (VSA-50).
10/23/80 Issued cloth and trimmings to produce one suit (VSA-13).
03/03/81 Deserted (Harding 1981: 29-30).

Lockard, Abraham [also Archibold]
06/09/80 Articles purchased for the State of Virginia from Archibold Lockard,
          five pair mill stones valued at 300 pounds (VSA-50).
07/15/80 Member, Captain Worthington's Company (MHS B1, F20; VSA-12).
07/17/80 Issued one check linen handkerchief, for honoring and setting public
          razors which were damaged (VSA-48).
08/27/80 Helped dig a well in fort with Matthew Jones and Ensign Gage during
          attack by the Chickasaws (VSA-12).
09/07/80 Issued one quart rum [tafia] for his sick family (VSA-13).
09/09/80 Sugar delivered to Abraham Lockard in Worthington's Company, for his
          sick family, two lbs (VSA-50).
10/28/80 Articles purchased for the State of Virginia from Archibold Lockard:
          one iron pick for keeping the hand mills in order valued at 1/2
          pound (VSA-50).

Lockard, [Family] [Mrs. and Child [ren]]
06/27/80 Paid one Indian handkerchief for making three plain shirts (VSA-
          48).

Long, Philip
06/04/79-12/03/81 Listed as a matross [corporal] in Captain Robert George's
          Company of Artillery (Harding 1981: 29-30).
06/12/80 Went on expedition with Captain Harrison to the Falls of Ohio;
          received clothing for the trip (VSA-11).
10/14/80 Deserted (Harding 1981: 29-30).

Lonian, Joseph
12/10/80 Enlisted in Captain Robert George's Company of Artillery (MHS: B1,
          F23).

Lovin, Richard [also Loving, Lovell]
Drummer designation (Harding 1981:21, 27).
09/10/80 Member, Captain Richard McCarty's Company (VSA-13).
09/10/80 Issued full clothing for enlisting (VSA-13).

Lowerback, Christopher
06/04/79-12/03/81 Listed as a matross [corporal] in Captain Robert George's
          Company of Artillery (Harding 1981:29-30).
03/15/80-05/10/80 Actual time of service (Harding 1981:31).
05/10/80 Deserted (Harding 1981:31).

Lunsford, Anthony and family
01/20/80-11/30/81 Listed as a private in Captain John Bailey's Company
          (Harding 1981: 45-46).
09/09/80 Issued two lbs sugar for sick family (VSA-13).
09/09/80 Sugar delivered to Anthony Lunsford and family, two lbs (VSA-50).
11/27/80 Sugar delivered to Mr. Lunsford and sick family, five lbs (VSA-50).

Lunsford, Mary [Mrs. Anthony and family]
06/16/80 Paid one India handkerchief and two linen check handkerchiefs for
          making five plain shirts (VSA-48).
09/09/80 Family is sick [husband given two lbs sugar] (VSA-13).
02/04/81 Made two shirts for Captain Worthington's Company at Fort Jefferson.
          Mr. Lunsford signed over payment to Mrs. Lunsford to Mrs. Francis
          Bredin (VSA-15).

Fort Jefferson Personnel

Lunsford, George
01/20/80-11/30/81 Listed as a private in Captain John Bailey's Company (Harding 1981: 45-46).
09/10/80 Issued 1/2 lb sugar for being very sick (VSA-13).

Lunsford, Mason
01/20/80-11/30/81 Listed as a private in Captain John Bailey's Company (Harding 1981: 45-46).

Lundsford, Moses
07/15/80 Listed in Captain Worthington's Company (MHS B1, F20; VSA-12).

McAuley, Pat
06/04/79-12/03/81 Listed as matross [corporal] in Captain Robert George's Company of Artillery (Harding 1981:29-30).
06/12/80 Went expedition with Captain Harrison to the Falls of Ohio; received clothing issue for the trip (VSA-11).
11/19/80 Deserted (Harding 1981:29-30).

McAuley, Mary [also McColey] [Mrs. William?]
12/02/80 Paid for making six soldier shirts for Captain George's Company (VSA- 14).
12/02/80 Mary McAuley received three yards white flannel in full of her demand for making six shirts (VSA-14).

McAuley, William
09/15/80 Sugar delivered to William McAuley of militia, one lb (VSA-50).

McCan, Moses
05/01/80-12/21/80 Listed as a private in Captain George Owens' Company of Militia (Harding 1981:48-49).
09/12/80 Moved (Harding 1981:48).

McCarty, Richard
05/30/79-06/02/81 Listed as a Captain (Harding 1981:27).
03/09/80 Ammunition delivered to Captain McCarty for his use, one lb gunpowder (VSA-50).
04/25/80 Captain Richard McCarty writes George Rogers Clark. McCarty congratulates Clark on his arrival at the Mouth of Ohio. Speaks of expected attack at McCarty's location; "health good but pockets is low." Wishes Clark was at McCarty's location (MHS: B1, F16).
04/29/80 McCarty writes to George Rogers Clark. Montgomery is sending something with Mr. Gratiot to Clark; Clark's presence is needed at Fort Clark (MHS: B1, F16).
07/11/80 Issued clothing he was entitled to by law (VSA-12).
07/12/80 Issued 1 1/2 yards of brown broadcloth 7 1/4 wide, 1 1/2 yards scarlet broadcloth 7 1/4 wide, issued for two pair breeches 2 1/2 yards thickset and 2 1/2 yards corded dimity, issued 2 1/2 yards shalloon, issued for four pair breeches and six vests 2 1/4 yards calender, four yards camlet, six yards calamanco, four yards toile gris, and three yards chintz, issued two dozen metal buttons, 21 yards white linen for six shirts, 3/4 yard fine holland for ruffling, two yards muslin for six stocks, two pair thread hose, one silk handkerchief, one Indian handkerchief, four linen handkerchiefs, two skeins silk, 12 skeins white thread, three yards coarse linen for lining, and three yards broadcloth 7/4 wide (VSA-48).
07/12/80 Issued four men of Major McCarty's Company, 14 yards blue cloth, 12 yards white flannel, four shirts, and 13 yards linen for four shirts (VSA-48).
08/08/80 Came to Fort Jefferson with ten whites and 65 Kaskaskia Indians (Draper Manuscripts 26J23).

09/10/80	Received for Col. Montgomery a set of treasury bills for $1000 for recruiting services in favor of Ensign Laurence Slaughter (VSA-13).
09/10/80	Received sixty-three yards blue cloth, 55 yards flannel, and thread for his company per his receipt (VSA-48)
09/10/80	Ammunition delivered to Captain McCarty's Company, 4 1/2 lbs gunpowder, nine lbs lead (VSA-50).
09/13/80	Issued three blankets and 14 shirts (VSA-48).
09/13/80	Sugar delivered to a man of Captain McCarty's Company, 1 1/2 lbs (VSA-50).
09/13/80	Soap delivered to Captain McCarty's Company, 15 lbs (VSA-50).
09/13/80	Listed as an officer of the mess; received a share of 60 lbs sugar (VSA-13).
09/15/80	Ammunition delivered to two men of Captain McCarty's company, one lb gunpowder and two lbs lead (VSA-50).
11/19/80	Soap delivered to Captain McCarty's Company, 1 1/2 lbs (VSA-50).
12/04/80	Stores issued to Captain McCarty's Company, one tomahawk (VSA-50: 40).
12/05/80	Soap delivered to a man of Captain McCarty's Company, 1 1/2 lbs (VSA-50: 52).
02/27/81-03/07/81	Court of Inquiry at Fort Jefferson, examined charges brought against Captain McCarty by Captain John Dodge; McCarty was found guilty and a general court martial was recommended (Draper Manuscripts 56J29).
06/02/81	Killed (Harding 1981: 27).

McCormack, John [also M Cormack, McCormick]

05/01/80-12/21[25]/80	Listed as a private in Captain George Owens' Company of Militia (George Rogers Clark Papers, I: 465; Harding 1981: 48-49).
09/01/80	Farmed one acre at Clarksville which would have produced 30 bushels of corn had the Indians not burned it (Draper Manuscripts 1M8).
09/07/80	Received one quart tafia for his sick wife (VSA-13).
09/09/80	Received one quart tafia valued at six shillings (VSA-13).
09/09/80	Listed as an "inhabitant" of this place" (VSA-13).

McCormack, E. [Mrs. John]

06/17/80	Paid 1 1/4 yards calico, one ivory comb, and one horn comb for making five ruffled shirts per receipt (VSA-48).
07/06/80	Paid six yards white flannel and one razor for making 14 plain shirts (VSA-48).
09/07/80	Husband received one quart tafia for his sick wife (VSA-13).

McCulty, Patt

12/10/80	Enlisted for three years in Captain Robert George's Company of Artillery (MHS: B1, F23).

McDonald, David

07/10/80	Member, Captain John Rogers' Company; issued two shirts and two stocks at Fort Jefferson for having more than one year to serve (VSA-12).

McDonell, James [also McDonald]

06/04/79-12/03/81	Listed as matross cCorporal] in Captain Robert George's Company of Artillery (Harding 1981:29-30).
06/19/80	Issued two shirts for enlisting during the war (VSA-11).
11/19/80	Deserted (Harding 1981: 30).

McGar, John [also McGarr]

06/04/79-12/03/81	Listed as a matross [corporal] in Captain Robert George's Company of Artillery (Harding 1981:29-30).
06/12/80	Went on expediton with Captain Harrison to the Falls; received clothing issue for the trip (VSA-11).
12/03/80	Issued John McGar eight yards linen for hunting with Major Harlan for one month (VSA-14).

Fort Jefferson Personnel

McGuire, John
07/13/80 Member of Captain Jesse Evans' Company; discharged at Fort Jefferson (Harding 1981:14).
07/14/80 Issued one shirt at Fort Jefferson (VSA-12).

McKensey, Mordiack
07/15/80 Member, Captain Worthington's Company (MHS B1, F20; VSA-12).

McLaughlan, Charles
07/12/80 Referred to as a private; received full clothing issue (VSA-12).

McMeans, Andrew [also M'Means]
Signed agreement [engagement] to settle near Clarksville. Business transaction occurred in Harrodsburg. "Signed the agreement with the company" (A. Jamison's Personal Narrative - Filson Club). Mr. McMeans' sister was Margery Young [wife of James Young].
05/01/80-12/21/80 Listed as a private in Captain George Owens' Company of Militia (Harding 1981:48-49).
06/26/80 Paid 1/2 paper pins, one pair scissors, 3 1/3 yards narrow ribbon, four linen handkerchiefs, and one paper pins for making two ruffled and nine plain shirts per receipt (VSA-48).
09/08/80 Issued three lbs sugar for family (VSA-13; 50).
09/12/80 Moved (Harding 1981: 48-49).

McMeans, Anne [Mrs. Andrew McMeans] [later became Jamison]
04/00/80 "Sailed to Fort Jefferson with husband and 7 children" (Personal Narrative, Filson Club).
Cleared land, planted corn and had hope for a prosperous settlement (Personal Narrative, Filson Club).
06/22/80 Paid 1 1/2 yards calico, two Indian handkerchiefs, and one linen handkerchief for making 12 plain shirts (VSA-48).
07/17/80 Paid one linen handkerchief, three yards ribbon, one pair scissors, one ivory comb, and one horn comb for making three ruffled and three plain shirts (VSA-48).
09/09/80 Received five lbs sugar and one pint tafia valued at 18 shillings (VSA-13).
09/12/80 Moved (George Rogers Clark, I: 464).
09/13/80 Left Fort Jefferson for Natchez. Thirteen families in her boat, 19 people total; only two were men (Personal Narrative, Filson Club).

McMeans, Fras
07/05/80 Paid one fine linen handkerchief and four coarse linen handkerchiefs for making six plain shirts (VSA-48).

McMeans, James
05/01/80-12/21/80 Listed as a private in Captain George Owens' Company of Militia (Harding 1981:48-49).
09/12/80 Moved (Harding 1981:48).

McMichael, John
07/12/80 Received clothing at Fort Jefferson as a member of Ensign Williams' Company [Captain Brashears'] (VSA-12).

McMullen, James
06/04/79-12/03/81 Listed as a matross [corporal] in Captain Robert George's Company of Artillery (Harding 1981: 31-33).
08/19/80 Issued one suit of clothes and one blanket by order (VSA-12).
08/25/80 Issued two shirts (VSA-12).
09/11/80 Issued one blanket (VSA-13).
06/01/81 Issued three lbs sugar (VSA-49).
11/04/81 Deserted (Harding 1981: 31-33).

Mackever, John
07/12/80 Issued two shirts as a member of Ensign Williams' Company [Captain Brashears'] (VSA-12).

Mains, Patrick and family
05/09/80-09/12/80 Member, Captain Edward Worthington's Company (Harding 1981:46-47; VSA-13).
07/28/80 Tobacco delivered to Sergeant Mains, two carots weighing six lbs (VSA-50).
09/08/80 Married with one child (VSA-13).
09/08/80 Received with Joseph Thornton, two lbs sugar, and one pint tafia, for use of Thornton and Mains' wife and child (VSA-13).
09/12/80 Discharged (Harding 1981: 46-47; VSA-13).

Mains, Mrs. Patrick and child
09/08/80 Received from husband one lb sugar for herself and her sick child (VSA-13).

March, John [also Marak]
06/04/79-12/03/81 Matross [corporal] in Captain Robert George's Company of Artillery (Harding 1981:29-30).
06/03/80 Died (Harding 1981:32).

Marr, Patrick
06/04/79-12/03/81 Corporal in Captain Robert George's Company of Artillery (Harding 1981:29-30).
11/29/79 Enlisted for three years Captain Robert George's Company of Artillery (MHS: B1, F23).
06/12/80 Went on expedition with Captain Harrison to Falls of Ohio; received clothing issue for the trip (VSA-11).
10/23/80 Issued cloth and trimmings (VSA-13).
12/03/81 Killed (Harding 1981: 29-30).

Martin, Charles
07/10/80 Member, Captain John Roger's Company; received two shirts and two stocks at Fort Jefferson for having more than one year to serve (VSA-12).

Matthews, Edward
06/04/79-12/03/81 Sergeant, Captain Robert George's Company of Artillery (Harding 1981:29-30).
07/13/80 Issued a flat bottomed boat and a swivel at the Falls of Ohio for carrying corn and other provisions to the troops at Fort Jefferson (VSA-12).
07/16/80 Received seven lbs gunpowder, two lbs of lead the boat crew (VSA-12).
07/16/80 Received at the Falls of Ohio 29 3/4 gal. good whiskey to be delivered to Fort Jefferson (VSA-12).
03/20/81 Was a prisoner in the quarter guard at Fort Jefferson (Draper Manuscripts 56J40).
05/0581 "Edward Matthews was confined [ms. torn]" (VSA-19).

Mayfield, "Cagy"/Micajah]
07/12/80 Issued clothing at Fort Jefferson as a member of Ensign Williams' Company (VSA-12).
07/27/80 Issued one carot tobacco with William Elms (VSA-12).
09/09/80 Issued two lbs sugar for sick family (VSA-13).
10/27/80 Issued two skeins of thread to repair his clothing (VSA-13).

Mayfield, Mrs. Micajah and family
09/09/80 Issued two lbs sugar for his sick family (VSA-13).

Fort Jefferson Personnel

Megarr, John
06/12/80 Member, Captain George's Company on an expedition up the Ohio River to the Falls with Captain Harrison (VSA-11).

Merrideth, Daniel
06/20/80-07/17/80 Private, Captain George Owens' Company of Militia (George Rogers Clark Papers, I: 465).
06/20/80-07/17/80 Actual dates of enlistment (Harding 1981:49).
07/17/80 Described by John Montgomery as "Killed by savages" (VSA-13).
07/17/80 Killed (George Rogers Clark Papers, I: 465; Harding 1981:49).
09/01/80 Had farmed 16 acres with eight others at Clarksville; total corn crops would have been about 320 bushels had the Indians not burned it (Draper Manuscripts 1M8).

Meredith, Mrs. Luvana [also Lorana] [widow of Daniel Meredith]
06/28/80 Paid one Indian handkerchief and one ivory comb for making four plain shirts (VSA-48).
07/06/80 Paid one coarse linen handkerchief for making one plain shirt (VSA-48).
07/17/80 Married to Daniel Meredith, who was killed by Indians (VSA-13).
08/18/80 Paid two linen handkerchiefs for making four hunting shirts (VSA-48).
08/22/80 Paid one paper pins for making one plain shirt (VSA-48).
09/02/80 Received two lbs sugar (VSA-13).
09/09/80 Received two lbs sugar at cost of ten shillings (VSA-13).
11/27/80 Sugar delivered to the Widow Meredith's family, sick, three lbs (VSA-50).
01/18/81 Paid two yards flannel for making three soldier shirts for Captain
06/07/81 Is taking care of Sergeant Miles child[ren]; received sugar for the use of the child[ren] (VSA-20).
George's Company (VSA-15).

Meredith, Lawrance [Mr.]
Furnished Fort Jefferson with cow valued at four shillings (George Rogers Clark Papers, II: 366).

Merriwether, James [Lt.]
06/10/80 Member, Captain John Rogers' Light Dragoons (VSA-12).
07/12/80 Issued to Lt. Merriwether, 1 1/2 yards scarlet cloth 7/4 wide, 1 5/8 yards brown broadcloth, 2 1/2 yards shalloon, issued for four vests and breeches two yards calender, four yards toile gris, three yards spotted flannel, and three yards gray cloth 7/8 wide; 19 1/2 yards white linen for six shirts, 3/4 yard fine holland for ruffling, two yards muslin for six stocks, six yards check linen for two vests and two breeches, four skeins silk, 12 skeins thread, one silk handkerchief, one Indian handkerchief, four linen handkerchiefs, and three yards white cloth 7/4 wide (VSA-48).
07/12/80 Issued one English blanket and 1/8 yd brown broadcloth (VSA-48).
09/09/80 Issued four lbs of sugar for his own use (VSA-13).
09/09/80 Sugar delivered to James Merriwether, Lt. of Cavalry, four lbs (VSA-50).
09/10/80 Issued one lb gunpowder, two lbs lead for his own use (VSA-13; 50).
09/13/80 Listed as "officer of the mess"; received a share of 60 lbs sugar (VSA-13).

Merriwether, William
07/10/80 Member, Captain John Rogers' Company; issued two shirts and two stocks at Fort Jefferson for having more than one year to serve (VSA-12).
12/03/80 Issued one check handkerchief to Sergeant Merriwether (VSA-48:44).

Fort Jefferson Personnel   135

Mershom, Nathaniel
07/10/80   Member, Captain John Rogers' Company; issued two shirts and two stocks at Fort Jefferson for having more than one year to serve (VSA-12).

Metivce, John
09/10/80   Member, Captain Richard McCarty's Company (VSA-13).
09/10/80   Issued full clothing for enlisting (VSA-13).

Metivce, Ps.
09/10/80   Member, Captain Richard McCarty's Company (VSA-13).
09/10/80   Issued full clothing for enlisting (VSA-13).

Miles, Michael [also Mills]
05/14/80   Sergeant Major, Captain John Girault's Company (Harding 1981:94).
01/00/81-02/00/81   Accompanied Captain Edward Worthington from the Falls of Ohio to Fort Jefferson (Draper Manuscripts 56J28).
02/12/81   Issued 1/2 pound sugar for his sick wife (VSA-16).
02/21/81   Issued liquor rations for one day for 50 men of the Illinois Regiment (VSA-16).
02/26/81   Arrived Fort Jefferson with Captain Edward Worthington and provided testimony on behalf of Captain Worthington during Worthington's Court of Inquiry (Draper Manuscripts 56J27).
03/01/81   Issued nine gills whiskey for nine men on fatigue (VSA-17).
03/07/81   Requested liquor issue for men of the Illinois regiment (one gill each) (VSA-17).
03/14/81   Requested tobacco issue for 50 men of the Illinois Regiment at 1/2 lb per man (VSA-17).
03/14/81   Issued one quart tafia for his sick wife (VSA-17).
03/17/81   Requested liquor issue for 90 men of the Illinois Regiment at one gill each (VSA-17).
03/19/81   Issued one musket or smoothed gun (VSA-50).
03/22/81   Requests issue of tobacco for nine men (VSA-17).
03/22/81   Received one quart tafia (VSA-17).
03/25/81   Received one quart tafia (VSA-17).
04/02/81   Receives one gallon rum (VSA-17).
04/17/81   Receives six skeins brown thread (VSA-18).
04/26/81   Request tobacco for 43 men of the Illinois Regiment (VSA-18).
04/28/81   Request one lb tobacco for one man of Captain Rogers' Company (VSA-18).
05/03/81   Request sugar for 76 men, nine women, and ten children of the Illinois Regiment (VSA-19).
05/11/81   Request tafia rations for 75 men of the Illinois Regiment (VSA-19).
05/13/81   Requests liquor for 30 men of the Illinois Regiment on fatigue (VSA-19).
05/17/81   Requests 10 gills tafia for one sergeant and nine men on fatigue (VSA-19).
05/21/81   Requests sugar for 69 men, eight women, and ten children of the Illinois Regiment (156 lbs) (VSA-19; 49: 67).
05/25/81   Requests tafia for 64 men of the Illinois Regiment (VSA-19).
06/02/81   Requests tobacco for 58 men of the Illinois Regiment, 1/2 lb per man (VSA-20).
06/04/81   Attested Rueben Kemp sawed 700 feet poplar plank (VSA-20).
06/05/81   Issued per order from day book, four lbs sugar (VSA-49).
06/07/81   Requests tobacco for 57 men of the Illinois Regiment (VSA-20).
06/07/81   Issued per order from day book, 12 lbs sugar (VSA-49).
06/24/81   Enroute to the Falls of the Ohio, Miles is issued five lbs sugar (VSA-20).
07/12/81   Received six pounds sugar upon arriving at the Falls of the Ohio (VSA-20).

Miles, Mrs. Michael [and child] [also Mills]
02/12/81   Mrs. Miles is sick (VSA-16).

03/14/81	Issued one quart tafia for sick wife (VSA-17).
03/28/81	Mrs. Miles is still sick (VSA-17).
06/07/81	Issued 12 lbs of sugar to Mrs. Meredith for Sergeant Miles' child (VSA-20).

Miller, Abraham
06/04/79-12/03/81	Corporal, Captain Robert George's Company of Artillery (Harding 1981: 29-30).
06/12/80	Went on expedition with Captain Harrison to the Falls of the Ohio; received clothing issue for the trip (VSA-11).

Miller, Daniel
09/01/80	Farmed 16 acres at Clarksville with eight others; would have yielded 320 bushels of corn had the Indians not burned it (Draper Manuscripts 1M8).

Moneral, Joseph
06/12/80	Member, Captain Williams' Company (VSA-12).
06/12/80	Issued cloth and trimmings for a complete suit of clothes, and two shirts having more than one year to serve (VSA-12).

Montbreuen, Timothe [also MonBreun, Mombrun]
05/16/80	Letter from Captain Valentine T. Dalton at Fort Clark to George Rogers Clark. Dalton has gone to O'Post from Fort Clark, to pick up salt. Letter mentions Montbreuen and his latest actions at Ouia (Seineke 1981: 435).
07/10/80	Issued full quota of clothing at Fort Jefferson as a Lieutenant (VSA-12).
07/12/80	Issued three yards broadcloth 7/4 wide, 2 1/2 yards shalloon, issued for six breeches and three vests, two yards calender, four yards camlet, two yards corded dimity, 1/2 yd camlet, two yards chintz, four yards toile gris, and 3 1/2 yards coarse linen for lining, one silk handkerchief, one Indian handkercheif, four linen handkercheifs, two yards muslin for six stocks, 19 1/2 yards white linen for lining, 3/4 yard fine holland for ruffling, 12 skeins white thread, two pair thread hose, one pair knee garters, 5 1/2 yards spotted flannel for three vests, three yards blue cloth 7/4 wide, and one hat (VSA-48).
08/05/80	Came to the relief of Fort Jefferson with Captain McCarty (Draper Manuscripts 26J23).
08/08/80	Arrived with ten whites and 65 Kaskaskia Indians (Draper Manuscripts 26J23)
09/10/80	Issued one English blanket (VSA-13).
09/11/80	Ammunition delivered to Mr. Montbreuen for his own use, one lb gunpowder, two lbs lead (VSA-50).
09/25/80	Issued ten weight sugar, and ten weight soap, six yards ferretting, one dressed deer skin, four weight sugar, and two weight coffee (VSA-48).

Montgomery, Hugh
12/22/80	Issued Hugh Montgomery 1/2 lb gunpowder and one lb lead for hunting with Major Harlan (VSA-14).

Montgomery, John
06/13/80	Furnished with Josiah Phelps, 1/2 lb gun gunpowder and one lb lead at Fort Jefferson (VSA-11).

Montgomery, John (Col.)
04/25/80	Col. Montgomery at Fort Clark writes George Rogers Clark at Mouth of Ohio. Montgomery is pleased Clark has arrived. Lt. Brashears delivers letter and awaits at Fort Jefferson for Clark's response. Montgomery states that the condition at Fort Clark is not good, but he will do all he can to bring Clark his goods (MHS: B1, F16).

Fort Jefferson Personnel 137

05/04/80   Letter from Oliver Pollack to Clark. Montogmery's bills of exchange are $60,000 and are unpaid (Draper Manuscripts 40J35).

05/06/80   In a letter to George Rogers Clark from Charles Gratiot in Kaskaskia, reference was made to Col. Montgomery's taking opinions of the officers to determine whether they wish to proceed with an expedition (MHS: B1, F17).

05/07/80   Letter from Col. Montgomery to George Rogers Clark. Trip planned will be delayed because inhabitants won't furnish Col. Montgomery with the needed supply of flour and corn to feed his troops for two months. Mr. Gillaspey will deliver to Clark part of the artillery, some salt, and 2,000 lbs lead (MHS: B1, F17; Seineke 1981:431-432).

05/15/80   Letter from Captain John Rogers at Fort Clark to George Rogers Clark. Rogers states that Col. Montgomery [on the Spanish side], is supposed to make an expedition with 100 men (MHS:B1, F17; Seineke 1981: 434).

05/15/80   Letter from Col. Montgomery at Fort Bowman to George Rogers Clark. Montgomery wishes to join the Spanish forces because of the approach of the enemy. They will try to prevent an attack upon the villages. Montgomery furnished 100 men with artillery and ammunition. He believes the expedition should begin in a few days with about 250 men (MHS: B1, F17).

06/03/80   Certified that Captain Brashears enlisted 24 men for his Company, and is therefore entitled to receive his commission (MHS:B1, F19).

07/11/80   Lt. Col. John Montgomery stated that Ann Elms attended the sick in the hospital at Fort Clark from 10 February until 5 June, and that she is entitled to receive the same pay as anyone else employed for the same purpose; she is to be paid out of the country store at Fort Jefferson. Montgomery wrote to Captain John Dodge to pay, at his leisure, Ann Elms and her daughter a petticoat each (VSA-12).

07/12/80   Issued to Lt. Col. John Montgomery: six yards brown broadcloth 7 1/4 wide, five dozen and five metal buttons, 2 1/4 yards fine cambric for six stocks, issued for six vests and six pair breeches; four yards white casernone, 2 1/2 yards white thickset, 2 3/4 yards cotton spotted velvet, 5 3/4 corded dimity, 3 3/4 sycee, 3 3/4 yards calender, and 2 1/2 yards calender chintz, issued to make up sundry garments; two sticks silk parit, seven skeins of silk, two pair knee garters (one pair overdrawn), and five yards of shalloon (2 1/2 overdrawn), issued 21 yards white linen for six shirts, one yard fine holland for ruffling shirts, five yards coarse linen damaged for lining, 11 skeins thread, three pair thread hose, two silk handkerchiefs, two Indian handkerchiefs, four linen handkercheifs (two overdrawn), one ivory and one horn comb (overdrawn), one brass ink stand (overdrawn) (VSA-48).

07/12/80   Articles overdrawn by Col. Montgomery, beyond his quota of clothing: one pair silk knee garters, 2 1/2 yards shalloon, two linen handkerchiefs, one ivory and one horn comb, one brass ink stand, one 2 1/2 point English blanket, one snaffle bridle, 5 3/4 yards muslin, one stick black ball, and 3 3/4 yards best ribbon (VSA-48).

07/12/80   Issued to Col. Montgomery for part of the clothing for four men of Captain Quirk's Company, 14 yards blue cloth, 12 yards white flannel, and four shirts, (13 yards linen for four shirts) (VSA-48).

07/13/80   Participant in court proceedings at Fort Jefferson looking into Captain John Dodge's character (Draper Manuscripts 56J22-24).

07/13/80   John Montgomery requests flour be issued one man for three days for "going up the river" (VSA-12).

07/14/80   Signs a return for ammunition for 14 men going to Kaskaskia, stating 1/8 lb gunpowder and 1/4 lb lead be issued to each of the 14 men (VSA-12).

Fort Jefferson Personnel

08/23/80	Issued 19 1/2 yards linen per order of Col. Montgomery to buy gunpowder (VSA-48).
09/08/80	John Montgomery writes a return for one pint tafia, one lb sugar, one lb coffee (VSA-13).
09/09/80	Sugar delivered by order of Montgomery to a man in Captain Bailey's Company, two lbs; to a man and his sick children, one lb; to eight sick people of the inhabitants, four lbs; to a sick woman and children of Captain Brashears' Company, two lbs; to two men of Captain Bailey's Company, two lbs; to two men of Captain Bailey's Company, one lb; to Col. Montgomery's order, one lb; to five men of Captain John Bailey's Company, 2 1/2 lbs (VSA-50).
09/09/80	Tobacco delivered to Indians by Col. Montgomery's order, two carots weighing, nine lbs (VSA-50).
09/10/80	Issued one boat and 23 oars for his trip to Kaskaskia (VSA-13).
09/10/80	Ammunition delivered by Col. Montgomery's orders to volunteers who came with Col. Montgomery, 1 1/2 lbs gunpowder and three lbs lead (VSA-50).
09/11/80	Present at Fort Jefferson (VSA-13).
09/11/80	Ammunition delivered by Col. Montgomery's orders to Col. Montgomery for his own use, one lb gunpowder, two lbs lead; to one man of Captain George's Company, 1/2 lb gunpowder, one lb lead (VSA-50).
09/12/80	Articles overdrawn by Col. Montgomery, beyond his quota of clothing; ten lbs coffee, one yard osnaburg for his saddle (VSA-48).
09/12/80	Issued ten lbs coffee for his own use (VSA-13).
09/12/80	Ammunition delivered to one man of Captain Worthington's Company, 1 1/2 lbs gunpowder, three lbs lead (VSA-50).
09/12/80	Sugar delivered by order of Col. Montgomery at Fort Jefferson, to two men of Captain Abraham Kellar's Company, one lb; to a man of Captain Bailey's Company, 1/2 lb (VSA-50).
09/13/80	Sugar delivered by Martin Carney by order of Col. Montgomery at Fort Jefferson: to Col. Montgomery for his own use, three lbs; to a man of Captain McCarty's Company, 1 1/2 lbs; to Col. Montgomery's order, two lbs; and to ten officers in Col. Montgomery's mess, 60 lbs (VSA-50).
09/13/80	Soap delivered by Martin Carney by order of Col. Montgomery and Captain George at Fort Jefferson, to Captain Bailey's Company, 12 lbs; to Captain Robert George's Company, 16 lbs; to Captain Edward Worthington's Company, 9 1/2 lbs; to Captain Brashears' Company, 8 1/2 lbs; to Captain McCarty's Company, 15 lbs (VSA-50).
09/13/80	Montgomery certifies that the "Destroyed corn" estimate written by William Clark and Leonard Helms, to be "true and just" and requests the State of Virginia to pay for the loss of the corn crop (VSA-20).
09/19/80	Wrote instructions to John Dodge to purchase $10,000 worth of supplies for Fort Jefferson troops, especially flour, salt, corn, furniture for Col. Clark, and blankets and shoes for troops (VSA-13).
09/22/80	Montgomery wrote to Geore Rogers Clark He has just returned from Fort Jefferson where he, ten men [whites], and 65 Kaskaskia Indians had relieved the fort noting that the channel of the Mississippi River has dried up. He plans to return to Fort Jefferson with all of his men except Captain Rogers (George Rogers Clark Papers, I:456-7).
10/05/80	John Montgomery [from Kaskaskia?] wrote John Dodge to replace 61 lbs flour to Thomas Kirk that Kirk lent to troops moving from Fort Jefferson to Kaskaskia (VSA-13).
10/17/80	John Montgomery wrote the Virginia Treasury to requesting $2,000 be paid to John Rogers for provisions for troops at Fort Jefferson (VSA-13).
10/18/80	John Montgomery wrote that he witnessed the accidental drowning of a brown horse by a soldier while the troops crossed the Ohio River enroute from Fort Jefferson to Kaskaskia (VSA-13).

Fort Jefferson Personnel

10/18/80	John Montgomery wrote from Kaskaskia to request John Dodge issue three hundred lbs flour and one-half barrock of tafia for the use of the troops at Fort Jefferson (VSA-13).
10/18/80	John Montgomery [at Kaskaskia] requests John Dodge issue two bags for transporting flour for the use of troops at Fort Jefferson (VSA-13).
10/24/80	Ammunition delivered to Col. Montgomery at Fort Jefferson for his journey to New Orleans, ten lbs gunpowder (VSA-50).
10/24/80	John Montgomery wrote Oliver Pollock to pay Valentine T. Dalton $1,860 and 1/6 for provisions (VSA-16).
10/24/80	John Montgomery wrote from Fort Jefferson to pay Valentine T. Dalton, 188 silver dollars (VSA-16).
10/28/80	Letter from Captain George to George Rogers Clark mentions Col. Montgomery was on his way to New Orleans and had stopped at Fort Jefferson (George Rogers Clark Papers, I: 461).
10/28/80	John Williams at Fort Jefferson writes to George Rogers Clark that Williams had arrived Fort Jefferson on October 23, to take command by order of John Montgomery (George Rogers Clark Papers, I: 463).
10/28/80	John Montgomery requests Martin Carney to send 50 lbs gun gunpowder to Kaskaskia with Captain Rogers via the first boat passage (VSA-13).
11/15/80	Reference to letter from Montgomery to George, advising George to purchase Barbours cargo. Montgomery met Barbour enroute on the Mississippi (George Rogers Clark Papers, I: 314).
12/05/80	Letter from John Donne at Fort Jefferson to George Rogers Clark. Donne suggests that Col. Montgomery might have done more to save Fort Jefferson (MHS: B1, F23).
12/07/80	John Montgomery, at Fort Jefferson, order the quartermaster to issue to John Ash, one gill tafia for every man belonging to the garrison (Reverse states 78 quarts and six gills; 152 1/2 persons) (VSA-14).
12/09/80	John Montgomery orders Captain Owens to make out a general return of Owens' men for those planning to stay and for those who are planning to leave Fort Jefferson. Any man who can be spared from duty, should help bring corn in from the fields (VSA-14).
12/24/80	Letter from Captain Robert George at Fort Jefferson to George Rogers Clark. George tells Clark he has received letters from Oliver Pollock and Col. Montgomery (MHS: B1, F23; Seineke 1981: 468-469).
01/08/81	Wrote to Thomas Jefferson advising of Fort Jefferson's poor condition [supplies and location] and suggested evacuation of fort. Montgomery had been to Fort Jefferson, but was now in New Orleans (George Rogers Clark Papers, I: 497-498).
05/10/81	Issued per order from day book, 12 lbs sugar (VSA-49).
05/15/81	Ammunition delivered to Col. Montgomery, 1/2 lb gunpowder, one lb lead (VSA-50).
05/17/81	Issued per order from day book, ten lbs sugar (VSA-49).
05/18/81	Omitted, issued per order from day book, two gallons rum (VSA-49).
05/30/81	Issued per order from day book, five lbs sugar (VSA-49).
06/05/81	Issued per order from day book, six lbs sugar and 20 lbs sugar (VSA-49).
06/05/81	Ammunition delivered by order of Captain Robert George and Col. Montgomery, to Captain Kellar for the use of hunting for the troops going to the Falls, one lb gunpowder, two lbs lead; to three men of Captain Worthington's Company, 3/4 lb gunpowder, 1 1/2 lbs lead; and to three men of Lt. Clark's, 1 1/2 lbs gunpowder, three lbs lead (VSA-50).
06/06/81	Ammunition delivered by order of Captain Robert George and Col. Montgomery to Col. Montgomery, one lb gunpowder, two lbs lead, two flints; to Captain Owens' Militia, four lbs gunpowder, eight lbs lead (VSA-50).
06/06/81	Stores issued to Col. Montgomery, one kettle (VSA-50).
06/07/81	Issued per order from day book, one carot tobacco (VSA-48).

06/07/81   Ammunition delivered by order of Captain Robert George and Col.
           Montgomery, to six men going to the Falls by land, three lbs
           gunpowder, six lbs lead (VSA-50).

Montroy, Anthony
06/02/80   Had served in Captain A. Kellar's Company (MHS: B1, F19).
06/18/79   Matross [corporal] in Captain Robert George's Company of Artillery
           (Harding 1981: 31-33; MHS: B1, F23).
07/12/80   Issued full clothing as a member of Captain Kellar's Company
           (VSA-12).
11/04/81   Deserted (Harding 1981: 32).

Moore, John [Sergeant]
07/10/80   Member, Captain Worthington's Company (MHS: B1, F20).
07/10/80   Delivered Louis Brown and David Allen to the commanding officer at
           Fort Jefferson (MHS: B1, F20).
07/15/80   Listed as Sergeant in Captain Worthington's Company (MHS B1, F20;
           VSA-12).

Moore, William
06/04/79-12/03/81 Matross [corporal] in Captain Robert George's Company of
           Artillery (Harding 1981: 29-30).
06/12/80   Went on expedition with Captain Harrison to Falls of Ohio; received
           clothing issue for the trip (VSA-11).
06/13/80   Received four, 2 1/2 point blankets (VSA-11).
09/25/80   Soap delivered to Sergeant Moore of Captain George's Company, 7 1/2
           lbs (VSA-50).
10/19/80   Ammunition delivered to Sergeant Moore of Captain George's Company,
           2 1/2 lbs gunpowder, five lbs lead (VSA-50).
11/01/80   Deserted (Harding 1981: 29-30).

Morgan, Charles
07/12/80   Issued clothing at Fort Jefferson as a member of Ensign Williams'
           (Brashears') Company (VSA-12).
08/19/80   Issued one suit of clothes and one blanket (VSA-12).
08/25/80   Issued two shirts (VSA-12).

Morgan, Charles
06/04/79-12/03/81 Sergeant, Captain Robert George's Company of Artillery
           (Harding 1981: 29-30).
09/11/80   Issued one blanket (VSA-13).
11/18/80   Soap delivered to Sergeant Morgan for Captain George's Company, 15
           lbs (VSA-50).
12/03/81   Discharged (Harding 1981: 29-30).

Morris, Graves
05/01/80-11/30/81 Listed as private in Captain John Bailey's Company in the
           Illinois Regiment (Harding 1981: 45-46).
07/12/80   Issued two shirts (VSA-12).
09/09/80   Sugar delivered to Graves Morris, a man in Captain Bailey's Company,
           two lbs (VSA-50).
09/10/80   Issued two lbs sugar for being sick (VSA-13).
09/13/80   Deserted (Harding 1981: 45-46).

Morris, James
05/30/80   Enlisted as a private in Captain Brashears' Company (Harding 1981:
           51).
07/12/80   Issued clothing at Fort Jefferson (VSA-12).
07/12/80   Received flannel, blue cloth, and thread and buttons as issue for
           clothing (VSA- 12).
11/12/80   Deceased (Harding 1981: 51).

Mulboy, James
07/10/80 Enlisted for three years into Captain Robert George's Company of Artillery (MHS: B1, F23).

Mulboy, William [also Mulby]
09/10/80 Member, Captain Richard McCarty's Company (VSA-13).
09/10/80 Issued full clothing for enlisting (VSA-13).

Murphy, John
07/10/80 Member, Captain John Rogers' Company. Issued two shirts and two stocks at Fort Jefferson for having more than one year to serve (VSA-12).

Murray, Daniel
No Date Paid two check handkerchiefs, one horn comb, and four skeins thread for writing paper (VSA-48).

Murray, Edward
05/24/79 Enlisted as a private in Captain John Bailey's Company (Harding 1981: 45-46).
09/15/80 Sugar delivered to Edward Murray, a soldier in Captain Bailey's Company, two lbs (VSA-13; 50).
10/01/80 Sugar delivered to Edward Murray, a soldier in Captain Bailey's Company, 1/2 lb (VSA-13; 50).
10/06/80 Issued 1/2 lb sugar (VSA-13).
10/09/80 Ten weight peltry for services (VSA-48).
06/05/81 Deceased (Harding 1981: 46).

Murray, Matthew (and family)
06/04/79-12/03/81 Matross [corporal] in Captain Robert George's Company of Artillery (Harding 1981: 31-33).
06/19/80 Issued two shirts (VSA- 11).
08/04/80 Tobacco delivered to Matthew Murray, a soldier in Captain Abraham Kellar's Company, 1/2 carot weighing 1 1/2 lbs (VSA-50).
09/08/80 Sugar delivered to Matthew Murray and family in Captain Kellar's Company, two lbs (VSA-50).
10/23/80 Issued cloth and trimmings to produce one suit each for enlisting (VSA-13).
01/20/81 Deserted (Harding 1981: 31-33).

Murray, Mary (Mrs. Matthew) [also Murry]
07/15/80 Paid one pair scissors and one linen handkerchief for making three shirts plain (VSA-48).
11/27/80 Made eight shirts for soldiers in Captain Kellar's Company paid four yards white flannel (VSA-14).

Nash, John
06/20/80 Member, Captain Shelby's Company. Received suit of clothes made by J. Bryan, tailor, at Fort Jefferson (VSA-11).

Nedinger, Nicholas
05/01/80-12/21/80 Listed as a private in Captain George Owens' Company of Militia (Harding 1981: 48-49).
09/12/80 Moved (Harding 1981: 48).

Nelson, Enoch
07/15/80 Member, Captain Worthington's Company (MHS B1, F20; VSA-12).

Nelson, John
07/15/80 Member, Captain Worthington's Company (MHS B1, F20; VSA-12).

Nelson, Moses
07/15/80 Member, Captain Worthington's Company (MHS B1, F20; VSA-12).

Nelson, William
06/23/80   Member, Captain Worthington's Company (VSA- 11; 48).
06/23/80   Issued two shirts (VSA-11; 48).

Oakly, John
06/04/79-12/03/81   Matross [corporal], Captain Robert George's Company of Artillery (Harding 1981: 29-30).
06/12/80   Went on expedition with Captain Harrison to the Falls of Ohio; received clothing issue for the trip (VSA-11).
12/03/81   Killed (Harding 1981: 30).

O'Bryan, John [also O'Brian]
06/04/79-12/03/81   Matross [corporal], Captain Robert George's Company of Artillery (Harding 1981: 29-30).
06/19/80   Issued two shirts (VSA-11).
11/19/80   Deserted (Harding 1981: 30).

O'Harrah, Mikel
07/10/80   Member, Captain John Rogers' Company; issued two shirts and two stocks at Fort Jefferson for having more than one year to serve (VSA-12).

Oiles, Mr. [also Oiler, Oialler]
09/07/80   Received one quart tafia for his sick family (VSA-13).
09/08/80   Received four lbs sugar for sick family (seven in number) (VSA-13).
09/09/80   Received four lbs sugar, valued at one pound (VSA_13; 50).
09/09/80   Called an "inhabitant of this place" (VSA-13).
09/09/80   Received one quart tafia valued at six shillings (VSA-13).

Oiler, Mrs. and family
09/07/80   Mr. Oiler received one quart tafia for his sick family at Fort Jefferson (VSA-13).
09/08/80   Issued four lbs sugar to Mr. Oiler's sick family (seven in number) (VSA-13).

Orbin, Philip
06/04/79-12/03/81   Matross [corporal], Captain Robert George's Company of Artillery (Harding 1981: 31-33).
12/31/80   Issued a coat, waistcoat, and pair of overalls for enlisting for three years (VSA-14).
03/03/81   Deserted (Harding 1981: 31-33).

Owens, George and family [also Oins, Oens]
No Date   Captain Owens was paid for beef, tallow, wild meat and bear meat he provided the troops at Fort Jefferson (George Rogers Clark Papers, II: 389-390).
No Date   Owens also provided testimony about Phillip Barbour (George Rogers Clark Papers, II: 314).
05/01/80-12/21/80   Listed as Captain of Militia (Harding 1981: 48-49).
06/07/80   First Lt. Mark Ker, Pvt. Henry Ker, and Conrad Ker were all killed; all were members of Captain Owens' Militia (George Rogers Clark Papers, I: 464).
06/08/80   Received 13 lbs gunpowder and 26 lbs lead for his Company at Clarksville (VSA-11).
07/03/80   Captain Owens and Captain George sign an issue for 1 3/4 lbs gunpowder, 3 1/2 lbs lead, two guns, and 45 gun flints for seven men of Owens' Company (VSA-12).
08/09/80   Ammunition delivered to Captain Owens' Company of Militia, 11 1/4 lbs gunpowder and 46 lbs lead (VSA-50).
09/09/80   Received two lbs sugar valued at ten shillings (VSA-13).
09/09/80   Sugar delivered to George Owens, Captain of Militia, two lbs (VSA-50).

Fort Jefferson Personnel 143

11/18/80 Sugar delivered to George Owens, Captain of Militia, three lbs (VSA-50).
12/09/80 John Montgomery ordered Captain Owens to make out a general return of men intending to stay, and one for those who are planning to leave Fort Jefferson. Also, any men that can be spared from duty shall bring corn in from the fields (VSA-14).
12/21/80 Service ended for Captain George Owens (George Rogers Clark Papers, I: 464-465).
12/26/80 Ammunition delivered to Captain Owens and Lt. Williams, two lbs gunpowder, four lbs lead (VSA-50).
01/08/81 Ammunition delivered to Captain Bailey and Captain Owens, going express to the falls, 1 1/2 lbs gunpowder, four lbs lead (VSA-50).
04/13/81 Ammunition delivered to Captain Owens of militia, one lb gunpowder (VSA-50).
05/05/81 Issued six lbs sugar (VSA-49).
05/14/81 Ammunition delivered to Captain Owens of Militia, 1/2 lb (VSA-50).
06/05/81 Issued one carot of tobacco, six lbs sugar, and 12 lbs sugar (VSA-49).
06/06/81 Ammunition delivered to Captain Owens' Militia, four lbs gunpowder, eight lbs lead (VSA-50).

Owens, Charaty (Mrs. George)
06/19/80 Paid five linen handkerchiefs for making ten plain shirts (VSA-48).
09/09/80 Received two lbs of sugar for her sick family (VSA-13).
01/09/81 Issued 4 1/2 yards flannel, 1 1/2 yards pamedor, one paper pens, 25 sewing needles, and three skeins thread (VSA-15).

Ouneler, Charles
07/12/80 Issued clothing at Fort Jefferson as a member of Ensign Williams' Company [Brashears'] (VSA-12).

Ozala, John [Captain]
04/20/80 Received 230 lbs Indian meal from Zephaniah Blackford for a command of 30 men going from Fort Patrick Henry to Fort Jefferson (VSA-10).

Pagan, David
07/10/80 Member, Captain John Rogers' Company issued two shirts and two stocks at Fort Jefferson for having more than one year to serve (VSA-12).

Panther, Joseph
06/29/80 Issued two shirts (VSA-11).
07/12/80 Member, Captain Abraham Kellar's Company; received clothing issue (VSA-12).
09/16/80 Sugar delivered to Joseph Panther, a soldier in Captain Kellar's Company, one lb (VSA-13; 50).

Papin, John [also Pepin, Jean]
05/30/79-06/02/81 Member, Captain Richard McCarty's Company (Harding 1981: 27-28).
09/10/80 Issued a full set of clothing (VSA-13).
10/10/80 Killed (Harding 1981: 28).

Parker, Edward
03/06/80-11/30/81 Sergeant, Captain John Bailey's Company of the Illinois Regiment (Harding 1981: 45-46).
07/12/80 Issued two shirts at Fort Jefferson (VSA-12).

Payne, Adam
06/04/79-12/03/81 Matross [corporal], Captain Robert George's Company of Artillery (Harding 1981: 29-30).
05/10/80 Deserted (Harding 1981: 30).

Pepin, Peter
05/30/79-06/02/81 Private, Captain Richard McCarty's Company (Harding 1981: 27-28).
09/10/80 Issued full set of clothing (VSA-13).
11/20/80 Deserted (Harding 1981: 27).

Perrault, Michael. [Perault]
05/30/79-06/02/81 Lieutenant Captain McCarty's Company (Harding 1981: 27).
07/11/80 Issued full quota of clothing (VSA-12).
07/12/80 Issued Lt. Michael Perrault, three yards brown broadcloth 7/4 wide, 2 1/2 yards shalloon, one stick silk twist, three skeins silk, 19 1/2 yards white linen for six shirts, 3/4 yd white holland for ruffling, two yards muslin for six stock, issued for 12 vests or breeches, two yards casimir, 2 1/2 yards chintz, 2 1/2 yards spotted flannel, three yards camlet, two yards shalloon, four yards toile gris, and 2 1/4 yards check linen; one silk handkerchief, one Indian handkerchief, four linen handkerchiefs, eight skeins thread, two pair thread hose, one hat, four yards damaged linen for lining, three yards broadcloth 7/4 wide (VSA-48).
09/06/80 Issued 20 lbs balls (VSA-13).
09/08/80 Issued one bottle tafia (VSA-13).
09/09/80 Issued one English blanket (VSA-48).
09/11/80 Issued 2 1/2 yards toile grise (VSA-48).
10/05/80 John Montgomery wrote to Oliver Pollock at New Orleans to pay Perrault $8,940 plus two bits and two quarters (VSA-16).

Phelps, Anthony
05/01/80-12/21 [25]/80 Listed as a private in Captain George Owens' Company of Militia (George Rogers Clark Papers, I: 465; Harding 1981: 48-49).

Phelps, Thomas and family
09/01/80 Farmed six acres at Clarksville which would have produced 200 bushels of corn had the Indians not burned it (Draper Manuscripts 1M8).
09/14/80 Issued six lbs sugar for his sick family (VSA-13).
10/24/80 The "beans and other vegetables" taken from Thomas Phelps' cornfield by the "troops at this post in distress" were valued at 1/2 the same value of corn raised in the same field (VSA-20).
11/21/80 Phelps' family six in number (VSA-25).
11/21/80 Sugar delivered to Mr. Phelps for his sick family, two lbs (VSA-50).

Phelps, George
05/01/80-12/21 [25]/80 Listed as private in Captain George Owens' Company of Militia (George Rogers Clark Papers, I: 465; Harding 1981: 48-49).

Phelps, Elizabeth [Mrs.] [Thomas?]
06/16/80 Paid five yards calico for making six ruffled and six plain shirts (VSA-48).
06/28/80 Paid four linen handkerchiefs, one pair scissors, and one ivory comb for making ten plain shirts (VSA-48).
07/14/80 Paid one pair scissors and two paper pins for making three plain shirts (VSA-48).
01/18/81 Made eight shirts for Captain John Bailey's Company and paid 4 3/4 yards and six sewing needles (VSA-15).

Phelps, Josiah
Not Dated Paid by Commissioners for loss of two horses, saddle, and bridle (George Rogers Clark Papers, II: 334).
05/01/80-12/21/80 Listed as a private in Captain George Owens' Company of Militia (Harding 1981: 48-49).

Fort Jefferson Personnel   145

06/00/80 Sent from the Falls to Clark at Fort Jefferson (Draper Manuscripts 26Ja4).
06/13/80 Ammunition delivered to Josiah Phelps and John Montgomery, one lb gunpowder and two lbs lead (VSA-11;50).

Philips, Henry
03/12/80-11/30/81 Listed as a private in Captain John Bailey's Company (Harding 1981: 45-46).
07/12/80 Issued two shirts (VSA-12).
11/09/81 Deserted (Harding 1981: 46).

Phister, John
05/01/80-12/21/80 Listed as a private in Captain George Owens' Company of Militia (Harding 1981: 48-49).
09/12/80 Moved (Harding 1981: 48).

Piggott, James [also Piggot, Pigot, Picket] [Magistrate]
05/13/80 Helped write a petition to government to make Clarksville and surrounding area a county. Piggott is listed as a magistrate and trustee of Clarksville (George Rogers Clark Papers, I: 425- 426).
07/03/80 Participant at Court of Inquiry at Fort Jefferson (Draper Manuscripts 56J22-24).
07/24/80 Paid seven yards damaged linen for making seven plain shirts (VSA-48).
12/01/80 Assigned a bond (VSA-14).
12/01/80 Received nine yards flannel and nine skeins of thread (VSA-14).

Piggott, Eleanor and family [Mrs. James]
Not Dated Assisted Mrs. McMeans [Jamison] with moving to Fort Jefferson until her husband arrived (Personal Narrative, Filson Club).
06/24/80 One Indian handkerchief, two linen handkerchiefs one paper pins, one ivory comb paid E. Piggot, for making three ruffled and four plain shirts (VSA-48).
Not Dated Mrs. James Piggott had two children, William, born 1773 and Levi, born 1775. She "died at Fort Jefferson while it was surrounded by Indians" (MHS: Steamboat File).

Piner, Jess [also Jesse]
05/30/79 Enlisted as a private in Captain Richard McCarty's Company (Harding 1981: 27).
09/10/80 Member, Captain Richard McCarty's Company (VSA-13).
09/10/80 Issued full clothing for enlisting (VSA-13).
11/26/80 Ammunition delivered to Jess Piner for two dressed deer skins for the use of the soldiers at this post, 1 1/4 lbs gunpowder, two lbs lead (VSA-50).
03/28/81 Killed (Harding 1981: 27).

Pines, Lewis
07/14/80 Issued one shirt at Fort Jefferson (VSA-12).

Pipes, Windsor
09/27/80 Paid twelve yards white linen, two gallons tafia, two check handkerchiefs, and 27 yards osnaburgs for 50 bushels Indian corn per receipt (VSA-48).

Pittman, Buckner [also Pitman]
Not Dated Boat master at Fort Jefferson (George Rogers Clark Papers, II: 333).
05/01/80 Enlisted as a sergeant in Captain George's Company (Harding 1981: 31-33).
10/04/80 Ammunition delivered to Sergeant Pittman 1/2 lb gunpowder, one lb lead (VSA-50).

01/01/81 Buckner Pittman received three barges and painters, 120 oars, one iron grapling hook, one pittaugree, one canoe, and 12 fathom new cable rope (VSA- 15).
01/01/81 Buckner Pittman signed request to issue tafia for 16 men on fatigue (VSA-15).
01/03/81 Stores issued to B. Pittman, Boat Master, one axe (VSA-50).
02/13/81 Stores issued to Buckner Pittman, Boat Master, one kettle (VSA-50).
02/22/81 Ammunition delivered to Buckner Pittman, Boat Master, 1/2 lb gunpowder, one lb lead (VSA-50).
04/24/81 Stores issued to Buckner Pittman, Boat Master, two tents or oil cloths (VSA-50).

Plant, Joseph
05/30/79-06/02/81 Listed as a private in Captain Richard McCarty's Company (Harding 1981: 27).
11/20/80 Deserted (Harding 1981: 27).

Plassy
10/09/80 Paid Captain Plassy for pitch and oakum, 84 livres peltry (VSA-48).

Pope, William
04/28/80 Sold to Martin Carney, one rifle and two muskets (VSA-50: 16).

Poston, William [also Pastin]
06/04/79-12/03/81 Listed as a gunner in Captain Robert George's Company of Artillery (Harding 1981: 29-30).
06/19/80 Issued two shirts (VSA-11).
07/26/80 Issued three carots of tobacco for six men (VSA-12).
10/14/80 Deserted (Harding 1981: 29-30).

Potter, James
07/13/80 Discharged at Fort Jefferson; had been a member of Captain Jesse Evans' Company (Harding 1981: 14).
07/14/80 Issued one shirt at Fort Jefferson (VSA-12).

Priest, Peter
06/04/79-12/03/81 Matross [corporal], Captain Robert George's Company of Artillery (Harding 1981: 29-30).

Pritchet, James
07/12/80 Member, Captain Abraham Kellar's Company.
07/12/90 Received clothing issue for having more than one year to serve (VSA-12).

Pritichett, Will [also Pritchet]
06/04/79-12/03/81 Corporal, Captain Robert George's Company of Artillery (Harding 1981: 29-30).
09/30/80 Issued one blanket (VSA-48).
12/26/80 Paid for making four suits of clothes for the use of Kellar's Company (VSA-14).
12/26/80 William Pritchett signed he received six yards toile gris for making the suits (VSA-14).

Pruit, Isaac
06/19/80 Member, Captain George's Company at Fort Jefferson; issued two shirts for enlisting during the war (VSA-11).

Pruitt, Joshua
04/05/80 Enlisted as a matross in Captain Robert George's Company (Harding 1981: 31).

Puccan, Francis
04/12/80 Enlisted for three years by Lt. Valentine T. Dalton into Captain Robert George's Company of Artillery (MHS: B1, F23).

Purcell, William [Pursley]
04/10/80 Enlisted as a matross in Captain Robert George's Company (Harding 1981: 31-33).
09/11/80 Issued one blanket (VSA-13).

Pursley, William
04/14/80 Enlisted as a matross in Robert George's Company of Artillery (Harding, 1981: 140, 156, 203).
09/10/80 Issued full clothing for enlisting (VSA-13).
10/23/80 Issued one suit due for enlisting; also received extra linen for two shirts (VSA-13).
04/23/81 Ammunition delivered to Mr. Pyatt going on command to the Falls, 12 flints (VSA-50).

Pyatte, Jacob [also Pyatt, Pyeatt]
04/17/80 Tobacco issued to Jacob Pyatte, three lbs (VSA-50).
08/01/80 Ammunition delivered to Mr. Jacob Pyatte on his way to the Falls of Ohio, 1/2 lb gunpowder and one lb lead (VSA-50).
04/11/81 In a letter to George Rogers Clark from William Clark, reference is made to Mr. Pyatte. William Clark and Captain John Dodge met Mr. Pyatte a little below the mouth of Salt River with letters from George Rogers Clark t Fort Jefferson (MHS: B2, F15).
04/20/81 Carried letters from George Rogers Clark to Fort Jefferson (MHS: B2, F15).
06/05/81 Per order exchanged for fatigue, liquor with Mr. Pyatte, 50 lbs sugar (VSA-49).

Quibea, Paul [also Quibeo, Quiyis]
06/04/79-12/03/81 Matross [corporal], Captain Robert George's Company of Artillery (Harding 1981: 29-30).
01/10/80 Enlisted for three years in Captain Robert George's Company of Artillery by Lt. Valentine T. Dalton (MHS: B1, F23).
08/12/80 Issued two shirts for enlisting (VSA-12).
08/14/80 Issued 1/2 carot of tobacco (VSA-13).
08/21/80 Issued one lb gunpowder (VSA-12).
09/11/80 Issued one blanket (VSA-13).
09/15/80 Sugar delivered to Paul Quibea of Captain George's Company, one lb (VSA-50).
11/15/81 Deserted [present?] (Harding 1981: 31).

Quirk, Thomas
07/12/80 Issued 14 yards blue cloth, 12 yards white cloth flannel, four shirts, and 13 yards linen for four shirts (VSA-48).
09/10/80 Listed as a volunteer with two children; received two lbs sugar for himself and his sick family (VSA-13).
09/10/80 Issued one plain shirts (VSA-48).

Quirk, Thomas (family)
09/10/80 Mentions two children (VSA-13).

Randal, Nathanal [also Randolph, N]
04/28/80 Appraised and taken into service, one rifle valued at 180 pounds, belonging to N. Randolph (VSA-50: 16).

Raper, Baptist [also Rahr?]
06/02/80 Served in Captain A. Kellar Company (MHS: B1, F19).
07/12/80 Received clothing issue for having more than one year to serve (VSA-12).

Ramsey, Jas [also James]
06/04/79-12/03/81 Matross [corporal], Captain Robert George's Company of
    Artillery (Harding 1981: 29-30).
10/23/80 Issued cloth and trimmings to produce one suit (VSA-13).

Reed, John
09/15/80 Sugar delivered to John Reed of militia, one lb (VSA-50).

Reid, William
05/01/80-12/21[25]/80 Private, Captain George Owens' Company of Militia
    (George Rogers Clark Papers, I: 465; Harding 1981: 48-49).
09/15/80 Issued one lb sugar for being sick (VSA-13).

Rey, Dr. Andrew [also Ray]
Not Dated Issued three weight sugar and 1 1/2 coffee to the hospital (VSA-48).
07/11/80 Issued his full compliment of clothing at Fort Jefferson as is
    allowed to officers by Act of Assembly (VSA-12).
07/12/80 Issued to Doctor Rey, 1 1/2 yards scarlet cloth 7/4 wide, 1 1/2
    yards brown cloth, 2 1/2 yards shalloon, one stick silk twist, three
    skeins silk, 19 1/2 yards white linen for six shirts, 3/4 yd fine
    holland for ruffling, two yards muslin for six stocks; issued for
    six vests and six pair breeches: two yards casimir, 2 1/2 yards
    chintz, 2 1/2 yards spotted flannel, three yards camlet, three yards
    shalloon, four yards toile gris, and 2 1/4 yards check linen, one
    silk handkerchief, one Indian handkerchief, four linen
    handkerchiefs, eight skeins thread, one skein thread, two pair
    thread hose, one hat four yards damaged linen for lining, and three
    yards broadcloth 7/4 wide (VSA-48).
07/13/80 Participant in Court Proceedings against John Dodge at Fort
    Jefferson (Draper Manuscripts 56J22-24).
07/13/80 Issued one box Jesuit Bark (VSA-12).
08/23/80 Paid Doctor Rey for medicines (VSA-48).
09/11/80 Issued 1/2 lbs gunpowder, one lb lead (VSA-13).
09/11/80 Issued one blanket (VSA-13).
09/13/80 Soap delivered to Captain Brahsears and Doctor Rey, one lb (VSA-50).
09/13/80 Listed as an "officer of the mess;" received a share of 60 lbs sugar
    (VSA-13).
10/09/80 Paid for the use of the sick, two weight coffee and two weight sugar
    (VSA-48).

Riely, John [also Riley]
06/04/79-12/03/81 Sergeant [gunner], Captain Robert George's Company of
    Artillery (Harding 1981: 29-30).
09/11/80 Issued two shirts for enlisting (VSA-13).
10/14/80 Deserted (Harding 1981: 29-30).

Rion, Mrs.
09/01/80 Helped farm 16 acres with eight others from Clarksville; would have
    yielded 320 bushels of corn had the Indians not burned it
    (Draper Manuscripts 1M8).

Roberts, Benjamin
12/22/79-11/30/80 Listed as a Captain in Major George Slaughter's Company
    (Harding 1981: 37).
12/20/80 Ammunition expended by the artillery by order of Captain Robert
    George at Fort Jefferson upon Captain Harrison and Captain
    Roberts' arrival from the Falls of Ohio, six lbs gunpowder, two lbs
    lead, and one yd flannel (VSA-50: 33).
12/20/80 Issued full quota of clothing (VSA-14).
12/22/80 Issued to Captain Roberts, two tents or oil cloths (VSA-50: 39).
12/23/80 Issued of two bags to Captain Benjamin Roberts to carry necessities
    to Col. Slaughter at the Falls of Ohio (VSA-14).

12/23/80	Issued for the use of the troops at Fort Jefferson and Col. Slaughter at the Falls: 157 3/4 yards linen, 23 1/2 yards fine linen, eight yards toile gris, two yards flannel, six skeins colored thread, 46 skeins white thread and two paper of pins (VSA- 14).
12/23/80	Issued 1 1/2 yards blue cloth, two yards coarse flannel, four skeins thread, and one skein silk thread (VSA-14).
12/23/80	Issued three dozen coat buttons and three dozen small buttons (VSA-14).
12/24/80	Ammunition delivered to Captain Benjamin Roberts, 24 flints (VSA-50: 31).
12/30/80	Ammunition delivered to Captain Roberts (of Slaughter's Company), 100 lbs gunpowder and 200 lbs lead (VSA-50: 30).
02/15/81	Ammunition delivered to Captain Roberts' Company going on command, 2 1/4 lbs gunpowder (VSA-50).
02/26/81	Served on Board of Court of Inquiry about Captain Worthington at Fort Jefferson (Draper Manuscripts 56J27).
02/27/81-03/07/81	Served on Board of Court of Inquiry at Fort Jefferson looking into Captain John Dodge's charges against Captain Richard McCarty (Draper Manuscripts 56J29).
03/09/81	Served on Board of Court of Inquiry at Fort Jefferson to examine conduct of Captain John Rogers while in command at Kaskaskia (Draper Manuscripts 56J45).
03/20/81	Served on Board for Court Martial proceedings at Fort Jefferson for David Allen and James Taylor (Draper Manuscripts 56J40).

Roberts, John
07/12/80 Issued full clothing for enlisting (VSA-12).

Robertson, James
06/04/79-12/03/81 Lieutenent, Captain Robert George's Company of Artillery (Harding 1981: 29-30).
05/22/80 Letter from Lt. James Robertson at New Orleans to George Rogers Clark. Robertson has just arrived in New Orleans; informs Clark of the Spanish plans in that location (Seineke 1981: 437).

Robison, John
07/15/80 Member, Captain Worthington's Company (MHS B1, F20; VSA-12).

Robinson, John (Jason) [also Robison]
Not Dated If this is James Robinson, had a Negro slave named Caesar.
01/08/81 Listed as a Captain; with John Montgomery when he visited Fort Jefferson. Went with Montgomery to New Orleans and carried letter from Montgomery to Thomas Jefferson (George Rogers Clark Papers, I: 497-498).

Robeson, William [also Robison]
04/12/80 Enlisted as a private in Captain Worthington's Company (Harding 1981: 47; 53).
06/23/80 Issued two shirts at Fort Jefferson (VSA-11).
09/28/80 Died (Harding 1981: 47 & 53).

Rogers, John
Not Dated Sent 224 weight flour, two bags, and four ells osnaburgs to Fort Jefferson by order of Captain Rogers, Commandant (VSA-48).
04/27/80 Signed a request with George Rogers Clark at "Camp on Mississippi" for 20 yards cloth with facings and trimmings for making clothing for part of Rogers' Company of Virginia Light Dragoons (MHS: B1, F16).
04/27/80 John Rogers and George Rogers Clark signed a request at "Camp on Mississippi" to deliver 30 yards flannel with thread to make shirts for part of Rogers' Company of Virginia Light Dragoons (MHS: B1, F16).
04/28/80 Received from Captain John Rogers two rifles (VSA-50: 16).

Fort Jefferson Personnel

04/28/80	John Rogers and George Rogers Clark signed a request for 40 yards cloth with trimmings and facings, for the purpose of clothing Rogers' Company (MHS: B1, F16).
04/28/80	John Rogers and George Rogers Clark signed a request for three hundred yards flannel for shirting overalls and over-jackets for the troops when cleaning their horses (MHS: B1, F16).
05/09/80	Letter from John Rogers at Kaskaskia to George Rogers Clark at Camp Jefferson. Rogers will be leaving May 10 for Cahokia with his Company. Mr. Dodge has purchased horses for Rogers. Rogers is asking for instructions to receive saddles, bear skins, and reams of clothing for his soldiers (MHS: B1, F18).
05/15/80	Letter from Captain John Rogers at Fort Clark to George Rogers Clark. Rogers speaks of the dirty conditions and need for repair of the fort at Cahokia, and his efforts to clean it. Rogers tells of Col. Montgomery on the Spanish side who is supposed to make an expedition with 100 men (MHS: B1, F17; Seineke 1981: 434).
06/06/80	Letter from Captain John Rogers at Kaskaskia to George Rogers Clark at Fort Jefferson. Rogers wants to go on a dangerous expedition to learn more about the service and to better serve his country (MHS: B1, F19; Seineke 1981: 442).
06/10/80	Issued for his company, two yards blue persian and one piece of silk ferret (VSA-48).
07/10/80	Signed order to issue 62 shirts and stocks with blackstuff to 31 of his men at Fort Jefferson; actually received 17 ruffled shirts; 45 plain shirts and 11 yards of black persians and 18 yards fine linen [damaged, for 62 stocks] (VSA-12).
07/10/80	Issued his full quota clothing at Fort Jefferson along with "his two officers" [Lt. James Merriwether and Coronet John Thruston] (VSA-12; Harding 1981: 109).
07/10/80	Issued two yards blue persian wool and some white narrow waisted binding to make a cape (VSA-12).
07/12/80	Issued 1 3/4 yards of broadcloth 7/2 wide, 1 1/2 yards blue bath coating 7/2 wide, 2 1/2 yards corded dimity for one vest or breeches, 1 1/4 yards sycee for one vest or breeches, 1 1/4 yards calender for one vest or breeches, four yards toile gris for two vests or breeches, 14 yards white linen for four shirts, two yards fine holland for six stocks, 1/2 yard cambric for ruffling, two linen handkerchiefs, two silk handkerchiefs, 1 1/4 yards blue persion, 12 skeins silk, one stick silk twist, 2 1/4 yards thickset for one pair breeches, two pair thread hose, 2 1/2 yards shalloon, three yards spotted flannel for two vests and breeches, three yards grey cloth for three vests and breeches, seven yards white linen for two shirts, 1/4 yard fine holland for ruffling, 2 1/2 yards of coarse linen for lining, two linen handkerchiefs, and 2 3/4 yards broadcloth 7/4 wide (VSA-48).
07/12/80	One English blanket, 3 3/4 ells ribbon, four skeins silk, one comb, and six lbs coffee issued to and overdrawn by Captain John Rogers (VSA-48).
07/12/80	Issued one pound lead and one pound gunpowder for four men of Captain Rogers Company (VSA-12).
07/13/80	Received 18 yards osnaburg for padding saddles; also one lb thread and 1 1/2 dozen course needles for the saddles (VSA-12; 48).
07/13/80	Served on Court of Inquiry Board investigating Captain Dodge's character at Fort Jefferson (Draper Manuscripts 56J22).
07/14/80	Received 11 coarse combs, 11 fine combs, three ink stands, two rolls black ball, 24 skeins fine thread to make officers shirts, two horse fleams, and 1/2 pound coarse thread for use of his company (VSA-12).
07/14/80	Received 27 1/2 yards blue cloth for making cloaks for 31 of his dragoons; also received one yard damaged thread (VSA-12).
07/14/80	Received three coverlids for himself and two officers (VSA-12).
07/14/80	Issued to Captain John Rogers' company: 78 1/2 yards blue cloth, two lbs thread, 11 coarse combs, 11 fine combs, three ink pots, two

Fort Jefferson Personnel 151

	sticks blackball, two pair horse fleams, 1/2 lb coarse thread, and 24 skeins fine thread (VSA-48).
07/14/80	Ammunition delivered to Captain John Rogers going to Cahokia, one lb gunpowder and one lb lead (VSA-50).
09/24/80	One unnamed soldier of Captain Rogers' Company dies (VSA-13).
09/25/80	The following were issued per order of Captain Rogers: two bags to John Goyles to transport flour to Fort Jefferson, 16 bags to John Goyles, five files to John Goyles and 15 weight steel to John Goyles sent to Fort Jefferson (VSA-48).
10/17/80	John Montgomery writes to the Virginia Treasury to pay $2,000 to John Rogers for provision supplies for troops at Fort Jefferson (VSA-13).
10/17/80	John Dodge received $2,000 from John Rogers to buy provisions for troops at Fort Jefferson (VSA-13).
10/27/80	Robert George at Fort Jefferson writes to John Rogers at Kaskaskia to inform him that Lt. William Clark had been sent to acquire a boat [to be returned], men [enough extra to return the boat], and provisions for Fort Jefferson. The Fort Jefferson boat is on dry land and immobile (Draper Manuscripts 50J72; George Rogers Clark Papers, I: 462-463; Seineke 1981: 465).
10/28/80	John Montgomery requests Martin Carney to send 50 lbs gunpowder to John Rogers at Kaskaskia via first boat passing (VSA-13).
10/28/80	Lt. Richard Clark signs he received 20 of the 50 lbs of gunpowder requested for John Rogers (VSA-13).
12/05/80	Letter from John Donne at Fort Jefferson to George Rogers Clark. Captain Rogers has been ordered from the Illinois to reinforce Fort Jefferson; the presence of his company will add 1,000 weight of meat to the monthly issue (MHS: B1, F23).
12/30/80	Ammunition delivered at Fort Jefferson: to two men of Captain Rogers' Company, 1/2 lb gunpowder and one lb lead (VSA-50: 30).
01/08/81	Ammunition delivered to Captain Rogers' Company, three lbs gunpowder, six lbs lead (VSA-50).
02/26/81	Served as President, Court of Inquiry investigating Captain Worthington's character at Fort Jefferson (Draper Manuscripts 56J27).
03/01/81	Provided testimony at Richard McCarty's Court of Inquiry at Fort Jefferson (Draper Manuscripts 56J33).
03/02/81	Provided testimony at McCarty's Court of Inquiry [McCarty] (Draper Manuscripts 56J34).
03/09/81	Requested Court of Inquiry at Fort Jefferson to examine his conduct while in command at Kaskaskia; Court approved of his conduct and dismissed unnamed allegations (Draper Manuscripts 56J45).
03/19/81	Ammunition delivered to Captain Rogers going to the Falls of Ohio, 25 lbs gunpowder, 20 lbs lead (VSA-50).
03/19/81	Stores issued to Captain Rogers going to the Falls of Ohio, two muskets or smoothed guns and five tents or oil cloths (VSA-50).

Rogers, Patrick
10/23/80	Member, Robert George's Company of Artillery; issued cloth and trimmings to produce one suit for enlisting (VSA-13).

Ross, Joseph [also Rofs]
07/12/80	Issued clothing at Fort Jefferson as a member of Ensign Williams' (Captain Brashears') Company (VSA-12).
09/18/80	Received a share of five lbs sugar for being sick (VSA-13).

Rubedo, Francis [Frank]
05/30/80	Enlisted as a private in Captain Brashears' Company (Harding 1981: 51).
07/12/80	Issued clothing at Fort Jefferson as a member of Captain Brashears' Company (VSA-12).
09/12/80	Deceased (Harding 1981: 51).

Rubedo, Jacke [James?]
05/29/79 James Rubedo enlisted in Captain John Williams' Company (Harding 1981: 26).
07/12/80 Issued cloth and trimmings for a complete suit of clothes and two shirts each having more than one year to serve (VSA-12).

Russill, David [also Rufsill]
07/12/80 Member, Captain Abraham Kellar's Company (VSA-12).
07/12/80 Received clothing issue at Fort Jefferson for having more than one year to serve (VSA-12).

Ryan, Lazurus
06/04/79-12/03/81 Matross [corporal], in Captain Robert George's Company of Artillery (Harding 1981: 29-31).
06/12/80 Went on expedition with Harrison to the Falls; received clothing issue for the trip (VSA-11).
10/03/80 Discharged (Harding 1981: 30).

Saintive, John
05/30/79-06/02/81 Private, Captain Richard McCarty's Company of the Illinois Regiment (Harding 1981: 27-28).
11/20/80 Deserted (Harding 1981: 28).

Scarcy, B.
02/14/81 Ammunition delivered to B. Scarcy, Express, 2 1/2 lbs gunpowder, five lbs lead (VSA-50).

Senet, Richard [also Sinnat, Sennet, Linnett]
06/23/80 Issued one shirt at Fort Jefferson to go to the Illinois for provisions. Formerly a member of Isaac Taylor's Company of Volunteers under Col. Montgomery (VSA-11).
07/14/80 Received one shirt or linen to make a shirt for going to Kaskaskia for provisions for Fort Jefferson [accompanied by Peter Freeman, James Ballenger, and Jacob Huffman] (VSA-12).

Serpy, M.
09/25/80 Issued twenty lbs lead and three bags for debarking goods (VSA-48).

Shaffer, David [also Shaver]
02/11/80-11/30/81 Listed as a private in Captain John Bailey's Company (Harding 1981: 45-46).
07/12/80 Issued two shirts (VSA-12).
10/26/80 Deserted (Harding 1981: 46).

Shank, John
06/02/80 Member, Captain Abraham Kellar's Company (MHS: B1, F19).
06/29/80 Issued two shirts (VSA-11).
07/12/80 Received clothing issue for having more than one year to serve (VSA-12).

Shannon, William
04/11/80 William Shannon received six land warrants containing 560 acres each from George Rogers Clark on this date, containing 560 acres each. Shannon promises to deliver one able bodied soldier per warrant (George Rogers Clark Papers, I: 412).
04/12/80 Abraham Kellar and William Shannon received from George Rogers Clark, four land warrants, containing 560 acres each, for recruiting four soldiers (George Rogers Clark Papers, I: 413).
04/12/80 Edward Worthington and William Shannon received from George Rogers Clark, 20 land warrants, containing 560 acres each, for recruiting 20 soldiers (George Rogers Clark Papers, I: 413).

Fort Jefferson Personnel

04/12/80	Letter from William Shannon at Falls of Ohio to Evan Baker, Commissary of Washington County, Virginia, to draw on Baker for six months provisions for 1,000 men to be at the Mouth of the Ohio by June 1, 1780 (George Rogers Clark Papers, I: 413-414).
04/12/80	William Shannon's deposition of August 25, 1781 states that he received 39 land warrants, containing 360 acres each, from George Rogers Clark to furnish provisions for use of the troops under his command in the Illinois Department valued at 8,771 pounds, 2 shillings, Virginia Currency) (George Rogers Clark Papers, I:593).
05/18/80	Captain Robert George at Fort Jefferson wrote to George Rogers Clark at Cahokia informing him that Captain Shannon and Doctor Smith arrived at Fort Jefferson a few days ago; Captain George is planning to keep the doctor at Fort Jefferson, but will send a letter with Shannon to Cahokia (MHS: B1, F17).
05/25/80	Letter from Captain William Shannon at Kaskaskia to George Rogers Clark. Shannon arrived at Kaskaskia after an eight day trip from Clarksville. He plans on seeing Clark in two days if his horse can hold out. Indians are daily being hostile with the inhabitants at the Falls, and Clark's return is much hoped for (MHS: B1, F17; Seineke 1981: 439).
06/01/80	Listed as Captain. Was supposed to supply Fort Jefferson Louisville (George Rogers Clark Papers, I: 413-414).
06/05/80	George Rogers Clark at Kaskaskia requests William Shannon to provide five gallons tafia to take to Fort Jefferson (VSA-11).
06/09/80	William Shannon at Fort Jefferson received six quire paper (VSA-11).
06/12/80	Furnish William Shannon with chintz for two pair trousers, cloth or other stuff for two waistcoats, two pair breeches, one breech cloth, one bridle, one blanket, one ink stand, one knife, one coarse and one fine comb (VSA-11).
06/12/80	Issued Captain William Shannon, Conductor General, five yards check linen for two pair trousers, 2 3/4 yards thickset for one pair breeches, 1 1/2 yards linen for lining, 1/2 yd blue bath coating for breech cloth, one 2 1/2 point blanket, one snaffle bridle, one clasp knife, one ink holder, one stick silk twist, one ivory comb, and one horn comb (VSA-11; 48).
06/13/80	Issued 1/2 yd white linen, 1/4 yd check linen, one Indian handkerchief, one silk handkerchief, one linen handkerchief, one pair scissors, and six skeins thread (VSA-11; 48).
06/14/80	Issued three yards fine ribbon (VSA-48; VSA-11).
06/14/80	Richard Harrison wrote a return for William Shannon for 27 gallons tafia for the use of his escort party [for Col. Walker] to the Falls from Fort Jefferson (VSA-11).
12/03/80	Letter from Captain Richard Harrison at the Falls to Col. Clark. Harrison tells Clark that Captain Shannon is taking a quantity of corn with him to Fort Jefferson (George Rogers Clark Papers, I: 468).
12/11/80	William Shannon at Louisville wrote letter to Thomas Jefferson. Shannon speaks of the distressed situation at Fort Jefferson; many have deserted. Shannon is expecting a boat to come down the river daily; he plans to purchase flour which he will send to Fort Jefferson. He mentions he already had sent flour and corn (George Rogers Clark Papers, I: 473-474).
05/21/81	Plans to send additional provisins to Fort Jefferson (apparently unaware of evacuation about to take place) (George Rogers Clark Papers, I: 554-555).

Shepeard, George

02/12/80-11/30/81	Listed as a private in Captain John Bailey's Company (Harding 1981: 45-46).
07/12/80	Issued two shirts at Fort Jefferson (VSA-12).

Shepeard, Peter
02/12/80-11/30/81 Private, Captain John Bailey's Company (Harding 1981:45-46).
07/12/80 Issued two shirts at Fort Jefferson (VSA-12).
09/09/80 Issued tafia and sugar for being sick (VSA-13).

Sherlock, James [also Shirlock]
06/20/80 Issued 2 1/2 yards osnaburgs and one yard linen exchanged for a set of buttons for the Interpreter's clothes (VSA-48).
07/13/80 Participated in Court of Inquiry at Fort Jefferson looking into Captain John Dodge's character (Draper Manuscripts 56J22-24).
07/16/80 Issued the Indian and French interpreter, for one coat: 1 1/2 brown broadcloth 7/4 wide, 1 1/2 yards shalloon, 1/8 yard scarlet cloth, 2 1/2 dozen buttons, three skeins silk, one stick silk twist, skeins thread, two yards damaged course linen damaged, issued for one capot: 3 1/2 yards grey cloth 7/8 wide, six yards silk ferret for binding, four skeins silk, and four skeins thread; issued for one summer coat, 2 1/2 yards chintz, 2 1/2 yards linen for lining, and four skeins thread, issued for three vests and two pair breeches, 4 3/4 yards corded dimity, 3 1/2 yards linen for lining, 2 1/2 yards grey cloth 7/8 wide, 1 1/4 yards cotton 16 sachaque, six skeins silk, and ten skeins thread; issued for two pair trousers, five yards cottonade, and four skeins thread; four ruffled shirts, four cambric stocks, one silk handkerchief, one romall handkerchief, two check linen handkerchiefs, two pair thread hose, and one hat (VSA-48).
08/03/80 Tobacco delivered to Mr. Sherlock, Interpreter to the Indians, two carots weighing six lbs; to Mr. Sherlock, Interpreter to the Kaskaskia Indians, one carot weighing three lbs (VSA-50).
08/28/80 Tobacco delivered to Mr. Sherlock, Interpreter for Indians, one carot weighing three lbs (VSA-50).
09/25/80 Issued two yards blue cloth, five yards linen, and 4 1/4 yards camlet (VSA-48).
11/02/80 Ammunition delivered to Mr. Sherlock for the use of the Kaskaskia Indians, 80 lbs gunpowder, 89 lbs lead (VSA-50).
11/23/80 Soap delivered to James Sherlock, Interpreter, for his use, six lbs (VSA-50).
01/12/81 Stores issued to James Sherlock, one sword (VSA-50).
03/01/81 Provided testimony in Court of Inquiry at Fort Jefferson regarding Captain Richard McCarty's character (Draper Manuscripts 56J31).
03/01/81 Sherlock was attached to the Indian Department under John Dodge and Lt. Leonard Helm (Draper Manuscripts 56J31).

Shillings, Jacob
05/01/80-12/21/80 Private, Captain George Owens' Company of Militia (Harding 1981: 48-49).
09/01/80[?] Farmed 16 acres at Clarksville with eight other people which would have yielded 320 bushels of corn had the Indians not burned it (Draper Manuscripts 1M8).
09/08/80 Received one quart tafia and two lbs sugar for use of his sick family (VSA-13).
09/09/80 Received two lbs sugar valued at 16 shillings from the quartermaster (VSA-13).
09/13/80 Moved (Harding 1981: 49).

Shilling, Mary (Mrs. Jacob and family
06/16/80 Issued 1 1/2 yards calico, one ivory comb, and 3/8 yard muslin for making three ruffled and three plain shirts (VSA-48).
06/21/80 Paid two Indian handkerchiefs for making six plain shirts (VSA-48).
09/08/80 Received one quart tafia and two lbs sugar for use of sick family (VSA-13).

Fort Jefferson Personnel   155

Shoemaker, Leonard [also Lenard
07/13/80   Private, Captain Jesse Evans' Comapny (Harding 1981: 14).
07/13/80   Discharged (Harding 1981: 14).
07/14/80   Issued one shirt (VSA-12).

Sinclair, Michael
06/04/79-12/03/81   Matross [corporal], Captain Robert George's Company of Artillery (Harding 1981: 29-30).
07/07/79-10/22/81   Actual dates of service (Harding 1981: 30).
10/22/81   Deserted (Harding 1981: 29-30).

Slaughter, George
01/01/80   Letter from Governor Jefferson to George Rogers Clark. Jefferson stated that 100 men will be stationed at the Mouth of Ohio under Major Slaughter (Seineke 1981: 418). There is no indication that activity ever occurred.
05/20/80   Colonel Broadhead at Fort Pitt wrote George Rogers Clark at Mouth of Ohio regarding primary forces. Broadhead told Major Slaughter will forward the letter and will join Clark with his 100 men (George Rogers Clark Papers, I: 419-420).
10/12/80   Slaughter wrote George Rogers Clark that Indians have paid five visits to the Falls area since Clark was at Fort Jefferson. They took nine horses from Spring Station. Mr. McConnell was killed yesterday below the Sandy Island (MHS: B1, F23).
10/29/80   Leonard Helm wrote a letter to George Slaughter. He congratulated Shannon on his success with the Shawnee expedition. He also thanks him for the balsam he sent. Tafia and other supplies needed at Fort Jefferson. He hopes Clark will return (George Rogers Clark Papers, I: 466).
12/10/80   George Slaughter at the Falls of Ohio wrote to George Rogers Clark in Richmond or "elsewhere." He tells that he has enclosed letters for Clark from the Mouth of Ohio wherein Clark will have a full account of affairs in the whole country (MHS: B1, F23).
12/23/80   Robert George requests two bags for Captain Benjamin Roberts to carry necessities to Colonel Slaughter at the Falls of Ohio (VSA-14).
12/23/80   Issued for the use of the troops and Col. Slaughter at the Falls: 157 3/4 yards linen, 23 1/2 yards fine linen, eight yards toile gris, two yards flannel, six skeins colored thread, 46 skeins white thread, and two papers of pins (VSA-14).

Slaughter, Laurence
04/26/80   Arms delivered to Captain John Bailey's Company: delivered to Ensign Slaughter, one rifle (VSA-50:4).
04/27/80   Laurence Slaughter received from George Rogers Clark, five land warrants, containing 560 acres each, and promises to return five able bodied soldiers to serve in Clark's battalion (MHS: B1, F16).
05/08/80   Arms delivered to Captain John Bailey's Company: one rifle for Slaughter (VSA-50:4; VSA-11).
05/19/80   Requests the armourer to please repair his rifle gun as quickly as possible (VSA-11).
06/04/80-11/30/81   Ensign, Captain John Bailey's Company (Harding 1981:45).
06/04/80   Enlisted (Harding 1981: 45).
07/12/80   Issued 1 1/2 yards broadcloth 7/4 wide, 1 1/2 yards scarlet 7/4 wide, one stick silk twist, four skeins silk, 2 1/4 yards thickset and two yards toile gris for one vest and one pair breeches; 2 1/2 yards shalloon, two yards toile gris, and 4 1/2 yards check linen for three vests or breeches; 3 1/8 yards calender for three vests for breeches, 5/8 yard sycee and two yards chintz for two vests or breeches, 19 1/2 yards linen for six shirts, two yards muslin for six stocks, 3/4 yard fine holland for ruffling, nine skeins thread, one silk handkerchief, one Indian handkerchief, four linen handkerchiefs, two pair thread hose, one hat, 3 1/2 yards

	coarse linen for lining, three yards blue cloth 7/4 wide, 2 3/4 yards calamanco for one vest, and 3/4 yard spotted flannel for one vest (VSA-48).
07/12/80	Issued Ensign Slaughter 44 shirts for 22 men of Captain John Bailey's Company (VSA- 12).
07/13/80	Participated in Court of Inquiry at Fort Jefferson looking into Captain John Dodge's character (Draper Manuscripts 56J22-24).
07/14/80	Ammunition delivered to Ensign Slaughter going to Cahokia, 1/4 lb gunpowder and 1/2 lb lead (VSA-12; 50).
09/10/80	Received two blankets, one for himself and one for Captain Bailey (VSA-13).
09/10/80	Received one blanket, 1 1/4 yards thickset, and five skeins silk overdrawn by Ensign Slaughter (VSA-48).
09/11/80	Soap delivered to Ensign Slaughter, two lbs (VSA-50).
09/13/80	Issued two lbs soap for his own use (VSA-13).
09/18/80	Issued eleven blankets (VSA-48).
10/19/80	Issued one comb, one knife, ten weight sugar, three weight coffee, six lbs soap, one deer skin, one bottle rum, and one ink holder overdrawn by Ensign Slaughter (VSA-48).
10/24/80	Received $400 from John Montgomery for recruiting service (VSA-13).
10/27/80	Ammunition delivered to Ensign Slaughter of his own use, 1/2 lb gunpowder, one lb lead (VSA-50).
11/15/80	Brass kettles delivered to Ensign Slaughter for Captain Bailey's Company, two kettles (VSA-50).
11/28/80	Sugar delivered to Captain Bailey and Mr. Slaughter, 12 lbs (VSA-50).
12/07/80	Soap delivered to Ensign Slaughter for his use, six lbs (VSA-50: 52).
12/27/80	Issued a set of buttons and mohair to make a suit of clothes (VSA-14).
12/27/80	Received two dozen and eleven large buttons, 2 1/2 dozen small buttons, and three skeins of mohair (VSA-14).
12/31/80	Received two pair shoes (VSA-14).
01/01/81	Issued two quarts tafia (VSA-15).
01/01/81	Issued one lb sugar (VSA- 15).
02/15/81	Ammunition delivered to Ensign Slaughter, 1/2 lb gunpowder, one lb lead (VSA-50).
05/28/81	Killed (Harding 1981: 45).

Smith, Daniel

01/29/80	Thomas Jefferson wrote a letter to Thomas Walker and Daniel Smith. Jefferson mentions proposes to fortify a post near the Mouth of the Ohio; it is necessary to know the exact latitude there. Jefferson requests that either Smith or Walker go to the Falls of Ohio where George Rogers Clark will furnish escorts and other necessities and then travel to the Mouth of the Ohio. Jefferson requests a return of one "plat" of work to him and one to Colonel Clark (George Rogers Clark Papers, I:392-393; Seineke 1981:420).
04/07/80	Daniel Smith and Thomas Walker about 160 miles east of the Cumberland River, received the January 29, 1780, letter from Thomas Jefferson from Colonel Henderson (Souissant 1915).
04/08/80	Daniel Smith and Thomas Walker recruit a guard to accompany them to the Falls of the Ohio (Souissant 1915).
04/25/80	Daniel Smith and Thomas Walker are 12 miles south of the Falls when informed by Captain Kellar that Colonel Clark left for the Iron Banks on April 14, 1780. Captain Kellar offers to take Walker and Smith with him as he was just leaving to go there (Souissant 1915).
04/26/80	"Left Louisville. Went with T. Walker and Captain Kellar to Fort Jefferson" (Souissant 1915).
05/03/80	"This morning at break of day opposite old Fort Massac. This afternoon at five o'clock got to the Mouth of Ohio; then down the Mississippi about five miles to Colonel Clark's encampment, who we

	saw this evening and had some conversation with respecting our business." Captain Kellar and untold number of individuals in party also arrives (Souissant 1915).
05/04/80	Daniel Smith and Thomas Walker "staid [sic] at the Intended Town" [Clarksville] (Souissant 1915).
05/05/80	"staid [sic] at the Intended Town." Note: journal entry combines May 4 and 5 as one entry (Souissant 1915).
05/06/80	"Went down to the Iron Bank, encamp'd on the Spanish Shore a little below---rather hazy" (Souissant 1915).
05/07/80	"Cloudy. Rain last night." (Souissant 1915).
05/09/80	"Cloudy, but being convinced we were north of the line moved to the South end of the Island about five miles" [Wolf Island?] (Souissant 1915).
05/10/80	"Observed" (Souissant 1915).
05/11/80	"Agreed with yesterday's observation. We were 3' 19" in Virginia (Souissant 1915).
05/12/80	"Got up to Col. Clarke" (Souissant 1915).
05/13/80	"Embark'd again for Kaskaskios" (Souissant 1915).
06/05/80-06/14/80	Returned to Fort Jefferson and stayed (Souissant 1915).
06/09/80	Issued Colonel Walker and Major Smith, four pair cotton overalls, two pair linen drawers, six linen shirts, one osnaburg shirt, and one pair scissors for them on their public service (VSA-11).
06/13/80	Daniel Smith and Thomas Walker wrote they received from the public stores: five pair of cottonade overalls, one pair brown linen drawers, six linen shirts [three ruffled, three plain], one pair blue leggings, one blue coating breech cloth, one scalping knife, 4 1/2 yards binding, one pair leg garters, one ivory comb, one linen shirt, and one osnaburg shirt (VSA-11).

Smith, Edmund
05/01/80-12/21/80	Private, Captain George Owens' Company of Militia (Harding 1981: 48-49).
09/13/80	Moved (Harding 1981: 49).

Smith, George
06/04/79-12/03/81	Matross [corporal], in Captain Robert George's Company of Artillery (Harding 1981: 29-30).
06/12/80	Went on expedition with Captain Harrison to the Falls of Ohio; received clothing issue for the trip (VSA-11).
01/02/81	Died (Harding 1981: 29-30 & 32).

Smith, George
07/12/80	Member Captain Abraham Kellar's Company (VSA-12).
07/12/80	Received clothing issue at Fort Jefferson for having more than one year to serve (VSA-12).

Smith, Henry
06/02/80	Signed testament at Fort Jefferson regarding arrival of Joseph Lindsey and Israel Dodge (VSA-11).
06/13/80	Helped write a petition as a trustee of Fort Jefferson to government seeking to make Clarksville and surrounding area a recognized county of Virginia (George Rogers Clark Papers, I: 425- 426).
07/13/80	Participant, Court of Inquiry at Fort Jefferson looking into Captain John Dodge's character (Draper Manuscripts 56J22-24).
09/01/80	Farmed five acres at Clarksville which would have yielded 125 bushels of corn had the Indians not burned it (Draper Manuscripts 1M8).

Smith, Joseph
07/13/80	Member, Captain Jesse Evans' Company (Harding 1981: 14).
07/13/80	Discharged (Harding 1981: 14).
07/14/80	Issued one shirt (VSA-12).

Fort Jefferson Personnel

Smith, Mary (Mrs.)
06/20/80 Paid four yards flannel for making one suit of soldiers clothes (VSA-48).
06/20/80 Paid 12 shillings and six pence, for making a suit of soldiers clothes for Jacob Wheat (VSA-11).
06/20/80 Received two yards of white flannel (VSA-11).
07/13/80 The daughter of Mary Smith [no name given] had been badly paid by Israel and John Dodge for making shirts according to Mary Smith's testimony at Fort Jefferson's Court of Inquiry looking into the conduct of Captain John Dodge (Draper Manuscripts 56J22-24).

Smith, Nicholas
Not Dated Paid 7 1/2 bushels corn for carting public goods (VSA-48).

Smith, Sarah
06/17/80 Paid 5 1/4 yards calico for making 19 plain shirts (VSA-48).

Smith, Sidy
06/05/80 Paid 2 1/4 yards calico and 2 1/2 yards ribbon for making six ruffled shirts (VSA-48).

Smithers, John [also Smothers]
06/04/79-12/03/81 Matross [corporal], Captain Robert George's Company of Artillery (Harding 1981: 29-30).
06/19/80 Issued two shirts for being enlisted during the war (VSA-11).
09/11/80 Issued one blanket (VSA-13).
09/12/80 Issued one lb sugar for being sick (VSA-13).
12/03/81 Killed (Harding 1981: 29-30).

Smyth, Samuel
05/18/80 Letter from Captain George at Fort Jefferson to George Rogers Clark at Cahokia, informing him of the arrival of Doctor Smith and Captain Shannon. The doctor is short of medicine. Captain George plans to keep the doctor at Fort Jefferson, but is sending a letter with Shannon to Cahokia. George refers to the sickly season approaching (MHS B1, F17).
06/10/80 Signed an invoice from New Orleans (VSA-11).
06/12/80 Issued Samuel Smyth, Surgeon Illinois Department: 1 3/4 yards blue bath coating, for three vests and three pair breeches, 7 1/2 yards spotted cotton velvet, one yard spotted persian, 2 1/2 yards gingham or check, and 7 1/2 yards linen for lining; 7 1/2 yards linen for three pair trousers, 9 3/4 yards for three shirts, one silk handkerchief, one romal handkerchief, one check linen handkerchief, 1 3/8 yards cambric for three stocks and ruffling three shirts, two sticks silk twist, 15 skeins thread, four skeins silk, one pair knee garters, six yards ferretting (VSA-48).
06/12/80 Furnish one clasp knive, two combs [one horn, one ivory], 1 1/4 yard white half-thicks for leggings, bath coating, breech cloth, four yards gartering, one brass ink stand, one pair 2 1/2 point blankets, and one bridle for the use of the expedition to the Fall (VSA-11).

Snellock, Thomas [also Snarlock]
06/04/79-12/03/81 Matross [corporal], Captain Robert George's Company of Artillery (Harding 1981: 29-30).
05/29/80 Discharged from Captain George's Company (Harding 1981: 30).
09/11/80 Issued, as a soldier in Brashears Company two shirts, one pair breeches, one jacket, and one coat (VSA-13).
09/18/80 One of five sick men in Captain Brashears' Company; received a share of five lbs sugar (VSA-13).
12/18/80 Issued eight yards linen for 31 days of assisting Major to Harlan on a hunting trip for Fort Jefferson (VSA-14).

Snow, George
07/10/80 Member, Captain John Rogers' Company (VSA-12).
07/10/80 Received two shirts and two stocks at Fort Jefferson for having more than one year to serve (VSA-12).

Spillman, Francis
07/10/80 Member, Captain John Rogers' Company (VSA-12).
07/10/80 Issued two shirts and two stocks at Fort Jefferson for having more than one year to serve (VSA-12).

Spillman, James
07/10/80 Member, Captain John Rogers' Company
07/10/80 Received two shirts and two stocks at Fort Jefferson for having more than one year to serve (VSA-12).

Springer, Enoch
05/01/80 - 12/21/80 Sergeant, Captain George Owens' Company of Militia (Harding 1981: 48-49).
08/16/80 Issued 1/2 yd blue stroud for plowing and harrowing a turnip patch for public use (VSA-48).
09/13/80 Killed (George Rogers Clark Papers, I: 464).

Stephensen, Stephen
09/10/80 Came to Fort Jefferson with Col. Montgomery (VSA-13).
09/10/80 Issued one shirt for serving 20 months in the service (VSA-13; 48).

Steward, Henry
05/01/80-12/21/80 Private, Captain George Owens' Company of Militia (Harding 1981: 45-46).
09/09/80 Received one pint tafia at a cost of two shillings; referred to as an inhabitant of this place (VSA-13).
09/09/80 Sugar delivered to Henry Steward, a militia man, one lb (VSA-50).
09/12/80 Moved (Harding 1981: 45-46).

Sutherland, Lawrence
07/15/80 Member, Captain Worthington's Company (MHS B1, F20; VSA-12).

Suverns, Ebenezer
07/14/80 Discharged at Fort Jefferson (Harding 1981: 2; VSA-12).
07/14/80 Issued one shirt (VSA-12).

Swordin, John [Snowden, Jonathon]
04/23/80 Enlisted in Captain Worthington's Company (Harding 1981: 47; 53).
06/20/80 Issued two shirts (VSA-11; 48).
08/27/80 Killed (Harding 1981: 47 & 53).
09/28/80 Discharged (Harding 1981: 47 & 53).

Taylor, Abraham
12/19/80 Ammunition delivered to Abraham Taylor, a militia man, 1/4 lb gunpowder and 1/2 lb lead (VSA-50: 29).
12/22/80 Issued Abraham Taylor, 1/2 lb gunpowder and one lb lead (VSA-14).
02/05/81 Ammunition delivered to Abraham Taylor, a militia man at this post, 1/4 lb gunpowder, 1/2 lb lead (VSA-50).

Taylor, Edward
02/24/79-07/14/80 Member, Captain Isaac Taylor's Company (Harding 1981: 13).
06/03/80 Paid 19 dollars for his service to Thomas Wilson by going express from Vincennes to Fort Jefferson, to Fort Clark, then to Fort Patrick Henry, and taking 19 days to do so (VSA-11).
07/14/80 Received one shirt at Fort Jefferson (VSA-12).
07/14/80 Discharged at Fort Jefferson (Harding 1981: 13).

Fort Jefferson Personnel

Taylor, James
06/04/79-12/03/81 Matross [corporal] in Captain Robert George's Company of Artillery (Harding 1981: 29-30).
06/12/80 Went on expedition with Harrison to the Falls; received clothing issue for the trip (VSA-11).
03/20/81 Court Martial proceedings were brought against him at Fort Jefferson. He was accused of having robbed Major Williams' kitchen, beaten his servants, and verbally abusing Major Williams after his arrest. He was acquitted of all charges (Draper Manuscripts 56J40).

Taylor, William
09/25/80 Paid for for making soldiers clothes, 2 1/2 yards linen, and three skeins thread (VSA-48).

Theel, Levi
03/24/80-11/30/81 Private, Captain John Bailey's Company (Harding 1981: 45-46).
07/12/80 Issued two shirts (VSA-12).
09/09/80 Listed as a sick member of Captain John Bailey's Company; issue tafia and sugar (VSA-13).
10/15/80 Issued cloth and trimmings for a suit of clothes in return for his enlistment (VSA-13).
10/15/80 Received three yards and one-half blue cloth, three yards flannel, six skeins thread, and ten dozen buttons (VSA-13).
12/03/80 Issued two yards damaged blue cloth for enlisting for three years (VSA-14).
05/28/81 Taken prisoner (Harding 1981: 46).

Thompson, James
12/08/79 Private, Captain Kellar's Company (Harding 1981: 24; MHS: B1, F19).
06/29/80 Issued two shirts (VSA-11).
09/14/80 Sugar delivered to James Thompson, a soldier in Captain Kellar's Company, one lb (VSA-50).
09/14/80 Issued one lb sugar for sickness (VSA-13).
10/20/80 Died (Harding 1981: 24).

Thompson, William
03/27/80-11/30/81 Private, Captain John Bailey's Company (Harding 1981:45-46).
07/12/80 Issued two shirts (VSA-12).
09/09/80 Listed as a sick member of Captain John Bailey's Company; received an issue of tafia and sugar (VSA-13).

Thornton, Joseph [also Thorninton and Thornington] [possibly two people]
05/08/80 Private, Captain Worthington's Company (Harding 1981: 47; 53; MHS: B1, F20; VSA-12).
06/20/80 Issued two shirts (VSA-11; 48).
07/25/80 Tobacco delivered to Thornton, 1/3 carot eqial to one lb (VSA-50).
08/24/80 Tobacco delivered to Thornton, one carot weighing three lbs (VSA-50).
09/08/80 Member, Captain Worthington's Company (VSA-13).
09/08/80 Received two lbs sugar and one pint tafia for his use and with Patrick Mains for use of his wife and children (VSA-13).
10/04/80 Killed? (Harding 1981: 53).
10/04/80 One of three men to receive one lb gunpowder and [illeg.] (VSA-13).
11/08/80 Soap delivered to Joseph Thornton, artificer for public work, two lbs (VSA-50).
11/16/80 Sugar delivered to Joseph Thornton, artificer, two lbs (VSA-50).
01/15/81-02/15/81 Worked as artificer (VSA-15).

Thruston, Cornet John
Under Capt. John Rogers' Light Dragoons (DMS 56J45).
04/11/80 William Shannon received six land warrants from George Rogers Clark containing 560 acres each. Shannon promises to deliver one able bodied solder per warrant. Signed by John Thruston, Sullivan, and William Shannon (George Rogers Clark, I: 412).
07/12/80 Issued to Cornet Thruston, 1 1/2 yds scarlet cloth 7/4 wide, 1 5/8 yds brown cloth, 2 1/2 yds shalloon, issued for four vests and four breeches two yds calender, four yds toile gris, three yds spotted flannel, and three yds gray cloth 7/8 wide, 19 1/2 yds white linen for six shirts, 3/4 yd fine holland for ruffling, two yds muslin for six stocks, six yds check linen for two vests and two breeches, four skeins silk, one silk handkerchief, one Indian handkerchief, four linen handkerchiefs, 12 skeins thread, three yds white cloth, one hat -- returned (VSA-48).
07/12/80 Capt. John Rogers, V. L. Dragoons, signed in behalf of Cornet Thruston that he received from Capt. John Dodge, Agent the quantity of goods, in part of the clothing allowed Thruston by law. J. Donne attested (VSA-48).
07/12/80 One English blanket per Capt. Rogers, and 1/8 yd brown cloth issued to and overdrawn by Cornet Thruston. The English blanket does not appear on the July 12th list of goods issued to Thruston (VSA-48).
02/26/81 Served on Court of Inquiry Board at FJ (DMS 56J27).
02/27/81-03/07/81 Served on Board of Court of Inquiry at Fort Jefferson regarding Capt. John Dodge's charges against Capt. Richard McCarty (DMS 56J29).
03/02/81 Provided testimony of no consequence during Court of Inquiry at Ft. Jefferson (DMS 56J233).
03/09/81 Served on Court of Inquiry at FJ regarding Capt. John Rogers' Conduct while in command at Kaskaskia (DMS 56J45).
03/20/81 Served on Court Martial Board during proceedings at FJ for David Allen and James Taylor (DMS 56J40).

Tinklee, Michel
06/12/80 Member of Capt. George's Co. going on expedition with Capt. Harrison to Falls of Ohio; among list of men receiving clohting issue for the trip (VSA-11).

Todd, John
03/00/80 Letter from George Rogers Clark at Louisville to Col. John Todd. Clark suggests that in order to maintain authority in Illinois, it may be necessary to evacuate the present posts and let the force center at the Mouth of Ohio. If militia families would station there, Clark feels they would be followed by two or three times their numbers of young men (Seineke 1981: 429).
06/14/80 Letter from Gov. Jefferson, In Council to the Speaker of the House. Mentions Ft. Jefferson and the building of another fort on the North side of the Ohio. Col. Todd is in possession of a grant of land for a fort. This grant was made on supposition that the post would be taken on the North side of the Ohio. These lands belong to the Chickasaw Indians now (Seineke, 1981: 443) (GRC, I: 427-428).
06/16/80 Lt. Wm. Clark writes to the State of Virginia [J. Dodge]. He wants payment in the form of 27 Spanish milled dollars in merchandise for the delivery of goods sent to J. Dodge by the orders of John Todd at the Falls (VSA-11a).
06/16/80 One pair 2 1/2 point blankets = 15 1/2 dollars, one check linen handkerchief = one dollar, one brass ink pot = one dollar, one large clasp knife = 1/2 dollar, four yds ribbon = two dollars. Total order = 20 dollars paid to William Clark by order of Col. John Todd in lieu of 20 Spanish milled dollars for his services in bringing to this place a quantity of cloth save from Col. Rogers' defeat (VSA-48) (VSA-11b).

Fort Jefferson Personnel

Todd, Robert
Not Dated Supposedly present at erection of Ft. Jefferson (DMS 32J42-44).
01/19/79 James Ballenger enlisted on this date as a member of Capt. Todd's Company. Believe Ballenger is later discharged at Fort Jefferson (Harding 1981:11-12).
01/20/79 Samuel Johnston enlisted on this date as a member of Capt. Robert Todd's Company. Later discharged at Fort Jefferson (Harding, 1981: 12).
04/11/80 Reference is made to Col. Todd in a letter from William Clark to GRC. William Clark wrote the letter in Louisville and plans on staying there several days. While he is in Louisville, he wants to see Col. Todd and try to make a settlement with him (MHS: B2, F15).
06/23/80 James Ballanger is issued a shirt at FJ to go to Illinois for provisons; was formerly a member of Capt. Robert Todd's Company of Foot under Col. John Montgomery; discharged at FJ (VSA-11).
10/09/80 One snaffle bridle paid Barbau per order Col. Montgomery on behalf of Col. Todd (VSA-48).

Tolley, Daniel
05/31/79 Discharged on this date from Capt. John Williams' Company (Harding 1981: 2).
07/14/80 Probably still a member of Capt. Williams' Co. when discharged (VSA-12).
07/14/80 Among list of men being issued one shirt per Col. Montgomery's orders at FJ (VSA-12).

Tonish, Madam
09/25/80 Paid Madam Tonish for hire of three horse to transport artillery to Cahokia 50 livres peltry (VSA-48).

Tourangean
08/23/80 Paid Tourangean for tafia for Indians, 100 and 30 (VSA-48).
09/09/80 Paid Tourangean for tafia for Indians, 100 (VSA-48).

Tratie, Francois
07/05/80 An invoice written of rations to Francois Tratie (VSA-13a, misfiled).

Trent, Beverly
11/17/79 Enlisted on this date as a sergeant in Capt. John Bailey's Company of the Illinois Regiment in the Virginia State Service (Harding 1981: 45-46).
04/12/80 Account of arms delivered to Capt. John Bailey's company: delivered to Sgt. Trent by Col. Clark's verbal orders, two rifles (VSA-50: 4).
01/21/81 Present at FJ. Married to Sarah (VSA-15).
07/20/81 Killed (Harding 1981: 45-46).

Trent, Sarah [wife of Beverly Trent]
01/06/81 Issued 17 yds white linen for making soldiers clothing per Capt. George's orders to Israel Dodge at FJ (VSA-15).
01/21/81 She is sick (VSA-15).

Tulfor, John [also Tulford]
07/15/80 Listed in Capt. Worthington's Co. (MHS B1, F20; VSA-12).

Turpin, Richard
06/04/79 Enlisted on this date as Matross [Corporal] in Capt. Robert George's Company of Artillery in Service to the Commonwealth of Virginia and Illinois Department (Harding 1981: 29-30).
09/25/79 Listed on payroll as being a private in Capt. John Bailey's Co. of the Illinois Regiment in the Virginia State Service (Harding 1981: 32).

	Fort Jefferson Personnel 163
06/19/80	Issued two shirts by order of Capt. George; among list of men receiving clothing issue for being enlisted during the war (VSA-11).
09/11/80	Issued one blanket with ten others by order of Capt. George (VSA-13a).
11/19/80	Died (Harding 1981: 29-30).

Tuttle, Nicholas

04/19/80-11/30/81	Listed as Private in Capt. John Bailey's Co. of the Illinois Regiment in the Virginia State Service. Payroll (Harding 1981: 45-46).
07/12/80	Capt. Robert George requests of John Dodge by order of Col. Clark, that Ensign Slaugther be given 44 shirts for 22 men of Capt. John Bailey's Company which are enlisted during the present war. Tuttle is among the list of 22 men (VSA-12).
12/18/80	Silas Harlan and Robert George sign request of Israel Dodge to issue Thomas Snellock, Nicholas Tuttle, and Thomas Hays eight yds of linen each for 31 days of assistance to Harlan on a hunting trip for Fort Jefferson (VSA-14a).
12/18/80	Thomas Snellock, Nicholas Tuttle, and Thomas Hays sign that they received of Israel Dodge the within contents (VSA-14b).

Tyger, Daniel

02/07/79	Enlisted as a private in Capt. Taylor's Co. of Volunteers in the Illinois (Harding, 1981:13).
04/21/80	William Bartholomew, John Breeding, George King, Bob Logan, William Bohman, John Deck, John Cowan and Daniel Tyger are mentioned as being at Ft. Clark, and some later at Ft. Jeff (VSA-10).
07/12/80	Among list of men being issued clothing at FJ as members of Ensign Williams' Company [Brashears] which they are entitled to by law (VSA-12).
07/14/80	Tyger is discharged from Taylor's Co. (Harding, 1981: 13).

Underwood, Richard (In Worthington's Co. Attached to Brashears)

07/04/80	Received a land warrant as bounty for enlisting in Capt. Richard Brashears' Company for three years or during the war (MHS B1, F20) (VSA-12).
09/09/80	Issued full clothing for enlisting, ordered by R. Clark, Lt., 3 1/2 yds blue cloth, eight yds white flannel, buttons and thread to make his clothing, and two shirts (VSA-13).
09/27/80	Lt. R. Clark requests [George signs], the Quartermaster to issue 1/2 lb sugar to Richard Underwood for sickness (VSA-13).

Valle, Madam [also Valley]

08/19/80	Twenty-nine ells blue cloth and 85 ells white flannel per Z. Blackford's receipt paid to Madam Valle for 52 bushels corn, 1417 weight flour and six empty barrels paid by order Lt. Col. Montgomery (VSA-48).
09/12/80	Thirty-six ells linen to Madam Valley for 26 dressed deer skins for the troops (VSA-48).

Vaughan, John

05/24/80-11/30/81	Listed as Sergeant in Capt. John Bailey's Co. of the Illinois Regiment in the Virginia State Service. Payroll (Harding 1981: 45-46).
07/12/80	Capt. Robert George requests of John Dodge by order of Col. Clark, that Ensign Slaughter be given 44 shirts for 22 men of Capt. John Bailey's co. which are enlisted during the present war. Vaughan is one of the 22 men (VSA-12).
08/01/80	Account of ammunition delivered by Martin Carney by Capt. George's order to Sgt. Vaughan of Capt. Bailey's Company, seven lbs powder and 14 lbs lead (VSA-50).

Fort Jefferson Personnel

08/05/80 Account of tobacco delivered by Martin Carney by order of Capt.
          Robert George at this place, to Sgt. Vaughan of Capt. Bailey's
          Company, 3 1/3 weighing ten lbs (VSA-50).
09/03/80 Account of tobacco delivered by Martin Carney by order of Capt.
          Robert George at this place, to Sgt. Vaughan for Capt. Bailey's
          Company, five weighing 16 lbs (VSA-50).
09/19/80 Rbt. George requests of John Dodge, by order of Col. Clark, to issue
          1/4 yd white cloth to John Vaughan to face a coat (VSA-13).
09/19/80 John Vaughan signs that he received cloth (VSA-13).
10/28/80 Account of ammunition delivered by Martin Carney by order of Capt.
          George, to Sgt. Vaughan of Capt. Bailey's Company, 1/4 lb powder,
          1/2 lb lead (VSA-50).

Villier, Francis [Sgt.]
03/10/79 Enlisted as a Sergeant on this date in Capt. Richard McCarty's
          Company (Harding 1981: 27).
07/12/80 Capt. Robert George requests that four enlisted men be issued to
          serve all during the war full clothing by Lt. Girault. The four men
          being: Francis Villier, Charls McLaughlan, John LaRichardy, Francis
          Bennoit. Lt. Girault certifies that the above mentioned men are all
          enlisted to serve during the war (VSA-12).
10/10/80 Killed at FJ (Harding 1981: 27).

Vonshiner, George [also Venshiner, Vinchinner]
06/04/79-12/03/81 Listed as Matross [Corporal] in Capt. Robert George's Co. of
          Artillery in the Service of the Commonwealth of Virginia and
          Illinois Department. Pay Abstract (Harding 1981:29-30).
06/19/80 Issued two shirts by order of Capt. George; among list of men
          receiving clothing issue for being enlisted during the war (VSA-11).

Wagoner, Peter [also Waggoner]
06/04/79-12/03/81 Listed as Matross [Corporal] in Capt. Robert George's Co. of
          Artillery in the Service of the Commonwealth of Virginia and
          Illinois Department. Pay Abstract (Harding 1981: 29-30).
09/25/79 Enlistment (Harding 1981: 32).
12/25/79 Enlistment (Harding 1981: 30).
06/19/80 Issued two shirts by order of Capt. George; among list of men
          receiving clothing issue for being enlisted during the war (VSA-11).
07/29/80 Issued one hat by order of Capt. George (VSA-12).
07/29/80 One hat per order and receipt of Peter Wagoner (VSA-48).
10/06/80 Account of sugar delivered by Martin Carney by orders of Capt.
          George, to Wagoner, a soldier in Capt. George's Company, 1/2 lb
          (VSA-50).
10/06/80 Robert George requests the Quartermaster to issue 1/2 lb sugar to
          Peter Wagoner of Robert George's Company (VSA-13a).
10/20/80 Died (Harding 1981: 30 & 32).

Walker, Doctor
06/13/80 Had 12 1/2 yds cottonade made into five pair overalls, 2 1/2 yds
          toile gris made into one pair drawers, 22 3/4 yds linen made into
          seven shirts, 3/8 yd muslin made into ruffling for three shirts, one
          yd blue cloth made into one pair leggings, 1/2 yd blue coating made
          into one breech cloth, one scalping knife, 4 1/2 yds worsted
          binding, one pair garters, one ivory comb and 3 1/4 yds osnaburgs
          made into one shirt for Doctor Walker and his party by order Col.
          Clark (VSA-48).
06/13/80 List of goods issued for Doctor Walker and his party by order of
          Col. Clark (VSA-48).

Walker, John
06/04/79-12/03/81 Listed as Sergeant in Capt. Robert George's Co. of
          Artillery in the Service of the Commonwealth of Virginia and
          Illinois Department. Pay Abstract (Harding 1981: 29-30).

Fort Jefferson Personnel 165

Date	
04/12/80	Account of arms delivered by Martin Carney to Capt. George's Company of Artillery on the Illinois Virginia Regiment: delivered to Sgt. Walker, two rifle guns (VSA-50: 3).
06/12/80	Going on expedition with Capt. Harrison to Falls of Ohio; among list of men receiving clothing issue for the trip (VSA-11).
06/12/80	Capt. Robt. George requests of J. Dodge by Clark's orders to furnish Sgt. Walker with two pr stockings, as much cottonade as will make two trousers, and 12 yds red tape (VSA-11a).
06/12/80	Two pair thread hose, 5 1/4 yds cottonade, and 12 yds ferret per order delivered to Sgt. Walker per receipt (VSA-48) (VSA-11b).
06/12/80	Sundry merchandise drawn out of the public store more than George's quota for which in part no returns or receipts have been issued or passed: two pair thread hose, 5 1/4 yds cottonade, 12 yds ferret per order, delivered to Sgt. Walker per receipt (VSA-48).
06/13/80	Received six carots of tobacco [18 lbs] from M Carney per Capt. George's orders for troops going up Ohio River with Capt. Harrison to Falls (VSA-11).
06/14/80	Received two shirts, one hat, one blanket, for use on trip to Falls (VSA-11).
06/14/80	One ruffled and one plain shirt, one hat, and one 2 1/2 point blanket per order and receipt of John Walker (VSA-48).
03/27/81	Ammunition delivered by order of Capt. George, to Sgt. Walker, 1/2 lb powder, one lb lead (VSA-50).
05/03/81	Per order brought from day book, two quarts and one pint rum (VSA-49).
05/14/81	Per order brought from day book, three lbs sugar (VSA-49).
06/01/81	Per order brought from day book, six lbs sugar (VSA-49).
06/07/81	Per order brought from day book, six lbs sugar (VSA-49).
10/08/81	Discharged (Harding 1981: 29-30).

<u>Walker, Thomas</u>

Date	
01/29/80	Jefferson's copy of a letter to Thomas Walker and Daniel Smith. Jefferson mentions proposing to fortify a post as near the Mouth of Ohio as the ground will admit and it is necessary to know the exact latitude there. Jefferson requests that either Walker or Smith go to the Falls of Ohio where George Rogers Clark will furnish escorts and other necessities and then travel to the Mouth of Ohio. Jefferson requests a return of one "plat" of work to him and one to Col. Clark (Seineke, 1981: 420) (George Rogers Clark Papers, I: 392-393).
04/07/80	Daniel Smith and Thomas Walker about 160 miles east of the Cumberland River, received the January 29, 1780 letter from Thomas Jefferson from Col. Henderson (Journal of Daniel Smith, <u>Tennessee Historical Magazine</u>, Vol. 1, No. 1).
04/08/80	Daniel Smith and Thomas Walker recruit guard to accompany them to the Falls of the Ohio [thinking they would meet with Col. Clark there to carry out Governor Jefferson's Jan. 29, request of them] (Journal of Daniel Smith, <u>Tennessee Historical Magazine</u>, Vol. 1, No. 1: 62).
04/25/80	Thomas Walker and Daniel Smith get within 12 miles south of the falls. Informed by Capt. Kellar that Col. Clark had left for the Iron Banks on April 14, 1780. Capt. Kellar offers to take Walker and Smith with him as he was just leaving to go there (Journal of Daniel Smith, <u>Tennessee Historical Magazine</u>, Vol. 1, No. 1: 63).
04/26/80	Daniel Smith, Thomas Walker, and Capt. Kellar embark for Iron Banks from Falls of Ohio (Journal of Daniel Smith, <u>Tennessee Historical Magazine</u>, Vol. 1, No. 1: 63).
05/03/80	"This morning at break of day opposite old Fort Massac. This afternoon at five o'clock got to the Mouth of Ohio; then down the Mississippi about five miles to Col. Clark's encampment, who we saw this evening and had some conversation with respecting our business." Capt. Kellar and untold number of individuals in party

Fort Jefferson Personnel

	also arrives (Journal of Daniel Smith, *Tennessee Historical Magazine*, Vol. 1, No. 1: 64).
05/04/80	Stayed at Ft. Jefferson (Journal of Daniel Smith, *Tennessee Historical Magazine*, Vol. 1, No. 1: 64).
05/05/80	"staid [sic] at the Intended Town." Note: journal entry combines May 4 and 5 as one entry (Journal of Daniel Smith, *Tennessee Historical Magazine*, Vol. 1, No. 1: 64).
05/06/80	"Went down to the Iron Bank, encamp'd on the Spanish Shore a little below---rather hazy" (Journal of Daniel Smith, *Tennessee Historical Magazine*, Vol. 1, No. 1: 64).
05/07/80	"Cloudy. Rain last night." (Journal of Daniel Smith, *Tennessee Historical Magazine*, Vol. 1, No. 1: 64).
05/08/80	"Clear in morning but cloudy at noon. Ran some lines to determine the width of the river" (Journal of Daniel Smith, *Tennessee Historical Magazine*, Vol. 1, No. 1: 64).
05/09/80	"Cloudy, but being convinced we were north of the line moved to the South end of the Island about five miles" [Wolf Island?] (Journal of Daniel Smith, *Tennessee Historical Magazine*, Vol. 1, No. 1: 64).
05/10/80	"Observed" (Journal of Daniel Smith, *Tennessee Historical Magazine*, Vol. 1, No. 1: 64).
05/11/80	"Agreed with yesterday's observation. We were 3' 19" in Virginia. From this point of the Island we ran east to the main land where I marked a buck eye elm and sugar tree. Then we surveyed south three miles, 265 poles; thence west 106 poles to the river [96 poles of which we mark'd]. New land is forming here; nothing to mark but cotton [wood?] trees. Moved up the river until we were about one mile below wt. clift. A cr: about 1-4 m. about wt. clift lay in the wet without fire" (Journal of Daniel Smith, *Tennessee Historical Magazine*, Vol. 1, No. 1: 64).
05/12/80	"Got up to Col. Clarke" (Journal of Daniel Smith, *Tennessee Historical Magazine*, Vol. 1, No. 1: 64).
05/13/80	"Embark'd again for Kaskaskios" [Leaving Fort Jefferson] (Journal of Daniel Smith, *Tennessee Historical Magazine*, Vol. 1, No. 1: 64).
06/05/80	Patt. Kennedy writes to certify that Col. Walker and son lived at Mr. Charlesvilles for 20 days at the rate of $2 per person per day from May 17 to June 5, 1780 (VSA-11).
06/09/80	Col. G.R. Clark requests of John Dodge to issue to Col. Walker and Maj. Smith, four pairs of cotton overalls, two pairs of linen drawers, six linen shirts, one osnaburg shirt, and one pair of scissors for them on their public service [Ft. Jefferson] (VSA-11a).
06/13/80	Dan Smith and Thomas Walker sign that they received from the public stores; five pairs of cottonade overalls, one pair of brown linen drawers, six linen shirts [three ruffled, three plain], one pair blue leggings, one blue coating breech cloth, one scalping knife, 4 1/2 yds binding, one pair leg garters, one ivory comb, one linen shirt, and one osnaburg shirt (VSA-11).
06/14/80	Rich. Harrison writes a return to Wm. Shannon for 27 gallons of tafia for the use of his escort party [for Col. Walker] to the Falls [Ft. Jeff]. J. Donne signs that the above was delivered (VSA-11a).

Wallace, Caleb
12/25/80 George Owens' Pay Abstract sworn before C. Wallace (GRC, I: 464-465).

Wallace, David
06/04/79-12/03/81 Listed as Sergeant in Capt. Robert George's Co. of Artillery in the Service of the Commonwealth of Virginia and Illinois Department. Pay Abstract (Harding 1981: 30).
05/29/80 Discharged on this date from Capt. George's Company (Harding 1981: 30).

Fort Jefferson Personnel 167

Wallis, David
Not Dated Three weight sugar to David Wallis per Col. Montgomery's order (VSA-48).
07/12/80 Among list of men being issued clothing at FJ as members of Ensign Williams' Company which they are entitled to by law (VSA-12).

Watkins, Elizabeth
03/20/81 Provided testimony during Court Martial proceedings at FJ stating she went to lay [sleep?] at Jones' where Taylor [James] lodges; sent her husband for their bedding at Maj. Williams' (DMS 56J41).

Watkins [no first name given] [probably Samuel]
06/03/80 Came from Fort Patrick Henry [Vincennes] with provisions for FJ (VSA-12).
07/03/80 Arrived at FJ from Fort Patrick Henry and issued linen and thread for two shirts per Capt. George's orders to Capt. John Dodge at FJ [traveled to FJ with J. Duncan and John Cox per Patrick Kennedy's orders] (VSA-12).
07/03/80 Issued one lb powder and two lbs lead balls for return trip (VSA-12).
07/03/80 16 1/4 yds white linen and 3 1/4 yds check linen per order Capt. George and receipt of Joseph Duncan, Sam. Watkins, and John Cox for bringing provisions (VSA-48).
03/01/81 According to testimony at FJ Court of Inquiry regarding Capt. Richard McCarty (DMS 56J33).
03/20/81 Mentioned by Mrs. Elizabeth Watkins during her testimoney in Court Martial Proceedings at FJ. He was sent by her to Maj. Williams to get their bedding and return it to Jones' where they would sleep [He apparently returned with wrong blanket] (DMS 56J41).

Welch, Dominick
07/10/80 Member of Capt. John Rogers' Co. Among list of men being issued two shirts and two stocks at FJ per Capt. George's orders to Capt. John Dodge for havimg more than one year to serve (VSA-12).

Wheat, Jacob
06/04/79-12/03/81 Listed as Sergeant [Gunner] in Capt. Robert George's Co. of Artillery in the Service of the Commonwealth of Virginia and Illinois Department. Pay Abstract (Harding 1981: 29-30).
06/12/80 Going on expedition with Capt. Harrison to Falls of Ohio; among list of men receiving clothing issue for the trip (VSA-11).
06/20/80 Provided with suit of clothes made by Mary Smith at FJ; Smith was paid in flannel for work (VSA-11).
10/20/81 Discharged (Harding 1981: 29-30).

Whit, Robert [Waitt, Wit]
04/24/80-11/30/81 Listed as Private in Capt. John Bailey's Co. of the Illinois Regiment in the Virginia State Service. Payroll (Harding 1981: 45-46).
07/12/80 Among list of men who are members of Capt. John Bailey's Company and receive two shirts each for being enlisted during the war (VSA-12).
09/09/80 Listed as a sick member of Capt. J. Bailey's Company; issued tafia and sugar with Levi Theel, Wm. Thompson, and Peter Shepard (VSA-13).

White, John
07/14/80 Eight yds white linen at 2 1/2 dollars = 20 dollars, one embroidered apron = 20 dollars, two paper pins = two dollars, one English blanket = 16 dollars, 9 1/2 yds white linen at 2 1/2 dollars = 23 3/4 dollars, 2 1/2 yds calamanco at 2 1/2 dollars = 6 1/4 dollars, thread = 4/3 dollars. Total order 88 1/3 dollars per order of Col. Clark in favor of John White for public serveces paid to John Williams per his receipt LL 26:10 V.C. (VSA- 48).
07/15/80 Listed in Capt. Worthington's Co. (MHS B1, F20) (VSA-12).

Fort Jefferson Personnel

White, Rand [also Randel]
05/25/80-11/30/81 Listed as Private in Capt. John Bailey's Co. of the Illinois Regiment in the Virginia State Service. Payroll (Harding 1981: 45-46).
07/12/80 Among list of men who are members of Capt. John Baiely's Company and receive two shirts each for being enlisted during the war (VSA-12).

White, William
06/04/79-12/03/81 Listed as Matross [Corporal] in Capt. Robert George's Co. of Artillery in Service of the Commonwealth of Virginia and Illinois Department. Pay Abstract (Harding 1981: 29-30).
06/12/80 Going on expedition up Ohio River to Falls with Capt. Harrison; among list of men receiving clothing issue for the trip (VSA-11).
10/03/81 Discharged (Harding 1981: 29-30).

Whiteacre, Daniel
02/16/79 Enlistment (Harding 1981: 31).
06/04/79-12/03/81 Listed as Matross [Corporal] in Capt. Robert George's Co. of Artillery in the Service of the Commonwealth of Virginia and Illinois Department. Pay Abstract (Harding 1981: 29-30).
06/04/79 Enlistment (Harding 1981: 30).
09/05/81 Killed (Harding 1981: 30 & 31).

Whitegar, Dapiae
06/07/81 Account of ammunition delivered by Martin Carney by order of Capt. Robert George and Col. Montgomery, to Dapiae Whitegar, one lb powder, two lbs lead (VSA-50).

Whitehead, Robert
10/26/79-11/30/81 Listed as Private in Capt. John Bailey's Co. of the Illinois Regiment in the Virginia State Service. Payroll (Harding 1981: 45-46).
07/12/80 Capt. Robert George requests of John Dodge by order of Col. Clark, that full clothing be issued for William Buchanan, Robert Whitehead, and William Whitehead who have enlisted druing the war and have never received any part thereof. Also issue the same for John Roberts who is enlisted for one year (VSA-12).

Whitehead, William
10/26/79-11/30/81 Listed as Private in Capt. John Bailey's Co. of the Illinois Regiment in the Virginia State Service. Payroll (Harding 1981: 45-46).
07/12/80 Capt. Robert George requests of John Dodge by order of Col. Clark, that full clothing be issued for William Buchanan, Robert Whitehead, and William Whitehead who have enlisted druing the war and have never received any part thereof. Also issue the same for John Roberts who is enlisted for one year (VSA-12).

Wigins, Barney
07/10/80 Member of Capt. John Rogers' Co. Among list of men being issued two shirts and two stocks at FJ per Capt. George's orders to Capt. John Dodge for having more than one year to serve (VSA-12).

Williams, Daniel
05/22/80 Enlisted on this date as a Private in Capt. Worthington's Company (Harding 1981:47 & 53).
06/23/80 Capt. Robert George requests of John Dodge by order of Col. Clark to issue 16 shirts to Reuben Kemp, Daniel Williams, Richard Bredin, Charles Evans, Andrew Johnston, Isaac Yeates, and William Nelson who are members of Worthington's Company (VSA-11) (VSA-48).
07/15/80 Listed in Capt. Worthington's Co. (MHS B1, F20) (VSA-12).
11/09/80 Dead (Harding 1981: 47).

Fort Jefferson Personnel 169

Williams, Ensign Jarret [Garritt]
05/26/80 Account of ammunition delivered by Martin Carney by order of Col. Clark: to Ensign Williams at Cahokia, 3 1/2 lbs powder and seven lbs lead (VSA- 50:8).
06/12/80 Issaac Allen is issued clothing at Ft. Jefferson as a member of Ensign Williams' Company (VSA-12).
07/09/80 Ensign Jarrett Williams requests provisions for three men [one officer and two privates] for four days [July 9 - July 12] going to Fort Jefferson (VSA-12).
07/12/80 Issued to Ensign Williams, 1 1/2 yds scarlet cloth 7/4 wide, 1 1/2 yds broadcloth, 2 1/2 yds shalloon, issued for five vests and five pair breeches two yds calender, four yds toile gris, eight yds toile gris, three yds gray cloth 7/8 wide, 19 1/2 yds white linen for six shirts, two yds muslin for six stocks, 3/4 yd fine holland for ruffling, ten skeins thread, 2 1/2 yds check for one pair breeches, 2 1/2 yds coarse linen for lining, one silk handkerchief, one Indian handkerchief, four linen handkerchiefs, four skeins silk, one hat, 2 3/4 yds black calamanco for breeches, three yds blue cloth 7/4 wide (VSA-48).
07/12/80 Ensign Jarret Williams, Ill Battalion signed that he received from Capt. John Dodge, Agent, the within mentioned quantity of goods in part of the clothing allowed Williams by law. Attested by J. Donne (VSA-48).
07/12/80 Williams signed, apparently in behalf of Capt. Brashears, for list of goods received from Capt. Dodge, Agent, in part of the clothing allowed Brashears by law. J. Donne Attested (VSA-48).
07/12/80 Jarrett Williams certifies that James Curry, William Elms, James Morris, William Bartholomew, James Dawson, James Elms, and John Elms are enlisted during the war (VSA-12).
07/12/80 Jarrett Williams signs that the previous order was received at FJ from Capt. John Dodge agreeable to the within order. Fourteen shirts, 21 yds flannel, 24 1/4 yds blue cloth with thread and buttons to make up the shirts. John Donne signs as attesting (VSA-12).
07/12/80 Capt. Robert George requests of John Dodge by order of Col. Clark, that Ensign Jarrett Williams be issued his full quota of clothing which he is entitled to by law (VSA-12).
07/12/80 Ensign Jarrett Williams certifies that a list of 18 men of George's Company are enlisted during the war and he signs that he acknowledged the receipt of the requeted number of shirts [two each] agreeable to the order (VSA-12).
07/13/80 Served on Board of Court of Inquiry at FJ (DMS 56J22).
07/13/80 Issued to Williams for 25 men of Capt. Richard Brashears' company, one ruffled shirt, 49 plain shirts, 21 yds flannel, 24 1/4 yds blue cloth, thread and buttons, and one ink pot to Sgt. Brown by Col. Montgomery's order (VSA-48).
07/14/80 John Montgomery requests of Capt. Dodge that Major Williams be issued one English blanket for Montgomery's use and also one 2 1/2 point blanket and one snaffle bridle for Williams' use at FJ (VSA-12).
07/14/80 Ensign Williams signed that he received the within articles from John Dodge (VSA-12).
07/14/80 Jarrett Williams and John Montgomery sign request for one man of Capt. Brashears' Company to be issued five days' provisions from July 14 - July 18 at FJ (VSA-12).
09/10/80 Issued one lb powder, two lbs lead for his own use (VSA-13a).
09/11/80 Account of ammunition delivered by Martin Carney by Col. Montgomery's orders, to Ensign Williams for his own use, one lb powder, two lbs lead (VSA-50).
09/13/80 Issued to Ensign Williams for 25 men of Capt. Brashears' Company, four blankets per receipt and order of Lt. Col. Montgomery (VSA-48).

09/13/80	Account of soap delivered by Martin Carney by order of Col. Montgomery and Capt. George at Fort Jefferson, to Lt. Williams for his use, one lb (VSA-50).
09/13/80	Listed as one "officer of the mess" who received a share of 60 lbs of sugar (VSA-13b).
09/16/80	Requested an issue of one qt. tafia for own use from Quartermaster M. Carney (VSA-13).
09/30/80	Issued to Ensign Williams for 25 men of Capt. Brashears' Company, ten lbs. soap per order Capt. Brashears and receipt of John Gils (VSA-48).
10/13/80	Account of soap delivered by Martin Carney by order of Col. Montgomery and Capt. George at Fort Jefferson, to Ensign Jarret Williams, four lbs (VSA-50).
10/13/80	Rbt. George requests of the Quartermaster to issue four lbs soap to Jarret Williams (VSA-13a).
10/24/80	J. Montgomery requests of the treasurer of Virginia to issue $1760 to Jarret Williams for recruiting services (VSA-13) (VSA-14a, misfiled).
10/24/80	Jarret Williams signs that he received money (VSA-14b, misfiled).
12/01/80	Account of sugar delivered by Martin Carney by order of Capt. George at Fort Jefferson: to Ensign Williams and Major Harlan, 12 lbs (VSA-50:28).
12/10/80	Account of soap delivered by Martin Carney by order of Capt. George at Fort Jefferson: to Ensign Williams, six lbs (VSA-50: 52).
12/28/80	Account of ammunition delivered by Martin Carney by order of Capt. Robert George at Fort Jefferson: to Ensign Williams and his hunting party, 22 flints (VSA-50: 31).
12/31/80	Jarrett Williams signed that he received of Israel Dodge one pair of shoes upon a certificate given Williams by John Dodge (VSA-14c).
01/01/81	Jarrett Williams requests of the Quartermaster to issue two quarts tafia for Williams' own use (VSA- 15).
02/19/81	Ammunition delivered by order of Capt. George, to Lt. Williams' hunting party, one lb powder, two lbs lead (VSA-50).
03/08/81	Ammunition delivered by order of Capt. George, to Ensign Williams' hunting party, one lb powder, two lbs lead (VSA-50).
03/23/81	Ammunition delivered by order of Capt. George, to Ensign Williams' hunting party, 1 1/2 lbs powder, three lbs lead (VSA-50).
05/03/81	Per orders brought from day book, one gallon and one pint rum (VSA-49).
05/05/81	Per orders brought from day book, eight lbs sugar (VSA-49).
05/15/81	Ammunition delivered by order of Capt. Robert George at Fort Jefferson, to Ensign Williams, 1/2 lb powder, one lb lead (VSA-50).
06/05/81	Per orders brought from day book, 20 lbs sugar (VSA-49).
06/06/81	Stores issued by order of Capt. Robert George, to Ensign Williams, one kettle (VSA-50).

Williams, John

Not Dated	Ten bags, 20 ells osnaburgs issued to the Commissary per order of Major Williams, Comdr., two bags, four ells osnaburgs issued per order Major Williams Comdr. for public use (VSA-48).
Not Dated	One hundred twenty-five weight pork issued per receipt of Major Williams 125 livres peltry (VSA-48).
Not Dated	A major Williams brought charges against David Allen and James Taylor at FJ; two were arrested and court martial held for Taylor and Allen who were accused of having robbed Maj. Williams' kitchen, beaten his servants, and for speaking disrespectful of Maj. Williams during their confinement (DMS 56J40).
05/29/79	James Rubedo enlisted on this date in Capt. John Williams' Company (Harding, 1981:26).
05/31/79	Ebenezer Suverns is mentioned as being discharged. Was formerly of Capt. John Williams' Company as Kaskaskia (Harding 1981: 2).

Fort Jefferson Personnel   171

05/31/79	Daniel Tolley is discharged on this date from Capt. John Williams' Company (Harding, 1981: 2).
06/02/80	Capt. Kellar listed 17 men who had served in his unit at one time or another during the war; John Williams is one of those men (MHS: B1, F19).
07/09/80	John Williams requests an issuance of 30 lbs flour for the detachment going to Camp Jefferson (VSA- 12a).
07/09/80	John Williams requests an issuance of 250 rations for his voyage to Camp Jefferson (VSA-12a).
07/09/80	John Williams requests an issuance of provisions for one soldier for 10 days [July 9 - July 18] at Fort Jefferson (VSA-12a).
07/12/80	List of sundry articles issued to Majr. John Williams; two yds of fine holland for six stocks, 3/4 yd of fine cambric for ruffling six shirts, issued for nine vests and breeches four yds cottonade, 2 1/2 yds sycee, 2 1/4 yds calender, 2 1/2 yds corded dimity, 2 1/2 yds thickset, and 2 1/2 yds spotted cotton velvet, three yds brown broadcloth 7/4 wide, three pair thread hose, six yds of cotton sycee for three vests and breeches, two dozen and nine metal buttons, 21 yds of white linen for six shirts, two sticks silk twist, six skeins of silk, one pr knee garters, ten skeins of white thread, two silk handkerchiefs, two Indian handkerchiefs, two linen handkerchiefs, 2 1/2 yds of shalloon, one fine hat, four yds of coarse linen for lining, three yards broadcloth 7/4 wide (VSA-48).
07/12/80	Major John Williams, Ill Battalion, received from John Dodge, Agent the within mentioned goods, in part of the clothing allowed him by law. Attested to by J. Donne (VSA-48).
07/12/80	Sundry articles overdrawn by Major Williams above the clothing allowed him by law; one 2 1/2 point blanket and one snaffle bridle issued by order Lt. Col. Montgomery, 5 1/2 weight soap and two weight coffee. None of these articles appeared on the July 12th list of sundry articles issued to Maj. Williams (VSA-48).
07/12/80	Signed in behalf of Majr. Richard McCarty for list of sundry goods in part of clothing allowed McCarty by law, received from Capt. John Dodge, attested by J. Donne (VSA-48).
07/12/80	Issued to Major John Williams for his company, two ruffled shirts, six plain shirts, 14 yds blue cloth, 12 yds white flannel, skeins thread, dozen buttons (VSA-48).
07/12/80	John Williams signs that one man of Capt. Brashears' Company be issued provisions at FJ (VSA-12).
07/12/80	John Williams certifies that he received cloth and trimmings for a complete suit of clothes and two shirts each for Joseph Momeral, Louis Lepaint, James Brown, and Jacke Rubedo of Capt. Williams' Company (VSA-12).
07/12/80	John Williams requests that he be issued ten lbs pork at FJ from Qtrm for his mess (VSA-12).
07/13/80	Also listed as Major John Williams; served as President of Court of Inquiry at FJ (DMS 56J22).
07/13/80	Issued in the Indian Department, 7 1/2 yds blue stroud, six plain shirts, 2 1/2 yds half-thicks, five yds ribbon - five ells, and two, 2 1/2 point blankets delivered Capt. Williams by Col. Montgomery's order (VSA-48).
07/13/80	Capt. Robert George requests of Capt. John Dodge at FJ to issue Major John Williams his full quota of clothing which he is entitled to by law and agreeable to Col. Clark's orders (VSA-12).
07/13/80	John Montgomery requests of Capt. John Dodge to issue to Major Williams for the use of Batist LeQuang, two shrouds, two blankets, two pair leggings, four shirts as he is entitled to them for his good service to the state on an expedition with Montgomery (VSA-12a).
07/13/80	John Williams signed that he received the above plus an addition of five ells ribbon to bind the leggings (VSA-12b).
07/13/80	Lt. Montgomery signs request of John Dodge to deliver to Major John Williams, one stroud [it being 2 1/2 yds] and one shirt which he

Fort Jefferson Personnel

	borrowed to bury an Indian which was killed by mistake by one of the Light Horse Men; also one stroud and a shirt which Montgomery borrowed for a chief of the Sauk nation in Dodge's absence at Cahokia (VSA-12a).
07/13/80	John Williams signs that he received the within account (VSA-12b).
07/14/80	Issued in the Indian Department, three yds blue persian at four dollars per yd = 12 dollars, 1/2 yd fine cambric at 12 dollars per yd = six dollars, 7 1/2 yds ribbon at one dollar per yd = 7 1/2 dollars, thread = one dollar, one ivory comb, two horn combs, 7 1/2 yds calamanco 2 1/2 dollars per yd = 18 3/4 dollars. Total order is 47 1/4 paid Major John Williams for liquor furnished for the Savages in lieu of 120 lbs peltry per receipt (VSA-48).
07/14/80	Eight yds white linen at 2 1/2 dollars = 20 dollars, one embroidered apron = 20 dollars, two paper pins = two dollars, one English blanket = 16 dollars, 9 1/2 yds white linen at 2 1/2 dollars = 23 3/4 dollars, 2 1/2 yds calamanco at 2 1/2 dollars = 6 1/4 dollars, thread = 4/3 dollars. Total order = 88 1/3 dollars per order of Col. Clark in favor of John White for public services, paid to John Williams per his receipt L 26:10 V. C. (VSA-48).
07/14/80	Twenty yds osnaburgs, 12 linen handkerchiefs, 3 3/4 yds ribbon and one paper pins paid John Williams for making 40 plain shirts (VSA-48).
07/14/80	Tolley is probably still a member of Capt. Williams' Company when he is discharged (VSA-12).
07/14/80	Capt. Dodge to John Williams: For four gallons of tafia delivered to Williams for the Indian Department at 30 weight peltry per gallon, 120 lbs peltry; John Williams signs that he received at FJ the full contents by Dodge (VSA-12).
09/04/80	Issued in the Indian Department, four shirts issued to Major Williams, Commandant at Cahokia per his order for the Potowatomee Chiefs 13 yds linen (VSA-48).
09/09/80	Eight weight coffee, six weight soap, and five weight sugar per order and receipt, issued to and overdrawn by Majr. Williams above the clothing allowed him by law. These articles did not appear on the July 12th list of sundry articles issued to Maj. Williams (VSA-40).
09/09/80	Fragment of a letter from Williams to someone gives reference to "my wife Nancy" and as postscript "pray send me a line" (VSA-13b).
10/02/80	5 1/2 quarts tafia issued to and overdrawn by Major Williams above the clothing allowed him by law. Tafia did not appear on the July 12 list of goods issued to Williams (VSA-48).
10/03/80	3 3/4 gals rum issued to and overdrawn by Major Williams above the clothing allowed him by law. This article did not appear on the July 12th list of sundry articles issued to Maj. Williams (VSA-48).
10/06/80	Williams requests of J. Dodge, by order of Col. Montgomery, to deliver to Sgt. Mccleever[?] for the use of Ft. Jefferson, 121 bushels of corn, 265 lbs flour, and three bags (VSA-13a).
10/23/80	Listed as Captain. Arrived at Ft. Jeff from Cahokia at request of Col. John Montgomery to take command from Capt. Robert George, Capt. George refused to give up command (George Rogers Clark Papers, I: 463).
10/28/80	Williams at Ft. Jefferson writes to GRC to inform that Williams arrived at Ft. Jefferson on October 23, to take command of fort at orders of John Montgomery; mentions there is hunger due to low water and inability to receive deliveries; has not taken command from R. George due to circumstances and will not take command until G. R. Clark arrives (George Rogers Clark Papers, I: 463).
10/28/80	R. George mentions in a letter to G. R. Clark that Capt. Williams had arrived and R. George had refused to relinquish command to Williams (George Rogers Clark Papers, I: 461-462; Seineke, 1981:465-466).
10/31/80	Account of ammunition delivered by Martin Carney by order of Capt. George, to Capt. John Williams one lb powder, two lbs lead (VSA-50).

Fort Jefferson Personnel 173

11/15/80 Account of brass kettles delivered by Martin Carney by order of Capt. George at Fort Jefferson, to Major John Williams for his use, one kettle (VSA-50).
11/29/80 Account of soap delivered by Marton Carney by order of Capt. George at Fort Jefferosn, to Major Williams for his own use, six lbs (VSA-50).
12/22/80 John Williams and Robert George sign request of the Quartermaster to issue three lbs of loaf sugar (VSA-14).
12/31/80 John Williams signed that he received of Israel Dodge one pair of shoes upon a certificate given Williams by John Dodge (VSA-14b).
01/01/81 John Williams requests of the Quartermaster to issue three quarts tafia for Williams' own use (VSA-15).
01/11/81 Stores issued by order of Capt. Robert George, to Major Williams, eight tents or oil cloths; to Major Williams, one swivel (VSA-50).
01/12/81 Account of ammunition delivered by Martin Carney by order of Capt. Robert George at Fort Jefferson, to Major Williams, six cartridges for swivel, four lbs powder, six lbs lead (VSA-50).
03/20/81 Court martial proceedings at FJ refers to his kitchen and servants [one of his servants was Rachel Yeats] (DMS 56J40).
05/03/81 Per orders brought from day book, one gallon, one quart, and one pint rum and ten lbs sugar (VSA-49).
05/31/81 Per orders brought from day book, one carot of tobacco (VSA-49).
06/01/81 Account of ammunition delivered by Martin Carney by order of Capt. Robert George and Col. Montgomery, to Major Williams, one lb powder (VSA-50).
06/06/81 Per orders brought trom day book, two lbs sugar and six carots of tobacco (VSA-49).

Williams, Zachariah
06/20/80 Capt. Robt. George requests of John Dodge to issue two shirts each to Joseph Thornton, John Sword, and Zachariah Williams of Worthington's Co. by order of Col. Clark (VSA-11;48).
07/15/80 Listed in Capt. Worthington's Co. (MHS B1, F20;VSA-12).
09/13/80 Issued one lb sugar for being a sick soldier in Capt. Worthington's Co. (VSA-13).
09/15/80 Account of sugar delivered by Martin Carney by order of Capt. George at Fort Jefferson, to Zachariah Williams, a soldier in Worthington's Company, one lb (VSA-50).

Willis, Jacob
07/15/80 Listed in Capt. Worthington's Co. (MHS B1, F20;VSA-12).

Wilson, Edward
05/01/80 Enlisted on this date as Ensign in Capt. George Owens' Company of Militia of the District of Clarksville in the State of Virginia (Harding 1981: 48-49; George Rogers Clark Papers, I:464).
09/01/80[?] Farmed two acres at Clarksville, would have yielded 60 bushels had Indians not destroyed it (DMS 1M8).
10/05/80 Killed (Harding 1981: 48).

Wilson, John
05/01/80-12/21/80 Listed as Sergeant in Capt. George Owens' Co. of Militia of the District of Clarksville in the State of Virginia [Jefferson Co.]. Pay Abstract (Harding 1981:48-49).

Wilson, John [Sgt.] [also Willson]
Not Dated Issued to 24 men just discharged [to take them home] by order of Col. Montgomery, 24 plain shirts per receipt of Sgt. John Wilson (VSA-48).
05/01/80-12/21/80 Listed as Sgt. in Capt. George Owens' Co. of Militia of the District of Clarksville in the state of Virginia [Jefferson Co.] Pay Abstract (Harding 1981: 48-49).

Fort Jefferson Personnel

07/11/80 John Donne attested to the list of articles that Thomas Wilson received from Henry Hutton at the Falls of Ohio on Jan. 5, 1780. The quantity of cloth received by Thomas Wilson was the same as what John Wilson measured. Articles included flannel, cloth, buttons, and thread (MHS: B1, F14)
07/14/80 Account of ammunition delivered by Martin Carney by Col. Montgomery's orders to Sgt. Wilson, Illinois Regiment, 5 1/2 lbs powder, 11 lbs lead (VSA-50).
07/14/80 John Montgomery requests of Capt. J. Dodge that one shirt be issued to a list of men. John Wilson is among the list (VSA-12a).
07/14/80 John Wilson signed that he received from Capt. John Dodge, 24 shirts for self and party within mentioned. John Donne attested (VSA-12b).
07/14/80 Discharged. Listed as Sergeant in Isaac Taylor's Co. (Harding 1981: 13).
07/15/80 Listed in Capt. Worthington's Co. (MHS B1, F20) (VSA-12).
11/21/80 Account of sugar delivered by Martin Carney by orders of Capt. George, to John Wilson, Capt. Worthington's Servant, one lb (VSA-50).
12/03/80 Issued to 24 men just discharged [to take them home] by order of Col. Montgomery: 24 plain shirts per receipt of Sgt. John Wilson (VSA-48:45).
12/21/80 Pay Abstract of a Company of Militia commanded by Capt. George Owens of the district of Clarksville in the state of Virginia. Service ended on this date for Sgt. John Wilson (GRC, I: 464-465).
12/22/80 Silas Harlan and Robert George sign request of the Quartermaster to issue Abraham Taylor, Hugh Montgomery, John Levrig, and John Wilson 1/2 lb powder and one lb lead for each man (VSA-14).

Wilson, Lt. Thomas
Not Dated Issued to Lt. Wilson by order of Col. Montgomery, 6 1/2 yds white linen and 4 1/2 yds toile gris per his receipt (VSA-48).
01/05/80 Thomas Wilson received 200 yds of flannel, 225 yds of cloth [blue and white], 227 buttons, and 320 skeins of thread from Henry Hutton, under the direction of George Rogers Clark. Transaction took place at the Falls of the Ohio (MHS: B1, F14).
06/03/80 Thomas Wilson requests that Edward Taylor, who is employed by Wilson, be paid for his service to Wilson by going express from Ft. Patrick Henry [Vincennes] to Ft. Jefferson, to Ft. Clark, and back to Ft. Patrick Henry and taking 19 days to do so (VSA-11a).
06/21/80 Account of ammunition delivered by Martin Carney by Capt. Robert George's order at Camp Jefferson, to Lt. Thomas Wilson, two lbs powder and four lbs lead (VSA-50).
06/30/80 Account of ammunition delivered by Martin Carney by Capt. Robert George's order at Camp Jefferson, to Lt. Wilson for a party of men going hunting, 2 1/4 lbs powder and 4 1/2 lbs lead (VSA-50).
07/08/80 Issued 1 1/4 lbs gunpowder for use of a scouting party at FJ per Capt. George's orders to Martin Carney, Quartermaster (VSA-12).
07/08/80 Account of ammunition delivered by Martin Carney by Capt. Robert George's order at Camp Jefferson, to Lt. Wilson going on command, 1 1/4 lbs powder and 2 1/2 lbs lead (VSA-50).
07/11/80 Thomas Wilson and John Donne attested to the issuance of cloth, flannel, buttons, and thread that was issued to Wilson at the Falls of Ohio on January 5, 1780. Wilson and Donne are in Clarksville now (MHS: B1, F14).
07/13/80 Account of arms received by Martin Carney in this department, the property of the Commonwealth of Virginia, received of Lt. Wilson at Fort Jefferson, five muskets (VSA-50).
07/14/80 John Montgomery requests of John Dodge that Lt. THomas Wilson be issued as much linen as will make two shirts and two pair of trousers which will be part of his clothing if acquitted, if not Lt. Col. Montgomery will see them paid as "it is impossible to keep a prisoner naked" (VSA-12a).
07/14/80 Lt. Wilson signed that he received the within conetents (VSA-12b).

Fort Jefferson Personnel

12/03/80 Issued to Lt. Thomas Wilson by order of Col. Montgomery: 6 1/2 yds white linen and 4 1/2 yds toile gris per his receipt (VSA-48: 45).

Wiley James [Ryly?]
Not Dated Five weight soap to James Wiley for liquor for the fatigue per Col. Montgomery's order (VSA-48).
05/01/80-12/21/80 Listed as Private in Capt. George Owens' Co. of Militia of the District of Clarksville in the State of Virginia [Jefferson Co.]. Pay Abstract (Harding 1981:48-49).
07/17/80 His house at Clarksville attacked by Indians or so mentioned by Capt. John Rogers writings to Clark (MHS B1, F21).
09/09/80 Fredrick Guion borrowed at different times 500, 200, and 50 dollars (VSA-13a).
09/13/80 Moved (Harding 1981:48-49).

Winn, S
06/21/80 One silk handkerchief paid S. Winn for making three ruffled shirts (VSA-48).
06/22/80 Paid 2 3/4 yds calico and one 1 1/4 yds ribbon to S. Winn for making six shirts and five pair trousers (VSA-48).
06/23/80 One Indian handkerchief paid S. Winn for making three plain shirts (VSA-48).

Win, Thomas [Winn]
06/19/80 Listed as member of Capt. George's Co. at FJ and issued two shirts by order of Capt. George; among list of men receiving clothing issue for being enlisted during the war (VSA-11).

Winston, Richard
06/25/80 Account of ammunition delivered by Martin Carney by order of Col. Clark, to Richard Winston at Kaskaskia, 50 lbs powder (VSA-50).
07/09/80 Document signed by Richard Winston written in other language (VSA-12).

Witzel, "The Widow" [Mrs.] [also Whitzell] (Husband probably member of George Owens' Militia)
06/22/80 Two Indian handkerchiefs and two linen handkerchiefs paid for making ten plain shirts to J. Witzel (VSA-48).
09/09/80 Received three lbs sugar at cost of 15 shillings by order of Col. John Montgomery; her bill was paid by Mr. Carney. Referred to as "an inhabitant of this place" (VSA-13).
09/09/80 Account of sugar delivered by Martin Carney by order of Col. Montgomery at Fort Jefferson, to Mrs. Witzel, a widow of militia, three lbs (VSA-50).
09/13/80 Account of sugar delivered by Martin Carney by order of Col. Montgomery at Fort Jefferson, to the Widow Witzel for a flat bottomed boat for public use, seven lbs (VSA-50).
10/20/80 Mr. Witzell alive and presumably well (VSA-50).

Wolf, E
06/17/80 Five yds calico and one paper pins paid E. Wolf for making three ruffled shirts and 15 plain (VSA-48).
08/26/80 Three yds white flannel paid E. Wolf for making five plain shirts (VSA-48).
08/26/80 One yd flannel and two yds ribbon paid E. Wolf for doubling and twisting six lbs twine for making a net for public use (VSA-48).

Wolf, Michael
05/01/80-12/21/80 Listed as Private in Capt. George Owens' Co. of Militia of the District of Clarksville in the State of Virginia [Jefferson Co.]. Pay Abstract (Harding 1981:48-49).

09/01/80[?] Farmed two acres at Clarksville that would have yielded 50 bushels had it not been burned by Indians (DMS 1M8).
09/12/80 Moved (Harding 1981: 48-49).

Worthington, Edward [Captain]

Not Dated Two dressed skins for Capt. Worthington's Co. per Col. Montgomery's order (VSA-48). Six check handkerchiefs, two yds check, and 18 livres peltry issued to Capt. Worthington on his own account per his receipt (VSA-48).
03/10/80 Page Certain enlisted on this date as a private in Capt. Worthington's Company (Harding, 1981:47).
04/12/80 Edward Worthington and William Shannon signed that they received of George Rogers Clark 20 land warrants containing 560 acres each for recruiting 20 soldiers during the war to serve in Col. Clark's regiment (George Rogers Clark Papers, I: 413).
04/12/80 William Robeson enlisted on this date as a private in Capt. Worthington's Company (Harding, 1981:47, 53).
04/15/80 James Brown enlisted as a private in Capt. Worthington's Co. (Harding, 1981:47).
04/22/80 Articles purchased by Martin Carney for the state of Virginia by order of Col. Clark: taken into service, two horses the property of Capt. Worthington, valued at 1800 pounds (VSA-50:2).
04/26/80 James Dean enlisted on this date as a private in Capt. Worthington's Company (Harding, 1981:47).
05/08/80 Joseph Thornton enlisted on this date as a private in Capt. Worthington's Company (Harding, 1981: 47, 53).
05/12/80 John Bailey signs that he received of Martin Carney, three fusees for Capt. Worthington's Company (VSA-11a).
05/17/80 Capt. Edward Worthington and Robert George sign request to Martin Carney to issue three pints tafia for Worthington's use (VSA-11).
05/20/80 Capt. Worthington at falls of Ohio writes to George Rogers Clark at Mouth of Ohio explaining why he did not accompany Col. Legras and Mr. Dejean from Williamsburg to Fort Jefferson. There are several dissatisfied people at the Falls of Ohio. Worthington speaks of supplies that are being prepared by the commissary in Clark's department that will be sent to Clark (MHS:B1, F17).
05/22/80 Daniel Williams enlisted on this date as a private in Capt. Worthington's Company (Harding, 1981:47, 53).
06/20/80 Issued to Capt. Worthington's Company, three ruffled and three plain shirts for Joseph Thornton, John Sword, and Zachariah Williams per order Capt. George and receipt Reuben Kemp (VSA-48).
06/23/80 Capt. Robert George requests of John Dodge by order of Col. Clark, to issue 16 shirts to Reuben Kemp, Daniel Williams, Richard Bredin, Charles Evans, Andrew Johnston, Isaac Yeates, and William Nelson who are members of Worthington's Company (VSA-11) (VSA-48).
06/23/80 Issued to Capt. Worthington's Company, 15 plain and one ruffled shirt per order Capt. George and receipt of Reuben Kemp (VSA-48).
06/23/80 William Robeson is issued two shirts at FJ from John Dodge per Capt. George's orders; member of Worthington's Company (VSA-11).
07/10/80 A. Gamelin signs he received of Sgt. John Moore of Capt. Worthington's Company, two soldiers of the same company: Louis Brown and David Allen. They are to be delivered to the commanding officer. [This probably occurred at FJ although not stated]. Not known if Allen and Brown went. There are references of them being at FJ after this date (MHS:B1, F20).
07/11/80 Lt. Richard Clark is issued his quota of clothing at FJ. Member of Capt. Worthington's Company (VSA- 12).
07/25/80 Account of tobacco delivered by Martin Carney by order of Capt. Robert George at this place, to Thornton, a soldier in Capt. Worthington's Company by Capt. George's order, 1/3 carot and one lb (VSA-50).

Fort Jefferson Personnel

07/28/80	Account of tobacco delivered by Martin Carney by order of Capt. Robert George at this place, to Sgt. Mains, in Capt. Worthington's Company, two weighing six lbs (VSA-50).
08/02/80	Issued to Capt. Worthington's Company, 14 plain shirts by order Capt. George issued to Lt. Clark (VSA-48).
08/12/80	Issued to Worhtington's Company, two plain shirts for David Allen per Lt. Clarks receipt and Capt. George's order (VSA-48).
08/17/80	Account of arms delivered by Martin Carney to Capt. George's Company of Artillery of the Illinois Virginia Regiment, delivered to Sgt. Anderson for "Sailor" Worthington, one rifle gun (VSA-50).
08/24/80	Account of tobacco delivered by Martin Carney by order of Capt. Robert George at this place, to Sgt. Reuben Kemp of Worthington's Company, 1/2 carot weighing 1 1/2 lbs; to Thornton a soldier in Capt. Worthington's Company, one carot weighing three lbs (VSA-50).
09/08/80	Account of sugar delivered by Martin Carney by order of Col. Montgomery at Fort Jefferson, to two soldiers in Capt. Worthington's Company, two lbs; to one woman and children of Capt. Worthington's Company, two lbs; to two soldiers of Capt. Worthington's Company, three lbs (VSA-50).
09/09/80	Issued to Capt. Worthington's Company, 3 1/2 yds blue cloth, three yds white flannel, two plain shirts, and buttons and thread for cloth issued by order of Lt. Col. Montgomery, for Richard Underwood, and per receipt of Lt. Richard Clark (VSA-48).
09/09/80	Account of sugar delivered by Martin Carney by order of Col. Montgomery at Fort Jefferson, to David Allen, a soldier of Worthington's, one lb; to Archibold Lockard in Worthington's Company, two lbs (VSA-50).
09/09/80	Account of sugar delivered by Martin Carney by order of Col. Montgomery at Fort Jefferson, to Charles Evans, a soldier in Capt. Worthington's, one lb (VSA-50).
09/13/80	Issued to Capt. Worthington's Company eight blankets per receipt of Richard Clark and order of Lt. Col. Montgomery, 18 3/4 yds blue cloth per receipt Richard Clark, 15 1/2 yds white flannel per receipt Richard Clark, thread and buttons for the above per receipt Richard Clark (VSA-48).
09/13/80	Account of sugar delivered by Martin Carney by order of Col. Montgomery at Fort Jefferson, to Reuben Kemp of Worthington's Company, one lb (VSA-50).
09/13/80	Account of soap delivered by Martin Carney by order of Col. Montgomery and Capt. George at Fort Jefferson, to Capt. Edward Worthington's Company, 9 1/2 lbs (VSA-50).
09/15/80	Account of sugar delivered by Martin Carney by order of Capt. George at Fort Jefferson, to Zachariah Williams, soldier in Worthington's Company, one lb (VSA-50).
09/18/80	Account of sugar delivered by Martin Carney by order of Capt. George at Fort Jefferson, to Andrew Johnston of Worthington's Company, one lb (VSA-50).
09/19/80	Account of sugar delivered by Martin Carney by order of Capt. George at Fort Jefferson, to Bredin of Worthington's Company, two lbs; to Edward Johnston a soldier in Worthington's Company, one lb; to William Crump, a soldier in Worthington's Company, two lbs (VSA-50).
09/19/80-04/07/81	Sometime between these dates, tobacco is issued to sundry persons per order of Capt. George, Commandant: to Edward Worthington, 3 1/2 lbs (VSA- 50: 13).
09/25/80	Capt. Worthington requests salt and corn to be issued for four weeks[?] (VSA-13a).
09/28/80	Account of sugar delivered by Martin Carney by order of Capt. George at Fort Jefferson, to one man of Capt. Worthington's Company, 1/2 lb (VSA-50).
10/04/80	Account of ammunition delivered by Martin Carney by Capt. George's order to three men of Capt. Worthington's Company, 3/4 lb powder and 1 1/2 lbs lead (VSA-50).

Fort Jefferson Personnel

10/09/80	One weight sugar and half a pound coffee to one sick man of Capt. Worthington's (VSA-48).
10/20/80	Account of ammunition delivered by Martin Carney by order of Cap. George, to Bryan a soldier in Capt. Worthington's Company, 1/4 lb powder 1/2 lb lead (VSA-50).
11/15/80	Account of brass kettles delivered by Martin Carney by order of Capt. George at Fort Jefferson, to Lt. Richard Clark for Capt. Worthington's Company, two kettles (VSA-50).
11/16/80	Account of sugar delivered by Martin Carney by orders of Capt. George, to a sick man of Capt. Worthington's Company, one lb (VSA-50).
11/17/80	Account of sugar delivered by Martin Carney by orders of Capt. George, to Andrew Johnston and family of Capt. Worthington's, 1 1/2 lbs (VSA-50).
11/18/80	Account of soap delivered by Martin Carney by order of Capt. George at Fort Jefferson, to eight men of Capt. Worthington's Company, eight lbs (VSA-50).
11/20/80	Account of sugar delivered by Martin Carney by orders of Capt. George, to a sick woman and sick child of Capt. Worthington's Company, one lb (VSA-50).
11/21/80	Account of sugar delivered by Martin Carney by orders of Capt. George, to John Wilson, Capt. Worthington's Servant, one lb (VSA-50).
11/23/80	Account of sugar delivered by Martin Carney by orders of Capt. George, to a soldier of Worthington's one lb (VSA-50).
11/30/80	Account of sugar delivered by Martin Carney by order of Capt. George at Fort Jefferson, to a woman and two children of Worthington's Company, two lbs (VSA-50).
12/07/80	Letter from Capt. Richard Harrison at the Falls to Col. Clark in Richmond or "elsewhere." Harrison mentions that Capt. Worthington is at Harrodsburgh and feels that Worthington has no intention of going to Fort Jefferson during the winter (GRC Papers, I: 468).
12/28/80	Stores issued by order of Capt. Robert George: to three men of Capt. Worthington's Company, one rifle and two muskets (VSA-50: 37).
12/29/80	Account of ammunition delivered by Martin Carney by order of Capt. Robert George at Fort Jefferson: to Capt. Worthington's Company, 32 flints (VSA-50: 31).
01/00/81-02/00/81	Traveled to FJ from Falls of Ohio (DMS 56J28).
01/12/81	Stores issued by order of Capt. Robert George, to Capt. Worthington's Company, 17 swords (VSA-50).
01/19/81	Account of ammunition delivered by Martin Carney by order of Capt. Robert George at Fort Jefferson, to three men of Capt. Worthington's Company, 1 1/2 lbs powder, three lbs lead (VSA-50).
02/04/81	Account of ammunition delivered by Martin Carney by order of Capt. Robert George at Fort Jefferson, to two men of Capt. Worthington's Company, one lb powder, two lbs lead (VSA-50).
02/13/81	Stores issued by order of Capt. Robert George, to Capt. Worthington's Company, two muskets; to Capt. Worthington for his use, one kettle (VSA-50).
04/20/81	Worthington is in Ft. Jefferson and writes a letter to GRC who is in Louisville. He writes of the poor situation at the Fort, the low provisions, and soldiers deserting their duties. He does say there are some officers and soldiers willing to stay there til they are down to one hours worth of provisions (MHS: B2, F2).
04/21/81	Ammunition delivered by order of Capt. Robert George at Fort Jefferson, to Capt. Worthington's Company, 1/2 lb powder, one lb lead (VSA-50).
05/11/81	Ammunition delivered by order of Capt. Robert George at Fort Jefferson, to one man of Capt. Worthington, 1/2 lb powder, one lb lead (VSA-50).
05/14/81	Per orders brought from day book, four gallons one quart, and one pint rum, and ten lbs sugar (VSA-49).

Fort Jefferson Personnel 179

05/17/81 Tobacco issued by order of Capt. George, Commander, to Capt. Worthington, three lbs (VSA-50).
05/19/81 Per orders brought from day book, two lbs sugar and ten lbs sugar (VSA-49).
06/01/81 Per order for hospital or sick accounts to two men of Worthington's company, four lbs sugar (VSA-49).
06/05/81 Account of ammunition delivered by Martin Carney by order of Capt. Robert George and Col. Montgomery, to three men of Capt. Worthington's Company, 3/4 lb powder, 1 1/2 lbs lead (VSA-50).
06/07/81 Per orders brought from day book, ten lbs sugar (VSA-49).
06/07/81 Per order to one of Capt. Worthington's Company, four lbs sugar (VSA-49).

Yeates, Isaac
06/23/80 Capt. Robert George requests of John Dodge by order of Col. Clark, to issue 16 shirts to Reuben Kemp, Daniel Williams, Richard Bredin, Charles Evans, Andrew Johnston, Isaac Yeates, and William Nelson who are members of Capt. Worthington's Company (VSA-11;VSA-48).
07/15/80 Listed in Capt. Worthington's Co. (MHS B1, F20;VSA-12).

Yeates, John
07/15/80 Listed as Drummer in Capt. Worthington's Company (MHS B1, F20;VSA-12).

Yeats, Rachel
06/16/80 One silk handkerchief paid R. Yates for making three ruffled shirts per receipt (VSA-48).
03/20/81 Supposedly was kitchen servant of Maj. Williams at FJ and testified at Court Martial proceedings at FJ as having been harassed by David Allen and James Taylor (DMS 56J40).

Young, James
Not Dated Married to Ann [McMeans] Jamison's sister, Margery (Jamsion Narrative, Filson Club).
05/01/80-12/21/80 Listed as Private in Capt. George Owens' Co. of Militia of the District of Clarksville in the State of Virginia [Jefferson Co.]. Pay Abstract (Harding 1981:48-49).
09/01/80[?] Farmed 16 acres of land with eight other people at Clarksville that would have yielded 320 bushels had it not been burned by Indians (DMS 1M8).
09/09/80 Received three lbs sugar from the Quartermaster by order of Col. John Montgomery; valued at 15 shillings. Referred to as "an inhabitant of this place [FJ]" (VSA-13).
09/12/80 Moved (Harding 1981: 48-49).
09/13/80 Account of sugar delivered by Martin Carney by order of Col. Montgomery at Fort Jefferson, to James Young a militia man (VSA-50).

Young, Margery [Mrs. James]
1780 James Young married to Ann Jamison's [McMeans] sister Margery (Jamison Narrative, Filson Club).
06/17/80 Issued 2 3/4 yds calico and one linen handkerchief for making nine plain shirts (VSA-48).

Young, John
05/01/80-12/21/80 Listed as Private in Capt. George Owens' Co. of Militia of the District of Clarksville in the State of Virginia [Jefferson Co.]. Pay Abstract (Harding 1981:48-49).
09/12/80 Moved (Harding 1981: 48).

Young, Hugh
05/01/80-12/21/80 Listed as Private in Capt. George Owens' Co. of the Illinois Regiment in the Virginia State Service. Payroll (Harding 1981: 45-46).

Fort Jefferson Personnel

07/12/80 Among list of men being issued two shirts each as members of Capt. John Bailey's Company being enlisted during the war (VSA-12).

Friendly Indians

Batisst [Chief of Kaskaskia Indians]

04/29/80 Letter from Batisst at Ft. Clark to George Rogers Clark. Batisst tells Clark he has heard of Clark's arrival at the Mouth of Ohio and Batisst plans to visit Clark along with Col. Montgomery (GRC, I: 418).

07/09/80 Writes to Capt. John Dodge at FJ stating he's waiting for the enemy at Ft. Clark but without powder and lead [Letter actually written by J. Clark] (VSA-12).

09/09/80 Issued one pint of tafia (VSA-13a).

"Joseph"

01/11/81 Issued two quarts of tafia to "Joseph" a friendly Indian by Capt. George's orders to Martin Carney, Quartermaster at FJ (VSA-15).

Unspecified by name

Not Dated Issued 13 1/2 yds osnaburg made into hunting shirts for use of our friendly Indian Chiefs (VSA-48).

06/21/80 Account of ammunition delivered by Martin Carney by Capt. Robert George's order at Camp Jefferson, to Indians going to Kaskaskia, one lb powder, two lbs lead and six flints (VSA-50).

07/14/80 Issued in the Indian Department, three yds blue persian at four dollars yd = 12 dollars, 1/2 yd fine cambric at 12 dollars yd = six dollars, 7 1/2 yds ribbon at one dollar yd = 7 1/2 dollars, thread = one dollar, one ivory comb, two horn combs, 7 1/2 yds calamanco at 2 1/2 dollars a yd = 18 3/4 dollars. Total order 47 1/4 dollars paid Major John Williams for liquor furnished for the Savages in lieu of 120 lb peltry per receipt (VSA-48).

07/20/80 Issued in the Indian Department to a party of friendly Kaskaskia Indians sent to hunt and scout for the garrison while it was weak, and deliverd by orders Col. Montgomery. 13 3/4 yds blue strouds for blankets and breech cloths, 6 1/4 yds white half-thicks for leggings, 12 yds white linen for shirts, two dark ground calico for shirts, three scalping knives, two horn combs, eight skeins thread, one bolt ravelled gartering, three linen handkerchiefs, 5 1/2 yds ribbon, one piece ribbon, one pair blue stroud leggings, one plain shirt, two scalping knives (VSA-48).

08/14/80 Stores issued by order of Capt. Robert George, to the Indians, three tomahawks (vSA-50).

09/04/80 Issued in the Indian Department, paid I. Camp for a keg for the savages, 12 livres peltry (VSA-48).

09/04/80 Issued in the Indian Department, three check handkerchiefs to Chapeau for carrying a speech to the savages, issued for a coat and jacket for a friendly Indian Chief eight yds red calamanco, 1/2 yd casimir, and three yds linen (VSA-48).

09/06/80 Issued five lbs of powder and ten lbs of lead for killing meat for the troops at FJ (VSA-13a).

09/07/80 Issued six gallons of tafia (VSA-13a).

09/08/80 Issued one gallon of tafia to Indians which had gone with Major McCarty (VSA-13a).

09/09/80 Issued two gallons of tafia to Indian allies by order of John Dodge, (VSA-13).

09/09/80 Issued 100 lbs powder, 200 lbs of lead to the friendly Indian allies who came to our relief when beseiged by the enemy. Received by James Sherlock (VSA-13a).

09/10/80 Issued ten lbs powder and 20 lbs lead and two carots of tobacco to a party of Indians going to revenge injuries to their father By Knifes (VSA-13a).

Fort Jefferson Personnel 181

09/10/80	Issued to 20 of the Kaskaskia Indians one barge and swivel to war against the Chickasaw Indians by order of Col. John Montgomery (VSA-13).
09/20/80	Issued in the Indian Department, three clasp knives and six pair scissors to the friendly savages, four shirts issued to Major Williams, Commandant at Cahokia per his order for the Potowatomee Chiefs, 13 yds linen, paid the sheriff for corn and two corn fields for the use of the friendly savages who came to our assistance in time of danger 554 continental dollars (VSA-48).
12/01/80	John Donne certifies that John Dodge paid money for corn, cornfields, and sudry other merchandise for the use of the savages (VSA-14).
12/03/80	John Dodge certifies from Kaskaskia that the State of Virginia is indebted to an Indian one stroud blanket for coming express from Fort Jefferson on public business (VSA-14).
01/01/81	Leonard Helm and Robert George sign request of the Quartermaster to issue to each of 25 Indians going to war against the Chickasaws, 1/2 lb powder, one lb lead, and two flints each (VSA-15).
01/08/81	Account of ammunition delivered by order of Capt. Robert George at Fort Jefferson, to the friendly Indians going to war, 12 1/2 lbs powder, 25 lbs lead, and 50 flints (VSA-50).
02/07/81	Account of ammunition delivered by order of Capt. Robert George at Fort Jefferson, to the Kickapoo Indians, seven lbs powder, four lbs lead (VSA-50).
02/13/81	Stores issued by order of Capt. Robert George, to Peorian Indians, seven swords (VSA-50).
02/22/81	Ammunition delivered by order of Capt. George, to Peorian Indians, 30 lbs powder, 30 lbs lead, and 30 flints (VSA-50).
03/10/81	Ammunition delivered by order of Capt. George, to the Kaskaskia Indians, 20 lbs powder, 40 lbs lead, and 50 flints (VSA-50).
03/13/81	Stores issued by order of Capt. Robert George, to Kaskaskia Indians, two swords (VSA-50).
03/19/81	Ammunition delivered by order of Capt. George, to the Kaskaskia Indians, 1 1/2 lbs powder, three lbs lead (VSA-50).
03/19/81	Stores issued by order of Capt. Robert George, to the Kaskaskia Indians, two swords (VSA-50).

Slaves

Cesar (served as artificer)
06/19/80	Listed as member of Capt. George's Co., at FJ and issued two shirts from VSA by order of Capt. George; among list of men receiving clothing issue for being enlisted during the war (VSA-11).

Unnamed
11/20/80	Account of sugar delivered by Martin Carney by orders of Capt. George, to Col. Clark's Negro, sick, one lb [assuming this is Cesar due to VSA-49 entry concerning Col. Clark's slave] (VSA-50).
12/10/80	Account of soap delivered by Martin Carney by order of Capt. George at Fort Jefferson: to Negro Ceaser, Artificer, 1 1/2 lbs (VSA-50: 52).
09/02/80	Letter to John Montgomery from Capt. George (VSA-13) (MHS B1, F20)
09/02/80	Letter from George to Montgomery stated that Capt. Smith owned a few [3-?] slaves of which one was female. Female slave killed by Indians Aug. 27, 1780 (MHS B1, F20).

Unspecified
01/07/80	Mention that Indians murdered three men near Ft. Jeff; two others missing; people in want of provisions (George Rogers Clark Papers, I: 426).
06/10/80	Issued to Col. GR Clark the following list for use of the slaves when setting off on Expedition: one check linen handkerchief, seven yds osnaburg for two shirts for Negro man, five yds Damaged linen

for Wench, seven yds osnaburg for Wench & boy, 2 1/2 yds dark ground calico for Wench, three yds spotted flannel for Wench, one Indian handkerchief for Wench, one check linen handkerchief for Wench, four skeins thread, one scalping knife for Negro man, 5 1/2 yds osnaburg for two pr trousers (VSA-49).

09/02/80 Letter from Robert George to Montgomery states that a female slave died 08/27/80 (MHS B1, F21).

Issues for Public Use

Not Dated Six yds black calamanco paid for a table for public use (VSA-48). Twenty weight thread issued at sundry times for public use, two boxes of wafers used issued for public use - five dollars (VSA-48).

06/20/80 Six yds osnaburgs made into bags for public use (VSA-48).

09/25/80 6 1/2 yds toile gris, one yd blue stroud, one yd white flannel, one scalping knife, two pair garters, two ivory combs, and four linen handkerchiefs paid for making a fish net for public use (VSA-48).

House Expenses [possibly Dodge]

06/10/80-03/20/81 Sometime between these dates, the following was issued under account of house expenses: 2 1/2 yds ribbon, two red handkerchiefs, one clasp knife, one ink pot, eight skeins thread, one ivory comb, one horn comb, one lb coffee, one scalping knife, two yds white flannel, two yds coarse linen, one yd osnaburgs, two scalping knives, one weight coffee, one yd ribbon, one Indian handkerchief, one check handkerchief, two dozen fine combs, one dozen coarse combs, one silk handkerchief, one snaffle bridle, eight yds camlet, one coarse check handkerchief, 3 1/4 yds black persian, 1 1/2 yds gauze, one ink holder, two yds linen, one yd ribbon, one check handerchief paid for two brooms for the store, two yds check, paid Gratiot for 70 weight sugar 105 livres peltry, ten weight coffee, 20 weight sugar, eight gallons rum, ten galls tafia, three ells osnaburgs for finding a horse, six yds camlet paid a woman for sundry kitchen services (VSA-48: 101-102).

Hospital

Not Dated One linen handkerchief and 1/2 yd linen for dressing a wounded man (VSA-48).

07/14/80 Eight yds white linen at 2 1/2 dollars = 20 dollars one embroidered apron = 20 dollars, two paper pins = two dollars, one English blanket = 16 dollars, 9 1/2 yds white linen at 2 1/2 = 23 3/4 dollars, 2 1/2 yds calamanco at 2 1/2 = 6 1/4 dollars, thread = 4/3 dollar total = 88 1/3 dollars per order of Col. Clark in favor John White for public services paid to John Williams per his receipt 26:10 V. C. (VSA-48).

07/15/80 Seven yds calico per order Col. Montgomery for Anne Elms Nurse in the hospital per her receipt (VSA-48).

07/17/80 5 1/2 yds linen damaged, one yd ribbon, and one piece gartering issued for use of wounded men (VSA-48).

09/13/80 1/2 yd white linen and one piece of ravelled gartering to dress a wounded man (VSA-48).

06/01/81 Per order to the hospital or sick accounts to two men of Worthington's company, four lbs sugar (VSA-49).

06/07/81 Per order to the hospital or sick accounts to one woman of Capt. Brashears', four lbs sugar; per order to one man and two children of Capt. George's Company, six lbs sugar; per order to one man and woman of Capt. George's Company, three lbs sugar; per order to one man of Capt. George, two lbs sugar (VSA-49).

Regiment and Fatigue

03/28/81 Ammunition delivered by order of Capt. George, to the Militia at Clarksville, 2 1/2 lbs powder, five lbs lead (VSA-50).

04/26/81 Tobacco issued to sundry persons per order Capt. George, Commandant, to Illinois Regiment, 21 1/2 lbs (VSA-50).

Fort Jefferson Personnel

05/03/81	Omitted, per order to regiment, 171 lbs sugar (VSA-49).
05/07/81	Per orders, nine carots of tobacco (VSA-49).
05/11/81	Per order for rations, two gallons, one quart, and 1/4 pint rum; per order for fatigue, three quarts and 1/4 pint rum (VSA-49).
05/12/81	Per order for fatigue, three quarts and 1/4 pint rum (VSA-49).
05/12/81	Per order for fatigue, one quart and 1/4 pint rum (VSA-49).
05/14/81	Tobacco issued by order of Capt. George, Commander, to Illinois Regiment, 27 lbs (VSA-50).
05/15/81	Ammunition delivered by order of Capt. Robert George at Fort Jefferson, to the Regiment, 113 lbs powder, 23 lbs lead (VSA-50).
05/17/81	Per order for fatigue, one quart and 1/4 pint rum (VSA-49).
05/21/81	Per orders to regiment, 156 lbs sugar (VSA-49).
05/25/81	Per order for rations, two gallons rum (VSA-49).
06/02/81	Tobacco issued by order of Capt. George Commander, to Illinois Regiment, 28 lbs (VSA-50).
06/07/81	Per order to the regiment, 9 1/2 carots of tobacco (VSA-49).

Miscellaneous

06/05/81	Per order to a soldier for burning four bushels of charcoal, four lbs sugar (VSA-49).
06/05/81	To a man for sawing four days, public works, four lbs sugar (VSA-49).
06/05/81	Per order a militia man for rowing 16 days up the Ohio, 16 lbs sugar (VSA-49).

INDEX

ALDAR, John xii xv 1
ALLEN, David x 1 Isaac ix 1 John 1
   Nathan 1 Samuel ix 1
ALLIN, Jon 2
ALISON, John 2
ANDERSON, John x xiii 2 Joseph 2
ANDRE, Jean xi 3
ANDREWS, Joseph viii
ANGLEY, Peter 3
ARCHER, Jane 3 Joshua xii 3
ARMSTRONG, George viii 4
ASH, John viii 4
ASHER, Mrs William xiv 5
BABER, Daniel 5
BABU, Daniel viii
BAILEY, John xi 5
BAKLEY, John viii
BALFAU, Petter 9
BALLANGER, James xiii 9
BALLENGER, Larken xi 10
BALSINGER, Valentine 10
BALSINKLEE, Valentine viii
BARBEAU, Jean 10
BARBOUR, Philip 10
BARNETT, James xii 11
BARNIT, Robert ix 11
BARTHOLOMEW, William ix 11
BATISST, xiv 180
BEAUVAIS, Marguerite 11
BELL, William xi xiii 11
BENDIT, Francis xi 11
BENTLEY, Thomas 12
BLACKFORD, Zephaniah xiv 12
BLAIN, Peter 13
BLAIR, John ix xv 13
BLANCHARD xi 13
BLANKINSHIP, Henry ix 13
BOHMAN, William 13
BOILS, John ix 13
BOLTON, Daniel viii 14 M 14
   Thomas 14
BOND, Shadrack 14
BOOFRY, Petter 14
BOOTIN, Travis ix 15 William ix 15
BOSSON, William 15
BOUDEN, John 15
BOWDERY, John x 15
BRADING, William x 15
BRADY, T 15
BRASHEARS, Richard ix xiv 15
BRAULEY, William xii xiii 19
BREDIN, Francis ix xiv 19
   Richard xiv 19
BREEDING, Hanah 19 John 20
BRIAN, John viii
BRIEN, Mary 20
BROWN, James ix xi xv 20 Lewis 20
   Loue xii 20
BRUIN, William x
BRYAN, John xiv 21 Mrs xiv 21

BRANT, James x 21
BUCHANNON, William xii 21
BURK, Charles viii 21 John xii xiv
   21 Elizabeth xiv 22 Nicholas xii
   22 Sarah 22
BURNEY, Simon 22
BUSH, Charles 22 Drury viii 22
   John viii 22 William 22
BUTCHER, Gasper xiv 23
CAILEY, Casper ix 23
CALLAGHAN, Patrick 23
CALVIT, Joseph 23
CAMP, Ichabod 24
CAMPBELL, William ix 24
CANADA, Nicholas 24
CANORE, Andrew 24
CARMACK, William 24
CARNEY, Martin viii xiv 24
CARR, William xii xv 29
CERTAIN, Page x xv 29
CESAR, v viii xiv 181
CHAPEAU, 29
CHAPMAN, Richard xii 29
CHAPPEL, John xi 29 119
CIMBLET, Francis xii 29
CLARK, Andrew viii xii xiv 29 George
   iii vi 30 John xii 35 Richard x
   35 William 36
CLARKSVILLE iv
COFFY, Samuel 38
COLBERT, James iv
COLEMAN, Frank 38
CONNOR, John xii 38
CONORS, Andrew 38
CONSOLE, Herman 38
COOPER, Barny xi 39 Joseph xi xv 39
   Samuel xii 39
COWEN, John ix 39
COX, John xiii 39 Thomas x 39
CRATEN, Robert xii 39
CRAWLEY, John xi xv 40
CRETON, William 40
CRUMP, Dan 40 William x 40
CRUTCHER, Henry 40
CRUTCHFIELD, Henry 40
CURRY, James ix 40 Patrick ix
CURTIS, Rice ix 40
DALTON, Hannah xiv xv 40, Valentine
   T xiv xv 41
DAMEWOOD, Boston viii xv 43 Mrs Mary
   xv 43
DATCHERUT 43
DAUGHTERTY, John viii xv 44 Mrs xv
DAVIES, James xi xv 44
DAVIS, Robert 44
DAWSON, James ix 44
DEAN, James xv 44
DECK, John 44
DECKER, Jacob xi xv 44 119
DEJEAN, Mr xiv 45

DELANEY, Thomas viii
DELEALE, Charles 45
DEMORE, Mary viii 45
DEWIT, Henry x 45
DITTERIN, Jacob viii xv 45
DIVENY, 45
DODGE, Israel xiv 45 John xiv 50
DOHATY, Frederick ix
DONNE, John Jr 63 John Sr xiv xv 59
  Mrs Martha xv 63
DORRELY, John 63
DOSSEY, Leaving 63 119
DRAGOON, Ephraim 63
DUFF, John 63
DULY, Haymore xi 63 Phillip xi 63
DUNCAN, Joseph xiii 63
DUPLASSE 63
EAGLE, Harmon xi 64
ELMS, Ann xv 64 Daughter 64 James ix
  xv 64 John ix xv 64 William ix xv
  65
ESTIS, James x xv 65
ETHERIDGE, Abner 65
EVANS, Charles x 65 Jesse xii
EYLER, 65
FABERS, William viii
FAGGIN, Abram 119
FAIR, Edmund viii xv 65
FEVER, William xv 66
FINN, James xiv 66
FITZHUGH, John 66
FLANERY, Daniel 67
FLARRY, James ix 67
FLEUR D EPEC 67
FLOR, Mary 67
FLOYD, Isam 67
FOLEY, Mark 67
FORD, Esther 67 John xii 67
  Joseph xii 67 R 67 Robert xii 68
FREEMAN, Eliasha 68 Peter xiii 68
  William 68
FROGGET, William x 68
GAGE, Ensign 68
GAGNIA, Louis xi 68
GAGNUS, Joseph xi 69
GAMLIN, Francis 69 Pierre 69
GARR, John 69
GEORGE, Robert iv viii 69
GEST, John 97
GILBERT, John viii 97
GILLASPEY, Mr 97
GILMORE, George x xv 97
GILS, John 97
GIRAULT, John xi 97
GLASS, Mikiel x 99
GLEN, David 99
GODIN, 99
GOODWIN, William x 99
GOYLES, John 99
GRAFFEN, Daniel xii 99
GRATIOT, Charles 99
GRIMSHAW, John viii 100
GROATS, Jacob xii 100

GROOTS, Mary 100
GROLET, Francis Sr xi 101
  Francis Jr xi 101
GRUIN, William 101
GUIRE, M. 101
GUION, Fred 101
HACKETON, Michael viii 102
HACKER, John viii 102
HALL, William xiii 102
HAMMIT, James x 102
HAUSLER, Charles 102
HARDIN, Francis xv 102
HARGIS, John x 102
HARLAN, Josiah 102 Silas xii 103
HARRIS, Francis x 104 John xiv 105
HARRISON, James xi 105 Richard viii
  xv 105
HART, Miles xiii 107
HARRY, James 107 John 107
HATTEN, Christopher x xv 107
HAUL, Henry xv 107
HAYS, James xii xiii 107 Thomas xi
  107
HAZARD, John viii 108
HELLEBRANT, Mary xv 108
  Peter xii xv 108
HELM, Leonard iv xiv 108
HELMS, Ann 108
HERN, Jeremiah viii xv
HOIT, George xi 119
HOLLIS, Joshua xii
HOPKINS, Richard viii
HORDEN, Frances xii
HOWELL, Peter ix 113
HUFFMAN, Jacob xii 113
HUGHES, Martha xv 113
HUMBLE, David xi 113
HUNTER, Joseph xii xv 113 Nancy xv
  114 Marah xv 114 Mary xv 114
HUPP, Philip viii 114
HUTCHINS, Thomas 115
HUTSEL, Madam 115
HUTSIL, John xii xv 115
  "The Widow" xv William xii
HUTTON, Henry 115
ILES, Mark 115
INDIANS Chickasaw iv Delaware iv
  Kaskaskia iv xiv Kickapoo iv
  Ottawa iv Peoria iv Sauk iv
IRWIN, Joseph x 115
JARRELL, James xii 115
JEFFERSON, Thomas iii
JEWEL, John x 116
JOHNS, John x 116
JOHNSON, E 116, Edward x 116
  Ezekiel xv
JOHNSTON, Andrew x 116 Mrs Ezekiel
  (Ann) xv 117 John xii 117 Samuel
  xiii 117
JOINS, John ix 117
JONEAST 117
JONES, Elizabeth xv 117 John 118
  Matthew viii xv 118

JOSEPH (a friendly Indian) xiv 180
KASKASKIA (Fort Clark), v
KEARNS, James xi 118
KEESEES, W 118
KEINON, Lawrence viii 118
KELLAR, Abraham 119 John xi 123
KEMP, Reuben x 123
KENING, Lazarous 123
KENNEDY, David 123 Patrick xiv xv 123 Rachel xv 123
KER, Conrad xii xv 124 Henry xii xv 124 Jonas xiii 124 Mark xiii xv 125
KERKLEY, James x 125
KEY, George x 125 Thomas x 125
KIMLY, Charlotte 125
KINCADE, James 125
KINDALL, William x 125
KING, B 125 Charles xiii 125 Charlott 125 George 125 James xiii
LAFORM xi
LAMARINE, John xi 127
LANEY, Thomas xv 127
LARICHARDY, John xi
LARISHARDIE, Alexis 127
LASTLY, John xii 127
LAYAROUS, Ryan viii 127
LAYCORE, Francis xi 127
LEER, William x 127
L'ENFANT, Francois xi 127
LECHAUNCE 127
LEGRAS, Col 127
LEPAINT, LOUIS ix 127
LEQUANG, Batist 128
LEVISTON, George x 128
LEVRIG, John 128
LEWIS, Benjamin 128 Nelly 128
LINCTOT, Geoffrey 128
LINDSAY, Joseph xiv 128
LINNETT, Richard 128
LITTLE, Francis viii 128
LOCKARD, Abraham 129 Mrs 129
LOCKART, Archibald x xv
LONG, Philip viii 129
LONIAN, Joseph 129
LOVIN, Richard xi 129
LOWERBACK, Christopher 129
LUNSFORD, Anthony xii xv 129 George xii 130 Mary xv 129 Mason 130 Moses x 130
MCAULEY, Mary xv 130 Pat viii xv 130 William 130
MCCAN, Moses xiii 130
MCCARTY, Richard iv xi xv 130
MCCORMACK, E 131 John xiii xv 131 Mrs xv
MCCULTY, Patt 131
MCDANIEL, James viii
MCDONALD, David x 131
MCDONELL, James 131
MCGAR, John 131
MCGUIRE, John xii 132

MCKENSEY, Mordiack x 132
MCLAUGHLAN, Charles xi 132
MCMEANS, Andrew v xiii xv 132 Anne Sr xv 132 Anne Jr xv Fras 132 Isaac xv James xiii xv 132 Jane xv John xv Mary xv Robert xv
MCMICHAEL, John ix 132
MCMULLEN, James viii 132
MACKEVER, John ix 133
MAINS, Patrick xv 133 Mrs xv 133
MARCH, John xv 133
MARR, Patrick viii 133
MARTIN, Charles x 133
MATTHEWS, Edward viii 133
MAYFIELD, Micajah ix xv 133 Mrs xv 133
MEADOWS, Josiah xiii
MEGARR, John viii 134
MERRIDETH, Daniel xiii xv 134 Lawrance xv 134 Luvana 134 Mrs xv
MERRIWETHER, James ix 134 William x 134
MERSHOM, Nathaniel x 135
METIVCE, John xi 135 Ps xi 135
MILES, Michael xv 135 Mrs xv 135
MILLER, Abraham viii 136 Daniel 136
MONERAL, Joseph ix 136
MONTBREUEN, Timothe 136
MONTGOMERY, Hugh 136 John xiii 136
MONTROY, Anthony xi 119 140
MOORE, John x 140 William viii 140
MORGAN, Charles viii ix 140
MORRIS, Graves xii 140 James ix xv 140
MULBOY, James 141 William xi 141
MURPHY, John x 141
MURRAY, Daniel 141 Edward xii xv 141 Mary 141 Matthew viii xv 141 Thomas xiii
NASH, John 141
NEDINGER, Nichols xiii 141
NELSON, Enoch x 141 John x 141 Moses x 141 William 142
OATER, Samuel xiii
OAKLY, John 142
OBRYAN, John xiv 142
OHARRAH, Mikel x 142
OILER, Mrs xv 142
OILES, Mr xv 142
ORBIN, Philip 142
OWENS, Charaty xv 143 George xii xv 142
OUNELER, Charles ix 143
OZALA, John xiii 143
PAGAN, David x 143
PANTHER, Joseph xi 119 143
PAPIN, John xi 143
PARKER, Edward xii 143
PAYNE, Adam 143
PEPIN, John xi xv Peter xi 144
PERRAULT, Michael xi 144
PHELPS, Anthony xiii 144 Elizabeth xv 144 George xiii 144 Henry 145

Josiah xiii 144 145 Thomas xv 144
PHILIPS, Henry xii 145
PHISTER, John xiii 145
PIGGOTT, Eleanor xv 145 James xv 145 Levi xv William xv
PINER, Jess xi xv 145
PINES, Lewis xiii 145
PIPES, Windsor 145
PITTMAN, Buckner ix 145
PLANT, Joseph 146
PLASSY, 146
POPE, William 146
POSEY, William ix
POSTON, William ix 146
POTTER, James xii 146
PRIEST, Peter 146
PRITCHET, James xi 146
PRITICHETT, Will 146
PRUIT, Isaac ix 146
PRUITT, Joshua 146
PUCCAN, Francis 147
PURCELL, William 147
PURSELY, William xi 147
PYATTE, Jacob 147
QUIBEA, Paul ix 147
QUIRK, Thomas xiii xv 147
RANDAL, Nathanal 147
RAPER, Baptist xi 119 147
RAMSEY, Jas ix 148
REED, John 148
REID, William xiii 148
REY, Andrew xiv 148
RIELY, John 148
RION, Lazarous xv Mrs xv 148
ROBERTS, Benjamin xiv 148 John xiii 149
ROBERTSON, James 149
ROBISON, John x xv 149
ROBINSON, John 149
ROBESON, William 149
ROGERS, John ix 149 Patrick ix 151
ROSS, Joseph ix 151
RUBEDO, Francis ix xv 151 Jacke ix 152
RUSSILL, David xi 152
RYAN, Lazurus viii 152
SAINTIVE, John 152
SCARCY, B 152
SENET, Richard xiii 152
SERPY, M 152
SHAFFER, David xii 152
SHANK, John xi 152
SHANNON, William xiv 152
SHEPEARD, George 153 Peter xii 154
SHERLOCK, James xiv 154
SHILLING, Mary xv 154
SHILLINGS, Jacob xiii xv 154
SHOEMAKER, Leonard xii 155
SINCLAIR, Michael 155
SLAUGHTER, George ix 155 Laurence x xv 155
SLAVES v xiv xv

SMITH, Daniel 156 Edmund xiii 157 George xi xv 157 Henry xv 157 Joseph xii 157 Mary xv 158 Nicholas 158 Sidy 158
SMITHERS, John ix 158
SMYTH, Samuel xiv 158
SNELLOCK, Thomas ix 158
SNOW, George x 159
SPILLMAN, Francis x 159 James x 159
SPRINGER, Enoch xiii 159
STEPHENSEN, Stephen 159
STEWARD, Henry xiii 159
SUTHERLAND, Lawrence x 159
SUVERNS, Ebenezer xiii 159
SWORDIN, Jonathan x xv 159
TAYLOR, Abraham 159 Edward xiii 159 Isaac xiii James 160 Travis ix William 160
TENNELL, Richard xiii
THEEL, Levi xii 160
THOMPSON, James xi xv 119, 160 William xii xiii 160
THORNTON, Joseph x xiv xv 160
THRUSTON, John ix 161
TIBURN, Christopher xiii
TINKLEE, Michel ix 161
TODD, John 161 Robert 162
TOLLEY, Daniel xiii 162
TONISH, Madam 162
TOURANGEAN 162
TRATIE, Francois 162
TRENT, Beverly xii xv 162 Sarah xv 162
TULFOR, John x 162
TURPIN, Richard ix xv 162
TUTTLE, Nicholas xii xiii 163
TYGER, Daniel ix xiii 163
UNDERWOOD, Richard 163
VALLE, Madam 163
VAUGHAN, John xii 163
VILLIER, Francis xi xv 164
VONSHINER, George 164
WAGONER, Peter ix xv 164
WALKER, Doctor 164 John 164 Thomas 165
WALLACE, Caleb 166 David ix 166 167
WATKINS, Elizabeth xv 167 Samuel xv xiii 167
WELCH, Dominick x 167
WHEAT, Jacob ix 167
WHIT, Robert xii 167
WHITE, John x xiv 167 Rand xii 168 William ix 168
WHITEACRE, Daniel xv 168
WHITEGAR, Dapiae 168
WHITEHEAD, Robert xii 168 William (American) xii 168 William (British) iv
WICKS, Mordicai
WIGINS, Barney x 168
WILEY, James xiii 175
WILLIAMS, Daniel x xv 168 Jarrett ix 169 John 119 170 Zachariah x 173

WILLIS, Jacob xi 173
WILSON, Edward xiii xv 173 John xi
    xiii 173 Thomas xiv 174
WIN, Thomas ix 175
WINN, S 175
WINSTON, Richard 175
WITZEL, Widow xv 175
WOLF, E 175 Michael xiii 175
WORTHINGTON, Edward x 176
YEATS, Rachel 179
YEATES, Isaac xi 179 John xi 179
YOUNG, Hugh xii 179 James xiii xv
    179 John xiii 179 Margery xv 179

www.ingramcontent.com/pod-product-compliance
Lightning Source LLC
Chambersburg PA
CBHW071438150426
43191CB00008B/1172